Alexander Hamilton

Alexander Hamilton (*Portrait by James Sharples, Prints Division, New York Public Library*)

Leaders of the American Revolution Series

North Callahan, EDITOR

ALEXANDER HAMILTON

The Revolutionary Years

BROADUS MITCHELL

Thomas Y. Crowell Company

NEW YORK   Established 1834

Designed by Vincent Torre

Manufactured in the United States of America
L.C. Card 70-106586
1 2 3 4 5 6 7 8 9 10

Foreword

During the American Revolution Alexander Hamilton commanded troops engaged in a military campaign during two periods, which, combined, amount to little more than one year. Yet, from early in 1776 until the surrender of Cornwallis late in 1781, with a single brief intermission, he was an officer immersed in the war. During most of this time, as an aide on General Washington's headquarters staff, he was as close as anyone, except the commander in chief, to the center of the struggle. That war, like all modern military contests, involved much more than fighting in the field. Just as the bulk of an iceberg is sunk below the surface of the sea, so in the Revolution the problems of recruitment of men and materials and keeping up of public morale—in a word, organization—underlay every clash of arms.

In the effort of the American Colonies to secure their independence, the support of troops in the field presented peculiar difficulties. The country was sharply divided between Whigs (patriots) and Loyalists, not to speak of those who were indifferent to the result. Some kind of all-Colonies government had to be created out of hand. Actually, until the fighting war was almost over, the Continental Congress was not constitutional at all, but was a continuation, with added functions, of the earlier protest conventions. Even when the Articles of Confederation were finally approved in 1781, the powers of Congress were inferior to its responsibilities. Thirteen states—unlucky number—were the real sources of funds and soldiers, and they acted or failed to act according to their separate inclinations. The states were strung along the Atlantic seaboard in a fifteen-hundred-mile line from Massachusetts (including what was later Maine) to Georgia. Not only did the geographic shape of the country, narrow and attenuated, hinder cooperation, the three sections—New England, middle states, and planting states to the south—were distinct in economic interests and social habits. The ideal of democracy, the first experiment in the world on such a scale, invited local self-direction, amounting at times to whim. No nation existed. The best that could be said was that a people, or a more or less determined contingent of people, was rebelling against the authority of mighty Britain.

We need not dwell on the handicaps of an agricultural country in obtaining war materials, not only munitions but clothing and shoes for soldiers—in fact, all military needs, except food, and even food presented problems of acquisition and transport. The enemy, to be sure, fought three thousand miles from base and relied in part on mercenary troops, but they had the advantage of an enormous navy and they could cope with their mounting debt.

The strictly military features of the Revolution, therefore, were subordinate to the governmental and economic requirements. America could not have achieved independence without foreign assistance in money, men, materials, and fleets, which came almost entirely from France. Without discounting the efforts of Congress, it is true to say that the prosecution of the war, domestic and diplomatic, rested in Washington's headquarters. In fact, Congress twice invested the commander in chief with dictatorial powers. Though this was a confession of the disability of Congress, Washington was too wise to supersede the civil authority, faltering as it was.

To state that the war hinged on public administration is to understate the crisis. Administration implies a going governmental concern, or management, within given determinations. The problem, rather, was one of summoning scarce resources before they could be usefully applied. The call was for constant leadership, in council as well as in camp and conflict.

In this demanding office Washington had eager and highly competent coadjutors. Of generals who exerted themselves in the public sphere in addition to the military field, it is enough to mention Major Generals Nathanael Greene, Henry Knox, Marquis de Lafayette, and Philip Schuyler. Of those in civil capacities immediately related to the war, one thinks of Benjamin Franklin, minister to France; Robert Morris, superintendent of finance; and John Jay, minister to Spain.

No one was more acutely aware of the needs of the situation than Captain Alexander Hamilton, commanding his New York artillery company, and later, for four years, a lieutenant colonel at Washington's elbow at headquarters. Most of his work, whether as courier, emissary, digester of information, or letter writer, was on Washington's order. But when else has a principal had such a second? A "word to the wise" was for Hamilton sufficient. Given the commander in chief's intention, he would convey it, in words penned or spoken, as accurately as though the message had originated with him, as frequently it had. Always his heart was in his assignment, his mind bent zestfully upon it. He and his superior thought alike, so that Hamilton's language for the general's signature is scarcely distinguishable from Washington's own composition. Amidst these duties as proxy, he made his own proposals to Washington, to friends in Congress, and to others of influence. These analyses and recommendations, where they dealt with public finance, transcended Washington's understanding of the subject. His pleas for improvement in the structure of government to forward the war were hardly less unique. After all, here at headquarters was a junior soon to become a principal agent in the molding of the nation. Hamilton directed his arguments with the precision he used in training his cannon on a target.

As will appear in the following narrative, Hamilton was not lacking in battle experience, for which he was always restive. However, his military contribution, whether as aide to Washington or, later, as major general and inspector general, embraced all aspects of the country's emergency. He had his demerits, but they were rarely military. More frequently his lapses were of a personal or political nature. A biographer must not see only the admirable and forget the errors. But the bullet that killed him was invited by his quarrel on behalf of America.

B. M.

New York City
November 1969

Contents

Illustrations

Maps

1

Artillery Captain

 A boy of fourteen on the Danish island of Saint Croix in the West Indies was writing to his chum in New York City. He may have perched on a high stool at the desk of the provision store where he worked. He would welcome his friend on a promised home visit,

tho doubt whether I shall be Present or not for to confess my weakness, Ned, my Ambition is prevalent [so] that I contemn the grov'ling . . . condition of a Clerk or the like, to which my Fortune . . . condemns me and would willingly risk my life tho' not my Character to exalt my Station. Im confident . . . that my Youth excludes me from any hopes of immediate Preferment . . . but I mean to prepare the way for futurity. . . . My Folly makes me ashamed and beg you'll Conceal it, yet Neddy we have seen such Schemes successfull when the Projector is Constant[.] I shall Conclude saying I wish there was a War.

The date was November 11, 1769.

In this earliest letter of Alexander Hamilton that we possess, he accurately sketched his temper. In the remaining thirty-five years of his life, his ambition was "prevalent"; his schemes, constantly pursued, were successful; and war provoked his achievements.

Like those of many other celebrated persons who rose from obscurity, Alexander Hamilton's beginnings are sketchy. He was born, probably, January 11, 1755, most likely on the British island of Nevis, across the narrow channel from the larger Saint Kitts. He was the younger son of James Hamilton and Rachael Faucette Lavien. His father was a young trader from a substantial family in Ayrshire, Scotland; his mother, of Nevis, was the daughter of John Faucette, a physician and planter of French extraction, and his wife, Mary Uppington, apparently English.

When Rachael was ten or eleven, in 1740, her parents separated; at the death of her father five years later, Rachael inherited his property and was living with her mother on Saint Croix. One of a number who transferred at this time from Nevis to Saint Croix was the planter-merchant Johan Michael Lavien (the first and last names are variously spelled), who, "attracted by [Rachael's] beauty, and recommended to her mother by his wealth, received her hand against her inclination."

The Laviens lived for three years on his cotton estate, misnamed "Contentment," where their son, Peter Lavien, was born. Then they moved to "Beeston Hill" with worsening of their disharmony. Here Lavien accused Rachael of adultery and had her jailed in the fort at Christiansted. He was prevailed upon to release her, but instead of returning to her husband and son, she went off, doubtless with her mother, to other islands, among them probably Saint Kitts. About 1752, a couple of years after she left Lavien, Rachael began to live with James Hamilton, by whom she had two sons: James, born in 1753, and Alexander, in 1755. These facts, without mention of the names, are from the suit Lavien filed for divorce from Rachael in 1759, lest if he died, she as his widow might claim, for her illegitimate children, what rightly should go to his son, Peter. Rachael did not answer her summons in the divorce hearing, and as the offending party in the decree granted Lavien, she was forbidden by Danish law to remarry.

Thus Alexander Hamilton was a "love child." In the face of

occasional unworthy taunts by his enemies in public life, this made him reticent about his origin, of which his own children had imperfect knowledge. Irregular unions, among high as well as low, were frequent in the islands. The common-law marriage of Rachael and James Hamilton lasted for a dozen years, with no visible objection by her relatives. She was a sprightly, talented woman, ever held in tender memory by her famous son, who received from her, we imagine, many of his gifts. Of James Hamilton we know little, except that he must have had engaging qualities to keep the affection of such a woman. Though he had served his apprenticeship in a Glasgow countinghouse, he failed to make his fortune as the employee of various merchants and planters in the West Indies. When an errand took him to Saint Croix in 1765, he brought his family there (Alexander was ten), but soon departed for other islands and never saw Rachael or his sons again. Alexander was filial; James Hamilton, in his last years, would have rejoined Alexander in New York, but before he could undertake the voyage, he died on Saint Vincent in 1799.

Alexander helped his mother in a little shop she opened in Christiansted until she died three years later, 1768. His older brother, James, was apprenticed to a carpenter, and Alexander, now thirteen, was employed by a friend of the family, the merchant Nicholas Cruger. In Cruger's business, importing plantation supplies and exporting island products, the youth, during four years, showed precocious competence. For some months, in Cruger's absence, he conducted the establishment, giving directions to sea captains with a maturity difficult to credit, except that we have his correspondence to prove his zeal and forethought. Besides earning the confidence of his employer, he attracted the attentions of the Reverend Hugh Knox, a Princeton-educated Presbyterian clergyman.

A hurricane that struck Saint Croix in 1772 is said to have "blown Alexander Hamilton into history." He wrote to his father a lurid description of the storm and its damage, which

Knox published in the local *Royal Danish-American Gazette,* in which other of Alexander's effusions had appeared. Actually the "hurricane letter" only confirmed the resolve of admiring friends and relatives to send Alexander, now seventeen, to the North American continent for his education. Knox supplied introductions to such New Jersey notables as William Livingston and Elias Boudinot. In New York the young West Indian was received by an associate of the Crugers, the redoubtable Hercules Mulligan, who placed him in the academy of Francis Barber, a Princeton graduate, at Elizabethtown, New Jersey. Alexander seems to have lived in the home of Boudinot and was a familiar in the household of Livingston. The former was to become president of the Continental Congress, the latter the first governor of New Jersey following independence. The notion that the orphan was cast up a waif on American shores is mistaken, for he had from the first powerful patrons, and he early came to know Lord Stirling, William Duer, John Jay, and others who figured intimately in his career.

He made such rapid progress at the academy with Barber that after less than a year, in 1773, he was ready for college. The solicitous Hercules Mulligan took him to the College of New Jersey (Princeton), Alexander's choice because it was more republican than King's College (now Columbia) in New York. President John Witherspoon—a flaming patriot earlier than others in his colony—examined the applicant and pronounced him eligible, but he could not accept the boy's proposal to complete the course as fast as possible without regard to class years. Alexander thereupon settled for King's, which he entered as a special student.

King's College, under President Myles Cooper, was Anglican and Loyalist, which did nothing to dampen, indeed may have provoked, the student's prompt espousal of the Colonies' cause against Great Britain. Urged to mount the platform in "the Fields" (City Hall Park) in support of patriot delegates to the First Continental Congress, Hamilton followed his oral outburst with anonymous pamphlets, in the winter of 1774–1775, replying to the Loyalist "Westchester Farmer" (Samuel Seabury). So spirited, informed, and cogent were these early productions that they were popularly attributed to John Jay and others of his elders. While many, now and afterward, were spokesmen of their particular colonies, Hamilton, foreign-born, ever retained a Continental outlook; proud of being a New Yorker, he was yet from the beginning a nationalist, which was his enduring strength.[1]

The collegian, fervid as he was, deplored punishing Tories with tar and feathers and such actions as scattering the type of the Loyalist printer James Rivington. Instead his ardor put him to drilling in Saint George's churchyard in the volunteer company of Major Edward Fleming, in which he "became exceedingly expert in the manual exercise." His first action under fire was on the August night in 1775 when the man-of-war *Asia* loosed broadsides at the Battery, and Hamilton, responding with his comrades, helped his friend Hercules Mulligan to drag guns of the fort to a place of safety from British seizure. As soon as the provincial congress, in January 1776, authorized the raising of an artillery company for defense of the colony, Hamilton prepared himself to obtain the command. He was coached in the mathematics necessary for gunnery by Robert Harpur, a professor at King's. Friends forwarded his ambition: Alexander McDougall, who had presided at the meeting in "the Fields," and John Jay, who had married the daughter of Hamilton's patron, William Livingston. Stephen Bedlam, captain of artillery, having furnished his certificate "that he has examined Alexander

[1] Almost two centuries later—the United States having purchased Saint Croix from Denmark—the waterfront area of Christiansted, where Alexander Hamilton had discharged duties for Nicholas Cruger, was declared a national historic site. When some objection was raised to expenditure in this behalf (as for putting telephone lines underground to preserve the integrity of the ancient scene), a newspaper correspondent pertinently observed that if a lad from that small island could do so much for the American continent, perhaps we should return the favor.

Hamilton and judges him qualified," the congress, March 14, 1776, ordered him "appointed Captain of the Provincial Company of Artillery of this Colony." He was two months over the age of twenty-one, of slight figure (about 5 feet 7 inches), but erect and vital; his boyish cheeks were of high coloring, his hair reddish brown, his eyes of a deep blue, almost violet.

While Hamilton's appointment was pending, his solicitous friend Elias Boudinot recommended him as "Brigade Major" (aide) to William Alexander, Lord Stirling.[2] Stirling agreed, but Hamilton politely declined, explaining that meantime he had been given command of an artillery company. Four years later, determined to quit Washington's staff, he said that early in the war he had refused invitations of two major generals (Nathanael Greene may have been the other one) because he preferred field duty. He always admired Stirling, whom he had first known when a schoolboy in Elizabethtown, as Stirling had married William Livingston's sister, and their friendship became close. Captain Hamilton's decision at this point to stick with the troops, though a small provincial unit, was more significant for his future than he could guess. If he had joined Stirling's staff, he would not have had his taste of active combat in the opening scenes of the war in New York and New Jersey. Further, in all likelihood he would have missed the long, intimate association with Washington, which led on to his role in the national government.

It was Hercules Mulligan's recollection that Hamilton's commission was not issued until he fulfilled the condition of recruiting thirty men for his company. The minutes of the provincial congress contain no such stipulation, and Hercules may have been confused by the requirement of seventy-two enlistees in New York companies to be taken into Continental service. In

---

[2] Readers may wonder how a British nobleman came to be a major general in the American Revolutionary army. William Alexander's claim to the succession as sixth earl of Stirling was disallowed by the House of Lords because, while his representations were pending, he was among the first to offer his services to the rebelling Colonies. Nevertheless, he was always given the title in America.

any event Hamilton recruited promptly and vigorously: The very first afternoon, Hercules, who helped in the endeavor, recorded, "we engaged 25 men." However, he soon encountered reluctance, and after two months of effort he complained to the provincial congress that he was unable to bring his company to full strength because he could not offer the higher pay of artillerists in Continental units. He objected that the New York Congress had not kept its promise to officers that "troops raised in this Colony will be placed precisely upon the same footing, as to pay, Cloathing &c. with other the Continental Troops." The discrimination caused "many marks of discontent" among his men. Captain Sebastian Bauman, enlisting men for the Continent at the higher scale, "makes it difficult for me to get a single recruit: for men will naturally go to those who pay them best." Also, could he be allowed the small "actual expenses" of sending recruiting officers into the country? And could his men be furnished with the frock given to other troops as a bounty? "This frock would be extremely serviceable in summer, while men are on fatigue; and would put it in their power to save their uniform much longer." Here spoke the economist, and with reason, for every man, in or out of uniform, that could wield pick and shovel was put to throwing up earthworks for the defense of lower Manhattan and the heights of Long Island facing the East River and Narrows.

The war had now moved into the young artillery captain's front yard. In mid-March 1776 Washington's surprise fortification of Dorchester Heights had confirmed General Sir William Howe's resolve to quit Boston. He loaded on the ships of Vice Admiral Samuel Graves his seven thousand troops, nearly a thousand Tories, all of his equipment, and such of his stores as he had not destroyed, and sailed for Halifax, Nova Scotia. Here many of the refugees were to settle, paying in hardships for their loyalty to King George. The completeness with which General Howe departed from Boston and its environs appears in a little joke he left behind him. Patriots believed he still held the hard-won Bunker Hill, for sentinels were spied there at their posts. On closer investigation these pickets proved to be "Images dressed in the Soldiers Habit with laced Hats and for a Gorget [crescent-shaped ornament at the throat] an Horse Shoe with Paper Ruffles, their Pieces Shouldered [with] fixed Bayonets, with this Inscription wrote on their Breast (viz.) Welcome Brother Jonathan."

Washington immediately shifted four brigades and Colonel Henry Knox's artillery to New York City, rightly suspecting that the enemy would attempt to seize and make that the base for future operations. Already the British government had doubled and redoubled preparations to subdue the rebellious Colonies. The army was to be recruited to 55,000 troops, almost a third of them "Hessians" hired from petty German princes. The navy was to get 12,000 more seamen, and the treasury was to be nicked to the tune of £850,000—call it, in today's purchasing power, more than $15,000,000.

After General Charles Lee left New York early in 1776 for the South, the command devolved on Stirling, who redoubled the digging when Washington arrived from Boston in mid-April. Discarding Lee's doubts—justified as it turned out—that New York could long be held against the British, Washington charged Stirling, "It is the Place that we must use every Endeavour to keep from them. For should they get that Town, and the Command of the North River, they can stop the Intercourse between the northern and southern Colonies, upon which depends the Safety of America." In the precious ten weeks before the enemy in late June began debarking 32,000 soldiers on Staten Island and the bay thronged with warships, Hamilton's men with all the others had to report for tools and instructions at five in the morning and labor until sunset. In spite of "the Greate Fatigue duty of this army," orders were that "the Evolutions" (drill) should not be neglected.

The authorities granted Captain Hamilton's requests, but he was obliged to use his credit with tailors and the commissary of clothing to provide uniforms for his men until the sums could be taken out of their pay, as was then the rule. From time to time between March and July 1776 Alsop and James Hunt delivered seventy-five pairs of buckskin breeches. The brisk demand for this article raised the price from thirty-six to forty-eight shillings,[3] so the thrifty Hamilton had old breeches repaired, and issued to one gunner a pair "half worn." He ordered "blue Strouds," "blue Shalloon" (coarse and finer woolens), "Oznabrigs" (osnaburgs, coarse linen), thirty gross and eight dozen buttons, and would pay, a friend remembered, when he had cash from his last remittance from Saint Croix. These materials were made into blue coats with buff cuffs and facings, the trimmings afterward changed to regulation artillery red. Hamilton later insisted that nothing contributed more to the morale of soldiers than proper uniforms complete to the last detail; distinctive dress was the badge of their commitment to the service. He set the example in his own outfit; he paid nearly twice as much for his own white buckskin breeches as for those of common quality, and several times as much for his shoes.

We know details of his recruiting and attention to the appearance of his company from his pay book, which has entries running from August 31, 1776, to relinquishment of his command on March 1, 1777. It is to be noted that on the pages left blank at the back he afterward, at Washington's headquarters, made memoranda of his current reading, which was mainly on economic and political subjects. This combination of the discharge of military duty and inquiry into the organization of society, as we shall see, marked his service throughout the war. Other officers, as the conflict proceeded—Washington not least, and Knox and Greene—pondered reforms in government as they bore upon the

[3] For many reasons it is difficult to make an accurate or even a meaningful comparison of the value of the monetary unit in this country in the period of the Revolution and the present. A pair of "buckskin" breeches, if such were made today, would cost at least five times as much as those furnished to Hamilton's artillerymen. This is in spite of superior modern methods of tanning and tailoring.

army, but Hamilton's diagnosis of needs was peculiarly acute.

Hamilton's artillery company numbered sixty-eight officers and men in October 1776. Their names were predominantly English, with some Irish, Scotch, and a few Dutch. Many in the ranks were illiterate, obliged to make their marks in the pay book. The roll calls show all officers present and fit for duty— James Moore, captain-lieutenant; James Gilliland, first lieutenant; John Bane (Bean?), second lieutenant; Thomas Thompson, third lieutenant; noncommissioned officers were Sergeants Samuel Smith, Richard Taylor, James Deasy, and Corporals Robert Barber, John Stakes, Martin Johnson. Next were listed bombardiers, gunners, drummers, fifers, and—most numerous—matrosses (gunners' mates). For all the captain's care, on October 4 eleven of the men were absent sick, two had deserted, and two were prisoners; perhaps one of these last was John Little, sentenced by court martial to receive thirty-nine lashes for abusing and striking Adjutant Henly. Maybe Hamilton's deserters were not as apt to be discovered and retrieved as one Thomsin Oddle of the "York Forces." He was advertised at this time (a twelve-dollar reward for lodging him in jail) as 6 feet 3 inches tall, twenty-six years old, apt to swear and blaspheme ("his common word, damn my wig"), fair complexion, black curled hair; made off in a light blue regimental coat trimmed with green, and "a pair of streaked trowsers."

Especially now, when men were hastily enlisted for the defense of New York, but also later, many of those most easily attracted were unreliable, insubordinate, and generally troublesome. Though Hamilton had taken some of this ilk, he strove to content them by filling their stomachs, petitioning for the Continental ration and not "almost a third less provisions than the whole army besides receives." Along with diet went discipline. Two friends recorded the zeal with which Hamilton trained his men, so that before long his company "was esteemed the most beautiful model . . . in the whole army."

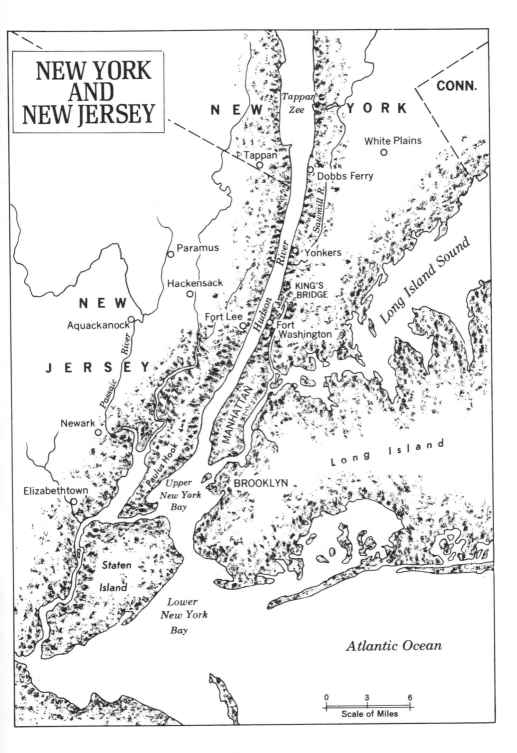

NEW YORK AND NEW JERSEY

CONN.

N E W   Y O R K

Tappan Zee

White Plains ○

Tappan ○

Dobbs Ferry ○

Sawmill R.

Paramus ○

Yonkers ○

Hackensack ○

KING'S BRIDGE

Hudson River

N E W

Fort Lee ○

Aquackanock ○

Fort Washington

Long Island Sound

Passaic River

J E R S E Y

MANHATTAN

Newark ○

Paulus Hook

Long   Island

Elizabethtown ○

Upper New York Bay

BROOKLYN

Staten Island

Lower New York Bay

Atlantic Ocean

0   3   6
Scale of Miles

II

When he gave over at the end of a year of command, his unit had its full complement of ninety-eight.

Captain Hamilton proposed to the New York Congress a particular means of rewarding good conduct and ambition in his unit. When First Lieutenant Johnson was promoted out of the company, Hamilton observed that the vacancy would best be supplied by advancing Mr. Gilliland and Mr. Bean, "and fill up the third lieutenancy with some other person." He urged for this commission Thomas Thompson, his first sergeant, who "has discharged his duty in the present station with uncommon fidelity . . . and expertness . . . and his advancement will be a great encouragement . . . to my company in particular, and will be an animating example to all men of merit to whose knowledge it comes." This policy of promoting from the ranks evidently struck the New York Congress as novel, deserving of report by Colonel (James?) Livingston when he had further inquired into it with Captain Hamilton. Livingston, besides discussing the propriety of the practice, was doubtless told what Hamilton remarked later, that Sergeant Thompson had been of more use to him in recruiting and training than had some of his officers. The New York Congress forthwith described the sergeant in Hamilton's words, promoted him to the lieutenancy, and erected this instance into the rule, "This Convention will exert themselves in promoting from time to time such privates and non-Commissioned Officers . . . as shall distinguish themselves by their Sobriety, Valour and Subordination," and further "Ordered that this Resolution be published in the newspapers of this State." Confirming his first judgment, Hamilton later recommended advancing Thompson over the heads of others to a captain-lieutenancy. Thompson, ever faithful, was killed leading his men in the action at Springfield, New Jersey, in June 1780.

Not to draw too much from this egalitarian precedent espoused by Hamilton, at a time when most men in authority, Washington included, preferred "gentlemen" for commissions, other examples of his democratic willingness could be added.

Most illustrative was his eagerness to receive Negro slaves into the army, to be freed on enlistment. He has so regularly been typed as aristocratic, distrustful, even scornful, of the common people, that he has not been credited with examples to the contrary.

Continental troops had been guarding the public records in the City Hall, but shortly after Hamilton was commissioned, the Committee of Safety judged that Hamilton's company was sufficiently recruited to perform that duty, at less expense to the colony. The City Hall, after the Constitution was adopted, became, with refurbishing by Major Pierre L'Enfant, Federal Hall, where President Washington was inaugurated. (This building was replaced by the Sub-Treasury, and here, in the national celebration of the two-hundredth anniversary of Hamilton's birth, the oldest military unit in the army, descended from his artillery company, was present for the occasion in resplendent array that would have pleased the first commander.) This interim tour of duty was brief, for Colonel John Lasher's City Battalion of Independents took over, and the records were moved to a less vulnerable place.

The provincial congress complained that the twelve hundred militia ordered by the Continental Congress to be raised in New York City and County was burdensome, so they counted Hamilton's company in the quota. It was incorporated into General John Morin Scott's brigade in August and encamped in Greenwich (Village), at that time separated from the city by some two miles. Prior to this, on July 12, Hamilton's battery was called on for its first action and suffered its first casualty. This was when the British warships *Phoenix* and *Rose* sailed up the North River, and Hamilton's two guns, with others stationed on both shores, opened up on the intruders. The American fire, which was returned, had no effect on the enemy vessels, but one of Hamilton's cannon burst, killing an attendant. After reaching miles above all American land defenses, and successfully escaping fireships sent after them, the *Phoenix* and

Rose returned to their anchorage. The proof that this penetration was feasible did not persuade Admiral Lord Howe and his brother, General Sir William, to land troops to the north of Manhattan Island and bottle up the American army. Instead, five weeks later, the thrust of the enemy was against Long Island.

Hamilton's company had helped Lasher's Independents construct the heptagonal fort on Bayard's Hill (now the intersection of Canal and Mulberry Streets). This was the highest ground overlooking the city of 25,000 people and 4,000 houses, which at that time did not extend above Chambers Street (in lower Manhattan). Known by various names (Independent Battery, Montgomery's, Bunker's Hill), it was enthusiastically described by Hamilton's schoolfellow Nicholas Fish as "a Fortification superior in Strength to any my Imagination could ever have conceived." Its ordnance was eight 9-pounders, four 3-pounders, and six royal and coehorn mortars. Washington had thanked the men of the fatigue parties "for their masterly manner of executing the work." It was the commanding redoubt in a line of earthworks reaching halfway across the island. Below, around the shore, a dozen defenses extended from Horn's Hook on the east to the Jersey battery on the west, the Grand Battery below Fort George being the strongest.[4]

---

[4] Artillery was of two main kinds, guns with relatively long barrels projecting solid shot, and mortars with short barrels throwing shells at high elevation. Guns were fieldpieces on wheeled carriages, or heavier siege guns, usually on fixed emplacement but sometimes maneuverable on carriages. Mortars were of various sizes, generally in fixed elevation at 45 degrees, though the elevation of some could be regulated by quoins (wedges) placed under the barrel. Guns were typically of cast iron, superior ones of the stronger bronze; mortars were bronze. Coehorns (the name corrupted from that of the Dutch military engineer Baron Menno van Coehoorn) were small mortars. Howitzers were intermediate in length of barrel, between guns and mortars, and like the latter fired shells at high angle.

Cannon ammunition was of three types: Solid cast-iron shot (cannon balls) varied in weight from three to forty-two pounds; fieldpieces were mostly three- to six-pounders, siege guns eighteen- to twenty-four-pounders. The lighter balls were trained on enemy personnel; the heavier were for battering defenses. Guns also fired scatter ammunition, either grape (a cluster of small shot contained in a cloth bag), or canister (small shot or various missiles, such as nails and bolts,

Washington, in general orders of August 8, 1776, warned that "the Movements of the enemy, and intelligence by Deserters, give the utmost reason to believe, that the great struggle, in which we are contending for every thing dear to us, and our posterity, is near at hand." At the Bayard's Hill fort the alarm should be given of the first approach of British transports, "A Flag in the day time, or a light at Night . . . with three Guns . . . fired quick, but distinct, is to be . . . a signal for the troops to repair to their . . . posts, and prepare for action." All drums would beat on the instant. Six days later the enemy, it was announced, were embarked, but were delayed by bad weather; our men must be on the alert, with food enough for two days and canteens filled.

During the battle of Long Island, August 27–29, 1776, Hamilton and his company were in the main Manhattan works on Bayard's Hill, for defense of the city, which Washington, until late in the disposition of troops, believed would be the enemy target at least equally with Brooklyn on Long Island. Everything went wrong for the Americans, except for Washington's extrica-

---

enclosed in a can). Shells or bombs were explosive. They were of cast iron, hollow, and filled with powder through a small hole into which the fuse was inserted. The fuse was a small wooden plug, several inches long, hollowed to a diameter of one-fourth inch, but widening at the top to form a cup. A powder composition was tamped into the tube, and, to give a larger igniting surface, the cup was filled with a fine ("mealed") powder moistened with alcohol. The time of explosion of the shell was regulated by cutting the fuse to the desired length; in any case it projected from the shell less than a quarter of an inch. The fuse was ignited by "slow match"—strands of cotton rope soaked in chemicals that burned surely but at the rate of only four inches an hour.

The range of guns (the distance from a horizontal barrel to the point where the projectile first touched level ground) during the American Revolution was about a mile; effective range was less, maximum range was greater. Shells from mortars, with high trajectory, had the advantage of reaching over intervening obstacles to the target. The effective range of mortars was somewhat greater than of guns firing solid shot. Mortars were aimed by varying the amount of the powder charge.

The short range of artillery (as compared with later development) was due principally to weak black powder. The usual composition of powder was six parts of saltpeter (postassium nitrate), and one part each of charcoal and sulphur. On burning, it liberated three hundred times its own volume in smoky gases.

tion of his beaten army in a masterly night retreat across the East River, from Brooklyn. The first miscalculation lay months in the past, when Washington resolved to protect New York City and its dependencies, in spite of Charles Lee's earlier judgment that it was not possible to hold off an attack here except temporarily, because the British fleet would command the surrounding waters. In that event, 10 British ships of the line and twice as many fast frigates would carry more than 1,200 guns, and would be accompanied by more than 450 transports and tenders, while the Americans had no navy whatever, unless we count John Glover's mariners and the boats they were able to collect. His decision was partly owing to the desire of Congress to defend this principal port, strategically situated, a most valuable base, the loss of which would be a blow to the country's cause, both militarily and in prestige. Then three days before the battle General Nathanael Greene, commanding on Long Island, fell sick abed. His superior skill and knowledge of terrain might have lessened the disaster, but General John Sullivan, appointed in his place, was not equal to the peril, and General Israel Putnam, who promptly succeeded Sullivan, was even less so. The town of Brooklyn was protected on the south by thickly wooded heights running northeastward across the island, behind which lay the American earthworks. The escarpment was insurmountable, but a road doubled the end of the ridge on the west, and two others penetrated it at the "passes" of Flatbush and Bedford.

American forces guarded these likely approaches. Stirling, on the coastal (Gowanus) road, was pounded by the British General James Grant, and Sullivan at the Flatbush pass was similarly confronted by General von Heister with his Hessians. But these assaults of the enemy were simply to occupy the Americans while through the night Howe, Cornwallis, and Lord Percy, with ten thousand troops and twenty-eight pieces of artillery, made a silent swing to the east to the unlikely Jamaica pass. At three o'clock on the morning of the twenty-eighth they scooped up the only Americans posted there, five young subalterns, including Hamilton's friend Robert Troup, stopped briefly for breakfast, then marched westward with the same caution to take the patriots in the rear. Thus enveloped, cut down by grape and canister, the uncaptured Americans made what escape they could to their entrenchments. Marylanders under Stirling, protecting withdrawal of their comrades, fought desperately, to their nearly total destruction. Both Sullivan and Stirling were made prisoners.

After this fighting, Washington's men were in their fortified works on Brooklyn Heights overlooking the East River. Reinforced from New York, they numbered some 9,500. The immediate storm by the enemy, which they expected, did not come, Howe preferring to dig trenches for a siege. The storm that did come was unexpected and from the skies, a drenching northeaster that kept up for three days and nights. The Americans' ammunition and arms were soaked and useless; their uncooked food was uneatable; they could not have withstood enemy bayonets. Thus facing disaster, Washington saved his army by retreat. Fortunately, among the reinforcements from Manhattan were Colonel John Glover's Cape Ann sailors and fishermen. The morning of the twenty-ninth Washington ordered every possible boat to be collected. They were brought to the Brooklyn side without interference from Lord Howe's ships, which were prevented by wind from entering the East River. That night, under cover of rain and blackness, Washington's forces filed off to the landing. Unsuspected by the enemy, the watermen manned the boats that took all—troops, guns, horses, baggage—to Manhattan. The few hundreds left in the lines to keep up a show of resistance were blessed by a dense fog, which allowed their early morning escape. Washington, who had hardly been out of his saddle for forty-eight hours and had supervised every aspect of the withdrawal, was the last to step into a boat.

That retreat, or secret night mass flight, was all the credit Washington could claim in the otherwise disastrous encounter on Long Island. Other American officers have been variously blamed for wrong decisions, and Putnam, chiefly, for no decision. Critics have held that General Howe, though victorious, could have finished off the Americans then and there by assailing the works. The American casualties were about a thousand (two hundred killed), the British casualties fewer than four hundred.

Hercules Mulligan, Hamilton's champion, missing no chance to give him merit, recorded long afterward that his young friend had drafted a plan of retreat "nearly the same" as that Washington used. According to Mulligan, he gave Hamilton's letter, written and read in Mulligan's presence, to Colonel Webb of Washington's staff for the general's perusal before the battle. But, despite his circumstantial recital, the cordial Irishman's memory was probably at fault.

General Howe, in one of those unaccountable lapses into which he frequently fell, did not at once follow up his success. Instead his army lay for two weeks on the Brooklyn end of Long Island, looking across at the disorder of the American force on Manhattan. Discipline was beyond Washington's efforts. The militia deserted in droves; officers failed to prevent looting. Men of every regiment, Washington complained, "are suffer'd to be continually rambling about, at such distances from their respective quarters and encampments, as not to be able to oppose the enemy in any sudden approach." Distrust of Washington's sole ability—for all seemed to devolve upon him—to rule this confusion produced the wish, "W'd to Heaven Genl Lee were here." Lee, professional soldier in British and other armies, was at this time admired, in competition with his chief, though later his reputation fell low indeed.

To Washington's question, September 2, whether New York, if evacuated, "ought . . . to stand as Winter Quarters for the Enemy?" Congress promptly answered that the town should not be burned. General Greene was of different mind. "The City and Island of New-York," he urged, "are no objects for us.

. . . A general and speedy retreat is absolutely necessary . . . I would burn the city and suburbs," for if the enemy were established there, "we can never recover the possession without a superiour naval force." The property belonged largely to Tories anyhow. Colonels Joseph Reed, adjutant general, and Rufus Putnam, chief engineer, agreed, as did John Jay. As though to confirm this advice, British warships sailed with impunity up both rivers.

A council of war, ten days after the retreat from Long Island, approved a compromise: disperse the army in three divisions— five thousand men under Putnam to defend the city, Heath with nine thousand to take post on the upper end of Manhattan Island, and Greene with six thousand (mostly militia) to protect the vulnerable waist of Manhattan. The danger of this dispersal of contingents was soon seen, but not soon enough to prevent attack at the weakest point.

On September 15 enemy navy and army struck at Kip's Bay (now East Thirty-fourth Street). Seventy heavy cannon of the ships pounded the trifling earthbank, from which the militia scampered wildly before troops from fourscore flatboats landed unopposed. Washington, alarmed by the cannonade, took horse at Harlem, met the frantic escapers in full flight. His desperate efforts to rally them (laying his riding cane on the backs of privates and officers alike) left him alone and exposed in his disgust and fury until an aide hurried him from the scene.

Hamilton's company, with Scott's brigade and Knox's artillery, was in lower Manhattan in peril of being cut off. Putnam, despairing of defense at Kip's Bay, chased to their rescue. Some were already streaming out by the time he reached the Bayard's Hill fort. The post road northward (now Lexington Avenue) was blocked by the enemy; Knox, though his artillery was already partly dismantled, was for fighting there, trapped or not. Captain Hamilton must have been active in rallying the fort for a stand. Putnam countermanded this forlorn hope. Fortunately his aide, Major Aaron Burr, knew a way of reaching the

Bloomingdale road up the western side of the island. Putnam rode back and forth along the two-mile column, urging speed in the escape. If the discouraged soldiers had been soaked by the downpours earlier, they were now parched with heat and clouds of dust raised by tramping feet and teams dragging the fieldpieces. Unless they hurried, there was danger they would be intercepted by the enemy contingents that were crossing Manhattan after the penetration at Kip's Bay. The retreaters did meet a small force, but beat it off. It was nightfall when Hamilton's company reached safety at Harlem Heights, where troops stationed there had already dug entrenchments.

Springing back from the disaster at Kip's Bay, Washington believed "the Enemy would meet with a defeat in case of an Attack" on his Harlem lines if his men recovered their courage. Egbert Benson, longtime friend of Washington and Hamilton, is credited with the story that here the young artillery captain first met the commander in chief. The general, struck by the diligence of Hamilton's men in throwing up an earthwork, invited their officer to his marquée.[5] Perhaps so, but Washington was probably too incessantly occupied for any sitdown conversation with a subaltern. It is likely that Washington did fix Hamilton in his eye before inviting him to the headquarters staff at Morristown, but more occasions offered, possibly at White Plains, in the retreat across New Jersey, or, especially, at Trenton, when the general commanded the attack at the spot where Hamilton had brought up his battery.

The armies took position, the American on Harlem Heights, the British on the lesser eminence to the south, with the "Hollow Way" between them. The locations, in terms of present-day streets, were about 147th Street for the first line of American entrenchments, while the British were encamped, river to river, in the neighborhood of the present 103rd Street. The center of the valley between is marked by 125th Street. These

---

[5] This was a large field tent. One used by Washington, doubtless the same here referred to, is in the museum at Valley Forge, Pennsylvania.

contemporary designations are apt to blot out in one's mind the extremely different terrain as it then was, for the most part broken, rocky, heavily wooded; only a remnant of the surface features remains, in Morningside Park, and even that is modified.

The morning after collecting his forces on Harlem Heights (about ten thousand effectives), Washington rose at five o'clock at his headquarters in the Morris (Jumel) House. He could not make out the enemy position and consequently could not guess what Howe would attempt. A scouting party of New England Rangers, under Lieutenant Colonel Thomas Knowlton, had crossed the valley before dawn. They were fired on by the British picket at what is now 106th Street and West End Avenue, more of the enemy came up, and a skirmish ensued. When the redcoats chasing them were seen from the American line, Washington called his men to arms. Provoked, it is said, by a bugle sounding enemy triumph—though the blast must have been thin by the time it reached two miles to the north—Washington suddenly decided on a limited sally. A small force in a frontal feint would ascend the hill and fall back in an effort to draw the enemy into the open valley. At the same time, Knowlton's Rangers, reinforced, would work through the woods around the British right and take them from behind. Premature firing by a few in Knowlton's party alerted the British to their danger. They attacked the flankers; Colonel Knowlton and Major Andrew Leitch fell, mortally wounded, but the company captains carried on valiantly. Washington ordered two thousand to their support, and the Americans, exuberant when the British backed up the slope, pursued them to a buckwheat field where now stands Columbia University, say between 116th and 120th Streets.

Here the British were reinforced from nearby units, and a standup fight lasted for two hours. The enemy were pushed back when their pair of small fieldpieces gave out of ammunition. But Washington was content with enough success and sent

Tench Tilghman with orders to withdraw. Not wanting a full-scale battle, he did the wise thing, for Cornwallis, with a powerful force of his own, and Hessian grenadiers were on their way to retrieve the day.

Hamilton was not in this action, but surely exulted, with the whole of Washington's army, at the Americans' courageous showing. Even Colonel William Douglas' militiamen, those "dastards" that had turned tail the day before at Kip's Bay, had defied British regulars, including the vaunted Black Watch. Some 130 casualties did not destroy enthusiasm, as the enemy suffered twice as many.

There were inconclusive clashes when the British landed in mid-October 1776 at Throg's Neck and Pell's Point, east of the Americans at Harlem Heights. Howe's purpose was to penetrate northwest to the top of Manhattan Island (Kingsbridge) and pin his enemy against the Hudson. Washington's council determined to withdraw fifteen miles northward to White Plains on the mainland. With this wise move was coupled the mistaken decision to leave two thousand men at Fort Washington, hopelessly cut off from rescue. Fort Washington and Fort Constitution (later called Fort Lee) across the Hudson, both on commanding heights, and overlooking obstructions in the river, were intended to prevent passage of British vessels, but this had already proved impossible.

The hilltops at White Plains, affording a naturally strong position, were hastily fortified with earthworks. Generals Sullivan and Stirling had been exchanged after their capture on Long Island and were back for the defense. Though the American center in front of the village of White Plains was the more vulnerable, Howe chose to attack Chatterton's Hill, to the left, beginning with a heavy cannonade from a wheat field in the flat below. Before troops could climb the hill, they had to cross the little Bronx River at its eastern foot, in flood but still only a few rods wide. The Hessians balked at the stream until they could fell trees and lay fence rails across for a bridge. While doing this work, they took the musket fire of the Americans on the hillside opposite, as did British regiments that plunged through the waters at a ford a short distance below. Once the attackers were on the hill, the American militia fired one volley against charging cavalry and then fled. They were cut down by sabers, or, most of them, captured.

General McDougall arrived with reinforcements, including two fieldpieces. Colonel John Haslet, of the valiant Delaware regiment, urged that they be brought immediately into play. In view of the subsequent action—or inaction—one hopes that these guns were not commanded by Captain Alexander Hamilton. McDougall ordered one gun forward, but the gun, said Haslet in disgust, was

so poorly appointed, that myself was forced to assist in dragging it along the rear of the regiment. While so employed, a cannon-ball struck the carriage, and scattered the shot about, a wad of tow blazing in the middle. The artillerymen fled. One alone was prevailed upon to tread out the blaze and collect the shot. The few that returned made not more than two discharges, when they retreated with the field-piece. At this time the Maryland battalion was warmly engaged, and the enemy ascending the hill.

Hamilton's son and biographer, claiming later that his father took a spirited and skillful part in this fight, must not have known of Haslet's damning experience. The performance is the opposite of what we would expect of Hamilton and his company. Indeed, no contemporary, so far as found, places Hamilton on Chatterton's Hill.

The Continentals of Delaware, Maryland, and New York fought bravely until compelled to retreat unpursued to their camp; they brought off the one remaining fieldpiece. The enemy were content to occupy the height they had won, and fortified it as the leftward defense in a crescent of earthworks threatening both flanks of the American lines. Washington prudently used the interval to withdraw to North Castle (now North White Plains), where Hamilton, we know from his company pay book, procured badly needed shoes for some of his men. Embankments were speedily thrown up. One, not the work of Hamilton's battery, was a sham, to impress the enemy or, at best, shelter musketmen. It was made of cornstalks, the clod-filled roots outward, with a covering of dirt.

The British, twenty thousand strong, did not attack North Castle, but moved westward to Dobbs Ferry. Would Howe invade New Jersey or drop down to storm isolated Fort Washington? He did both. Washington had doubted the utility of the fort after enemy ships proved they could pass up the river, but until too late he listened to the insistence of Greene, Putnam, and Colonel Robert Magaw, the commander there, that the place should be held. The Americans were hampered by their troops from other posts overcrowding the works, which made their losses in prisoners—some twenty-eight hundred—and in weapons and supplies greater when the fierce enemy assault of November 16 succeeded. More than one biographer has advanced the fiction that Captain Hamilton begged to be allowed, if he could share the adventure with Major Ebenezer Stevens, to re-take Fort Washington. The fact is that Hamilton was at Hackensack, Washington was drawing his main force into New Jersey, and, even could the exploit have been mounted, the disastrous defeat of Magaw's garrison proved that the place could not have been defended. A few days after the fall of Fort Washington, Cornwallis landed three thousand troops at Alpine, New Jersey, opposite Yonkers (November 19). Next morning they clambered up the Palisades and descended the few miles to Fort Lee. General Greene, in command there, had been warned in time to evacuate, but he had to leave in such haste that all ordnance, equipment, and stores were abandoned—146 cannon, 12,000 shot and shell, 1,000 barrels of flour, besides 2,800 muskets, 400,000 cartridges, all tents, blankets, and—a loss especially felt in succeeding weeks—all entrenching tools.

2

Retreat and Triumph
in New Jersey

 Hamilton, we know from his artillery company pay book, was at Peekskill, whence his company, as part of Stirling's detachment, crossed the Hudson to Haverstraw, November 9, and passed through the Clove, a gap in the Palisades, to Hackensack. The next day Washington followed on the same route. He had left General Lee with a force at North Castle to protect New England against an upward move of the enemy, and General Heath at Peekskill to guard the highlands. Lee had 10,000 men, Heath 5,400, but in neither case did the effectives number many more than half the paper strength. As cold weather came on, and periods of enlistment neared expiration, desertion of the thinly clad, oftentimes shoeless, men became epidemic; one regiment shrank to a single company. This was before the fall of the river forts.

Since Hackensack was "a dead Flat," Washington could not fortify it. He had "not above 3000 men and they much broken and dispirited." When joined by Greene's regiments, which had fled Fort Lee, the army with Washington was brought to

5,400, but all the picks and shovels had been left behind. The British were pressing on to trap the Americans between the Hackensack and Passaic rivers. Captain Hamilton's battery doubtless continued with Stirling's brigade of 1,200 when it was sent forward across the Passaic at Aquackanock and down to Newark, Washington following. The rear guard left at Hackensack had not long to wait before they destroyed the bridge at approach of the enemy columns.

Still in the advance with Stirling, Captain Hamilton marched the twenty-odd miles to the Raritan and crossed the wooden bridge into (New) Brunswick. Washington remained five days at Newark with "the wretched remains of a broken army." He had every cause for apprehension. Soon he would have no army at all, for two thousand of the men would be free to leave him December 1, and most of the others a month later. His call on Governor Livingston to rouse the militia to his aid was in vain, for Jerseymen took Howe's protections (signed oaths of British allegiance) instead of rallying to the dwindling patriot force. About to begin his desolating trek across New Jersey, with small prospect of preventing the enemy from occupying Philadelphia, where the Congress sat, Washington was resolved to keep up a resistance. If we may believe Dr. William Gordon, a contemporary historian, Washington asked Adjutant General Joseph Reed, of Philadelphia, whether, if he were driven to retreat "to the back parts of Pennsylvania," the inhabitants would support him? Reed answered that if the eastern counties were overrun by the enemy and gave up, "the back counties will do the same." In that case, Washington replied, he would take refuge in mountainous western Virginia, and if pushed from there, he would cross the Alleghenies and persist with whatever band stuck to him. It was truly said that at certain desperate times all that remained of the American Revolution was the unconquerable courage of George Washington. Though matters worsened before they improved, he was not to be reduced to lone guerrilla defiance.

Since the British were in New Jersey and aiming at Philadelphia, General Charles Lee's force was no longer needed at North Castle to repel a march into New England. Washington had instructed Lee that if the enemy crossed to New Jersey, "I have no doubt of your following with all possible dispatch." Then, on the day that Cornwallis took Fort Lee, Colonel William Grayson, aide to Washington, notified Lee that the time had come: "His Excellency thinks it would be advisable in you to remove the troops under your command on [i.e., to] this side of the North River." This was urgently repeated the next day: "I am of opinion . . . that the public interest requires your coming over to this side." But Lee's dilatory response was maddening in the face of Washington's imperative need. Lee, one of the few professional soldiers in the army, was scornful of the amateur American commanders, Washington included, and was encouraged in his vanity and willfulness by the praise he received from officers, Joseph Reed among them, who at this juncture lamented that Washington's temporizing had doomed the forts on the Hudson.

The day after the second stronghold was forfeited, Lee wrote General William Heath at Peekskill, "I have just received a recommendation, not a positive order, from the General, to move the corps under my command to the other side of the river." He gave his reasons for preferring that Heath would send two thousand from Heath's division under a brigadier to join Washington at Hackensack. If others disparaged Washington in favor of Lee, Heath was not one of them. He immediately answered that the commander in chief's orders did not "admit of moving any part of the troops assigned to me." When Lee remonstrated, Heath repeated that he would not deviate from orders "positive and poignant," and took a jab at Lee's avoidance of Washington's wishes. "I have the salvation of the General and army so much at heart," Heath wrote, "that the least recommendation from him to march my division, or any part of them, over the river, should have been instantly obeyed, with-

27

out waiting for a positive order." Heath sent these exchanges to Washington at Newark, but had hardly received the commander in chief's approval of his conduct when Lee descended on him at Peekskill, asserted his superior rank, and ordered the regiments of Wyllis and Prescott to march with him. However, shown Washington's letter supporting Heath, Lee revoked his order, and, after further procrastination, took his own division to Chatham, New Jersey. From there, December 9, which was four days after Washington had reached across the state to the Delaware River, Lee boasted to Heath, "I am in hopes . . . to re-conquer (if I may so express myself) the Jersies," which were "really in the hands of the enemy before my arrival." This was pride that goeth before a fall, for Lee was promptly captured (December 13) at a tavern at Basking Ridge, where he had slept the night at a distance from his troops. A detachment of British horsemen, guided by an informer, grabbed him in bed and took him off, hatless and in his slippers. General Sullivan brought on Lee's two thousand men. Hamilton, like everybody else, knew Lee had been bagged; later what he learned of Lee's postponements added to his distrust of that gentleman.

Washington lacked more than Lee's assistance. Scarcely had he left Newark, to follow Stirling toward New Brunswick, than Cornwallis was treading on his heels. Three days later two thousand Maryland and New Jersey militiamen, their enlistments up, made off. In stately language, which concealed near heartbreak, Washington deplored that "being applied to they refused to continue longer in service." Worse, Pennsylvanians anticipated their release January 1 by "deserting in great numbers." The Philadelphia Associators, volunteers a thousand strong, did respond to the call of Congress, but had not yet arrived.

Captain Hamilton, with Stirling's advance, had been waiting several days at New Brunswick for Washington's columns to catch up, which they did about noon of November 29. Immediately after he arrived, Washington directed Colonel Richard

Humpton, of a Pennsylvania Continental regiment, and General William Maxwell, of the New Jersey line, to collect all boats then on the Delaware River at the west bank opposite Trenton, to be prepared to take the troops across.

Washington tarried two days at New Brunswick. December 1 he wrote Congress that the enemy, twice his numbers and more than twice his strength, had reached Bonum Town. Then in a postscript in the afternoon, "The Enemy are fast advancing, some of 'em are now in sight." With Cornwallis was Colonel Carl von Donop and his brigade of Hessians. It must have been at this time or shortly before that the Americans partially destroyed the bridge. That same afternoon Washington pursued his march to Princeton; when halfway to that town he further reported to Congress, "the enemy appeared in several parties on the Heights opposite Brunswic [*sic*] and were advancing in a large body towards the crossing place. We had a smart canonade whilst we were parading our Men but without any or but little loss on either side. It being impossible to oppose them with our present force . . . we shall retreat to the West side of Delaware."

Captain Hamilton's battery was part of this "smart canonade" to cover Washington's withdrawal. Hamilton placed his guns on the high west bank a few hundred yards from the Raritan River.[1] He must have continued firing until the American troops were well on their way, since Washington, some hours later, had uncertain knowledge of casualties. Every fieldpiece must have been engaged in lobbing shot over the Raritan. Two contemporaries, though neither was on the scene, singled out Hamilton's service. G. W. P. Custis, as Washington's step-grandson, may have had special knowledge when he reported that the commander in chief, "charmed by the brilliant courage and admirable skill" of Hamilton, sent an aide to discover who he was and at an interview at the first halt "marked him for his

[1] The location, as recited in a historical marker, is on the main campus of Rutgers University.

own." James Wilkinson simply followed Washington's report, but he himself praised Hamilton's work that day. It is pleasant to credit these special commendations, but we must remember that they were written long after the event, when the New York artillery captain was a prominent figure. Further, Egbert Benson reputedly declared that Washington first approved of Hamilton's conduct at Harlem.

Perhaps a more authentic impression of Hamilton was made upon "a veteran officer" as the young captain, with other artillerists, was hastening from New Brunswick to rejoin retreating comrades. This informant "noticed a youth, a mere stripling, small, slender, almost delicate in frame, marching . . . with a cocked hat pulled down over his eyes, apparently lost in thought, with his hand resting on a cannon, and every now and then patting it, as if it were a favorite horse or a pet plaything." And similarly "a friend" recalled "the day when Hamilton's company marched into Princeton. It was a model of discipline; at their head was a boy, and I wondered at his youth; but what was my surprise when . . . he was pointed out to me as that Hamilton of whom we had already heard so much."

Friends and foes wondered at the time why the British did not exert themselves to overtake Washington's retreat and finish off his diminished army before the Americans could reach the relative safety of Pennsylvania. Instead the king's men, Howe now in command of them, lingered on the Raritan five days after their arrival. Then they moved in two columns, under Cornwallis and von Donop respectively, to Princeton, to which they soon returned to sit for a solid month. Indeed Howe's own deputy adjutant, Major Stephen Kemble, in his journal queried, "Why not pursue Washington from Brunswick with more Spirit? His Cannon and Baggage must have fallen into our hands." Cornwallis, as shown by a debate in Parliament, was interrogated and answered for himself:

I could not have pursued the enemy from Brunswick . . . without distressing the troops under my command. . . . We had marched that day twenty miles through exceeding bad roads. We subsisted only on the flour we found in the country; and as the troops had been constantly marching ever since their first entry into the Jerseys, they had no time to bake their flour; the artillery horses and baggage horses of the army were quite tired; that sufficiently proves that we were not in a good condition to undertake a long march. The bridge over the Raritan was broken, which caused a necessary delay of one day.

Possibly Cornwallis was finding excuses for his superior, Howe. The latter, though with spurts of energy, as on Long Island, was notably leisurely in his American campaigns. This was partly due to his love of ease, including amusement with his mistress. But the suspicion, more to his credit, is that, on prompting from the British ministry, Howe did not want to end the Americans' resistance by destroying their army. Rather he expected that their military rebellion would fade from reluctant recruiting and poor supply, to the point where they would accede to a peace acceptable to the mother country. General James Grant, in command in New Jersey, immediately following Washington's capture of the Hessians at Trenton, illustrated the frequently expressed contempt for his enemy. Grant assured von Donop, who remained on the Delaware, "After all that has happened if I was with you, your Grenadiers and Yagers I should not be afraid of an attack from Washington's Army, which is almost naked and does not exceed 8000 men." Furthermore, at just the time when Washington could have been cut off in his New Jersey retreat, Howe sent Sir Henry Clinton with a division by sea to Newport, Rhode Island, where Clinton remained inactive for three years. This force could have been used to cut Washington off in New Jersey, or thereafter in Pennsylvania.

However that may be, Hamilton's battery likely caught up with Washington's march by the time Princeton was reached

This portrait of General George Washington shows him as commander in chief of the Revolutionary army. Washington's sponsorship was of foremost influence in Alexander Hamilton's career. In turn, Hamilton rendered superior service as military aide, and later, as secretary of the treasury, was a chief support of Washington's presidency. (*Portrait by Charles W. Peale, Prints Division, New York Public Library*)

Major General Charles Lee was next in command under Washington after the resignation of Artemus Ward in 1776. An English soldier of fortune, he espoused the Colonies' cause, but with
more fanfare than faithfulness. In his court-martial for disobedience to orders in the battle of Monmouth, Hamilton testified
against him. Lee was suspended from any command and later
dismissed from the army. (*Caricature by B. Rashbrooke, engraving by A. H. Ritchie, Prints Division, New York Public Library*)

Major General Henry Knox, commander of the artillery, was one of Washington's most valued subordinates. As an artillery captain Hamilton served under Knox, and they were close friends for two decades until Hamilton offended Knox by seeking precedence over him in the quasi-war with France. (*Portrait by Gilbert Stuart, courtesy of Museum of Fine Arts, Boston*)

"Never leave an enemy castle in your rear" was the military maxim obeyed by Henry Knox when he insisted on halting, in the battle of Germantown, to bombard the Chew house in which a British force had taken refuge. Hamilton, Pickering, and others vainly urged that the house should be simply sealed off while the advance against the main enemy position was pressed. The delay at the Chew house helped lose the day for the Americans. (*Painting by Alonzo Chappel, courtesy of Chicago Historical Society*)

Major General William Alexander was generally known in America as Lord Stirling, though the House of Lords did not confirm his claim to the title, which was pending at the outbreak of the Revolution. He and Alexander Hamilton had cordial ties; it may have been Stirling who recommended young Hamilton to Washington for appointment as one of the commander in chief's aides. (*Prints Division, New York Public Library*)

Major General John Burgoyne was as handsome as he was har-
ried. Leading his army of English and Germans southward from
Canada in an attempt to split the Colonies on the line of the
Hudson, he was compelled to surrender to Major General
Horatio Gates at Saratoga, October 17, 1777. Burgoyne's defeat
was decisive in bringing France to fighting partnership with
America. Hamilton was emissary in drawing Gates's victorious
troops to reinforce Washington in Pennsylvania. (*Portrait by
Joshua Reynolds, The Frick Collection*)

Major General Horatio Gates, the "Hero of Saratoga," was the candidate of his partisans to supersede Washington in supreme command. Hamilton, accidentally, figured in disclosure of Gates's complacency in receiving flattery to the prejudice of Washington. Hamilton was wrongly accused of prying in Gates's private correspondence, and later made ironic comment on the nimbleness with which Gates fled following defeat in the battle of Camden. (*Engraving by C. Tiebout from Gilbert Stuart painting, Prints Division, New York Public Library*)

If Hamilton's early impression of one was unfavorable, the relationship did not improve. James Wilkinson was an exception. Early in the war, as adjutant to General Gates, he provoked Hamilton by false insinuations. Years later, in spite of worse conduct (he accepted pay from the Spaniards against whom he was supposed to guard the southwestern frontier), he established himself in Hamilton's confidence. (*Portrait by C. F. Pidgin, Prints Division, New York Public Library*)

The encampment at Valley Forge, Pennsylvania, in the winter of 1777–1778 has become the symbol of hardship of Washington's army, though actually severer suffering was endured at Morristown, New Jersey, two years later. This house, preserved as a national shrine, was the commander in chief's headquarters at Valley Forge. (*Valley Forge State Park*)

Baron Friedrich Wilhelm von Steuben joined Washington at Valley Forge in February 1778. He will always be remembered for his success in training the troops, a service in which Hamilton assisted him in several ways. Later Hamilton exercised a kindly discipline in the old baron's private affairs. (*Portrait by Ralph Earl, courtesy of New York State Historical Association, Cooperstown, New York*)

around eight or nine o'clock the morning of December 2. After a short halt they hurried on to arrive at Trenton before noon. Here Washington learned that Cornwallis had halted at Brunswick. Washington did not know that Cornwallis stopped as long as he did against his will, on orders of Howe, who promised to join him with Grant's brigade, including Colonel Johann Rall's Hessians. Howe did not come until December 6. However, Washington felt sufficiently safe for the moment. He even started back toward Maidenhead (now Lawrenceville) and Princeton, but met Greene retreating to Trenton and turned back. He left Stirling and Stephen with fourteen hundred troops to remain near Princeton to watch the enemy and cover passage of the stores and baggage to the Delaware.

Washington was blamed for taking three weeks in the hundred-mile march across New Jersey and for then remaining several days at Trenton. Tom Paine, in the general's defense, praised the retreat as most orderly and explained that Washington proceeded slowly "that the country might have time to come [opportunity for militia to gather]." He posted Brigadier General William Maxwell at Morristown with a sizable contingent to harass the enemy and encourage the New Jersey people to be patriotic and refuse British protection. Similarly he wrote to the chairman of the Committee of Safety at nearby Easton, Pennsylvania: "I most earnestly entreat you . . . to exert your influence among the people of the County and endeavour to make them turn out generally. . . . Those who are so far lost to a love of their Country, as to refuse to lend a hand to its support, at this critical time, may depend upon being treated, as their baseness and want of Public Spirit, will most justly deserve."

Washington had barely crossed the Delaware River into Pennsylvania the morning of December 8 when Cornwallis' advance entered Trenton, to be met with grapeshot from across the stream. Had the king's men not been delayed twenty hours at Princeton to rebuild the bridge over Stony Brook, which the

Americans had destroyed, Washington would have been caught defenseless in the act of crossing the Delaware. Shortly after midnight Cornwallis set out with a strong detachment for a point near Coryell's Ferry, twelve miles above Trenton, intending to capture boats to carry over his whole army. But finding all boats on the Pennsylvania shore under Stirling's guard, Cornwallis returned to Trenton. Nor did another detachment sent to Bordentown have better luck in finding transport. Due to Washington's precaution the enemy, if they aimed to attack Philadelphia, must wait on the Jersey side for the river to freeze.

The attack on the Hessians at Trenton the morning after Christmas 1776 is to Americans the best-known action in the Revolution. The siege of Yorktown is held in remembrance, but that was long drawn-out and not a sudden dramatic stroke. Valley Forge has become a byword for steadfast suffering, but that, to outward appearance, was inaction rather than action. Alexander Hamilton figured vividly at both Trenton and Yorktown, and had a part in less spectacular happenings at Valley Forge.

Washington had been on the Pennsylvania shore of the Delaware only a few days when he began to design an assault on one or more of the enemy garrisons on the opposite side of the river. Howe's disposition of his troops in New Jersey, in scattered cantonments, invited American attack. Howe himself had returned to New York, and Cornwallis had received permission to go to England, and had actually put his baggage on board the vessel. General James Grant was left in charge of the main British post at New Brunswick, but it was a long day's march to bring relief to the Hessian brigades at Bordentown and Trenton. An enemy push against Philadelphia was still possible when the river froze, allowing them to get over it. Congress, to keep up patriot morale, had promised, December 11, not to quit Philadelphia, but two days later, with Washington's approval, they moved to Baltimore. Soon Washington was writing to Robert Morris, chief of the committee of Congress remaining in the capital, "I will give you the earliest information in my power of immediate danger; in the meantime, I advise . . . that you detain no Papers you can possibly do without, for I am satisfied the Enemy wait for two events only to begin their operations upon Philadelphia, Ice for a passage, and the dissolution of the poor remains of our debilitated Army." We know that Washington's surmise was correct. Von Donop, the Hessian commander at Bordentown, did not consider that he was settled into winter quarters, but hoped for the opportunity to subdue Philadelphia.

Adjutant General Joseph Reed's plea to Washington three days beforehand for a saving blow has sometimes been taken as prompting the general to the attack on Trenton. "We are all of Opinion," Reed urged,

that something must be attempted to revive the expiring Credit give our Cause some degree of Reputation and prevent a total Depreciation of the Continental Money . . . even a Failure cannot be more fatal than to remain in our present Situation in short some Enterprise must be undertaken . . . or we must give up the Cause. Will it not be possible . . . to make a Diversion or something more at or about Trenton. . . . Our Affairs are hasting fast to Ruin if we do not retrieve them by some happy Event.

The fact is that Washington, as usual, was ahead of those around him in forming his plans to seize a favorable chance. A week earlier he had written to Horatio Gates, "If we can draw our forces together, I trust, under the smiles of Providence, we may yet effect an important stroke." And similarly to Governor Trumbull of Connecticut, he spoke of "a stroke upon the forces of the enemy, who lie a good deal scattered, and to all appearances in a state of security. A lucky blow in this quarter . . . would rouse the spirits of the people, which are quite sunk by our late misfortunes." At the same time General Heath received notice of the commander in chief's resolve. Finally, four days later (December 18) he imparted to his brother

Augustine that something must be attempted to brighten the American prospect: "If every nerve is not strained to recruit a new army . . . I think the game is pretty nearly up."

Washington was better off for troops than he feared would be the case. The Philadelphia Associators arrived, Sullivan brought 2,000 of Lee's division, Schuyler sent down 500 New Englanders with Gates, and the Pennsylvania militia turned out in response to Thomas Mifflin's eloquence. Of some 8,000 total, 6,000 were effectives, strung out for thirty miles along the west bank of the river, guarding every ferry. Many contingents were not equipped for a winter expedition; indeed among the 2,400 he selected for sally against Trenton were numbers thinly clad and marching in broken shoes.

The general had taken every means to inform himself of the strength and outposts of the Hessians at Trenton and Bordentown. His scouting parties had been in the vicinity. Some of the "hard Money, to pay a certain set of People who are of particular use to us"—£124.7.6. which Robert Morris sent him in two canvas bags—went to reward one John Honeyman, a butcher and cattle dealer of Griggstown, Somerset County, New Jersey. Honeyman had been with Wolfe at Quebec; Washington had met him at Hackensack in November and arranged for him ("talking Tory") to ply his trade among the enemy in Trenton. There he gathered information, allowed himself to be captured by American scouts, and was whisked over the river to Washington as a suspicious character. After questioning Honeyman, Washington ordered him held in confinement, from which he "escaped" back to the Hessians for further services. The layout of the village of Trenton was familiar to Washington, some hundred houses on two principal streets—King Street and Queen Street—running almost parallel north and south and coming together at the northern edge of the town. Colonel Johann Gottlieb Rall, for his brave work at White Plains and Fort Washington, had been placed in command of the garrison of fourteen hundred troops—three regiments of Hessian infantry, a detachment of artillerymen with six guns, another of jaegers (rangers), and twenty British light dragoons. Many of the villagers having fled, the soldiers filled their houses, as well as the churches. Colonel Carl von Donop, with fifteen hundred Hessians at Bordentown, six miles downriver, as the superior officer in the vicinity had sent an engineer to Trenton to indicate to Rall the strategic points to be fortified. But Rall was contemptuous of the nondescript army across the river and neglected these precautions. He did post pickets half a mile from the village in various directions, and once in a while he sent a party as far upstream as McKonkey's Ferry to report any enemy movement. He had given no orders to be followed in case of attack. He was himself an aggressive, fearless attacker, with less thought for defense.

Washington divided his forces to cross the river at three points: Lieutenant Colonel John Cadwalader with a couple of thousand was to engage von Donop at Bordentown, Brigadier General James Ewing with a third as many would land just south of Trenton to cut off escape. The main attack, under Washington, would approach Trenton from upriver. If these assaults succeeded, the Americans would push inland to Princeton and New Brunswick.

Washington had collected Durham boats on the Pennsylvania side. These were commodious craft, forty to sixty feet long, not the smaller variety shown in the famous painting by Emanuel Leutze of *Washington Crossing the Delaware*. The afternoon of Christmas Day Washington's troops formed a mile back of McKonkey's Ferry. Colonel Henry Knox in his artillery voice announced the order of march to the boats. The early dark had fallen when embarkation began. Previously the river had been free of ice, but now was choked by obstinate, jagged cakes from frozen reaches upstream. It was all Glover's Marblehead sailors could do to fend off the blocks of ice in repeated crossings with men, horses, and eighteen fieldpieces. The commander in chief reached the Jersey shore with the first contingent,[2] but the last got over three hours behind schedule.

Instead of midnight, as planned, it was four o'clock in the morning before the nine-mile march to Trenton began. A snowstorm, changing at times to driving sleet, added to the ordeal. This was no night for Tom Paine's "summer soldier." Hamilton, with his two guns, seems to have been with Stirling's brigade in the division under Greene, which took the upper road through Pennington; the other division, under Sullivan, traversed the same distance by the river road. The surprise of the Hessian garrison could have been foiled because "day had broke" when Greene's advance drove in the picket on the Pennington road. Lieutenant Andreas Wiederhold raised the alarm with the cry of "Der Feind! Der Feind! Heraus! Heraus!" (the enemy! the enemy! all out! all out!), but the shots exchanged, and more firing when the retreating guard fell back on Captain Altenbockum's post nearer the village, did not waken Colonel Rall. He had been convivial in the Christmas celebration till near dawn, then slept deeply until one of his officers, banging on his door, brought him to the window in his nightclothes. The story that the whole garrison was sodden from drunken revels is not true. The usual guard duty had been performed, but the post, also as usual, was not prepared to meet attack.

In minutes Colonel Rall was on his horse. As Washington related, "We presently saw their main Body formed, but from their Motions, they seemed undetermined how to act."

The Hessians were confused in their sudden peril. Hemmed in by the houses, Rall's regiment and part of Lossberg's had not advanced forty paces up King Street when the balls from Hamilton's cannon ripped through their ranks. Those in Queen Street were stopped by discharges from the four guns of Cap-

[2] The scene is little changed today; the central room of the Dutch-style ferry house has the great hearth where a log fire warmed the worst sufferers that bitter night; reached by a winding stair is the chamber where Washington is said to have tarried briefly in the midst of his many duties.

tain Thomas Forrest beside Hamilton's battery at the junction of the two thoroughfares. Hessian artillerists fired two brass pieces planted in King Street, but were killed before they could repeat the volley, and their guns were promptly captured. The Americans in a twinkling swarmed into the houses, shot from windows and doorways. In the confined space the air was dense with smoke and snow. After the Hessian bayonet charges failed, Rall was leading his men out of the deadly streets when he fell from his horse with fearful wounds in his side. Drawn up in an orchard, his troops were closely surrounded, and they surrendered. Major von Dechow was mortally wounded making a dash for the bridge across Assunpink Creek, which was hopeless because Brigadier General Arthur Saint Clair's corps blocked escape from destruction, except by surrender.

Some three hundred of the garrison had earlier got over the Assunpink toward Bordentown; but these too would have been bagged if ice, backed up by the tide, had not prevented Ewing and Cadwalader from crossing the river.

After an hour's fight the Americans had captured 918 of the enemy, including thirty officers, six brass cannon, as many muskets as men, and four of the prized Hessian standards. Since, as Washington reported to Congress, the Hessians "never made any regular Stand," they had only thirty killed and three times as many wounded. No American was killed, four were slightly wounded.

Burdened with prisoners and menaced by von Donop's troops at Bordentown, Washington abandoned thought of penetration to Princeton and Brunswick. The snowstorm continuing, it was enough to retrace the toilsome miles to McKonkey's, where the river crossing was worse than before. The last of the weary men did not reach their quarters in Pennsylvania until forty-eight hours after they had set out to attack Trenton. Though at another time of less exertion in the military field Hamilton pushed his strength beyond the limit, we hear nothing of his succumbing to the fatigue of the Trenton exploit.

46

Doubtless his eager spirit buoyed his body. He must have shared Washington's resolve. The general explained that when the delayed start seemed to rule out his planned surprise, "there was no making a Retreat without being discovered, and harassed on repassing the River," therefore "I determined to push on at all Events."

An ironic footnote: When attendants undressed the dying Colonel Rall, they found in his pocket, certainly unread, a scrawled note from a Bucks County Loyalist giving the Hessian commander word, hours in advance of the attack, that Washington was on his march.

The desperate, brilliant stroke at Trenton reversed the patriots' gloom and brought to Washington's camp more recruits than he could arm. The shamefaced General Howe countermanded Cornwallis' departure. General James Grant, commanding at New Brunswick, and responsible for the safety of the Hessians in the river posts, commiserated with von Donop on "a most unfortunate business. I did not think," he confessed, "that all the Rebels in America would have taken that Brigade prisoners." William, count of Hesse-Hanau and son of the landgrave of Hesse-Cassel, had sold his conscripted countrymen to fight and die in an alien cause. This did not prevent that princeling from going into mock fury. He wrote to General William von Knyphausen, commanding his mercenaries, "The death of Colonel Rall has taken him away from my wrath which he so well deserved in allowing himself to be so inexcusably surprised." He ordered courts martial—delayed because the accused officers were prisoners—which blamed Rall for not hastening his troops out of Trenton instantly he saw that the place was in possession of the enemy.

Obliged to depart New Jersey as suddenly as he had entered for his brilliant coup at Trenton, Washington did not abandon his "purpose of attempting a recovery of that country from the Enemy." His second sally into New Jersey within a week was as surprising as his descent upon the Hessians. He wrote

47

Robert Morris, "I am taking every Measure to improve our late lucky Blow, and hope to be successful." Morris, on the general's appeal, had taken the necessary measure of sending him fifty thousand dollars, paper of course, but promptly raised in Philadelphia on Morris' personal credit. On December 29 from his headquarters at New Town, Pennsylvania, Washington informed Congress, "I am just setting out, to attempt a second passage over the Delaware, with the Troops that were with me on the Morning of the 26th. I am determined to effect it, if possible" in spite of the mini-icebergs. He would be joined in New Jersey by Cadwalader's eighteen hundred men, who had got over two days before. Mifflin had sent across five hundred militia and was following with seven or eight hundred more. So Washington would have five thousand men for the expedition. Besides, the corps at Morristown under Maxwell was to proceed southward. But the enemy had a force of eight thousand, trained and fit, more than a match for Washington's raw militia and a few weary Continentals. The enlistment of the latter was expiring December 31; they were mostly New Englanders, far from home, and were about to decamp at this critical moment. The eloquence of Quartermaster-General Thomas Mifflin, which had already drummed up the Pennsylvania militia, saved the day with the restless Continentals at Crosswicks, New Jersey. His appeal to them to stay on for another six weeks took color from his "overcoat made up of a large rose blanket." Robert Morris' purse would furnish a bounty of ten dollars each, and there would be booty besides. When the commander in chief reached Trenton after a two-day struggle with the river, he was cheered by the news that Mifflin's hearers had responded to a man.

Congress, at length confessing its failure to support the campaign, now gave Washington for six months the dictatorial powers to raise troops and impress supplies. Civil government, so far as the war was concerned, was for the nonce in abeyance. Washington in the emergency did use the authority shifted to him, but, characteristically, no further than he was compelled by exigency in the field. Throughout the war he scrupulously deferred to Congress, though that body summoned resources in inverse ratio to its responsibility for conducting the war. We shall see that the present instance of virtual abdication and further examples of the incompetence of Congress were not lost on Alexander Hamilton. On the eve of the conflict he had rallied resistance with political reasoning, and in the midst of fighting he was eager for the better deployment of legislators.

On January 1 Washington had sent a corps toward Princeton. The next day Cornwallis, posting strong detachments, 1,200 each at Princeton and Maidenhead, marched from the former place with 5,500 troops and a train of artillery through heavy roads for Trenton. The Americans, with only two fieldpieces, at every vantage point bravely disputed his progress and were not forced back to the south of the Assunpink Creek at Trenton until early darkness was falling. They found refuge with Washington's army, which had taken that position and held the bridge and fords above against brisk British attack. Cornwallis, usually more aggressive, preferred to postpone the battle until dawn. His enemy, he saw, was trapped in low ground between creek and river, and could be dispatched the next day. Sir William Erskine, in the consultation, objected, "If Washington is the general I take him to be, he will not be found there in the morning."

In spite of this prophecy, the British and Hessians bedded in the town, assured by the Americans' blazing campfires and ringing entrenching tools that their quarry remained at hand.

Captain Hamilton, when ordered an hour past midnight to hitch his horses and wrap the wheels of his gun carriages with rags to silence them on the now frozen roads, could not have known Washington's design to detour the enemy for a strike at Princeton. Only the general officers knew the strategy. A nimble rear guard was charged to keep up the fires, protect the bridge, and thus deceive the British picket until the army was withdrawn. Avoiding the highway, they traveled a new woods road, stump strewn, via Sandtown.

After stumbling a dozen dark miles, with the artillery particularly impeded, the Americans emerged from the forest a short distance southwest of Princeton as the sun rose. For a moment they took in the scene of Lieutenant Colonel Charles Mawhood riding at the head of his regiments down a slope into an open meadow, a couple of spaniels frisking about him. He had been ordered to leave a guard in the village of Princeton, pick up General Leslie's corps at Maidenhead, and join Cornwallis at Trenton. But this picture, as of a parade, suddenly changed as both Americans and British dashed for high ground in an orchard. The Americans, closer, gained it first, and the enemy was forced to face them in the field below. The principal fighting was in a small space, maybe three hundred yards both ways. The two American guns in action were not Hamilton's, for his battery had been sent around with Sullivan's division to attack Princeton. After two volleys General Hugh Mercer's men broke before Mawhood's bayonet charge. Mercer's horse was wounded; dismounted, he strove to recall his fleeing troops; knocked down, he rose sword in hand, but fell again with seven bayonet wounds.[3] Colonel John Haslet, whose own Delawareans had gone home, was leading some of Mercer's militia back to the field when he was killed instantly by a bullet through his head. Mawhood pursued Mercer's demoralized companies until met by Cadwalader with a fresh force. The Philadelphians formed in the face of artillery and musket fire, but after a few volleys took to the woods.

Washington was with the division that had detoured to Princeton. At the firing, he galloped back to the battle, which

---

[3] One is shown today the small room in the adjacent farmhouse where he died. He was an exemplary patriot. Born in Aberdeen, Scotland, he was a surgeon with the clansmen of "Bonnie Prince Charlie" until Culloden finished the Young Pretender's hopes. Coming to Virginia, Mercer fought under Generals Edward Braddock and John Forbes in the Seven Years War. At the outbreak of the Revolution he organized his neighbors in militia and offered himself in any capacity.

seemed lost. As at Monmouth, later, he exposed himself to the greatest danger, in even closer quarters, to hold his panicky lines. From the troops that had already reached the village came Rhode Island and Virginia Continentals and Pennsylvania riflemen to his support. Some of the retreaters returned, and Captain Joseph Moulder's battery came into play from the ridge where Mercer had first stood. Mawhood's men broke through the surrounding cordon, but did not keep their orderly retreat toward Trenton when hotly pursued by American horse and infantry. Those not killed or captured scattered in every direction.

The British in the village of Princeton either made off for New Brunswick or forted themselves in the college building, Nassau Hall, which was promptly surrounded. The story is that Captain Hamilton fired a ball that entered the chapel and pierced a portrait of George II. However, other accounts differ. James Wilkinson, without identifying Hamilton's battery, declared there was but a single gun fired at Nassau Hall; if one ball found an appropriate target in the royal visage, he knew nothing of that, but remembered sourly a shot that "recoiled, and very nearly killed my horse as I passed in rear of the building." True or not, Hamilton later, as we shall see, made some verbal discharges that very nearly unhorsed Wilkinson. The number of the enemy who surrendered in Nassau Hall is variously reported between 60 and 200. As usual, the casualties on both sides are uncertain, perhaps 40 Americans and twice as many of the king's men killed or wounded, plus some 185 of the latter missing.

Washington's ambition was to press on and repeat his success at New Brunswick, the enemy's headquarters in New Jersey. He did go three of the eighteen miles toward this objective, chasing Mawhood's retreaters as far as Kingston. But his men were exhausted from two days of continuous exertion—crossing the river, holding back the enemy at Trenton, the bitter night march to Princeton, and fierce fighting there, all with no proper food. Leslie would be after them from Maidenhead; actually the last

Americans quit Princeton in sight of Cornwallis' advance. His lordship had made double time to retrieve his mistaken trust that his enemy would stay put at Trenton; the bridge over Stony Brook had broken again, but the British breasted the icy waters in their haste.

Washington's anxious council with his officers at Kingston decided to call it enough and turn off for the American post already established at Morristown. Fortunately Cornwallis thought Washington was making a detour to New Brunswick, and pushed on to defend that valuable depot. Washington regretfully told Congress that with "six or seven hundred fresh troops, upon a forced march," he could have "destroyed all their Stores, and Magazines, taken . . . their Military Chest, containing seventy thousand pounds, and put an end to the War." As it was, his road lay by Somerset Courthouse, reached for a bleak camp that night, then on to Pluckemin and a two-day rest before marching to Morristown January 6.

Here in winter quarters began a new chapter in Alexander Hamilton's military career.

3

Aide to
Commander in Chief

 We are told that General Greene, in New York in the summer of 1776, on his way to Washington's headquarters, was impressed by the brisk drill of an artillery company and by the competence and bearing of their commanding officer. He sent a messenger to compliment Captain Hamilton and to invite him to dinner. Thus began a friendship that ended only in Greene's untimely death; Hamilton pronounced his eulogy in Saint Paul's Chapel. General Greene may have recommended Hamilton for Washington's staff; Boudinot, continuing his good offices, may have done so; Knox, impressed by Hamilton's spirited performance at Trenton and Princeton, may have passed on word that here was a young fellow eligible for preferment. All three of these possible sponsors would have known of Hamilton's studies and aptitude with the pen, besides his efficiency as a junior commander in the field. Perhaps more than one of these friends, aware that the commander in chief was shorthanded at headquarters, may have suggested that Hamilton be employed. George Baylor, though "not in the

smallest degree a penman," had been useful on the staff until he took the Hessian colors, captured at Trenton, to Congress, and then chose a command in the cavalry. Robert Hanson Harrison, entirely dependable as a secretary, was absent from camp because of illness. Richard Meade was added to the staff within a fortnight of Hamilton's appointment. John Walker of Virginia, in the Morristown camp in a civilian capacity, was taken as an extra aide. Doubtless if we had the letter that Washington asked Harrison to "forward . . . to Captn. Hamilton," we should find it was the invitation to join the general's staff, and gave the reasons for Washington's choice.

The close association with the commander in chief, thus commenced and continuing for four years, was serviceable in all the business of headquarters and determined Hamilton's career in the nation after the war. At the center of the struggle, in campaigns and camps, the aide knew and was an agent in all of the complex operations. His duties extended to every sort of service, as Washington's assistant or proxy. Not only was he depended on at headquarters and as an aide conveying orders in battle, but the general charged him with missions, as much diplomatic as military, in which he had to use his own discretion.

The passing scene meant more to Alexander Hamilton than the day's work. He reflected on what the commander in chief, the country at war, and he himself were experiencing. Others on the staff for different periods, who later entered public life —Thomas Mifflin, James McHenry, and David Humphreys, for example—were similarly informed, but Hamilton particularly drew from the conflict original lessons for the future of America. Not content with laments at trials, and efforts at the moment to cope with them, Hamilton, while still in uniform, analyzed causes and formulated reasoned remedies for wartime and when peace should be achieved.

Mrs. Emily Whiteley, in her agreeable picture of life at headquarters,[1] says no one assistant was placed above others in the

[1] *Washington and His Aides-de-Camp* (New York, Macmillan Company, 1936).

general's reliance. He undoubtedly appreciated the qualities of individuals, was companionable with them, and promoted their prospects when the war was won. "Friend Dick" (Richard Kidder Meade) was often the choice for riding assignments; after Meade's marriage he followed the general's advice to become a planter in Virginia, and visited Mount Vernon when Washington resumed farming. Robert Hanson Harrison, the "Old Secretary," young in years but senior in service to most of them, was cordially known to Washington in Alexandria before the war, and was always able to transmit his superior's wishes; he became chief judge of the Maryland General Court, and only ill health prevented him from accepting President Washington's appointment to the Supreme Court of the United States. Tench Tilghman of Maryland early volunteered as a secretary, long refused pay or rank, was honored with taking to Congress the news of Cornwallis' surrender, and accompanied the general when he resigned his commission. As modest as he was faithful, he held a special place in the commander in chief's affections, to which Washington feelingly testified when Tilghman, in merchant partnership with Robert Morris, died soon after the peace.

Washington explained, at Cambridge in 1776, "at present my time is so taken up at my desk, that I am obliged to neglect many other essential parts of my duty; it is absolutely necessary . . . for me to have persons that can think for me, as well as execute orders." This was Hamilton's particular contribution, as shown in the use Washington made of his talents, and which induced observers of headquarters and Washington himself to refer to Hamilton as the commander in chief's "principal confidential aide." Everything fell upon Washington; "the Weight of the whole War," said Tilghman, "lay upon his Shoulders." His direction was required in every quarter: a floating militia indifferently officered; departments of supply, intelligence, and hospitals disorganized; Congress and states jealous of their authority. Hamilton could suggest ways and means, as well as, at the general's command, embody them in policy. We have sufficient evidence of this in the headquarters years; if needed, we have only to argue backward from their association in the cabinet, Hamilton's continuing assistance to the President after leaving the Treasury, and Washington's wish that Hamilton be his second in command in preparing for war with France in 1798.

It is not necessary to say that Washington—personally and in position and prestige—was of enormous importance in forwarding Hamilton's career. Among the juniors at headquarters Hamilton was not the most emotionally attached to the commander in chief. The general had Hamilton's trust, admiration, and deep respect, but not his affection to anything like the extent that the hearts of Tilghman, Meade, John Laurens, Knox, and others went out to their superior. Hamilton could and did lose himself in love of country, but in relations with individuals, unless the nearest and dearest, his self-esteem and ambition got in the way of unselfish devotion.

Some biographers of Hamilton have suggested that Washington's solicitude for him was because Washington sought in him a foster son. Not only was Washington childless, but his stepson, John Parke ("Jacky") Custis, was far from satisfactory. One romanticist has gone so far as to venture that Hamilton was, in fact, Washington's natural son. The sole basis for this flight of imagination is the conjecture that Hamilton's mother may have been in Barbados in 1751, when Washington was there in attendance on his brother, Lawrence Washington, who was suffering from tuberculosis. Rachael Lavien's husband, in his application for divorce, complained that she had left him (probably in 1750) and gone off to "an English island," where she was guilty of shameless conduct. The whole imputation is not worth the space required to mention it. Even had George Washington, worried about Lawrence, and himself attacked by smallpox, been gallivanting on Barbados, supposing he found Rachael Lavien there and similarly inclined, their casual union would have made Alexander at least three and possibly five years older than we believe him to have been. The two men differed in physical frame—Washington 6 feet 2 inches, Hamilton 5 feet 7—and in temperament.

On the theme of Washington looking for an adoptive son, his attachment for John Laurens, another of his aides, is more plausible. Laurens, in addition to his gifts, was personally devoted to Washington, and fought a duel with Charles Lee who had spoken disrespectfully of his hero. Outside of the immediate military family, the most filial of Washington's juniors was Lafayette, whose feelings of attachment the commander in chief returned. Ironically, in later years due to party antagonisms in this country, President Washington was unable to receive Lafayette's son, George Washington Lafayette, as soon as the youngster arrived with his tutor in 1795. Hamilton, acting for Washington, was obliged to keep the visitors at a distance for six months before political reasons for sequestration could yield to personal cordiality.

Unresponsive real sons are plentiful, but proxy ones who do not warm to the foster parent must be rarer. Hamilton's admiration for Washington was as a public figure; his lament at Washington's death was that he had lost a valuable patron, not a cherished would be father.

Fortunately for their long, fruitful collaboration, Washington and Hamilton were alike, practically identical, in political principles. They rarely disagreed on aims. In charting a course to accomplish common ends, Washington was the more deliberate and wiser. Almost anyone was second to him in these qualities. Hamilton frequently, in youth and in maturity, acted on impulse. He might correct himself, or be checked by the judgment of others before harm was done. Some mistakes he lived down, but on occasion his indiscretions were irretrievable. This is not to say that he was prone to act hastily, without pondering all the elements in a situation. But in comprehensive awareness of a problem, Washington's grasp was superior.

Hamilton was twenty-two on joining the staff, but, with his small stature, high coloring, and debonair manner, he seemed even younger. A miniature on ivory by Charles Willson Peale is supposed to be of Hamilton just at this time. He wears across his breast the green ribbon that was the insignia of an aide; the face is handsome, delicate, exceedingly youthful. If the artist had presented him otherwise, it would have been to belie his precocity. A favorite with his fellows, Harrison, ten years Hamilton's senior, called him the "Little Lion," a sobriquet that stuck.

Washington several times described the qualifications of an aide; he should have education, sense, and good temper. "As to Military knowledge, I do not expect to find Gentlemen much skilled in it. If they can write a good Letter, write quick, are methodical, and diligent, it is all I expect to find in my Aids." During the war he had thirty-two in all, though generally only five or six at any one time. If in winter camp, and the headquarters house permitted, the aides had a room where they wrote and another where they slept. When Hamilton commenced at Morristown, New Jersey, headquarters were in the Arnold Tavern on the west side of the village green. That building has disappeared; perhaps Washington and his "family" were more cramped there than in the Jacob Ford mansion, which they later occupied. It is standing in the Morristown Historical Park, has been kept in original condition, and is suitably furnished. Even that spacious dwelling was crowded, for Mrs. Ford and her children needed half of it. The front room to the left of the entrance was Washington's office, where he wrote and received the stream of visitors who could not be diverted to his aides. Behind was the apartment, convenient at hand, with the aides' desks. The chamber of the young men was on the second floor, across the hallway at the rear. His aides had to be always within call.

"I give in to no kind of amusement myself," said Washington,

and consequently those about me can have none, but are confined from morning till eve, hearing and answering the applications and letters. . . . If these gentlemen had the same relaxation from duty as other officers have in their common routine, there would not be so much in it. But, to have the mind always upon the stretch, scarce ever unbent, and no hours for recreation makes a material odds.

"Winter quarters," Tilghman reported to his friend Robert Morris, "[brings] an increase in business in the way of paper, pens and ink." He assured his father, "you need be under no Apprehension of my losing [my health] on the Score of Excess in living. . . . Vice is banished from . . . the General's Family. . . . We never sup, but go early to bed and are early up." Pressing demands on the aides, particularly when Hamilton was absent on his mission to Horatio Gates, prevented John Laurens from asking leave for the briefest visit away from camp. From White Marsh, sitting "in a small noisy crouded room," he wrote his father: "Between copying and composing I have inked a great deal of paper and it begins to be time for me to join . . . my snoring Companions, who are extended before the fire in the Style which we practiced formerly in the interior parts of So Carolina." Hamilton often spoke of "hurry of business" that prevented him from writing at length, or explained that Washington was so engaged that he had not been able to bring an important matter to the general's attention.

Actually, this regimen, while strict enough, was relieved by outside assignments, by occasional rides with the general, and by dances when the wives of principal officers, joining their husbands in winter quarters, inaugurated what passed for a social season. General and Mrs. Henry Knox, in spite of famous bodily bulk, were among the liveliest in a cotillion. And Washington did sometimes allow himself amusement, evidently concentrated when he indulged, for he once danced with the animated Mrs. Nathanael Greene for three hours.

Dinner at headquarters, though there might be little to eat or drink, preserved the amenities. The officer of the day was always expected, the current adjutant general probably came, and distinguished visitors to camp were guests, along with a sprinkling of ladies, if available. Alexander Graydon gives us a glimpse of Hamilton in the first winter at Morristown. He "presided at the general's table, where we dined; and in a large company in which there were several ladies, among whom I recollect one or two of the Miss Livingstons and a Miss Brown, he acquitted himself with an ease, propriety and vivacity, which gave me the most favourable impression of his talents and accomplishments." That evening Hamilton and Tilghman took Graydon to drink tea with the ladies in the village, including those with whom they had dined. Three years later, again at Morristown, Hamilton discovered intervals in which to court Elizabeth Schuyler, who was visiting her aunt, Mrs. John Cochran.

In temporary camps during campaigns, secretarial work had to go forward under awkward conditions. Perhaps in a tent and perched on a cot, Hamilton wrote on a portable desk, which now belongs to Hamilton College, at Clinton, New York. Compact, and a fine specimen of cabinet work, it came through many loadings on baggage wagons with no damage.

In conduct of his correspondence by his assistants, Washington adapted his directions to the nature of the matter in hand and the experience and aptitude of the aide. His instructions might be more or less specific. To a beginner he might practically dictate what was to be said. A practiced helper might wish for more pointers than were given him. Thus Harrison, coming down from Washington's room at Valley Forge, complained to Pickering, "I wish to the Lord the General would give me the heads or some idea, of what he would have me write." As it happens we have just such an outline, in Harrison's hand, jotted down, on the back of a letter from William Duer, at Morristown the day after Hamilton entered the staff. The memo runs:

The forage in West Chester. The consequence resulting from the retreat of Heath and Wooster for mtg. [mustering] Militia to prevent outrages of Rangers. Calling Conl. [Continental] Troops by parts injuerious. Forage should be got off soon as possible or sooner. The Enemy drawn their Force from N. York and design Phila. The Enemy going up North River. The Convn. should certly. [sic] interpose about purchase of provision. Expedn. to Long Isld. Mr. S.

Not having the letter, we do not know how this brief was expanded. In Hamilton's case, as time passed, Washington trusted more and more to his aide's knowledge and discretion concerning content, especially where Hamilton had been dealing with a problem over a period. Hamilton came to understand Washington's intentions so well that he could often anticipate them in a given instance, and express them in language such as the commander in chief himself would use.

We have means of knowing what were Hamilton's own contributions to letters and documents he prepared at Washington's direction and for his approval. Of course when Washington, after careful reading and frequently some revision, affixed his signature, these papers became his own. In editions of Hamilton's writings, those that received Washington's name are properly calendared (identified as to date and subject), and only what Hamilton signed is credited to him. Still, one who has read extensively in Hamilton's writings has little difficulty— usually, not always—in recognizing his native style of expression and thought. Where he wrote for Washington two or more letters, say, on the same subject, differences in phraseology or emphasis may reasonably be attributed to his own choice. In other instances, which multiplied as time went on, where the materials or argument were best known to him, though Washington gave his authority, we cannot mistake Hamilton's originality. The chief example is the instructions to John Laurens (January 15, 1781) for his representation to the French court of the critical need of America for financial and naval aid.

Others of Washington's secretarial assistants at headquarters were young men of education and abilities in conveying accurately the intentions of the commander in chief, and their postwar careers, if we required any proof beyond Washington's confidence, demonstrated their worth. Two particularly, besides Hamilton, possessed literary talents. These were David Humphreys, remembered for his copious patriotic poetry, and James McHenry, also a versifier, who wrote the response of Congress to Washington when he resigned his commission. But

Hamilton's associates on the staff, even at that early day, would be the first to agree that he had a "power of statement," as Henry Cabot Lodge put it, that was surpassing. From the time he was a boy he had taken a delight in wording his thoughts on paper; in joining Washington's staff at the age of twenty-two he was advanced in this respect beyond his years. It is sufficient to allude to his *Federalist* papers, his Treasury reports, and finally, Washington's choice of Hamilton to develop and polish his "Farewell Address." To excellent thought and expression Hamilton added, we may agree, the touch of genius.

Years later (in 1798), when Washington was commander in chief of the provisional army to be raised for expected defense against France, many applied to become aides in his military family. These well-meaning requests he politely deferred while he took his time to choose fit characters.

The variegated, and important, duties of the Aids of a Commander in Chief, or, the Commander of a separate Army [he observed] require experienced Officers, men of judgment, and men of business, *ready pens* to execute them properly, and with dispatch. A great deal more is required of them than attending him at a Parade, or delivering verbal orders here and there; or copying a written one. They ought if I may be allowed to use the expression, to possess the Soul of the General; and from a *single* Idea given to them, to convey his meaning in the clearest and fullest manner. This, young men unacquainted with the Service and diffident, would not do; be their abilities what they may.

The capacity he needed he found, during the Revolution, in several tried aides, foremost in Alexander Hamilton. This knowledge of the qualities displayed by his chief headquarters assistant, with much besides, figured in Washington's designation of Hamilton to stand next to him in command of the provisional army.

The notion that Hamilton, in his first weeks after joining Washington's headquarters staff, was assigned only to routine or simple correspondence (Whiteley, *Washington and His Aides-de-Camp*) is not borne out by careful reading of the letters. It may be said at once that they required not only grasp and accuracy, but tact in expression. That he was entrusted with drafting important missives for the commander in chief is to be expected. Washington chose the members of his "military family" with care; they must have fitness for his work and be "perfectly confidential." If he did not know beforehand, he soon discovered which of the young men about him were better as "riding aides" and which had the faculties for "writing aides." Actually Hamilton served in both capacities. Though Hamilton was appointed to the staff and commissioned lieutenant colonel March 1, 1777, as was announced in general orders that day, Pickering had found him at headquarters in February, and then received the impression "that Hamilton was a very extraordinary young man." This prior acquaintance (during which we have no letters in his hand), gave him an opportunity to see what others did, and permitted Washington to judge his capacities. Tilghman also had been at headquarters a while before he was formally appointed in the previous August. From several persons—Boudinot, Stirling, Greene, Benjamin Lincoln—Washington may have known of Hamilton's turn for the written word, and he may even have heard of his patriotic pamphlets, which had attracted notice a couple of years earlier.

Hamilton's first letter for the commander in chief, the day he entered on his service, was to mollify Lieutenant Colonel Archibald Campbell, a prisoner. British headquarters had complained that Campbell, along with five Hessian field officers, was being harshly treated in retaliation for Britain's refusal to parole General Charles Lee. The day before, Washington had written his remonstrance to Congress, stressing the impolicy of such action, especially while the British held three hundred American officers, and the Colonials had only fifty of theirs. Campbell was a member of Parliament from Dunfermline, Scotland. Pending an answer from Congress (which was a refusal to alter the order), Hamilton, for Washington, assured Campbell, "I shall always be happy to manifest my disinclination to any undue severities towards those whom the fortunes of war may chance to throw into my Hands." This was early in a long correspondence concerning Lee's status in British hands—whether they would try him as a traitor or treat him as an ordinary prisoner of war and subject to exchange. For a time Campbell and the Hessians were offered to be released in return for Lee, since the Americans held no enemy major general, but this was unacceptable to Howe. Later, Washington's bargaining position was improved by the capture of the British Major General Richard Prescott. The pending swap involved the negotiation of a general cartel for the exchange of prisoners, in which Hamilton with others was to act for Washington.

That same day the new aide drafted a correction, or at least admonition, to General Horatio Gates. The "very extraordinary . . . returns of desertion given in to you, appear to be utterly impossible; should therefore be glad you would call the Colonels together, and endeavour to find out the source of this iniquitous Scheme; and if you are fortunate enough to fix it on any person, to bring him to the most exemplary punishment." (What was happening, as Washington soon explained to Brigadier General John Cadwalader, was that "the infamous practice of peculation has found its way into the Recruiting Service and . . . much money [recruiting allowance plus bounty] is received for Deserters that never were Inlisted"; also bounty-jumping, frequently several times repeated, was prevalent among pretended recruits.) The implied censure of Gates went on: "You can at least fall upon some plan for discouraging such proceedings, in future, such as reviewing the Companies at certain times." Scolding a major general for neglect demanded delicacy as well as clarity from the commander in chief's draftsman. Before the year was concluded, Hamilton was reporting to Washington his own complaints about the conduct of Gates.

Hamilton and Harrison combined their skills in a brief letter for Washington to General Artemus Ward (March 3, 1777), relieving him, at his own request, of his command in Boston, and notifying him that General William Heath would take his place.

Ward had been regarded as commander in chief of American forces before Washington arrived at Cambridge, but now his decision to resign his commission was acceptable, as age and ill health hindered his usefulness. Courtesy with restraint seemed the right form of acknowledgment: "I beg you will accept my thanks for your Zeal and Services, and believe me to be with all due respect &c." Washington at once, in Hamilton's words, ordered Heath to succeed to Ward's post.

Next came cautions in a proposed attack on the enemy in Rhode Island: first to Major General Joseph Spencer, about the enterprise he had in view, "as it may be productive of consequences importantly beneficial, so it may be attended with effects the most importantly injurious." The same day (March 3) Washington, with Hamilton again his scribe, was more particular with the audacious Benedict Arnold on the same topic, and broached a question touching Arnold's pride. Arnold was already known for his brave but often opinionated initiative.

I must recall your attention [Washington enjoined] to what I have before said on the Subject of your intended attack. You must be sensible that the most serious ill consequences may and would, probably, result from it in case of failure, and prudence dictates, that it should be cautiously examined in all its lights, before it is attempted. Unless your Strength and Circumstances be such, that you can reasonably promise yourself a *moral certainty* of succeeding, I would have you by all means to relinquish the undertaking, and confine yourself, in the main, to a defensive operation.

He had addressed Arnold as "Major General," but this was provisional, as at once appeared.

We have lately had several promotions to the rank of Major General, [the commander in chief continued] and I am at a loss whether you have had a preceeding [sic] appointment, as the news papers announce, or whether you have been omitted by some mistake. Should the latter be the case, I beg you will not take any hasty steps in consequence of it; but allow proper time for recollection, which, I flatter myself, will remedy any error that may have been made. My endeavours to that end shall not be wanting.

In promotions voted by Congress a fortnight earlier (February 19), Brigadier General Arnold was passed over, and five brigadiers, junior to him, were advanced to the higher rank; they were Stirling, Mifflin, St. Clair, Adam Stephen, and Benjamin Lincoln.

It is well known that this slight to Arnold was an ingredient in his resentment, which nearly three years later prompted him to treason. Answering Washington's appeal, however, he requested a court of inquiry on his conduct, but promised, "I shall Cautiously avoid any hasty Step (in Consequence of the Appointments which have taken place) that may tend to Injure my Country." Meantime Washington inquired of Richard Henry Lee—still in Congress and who had been a member of the committee which placed Washington in supreme command—whether Arnold had been passed over by accident or design. "Surely," he declared, "a more active, a more spirited, and sensible officer, fills no department in your army."

Just as Washington exhorted Benedict Arnold to put patriotism above reward in rank, so at the same time (in Hamilton's words) he enlarged on the theme to William Woodford, who should accept appointment as brigadier, though dated after similar commissions of Peter Muhlenberg and George Weedon, formerly his juniors. This was because Woodford had resigned his former rank in Continental service, but Washington urged,

If smaller matters do not yield to greater, If trifles, light as Air in comparison of what we are contending for, can withdraw or withhold Gentlemen from Service, when our all is at Stake and a single cast of the die may turn the tables, what are we to expect! It is not a common contest we are engaged in . . . and . . . success depends upon a Steady and Vigorous exertion. Consider twice therefore, before you refuse.

In the fervor of this appeal the aide's own dedication to the American cause was evident.

A week after assuming his duties as aide to General Washington, Hamilton wrote to the New York Provincial Congress, in effect resigning his commission as captain of the state artillery company. What with deaths, desertions, and expiration of enlistments, the company was reduced "at present to the small number of 25 men." If the state wished to retain it, he recommended that Lieutenant Thomas Thompson be advanced to a captain-lieutenancy; he could not urge Lieutenant John Bean for preferment beyond his present rank. Four new officers should be appointed, the full complement of rank and file be completed, and the pay of all, under the new arrangement for the artillery, should be raised to a fourth more than the other troops. However, as the company could hardly answer any good purpose to the state, he supposed it should be transferred to the Continental establishment, with no difficulty. The New York Congress deputed Gouverneur Morris to inform Hamilton of its resolve "that the . . . company be permitted to enlist in the service of the Continent." [2] Morris asked Hamilton to take the necessary steps.

Of course the authorities of the different states were anxious for frequent and reliable news from Washington's headquarters. Since the commander in chief could not write often, the Virginia legislature sent John Walker, a well-recommended young man, to camp to keep it informed. General Washington wrote Governor Patrick Henry (February 24, 1777, a few days before Hamilton joined the staff) that he had appointed Walker an extra aide. In this capacity he

may obtain the best information, and, at the same time, have his real design hid from the World; thereby avoiding the evils which might otherwise result from such Appointments if adopted by other States. It will naturally occur to you, Sir, that there are some Secrets, on the keeping of which . . . depends, oftentimes, the salvation of an Army:

[2] The last entries in the pay book of the New York Company of Artillery were made May 23, 1777. In turning over the company, Hamilton was to inquire about the guns belonging to New York, lest "we may perhaps never see them again." General Knox promptly assured him "that he had still your six pieces in his hands" and that "he considered the Continent at all times bound to make good the number borrowed from your state."

Secrets which . . . ought not to be intrusted to paper; nay, which none but the Commander in Chief at the time, should be acquainted with.

If Walker's assignment from Virginia were known, other states would send their reporters, who would "be no better than so many marplots." Some months earlier (September 17, 1776) the New York Provincial Convention had appointed a committee, which by daily expresses to and from headquarters should "write letters to any correspondents, and take every other proper means to obtain intelligence." In this case also it was arranged that the informant be confidential, a member of Washington's military family, Tench Tilghman.

When Gouverneur Morris was named to the New York committee of correspondence, March 14, 1777, it was doubtless he who suggested that Alexander Hamilton take over the duties previously performed by Tilghman. Morris, when the convention was notified of Hamilton's appointment as an aide-de-camp, had handled the transfer of his artillery company to the Continental service. Two members of the convention, Jacob Cuyler and John Taylor, who had recently been at headquarters, likely brought word that Hamilton would be an eligible correspondent, and indeed must have discussed the possibility with him. Morris and William Allison, for the committee, [3] wrote Hamilton (from Kingston, March 17) that he was their choice to communicate "Any Occurrences in the Army which may have happened." Another letter, two days later (which we do not have) evidently gave particulars of the arrangement, [4] but without waiting for that, Hamilton replied: "With cheerfulness, I embrace the proposal of corresponding with your convention, through you, and shall from time to time as far as my

[3] The other member of the correspondence committee was Robert R. Livingston, Jr.; Gouverneur Morris had been appointed to the place of Henry Wisner, Jr.

[4] The N.Y. Convention had voted Tilghman, for his services, a present of the value of £80.

leisure will permit, and my duty warrant, communicate . . .
such pieces of intelligence as shall be received and such comments upon them as shall appear necessary, to convey a true idea
of what is going on in the military line."

These exchanges between Hamilton and Morris—the latter
usually answered for the legislature—brought together two of
the most practiced writers of the time, whose association was
to continue for many years. Partly because he was born and
spent his early youth outside of this country, Hamilton, as contrasted with many in public life, had a Continental loyalty. He
did not allow attachment to New York, his home state, to
compromise the interests of the nation as he saw it. Information from headquarters that he relayed to the committee of correspondence at Kingston concerned especially military movements affecting New York. The committee was of course apprehensive, since New York City was the base of enemy operations.

Hamilton more than once warned that "whatever opinions I
shall give, in the course of our correspondence, are to be considered merely as my private sentiments, and are never to be interpreted as an echo of those of the General; since they will not be
really so, and a construction of the kind may lead into errors."
He ventured (March 22, 1777) that the enemy could not open
their campaign before the first of May, due to badness of the
roads and tardy reinforcement. Their object would probably be
the capture of Philadelphia, their land and sea forces cooperating. No mention should be made of his forecast, though only his
personal guess, that the British would lie inactive for six
weeks, lest it relax vigilance.

In reply Gouverneur Morris made light of "a little Expedition
[by the British] against Peeks Kill," which if "intended as a Diversion . . . is a ridiculous one." Actually it was anything but
an empty gesture, as Hamilton at headquarters soon knew. In
spite of Washington's efforts to strengthen the garrison, valuable
stores at Peekskill were guarded by only 250 troops under Brig-

adier General Alexander McDougall. On March 23 enemy vessels disembarked twice as many men, who drove out McDougall's force and, before Colonel Marinus Willett could arrive from Fort Montgomery across the Hudson with an energetic detachment, laid the village in ashes. The loss by fire included provisions, 400 hogsheads of rum, 150 wagons, and several boats; other equipment and ammunition was carried off. Willett, without help from McDougall, charged the pillagers with the bayonet, compelling them to fall back to their ships, but the raid was an accomplished success. McDougall was replaced in command by General Israel Putnam.

Next from the Committee of Correspondence at Kingston came a letter, dated March 29, 1777, from Robert R. Livingston, Jr., alarmed by "the Enemy's little excursion to Peeks Kill," and equally disturbed because Indians on the New York frontier had left their villages to be harangued by the formidable Joseph Brant, the Mohawk chief who was a pertinacious ally of the British. Also, most critically for New York, might not the British, instead of pointing toward Philadelphia, sail northward, up the Hudson? The committee was anxious for any knowledge Washington's headquarters might have about the latter possibility. The enemy could extend ravages into western Connecticut where, sour comment, they would find disaffected people to befriend them. If they destroyed boats in the river, Washington's army could not cross short of Albany, which would involve a march impracticable in the condition of the roads. Thus fearful, the convention had empowered Governor George Clinton to draft for the militia every third man from the southern counties and every fifth man from the northern. The convention sent, for delivery to General Washington, resolutions for punishing spies and others assisting the enemy, after conviction by courts-martial.

Hamilton answered from headquarters (April 5, 1777) that the British were astir earlier than expected. They were embarking three thousand men on transports at Sandy Hook, evidently destined for the Delaware, because they were trying to bribe pilots in that river. With such a small force it would be a desperate attempt, but they might be provoked to it by learning that reinforcements were finally coming to Washington. Also, Philadelphia had been the main source of supplies for the American army, and was "a wheel we could very badly spare in the great political and military machine." The enemy would be following the "well grounded rule in war, to strike first . . . at the capital towns and Cities in order to the conquest of a country."

This quieted fears for the Hudson. Mere devastation could answer no end, and to form a junction with their northern army and cut off communications between the eastern and other states would require more troops, for a chain of posts, than the enemy could command. Nevertheless General Washington would collect a good body at or near Peekskill, ready to move north or south as signs of enemy intention might require. The recent raid on Peekskill showed the folly of forming magazines near the water. Hamilton warned the New Yorkers that at first notice of danger all boats should be brought under cover of the forts.

He had other reassuring news. Six Oneida chiefs, brought to headquarters by the missionary the Reverend Samuel Kirkland, had been entertained by the general for two days and sent back to their nation firm friends of the Americans. Congress had obtained a credit in France, £100,000 sterling. New troops were coming in, and if the flow continued, the army might be able to deliver a brilliant stroke.

A particular problem arose in the exchange of prisoners in the absence of a general agreement for that purpose. A few days earlier Hamilton had written that efforts of American headquarters "to negotiate a regular Cartel" had been broken off because General Howe would not permit his prize prisoner, General Charles Lee, to be included in a comprehensive arrangement. Hamilton conducted some of Washington's correspondence concerning Lee, and later was deputed to meet with British commissioners to form a cartel.

Hamilton reported to the New York committee what appeared to be reliable information that the enemy had "constructed a bridge to be laid on boats" for crossing the Delaware. Congress wished Washington to concentrate troops, including three thousand militia sought from Pennsylvania, on the west side of the river. Hamilton repeated his own concern for the safety of Philadelphia, "a place of infinite importance." This view did not coincide with that of Washington, who objected to forming an army in Pennsylvania.

Hamilton's advice for treatment of suspected Tories was to punish serious offenses severely, and ignore minor disaffection. He felt that those of doubtful guilt would complain that they were persecuted, would excite pity for themselves and hostility toward the authorities.

Hamilton had opportunity, at Morristown headquarters, to practice what he preached to the New York committee. He had a leading part in the examination of accused Jerseymen who had been brought to General Washington. The purpose was to discover "who of them were subject to a military jurisdiction, & who came properly under . . . the civil power; also to discriminate those who were innocent, or guilty of trivial offences from those whose crimes were of a . . . capital and heinous nature." Following the enquiry he gave Governor Livingston the recommendation of General Washington that those of no deep die should be dismissed, while "daring offenders" should meet exemplary punishment. In sending prisoners and pertinent papers to the governor, Washington wanted to avoid "the least encroachment either upon the rights of the citizen or of the Magistrate."

Washington's aide was on the same theme in telling the New Yorkers that some sentences passed by courts-martial, under the convention's resolve, had been improper. Confiscation of the estates of offenders "is not cognizable by martial law." In crimes of enormity "an execution or two, by way of example, would strike terror, and powerfully discourage the wicked practices going on." Lesser sentences should take the form of fines or imprisonment rather than whipping; "corporal punishment . . . is apt to excite compassion and breed disgust." These were the commander in chief's sentiments, conveyed to prevent mistakes.

As Hamilton was an artilleryman, the New York committee asked his opinion of field cannon of wrought iron produced by Colonel Robert Livingston. He answered that such a piece at the Morristown encampment weighed 227 pounds, was hooped and welded, and carried a three-pound ball. It had withstood firing twenty times as fast as possible, and Washington and others thought it a great acquisition. Hamilton, however, had proposed that it be tested by fifty discharges instead of twenty. "If she would stand that, her sufficiency would be as certained beyond a doubt, and her value would be immense," and Livingston would render essential service by constructing more of the same kind.

Hamilton noticed the enemy's "attempt upon the stores at Danbury," of which, he rightly said, the New York committee was as well informed as headquarters. At the time he wrote (April 28, 1777), this foray, costly to the Americans, had not played itself out to its conclusion. Two thousand British, under Major General William Tryon (who was also royal governor of New York), disembarked from their ships at Norwalk April 25. They marched unopposed to Danbury, where the garrison of 150 Continentals, having removed what stores they could, withdrew. In a day and night of destruction the enemy burned a score of dwellings and as many warehouses containing provisions, clothing, and tents. The return to their ships, however, was not so easy. Brigadier General Benedict Arnold was at New Haven, smarting under the recent action of Congress in advancing five brigadiers, junior to him, in disregard of his superior claim. However, his itch for a fight overcame his resent-

73

ment of neglect. As soon as he knew of the raid, he rode with all speed to Redding, where he joined Generals David Wooster and Gold S. Silliman with their seven hundred troops, mostly militia. They pressed toward Danbury, too late to save the town, but resolved to attack the enemy in march back toward Norwalk. In several spirited engagements the Americans inflicted two hundred casualties on the British and lost a third as many men themselves. General Wooster was mortally wounded, and Arnold, narrowly escaping capture when his horse was killed, rallied his troops for further resistance.

Tryon's force got away, but Congress thanked Arnold for his spontaneous service, and promoted him to major general. However, he again offered his resignation, for, by later dating of his commission, he was ranked below the others. Immediately Washington, who had all along tried to mollify Arnold, urged Congress to attach him to the northern army opposing Burgoyne's invasion. Arnold swallowed his pride and accepted the assignment, in which he was to win laurels at Saratoga. In spite of Washington's praise, Arnold continued to brood, and in several ways abused his trust before his act of treachery at West Point two years later.

The New Jersey prisoners charged with aiding the enemy were still held at Morristown, awaiting trial. As a youthful friend of Governor Livingston, Hamilton felt free to caution him against misplaced severity. In the manuscript, this paragraph years later was crossed out by somebody else, doubtless Hamilton's son and editor, who probably thought it presumptuous. In the examination ordered by Washington "it appeared, that private pique and resentment had had their influence in causing some innocent persons to be apprehended," and Hamilton descanted on the impolicy of prosecuting these victims of mean accusation. Though he apologized for gratuitous urgings, his plea showed the sensitivity to the workings of public opinion for which he became notable.

Unfortunately we do not have Hamilton's letters from headquarters to his old patron in Saint Croix, Dr. Hugh Knox, who assured him they contained "a more true, circumstantial & Satisfactory acct. of matters . . . than all the public & private Intelligence we had received here." Knox insisted that "You must be the Annalist & Biographer, as well as the Aid de Camp, of General Washington, & the Historiographer of the American War! . . . I hope you will take Minutes and Keep a Journal! . . . This may be a new & Strange thought to You, but if you Survive the present troubles, I Aver few men Will be as well qualified to Write the History of the present Glorious Struggle." And again Knox declared, "I feel . . . under a strong Impulse, to *prophesy* that *Washington* was born for the Deliverance of America; that . . . Providence will Shield his head in every Day of Battle, *Will Guide* him to See America *free, flourishing & happy*." He added, in prescient admonition to Hamilton, "depend upon it the Very Minutiae of that incomparable man Will be read with Avidity by posterity."

This injunction Hamilton never fulfilled, though his voluminous papers, private and public, are much to that purpose.[5] He did assist Washington to compress, in the "Farewell Address," the lessons of the Revolution and the first Federalist administrations.

[5] His son, John C. Hamilton, published *History of the Republic of the United States. . . . as Traced in the Writings of Alexander Hamilton* (New York, Appleton, 7 vols., 1857–64).

4

Washington Is Disparaged;
Gates Is Adulated

 Hamilton shared Washington's Fabian tactics. The American army, ill equipped and in great part newly collected for each campaign, should wear down the enemy by worrying resistance, not by seeking full-scale battle. America had resources of men and food at hand, while the British had to transport theirs across three thousand miles of ocean. The enemy must keep garrisons in cities they captured, and thus reduce their strength in the field. This apparent dominance, however, hurt American popular morale, on which depended the program of inveterate badgering and attrition. Inflation—the enemy within—was increased by loss of confidence.

Earlier Hamilton had held that capture of the Philadelphia capital would gain General Howe nothing militarily, and thus was not to be lamented. Now, however, in August 1777, as the British approached the city, he, like General Washington, was persuaded, by the knowledge that there would be injurious economic and political effects, to block their progress by open combat.

When it was evident, after the month-long wanderings of their great flotilla, that the British were making for Philadelphia from Head of Elk, Maryland, Washington broke camp on the Neshaminy (then Cross Roads, now Hartsville, Pennsylvania) and marched toward the capital with all the troops he had been able to collect. Stopping the night of August 23, 1777, near Germantown, the army the next day paraded through Philadelphia. The general took pains to make the best possible show of strength to intimidate the Tories and hearten the patriots of the city. The contingents of his army of sixteen thousand were so spaced that they took two hours to pass a given point in Front or Chestnut streets. Washington and Lafayette, accompanied by their aides, all mounted, took the lead.

John Adams, the New Englander, at this time not as cordial toward Washington's efforts as he might have been, caviled that the troops lacked "quite the air of soldiers. They don't step exactly in time. They don't hold up their heads quite erect, nor turn out their toes exactly as they ought. They don't all of them cock their hats. . . ." Alexander Graydon, a better judge of military sufficiency, also surveyed the men from head to foot; he remarked that "though indifferently dressed, [they] held well burnished arms and carried them like soldiers." [1]

The army camped that night at Darby, on the next night, of August 25, at Naaman's, but Hamilton, with others of the staff, rode on past Naaman's to establish headquarters at Wilmington. Here Washington learned that the British were disembarking at Head of Elk (Elkton, Maryland, and nearby).

Promptly next day the commander in chief, his aides, and Generals Greene and Lafayette, with a guard of cavalry, set out for the district a few miles south of Newark, Delaware, to reconnoiter the position and movements of the enemy. From a couple of hillocks, which rise from the otherwise level country, they could look down on the temporary British camp. They

[1] These sideline observations were culled by Christopher Ward, *The War of the Revolution* (New York, Macmillan Company, 1952), I, 334–35.

would have returned that night except for a torrential rain, Washington preferring the shelter of a farm house. His guards stood about the dwelling, for, so near the enemy, the general might be captured à la Charles Lee at Basking Ridge. The next day brought more reconnaissance by Washington's party.

A few days later (September 1, 1777) Hamilton gave news to Gouverneur Morris

of. Howes coming into Chesapeake bay; where he has landed his whole army within about four miles from the head of Elk; a day or two, after his landing, he marched from his first position and extended his van as far as Gray's-Hill. He still lies there in a state of inactivity; in a great measure I believe from the want of horses, to transport his baggage and stores. It seems he sailed with only about three weeks provendor and was six at sea. This has occasioned the death of a great number of his horses [actually about three hundred] and has made skeletons of the rest. He will be obliged to collect a supply from the neighbouring country before he can move.

(The British, and especially the Hessians, were active in foraging, bringing in quantities of needed horses besides cattle and sheep, and possessed themselves of stores the Americans had not been able to remove from Elkton. After the enemy troops had been cooped up so long in their stifling ships, they required fresh food before they could march.)

Hamilton was cheered by the strokes of John Stark at Bennington, the check by Nicholas Herkimer to the enemy at Oriskany, and Benedict Arnold's relief of Fort Stanwix. The first of these American successes, in southern Vermont, reduced General John Burgoyne's force penetrating the Hudson Valley from Canada, while the others, along the Mohawk, turned back Colonel Barry St. Leger, who meant to join Burgoyne from the west. As Howe was "now fairly sat down to the Southward" and no longer threatened the New England states, Hamilton hoped that they would rally to the defeat of Burgoyne. The main American army held the heights of Wilmington, determined by Washington after two days more of scouting to be the best of poor posts for defense. Little dependence could be put on this position, and the "enemy will have Philadelphia, if they dare make a bold push for it, unless we fight them a pretty general action. I opine we ought to do it, and that we shall beat them soundly if we do," the Americans being "in high health & spirits."

The first attempt to stop the British advance on Philadelphia, from Kennett Square, was at the Brandywine, September 11, 1777. The Nottingham Road (later Baltimore Pike, or U.S. 1) crossed the stream at Chad's Ford. Howe's successful strategy was a repetition of his tactics on Long Island. Knyphausen, with a large force of British and Hessian regiments, batteries of artillery, and flanking dragoons (some five thousand troops in all), on the west bank of the stream at Chad's Ford, confronted the main American position on the opposite shore. When the enemy cannonade died down in midmorning of that hot day, and yet Knyphausen, his men marshaled in full array, made no move to cross to the attack, Washington might have suspected that he was to be assailed from another quarter. Indeed, at his undisturbed headquarters a mile east of Chad's Ford, he was twice definitely notified of the march of Howe and Cornwallis, with a force equal to Knyphausen's and a large train of artillery, up the west shore. They had left Kennett before Knyphausen, to circle the American position by way of lightly guarded fords four miles above. Washington gave orders to Sullivan, Stirling, and Stephen to shift northward, cross the stream, and fall on Howe's rear. But this disposition was countermanded when Sullivan, who had relayed news of the enemy's maneuver, sent word that earlier reports were mistaken.

More waiting followed. Headquarters seemed unconcerned at the breathless insistence of a patriot farmer that on a volunteer scout he had seen the British on a hill near the Birmingham Meeting House, far to Washington's right and rear. We do not know whether Hamilton was one of the headquarters aides who joined in discrediting the man as probably a deceiving Tory. But the exact truth of his tale was quickly confirmed (at

two o'clock in the afternoon) by a dispatch from Colonel
Theodorick Bland, stationed with his dragoons on the west
side of the Brandywine and instructed to inform headquarters
of any movement of the enemy across the upper fords. Now
Washington, finally convinced of what was happening, ordered
his right wing, Sullivan in command, to leave the river and hasten northeastward to oppose the enemy advance. They did that
in a fierce fight of nearly two hours before they fell back toward Dilworth on the road leading to Philadelphia, for which
Cornwallis aimed. The cannonade signaled Knyphausen to vigorous attack at Chad's Ford. Washington hesitated between
keeping Greene in reserve there, to support Wayne and Proctor,
or hurrying to the aid of Sullivan three miles away. Deciding
for the latter, but late, he pressed a countryman into service as
guide to the shortest way. But when he arrived near Dilworth, it was only to open ranks to let the beaten Americans
through, to be formed, hopefully, to the rear. Greene renewed
the resistance till sundown, when he too was obliged to retreat; thankfully, he was not pursued. Knyphausen, similarly,
drove the Americans before him until darkness ended his advance. The fugitives, in a confused mass, jammed the roads to
Chester, where Lafayette, Washington, and Greene brought sufficient order for encampment after the disastrous defeat.

In the three weeks after Brandywine Washington was ma-
neuvering to keep between the British and Philadelphia. It
was a wet time. Equinoctial rains soaked the tentless troops,
making their ammunition useless. They forded breast-high
streams. For the thousand men who were barefoot the mirey
roads were more welcome than frozen ground. The surprise of
Wayne's division near the Paoli Tavern was a blow. Wayne,
with fifteen hundred men and four fieldpieces, had secretly
taken a position from which to attack the enemy's rear guard.
Tories disclosed his intention to the British, and Major General
Charles Grey, with four regiments and some light infantry and
dragoons, after a silent night march (September 20, 1777),

charged Wayne's hastily formed line with bayonets. The Americans' loss in killed and wounded, claimed by the British to number three hundred, plus seventy prisoners, was suffered mainly in the confused retreat. Wayne's fleeing troops abandoned a thousand muskets and eight or ten loaded wagons.

It was only a question of time before the British would invest Philadelphia. In spite of all, the army was in high spirits and, if Hamilton's mood was typical, was anxious for another stroke at the enemy. Washington summoned reinforcements all the way from New England to Virginia, including Colonel Daniel Morgan's riflemen, who had helped defeat Burgoyne at Saratoga. For Washington, from Yellow Springs on September 17, Hamilton described the situation to the apprehensive Congress, which was poised for flight. John Adams, exultant at Gates's triumph, correspondingly despaired of Washington's efforts. He deplored "the . . . timorous, defensive part, which has involved us in so many disasters," and exclaimed "O, Heavens! grant us one great soul! One leading mind would extricate the best cause from . . . ruin which seems to await it." Congress itself discovered no "active, masterly capacity" to "bring order out of confusion." The best it could do was furnish to the waterlogged troops each a gill of rum a day, in default of blankets, which Washington had vainly begged. Washington must be both commander and Congress, using dictatorial power, again conferred on him, "to take wherever he may be, all such provisions and articles as may be necessary for the comfortable subsistence of the army . . . paying or giving certificates for the same."

The enemy, in a stop at Valley Forge, seized supplies, which Washington sorely needed, including "3800 Barrels of Flour, Soap and Candles, 25 Barrels of Horse Shoes, several thousand . . . Kettles and Intrenching Tools." Washington was obliged to destroy other stores that lay in the British path to the capital. He sent Hamilton, with a body of horsemen under Henry Lee, for this purpose to flour mills at Deviser's Ferry on the Schuylkill. The mission was barely accomplished when mounted sentries, posted at the top of the hill, warned by their shots that the enemy would be upon Hamilton's party. To provide against this danger, Hamilton had drawn a flat-bottomed boat to the shore, and he and four companions sprang in and shoved off just ahead of the galloping dragoons. Volleys from the bank killed one of his men, wounded another, and disabled Hamilton's horse. Worse would have happened except that Lee's detachment attracted some of the fire.

No sooner was he safe on the opposite shore than Hamilton got off a note to John Hancock: "If Congress have not yet left Philadelphia, they ought to do it immediately . . . for the enemy have the means of throwing a party this night into the city." A few hours later, as double precaution, he dispatched another messenger with more particulars. The main body of the enemy was only four miles from Swede's Ford. In the haste of his departure he had left a boat on their side of the river, with which they could secure the one he had used, and thus be able to ferry across fifty men at a time, "in a few hours . . . perhaps sufficient to overmatch the militia who may be between them and the city. This renders the situation of Congress extremely precarious."

In consequence of Hamilton's warning, Congress immediately prepared to leave for Lancaster. John Adams was as quick as any to mount his horse, avoiding all danger by a wide circuit through Trenton and Bethlehem, but he was soon blaming Hamilton for his "false alarm which occasioned our flight from Philadelphia. Not a soldier of Howe's has crossed the Schuylkill." Hamilton, September 22, explained to the president of Congress why the enemy had not entered Philadelphia. Instead of moving south as expected, Howe at midnight began a twelve-mile march up the river, "on their old scheme of gaining our right." To prevent this, Washington at once marched fifteen miles north on his side of the river to the present Pottstown. Hamilton did not know Howe's ruse to draw Washington's force away from the city. That done, Howe suddenly backtracked, chased off the weak American detachments at the lower fords of the Schuylkill, and crossed his whole army. Philadelphia, unprotected, lay before him.

In these precious days Hamilton, in orders drawn by himself, was sent by the commander in chief to the capital to impress blankets, clothing, shoes, and horses. He begged patriotic response to the demands of his collecting parties, but, as John Marshall recorded, "this very active officer could not obtain a supply, in any degree, adequate to the . . . wants of the army." However, he sent vessels with military stores up the Delaware "with so much vigilance, that very little public property fell, with the city, into the hands of the British general." Hamilton had less than two days for this rescue before Cornwallis, on September 26, 1777, came into the city with British and Hessian battalions; Sir William Howe had encamped the main army at Germantown, seven miles north of the capital. If the forts in the Delaware River below Philadelphia withstood attack, thus preventing Howe from getting supplies by water, Washington might yet seal him in the city. Howe's success might "instead of his good fortune, prove his ruin." Howe was obliged to send three thousand troops to escort supplies up from Elkton, and Cornwallis had weakened himself by detaching troops for an expedition against an American fortification on the Jersey side. Washington had moved down the Reading (Skippack) Road to within sixteen miles of Germantown. With eleven thousand men, two thousand more than were with Howe, Washington, supported by his council of war, determined on attack.

Washington's plan for the battle of Germantown was too complicated to succeed unless every feature developed just as hoped. Beginning at seven o'clock in the evening (October 3, 1777) the Americans were to march sixteen miles by four roads for simultaneous attacks. The enemy lines ran east and west across the center of the village. The most direct approach was from the northwest by the Skippack Road, to be taken by a column under the immediate command of Major General John Sullivan, Washington and his staff accompanying this column. Next, to the east, was the Limekiln Road; Major General Nathanael Greene commanding the divisions, amounting to two-thirds of the American army, was to follow that route. A mile farther to the east Generals William Smallwood and David Forman, with Maryland and New Jersey militia, would reach the battle by the Old York Road. The extreme western route, on the far side of the Wissahickon Creek, was by the Manatawny or Ridge Road, at places six or seven miles distant from the Old York Road, the easternmost of the four. Major John Armstrong would lead Pennsylvania militia on the Manatawny Road.

The four columns were to halt when they reached within two miles of the enemy's pickets, judged to be at two o'clock in the morning. At five o'clock they would make simultaneous bayonet attacks: the Continentals under Sullivan and Greene against the British center; the militia on the extreme east (Smallwood and Forman) would fold back the enemy's right flank; the militia on the west (Armstrong), having crossed the Wissahickon Creek, would turn the left flank. Thus these two columns of militia, in a pincers movement, would meet to the rear of the British, who, presumably, would be quailing from the main frontal assault.

However, when it came to doing it, the timing went wrong. The troops were mostly inexperienced—even many of the Continentals—and columns had to halt while shoeless men caught up in the fatiguing march. Guides lost their roads in the darkness. Communication between the widely separated bodies was impossible.

The main column had reached only to Chestnut Hill, four miles from the enemy position, when the sun rose, destroying all chance of surprise. Early mist turned to dense fog, which hindered identification of friend and foe. At Mount Airy (roughly midway between Chestnut Hill and Germantown) the picket was driven in, but only to have the forward enemy post fire two fieldpieces, which alerted the whole British

army. The post was promptly supported, and stiff fighting ensued, ending in slow enemy retreat. General Sir William Howe
had ridden to the front, but was unable to stop the backward
movement. Colonel Musgrave, commanding the Fortieth British
Regiment, accomplished more than he knew at the time by
lodging better than a hundred of his men in the Benjamin
Chew house. This solid stone structure, set in a large yard,
which furnished a field of fire, became their fort, from which
their musket shots dealt death among the Americans surging
past.

Washington and his staff came up. Hamilton and Pickering
urged pressing forward, detailing only a sufficient force to seal
off the enemy stronghold. But Washington listened to the insistence of Henry Knox that a hostile castle—he was remembering
his military reading—should never be left in the rear. The garrison of the house must, in form, be summoned to surrender before the six-pounders were turned on it. Hamilton and Pickering remonstrated that this would only delay the advance to the
main battle, which lay at School Lane a mile ahead. In vain
they pled that Adjutant General Pickering's assistant, Lieutenant
William Smith, who volunteered to advance with the flag to
deliver the summons, would be fired upon. Their prudence
was justified when the brave young officer was promptly mortally wounded. Knox then battered with his light cannon with
no effect on the stout walls of the mansion. The front door
was blown in, but a barricade of furniture, backed by bayonets,
prevented a storm of the place. When a first attempt to set the
house afire failed, Hamilton's friend John Laurens got straw
from the stable and with no better shield tried to thrust it
through shutters, which Mauduit de Plessis had forced open. A
shot aimed at the Frenchman missed the mark, but another hit
Laurens in the shoulder. Knox renewed his bombardment, and,
joined by Woodford's artillery, which should have been hastening to the front, consumed an hour, which lost the battle.

Greene, Sullivan, and Wayne did drive through the main

enemy line, and "soon were in possession of a part of their artillery,—about thirty pieces,—and among their tents." But they were not supported. Major General Adam Stephen, drawn by the uproar at the Chew house, had disobeyed orders and wheeled his division to the right to that scene of action. American contingents cutting through enemy lines beyond School Lane, in what had become the real contest, were so enveloped in fog and powder smoke that they could not see each other, much less act in unison. Hearing the tumult at the Chew house, Wayne feared that Sullivan—actually thrusting forward near him—was having a hard time to his rear. He reversed his troops to give relief. Before he could get back to the Chew house, he met Stephen's men belatedly advancing. Each division of Americans took the other for the enemy, and tragically exchanged fire before all fled in panic. Wayne later recorded that when

the Enemy were broke, Dispersed & flying on all Querters . . . a *Wind Mill* attack was made on a House into which Six Light Companies had thrown themselves to Avoid our Bayonets.—this gave time for the Enemy to Rally—our Troops . . . fell back to Assist in what they deemed a Serious matter—the Enemy finding themselves no further pursued and believing it to be a Retreat followed—Confusion ensued, and we ran away from the Arms of Victory ready Open to receive us[.]

Hamilton and the other aides surely did their best in General Washington's exertions to stay the pell-mell push away from the conflict, but the thronging escape was out of hand. Ironically, the retreat was more irresistible because in slow motion. The men were too exhausted to do other than stumble for safety. Cornwallis, with fresh battalions from Philadelphia, pursued for eight miles, but even he "kept a civil distance behind."

The Americans might have stopped at their last camping ground, from which they had marched sixteen miles to Germantown, fought more than two hours, and trudged back that weary road. But in fact they kept on going eight miles farther to their base at Perkiomen. Said Captain Anderson of the Delaware Regiment, "Here we . . . had marched forty miles. We eat nothing and drank nothing but water on the tour."

A planned pincers action by the Americans did not work. The Pennsylvania militia under Armstrong, advancing west of the Wissahickon, were stopped by the Hessians from crossing the creek. The Maryland and New Jersey militia under Smallwood did arrive by the Old York Road, but only in time to join in the retreat. Still, with all of its mischances, the Germantown battle was a near success for the Americans, though undoubtedly a defeat as it stood. Hamilton drafted Washington's report to Congress; retreat "at the instant when Victory was declaring herself in our favor" was due to "the extreme haziness of the weather."

The British could not maintain themselves in Philadelphia unless they opened the river to their shipping, for the Americans would combat their foraging parties. While Admiral Lord Howe's fleet lay long at Head of Elk in the Chesapeake and then made its slow sail into the Delaware, the Americans had obstructed the channel with *chevaux-de-frise* and constructed forts at two places below the city. The *chevaux* were cribs of heavy timbers filled with stones and sunk a few feet below the surface; from them projected, downstream, pointed logs, iron shod, at an angle to impale vessels coming against them. The lower double line of *chevaux* was guarded by a redoubt at Billingsport on the Jersey shore. The British took the redoubt and broke through the *chevaux* October 2. American hopes then depended on stronger defenses farther north—triple ranks of *chevaux* and forts on Mud Island and at Red Bank on the Jersey side.

On October 15, at Washington's direction, Hamilton ordered Colonel Christopher Greene, commanding Fort Mercer at Red Bank, to detach as much as possible of his garrison to strengthen that of Fort Mifflin on Mud Island, against which the enemy appeared to be "preparing a . . sudden & violent" attack.

Greene's force, thus depleted, would be reinforced by Colonel Israel Angell's Rhode Island regiment. Hamilton urged that the enemy's choice of "keeping or evacuating Philadelphia materially depends upon their having the communication with their shipping immediately opened." He repeated "the prodigious importance of not suffering the Enemy to get entire possession of the Delaware." The strengthening of Fort Mifflin was not too soon, though the first assault was on Red Bank. Washington was not alerted to this until the very day, October 21, that Colonel Carl von Donop moved against Fort Mercer with two thousand Hessians. Hamilton's letter, for Washington, of that date, soliciting Brigadier General David Forman to bring New Jersey militia to the aid of Fort Mercer was too late. However, Chevalier de Mauduit du Plessis, the French engineer, had improved the works and the small garrison beat off the assault with heavy loss to the enemy.

Three weeks later Fort Mifflin on Mud Island, mainly relied upon, told a different story. In five days of incessant cannonading from land and floating batteries, joined at the last by guns of the ships (some 275 pieces total), the fort was reduced to rubble. The few American ships stationed above gave no help. The gallant defenders escaped to Fort Mercer at Red Bank, but Cornwallis stormed that with 2,000 troops, placing the whole river in enemy hands. Sir William Howe, withdrawing his main force left at Germantown, collected his whole army in Philadelphia, which he strongly fortified.

Meantime Washington had been shifting his camp from one place to another some dozen miles north of Philadelphia. By October 29, 1777, when Washington called a council of war at Whitpain, he knew reliably of the surrender of Major General John Burgoyne to the Americans at Saratoga twelve days earlier.

Burgoyne's expedition from Canada, aimed at Albany, New York, consisted of 6,985 rank and file (nearly 4,000 British and 3,000 Germans), plus 150 Canadians, 100 Tories, and 400 Indians, a total of 7,635. The enterprise was conceived and conducted with insouciance. Lord George Germain, secretary for the Colonies, and therefore in charge of military operations, was too distant, uninformed, and careless for that responsibility. "Gentleman Johnny" Burgoyne, hail fellow well met, lacked judgment to match his bravery, and was too obedient to Germain's mistaken orders. The plan to sever New England from the remainder of America by attacks on the Hudson from north, west, and south invited mischances. The movement up the river from New York was only vaguely suggested to Sir William Howe, and belatedly too, for he received Germain's letter when he was already on his way by sea to the Chesapeake to capture Philadelphia. Howe passed word back to Sir Henry Clinton, left in command at New York, but Clinton only partially executed the recommendation.

Leaving Saint Johns, New Brunswick, to ascend the Richelieu River to Lake Champlain, the outfit was unsuited in all its parts to laborious penetration of woods and swamps in summer heat. The regular troops were burdened with heavy uniforms and packs; the great jackboots of the dismounted German dragoons weighed twelve pounds, to which add worse than useless brass spurs. The train of artillery numbered forty-two pieces. In a varied flotilla, ranging from Indian canoes to full-rigged ships, the equally varied force descended Lake Champlain to attack Ticonderoga. It was not the fortress that hopeful New England supposed. Only partially repaired, it was garrisoned by 2,500 ill-equipped troops under Major General Arthur St. Clair. An earlier project to fortify Sugar Loaf (later called Mount Defiance), rising 750 feet a mile to the southwest of Ticonderoga, had been rejected because it was thought to be unscalable with artillery. When British Major General William Phillips nevertheless perched two heavy guns on that commanding height, St. Clair had no choice but to contrive a night evacuation of his small force (July 5, 1777).

New Englanders, now terrified at the prospect of invasion, blamed Major General Philip Schuyler, in command of the

American northern department, though he had no foreknowledge of St. Clair's abandonment of Ticonderoga. The chief personage, military and political, in upper New York, Schuyler was deeply disliked and distrusted by the Yankees. Wealthy, aristocratic in the Dutch tradition of patroonship, he was the protagonist of New York in the controversy with New Hampshire over land grants in the Green Mountain area west of the Connecticut River. His long-standing influence with the Indians who supplied the coveted fur trade made him an object of jealousy with New England frontiersmen. As one of the three original major generals, he was the friend of Washington, who after expelling the British from Boston had withdrawn from the New England capital to defend New York, which he could not hold. Schuyler incurred the antagonism of Samuel and John Adams, partisans of Major General Horatio Gates. That New Englanders had been backward in assisting Schuyler's efforts to impede the march of Burgoyne gave him no more credit in their eyes. Hamilton, for Washington, had conducted the headquarters correspondence that sought to heal this schism. Washington encouraged Schuyler's activity in resisting Burgoyne's penetration, and at the same time courted New England aid by assigning to the northern force New England commanders, Major General Benjamin Lincoln, Brigadier Benedict Arnold, and Brigadier John Glover.

This was not enough for the Yankees. At the end of July 1777 Congress demanded an investigation of the forfeit of Ticonderoga, remanded Schuyler to headquarters, and directed Washington to name his successor. Washington relieved his embarrassment for the moment by reminding that Congress had assumed separate responsibility for the northern department, and therefore the choice of a substitute general must be theirs. Samuel Adams in the name of New England urged Gates, who was promptly appointed. As some offset, Washington (Hamilton his draftsman) comforted the New York Council of Safety with sympathy for the distresses of that state; he deplored jealousy hurtful to the common cause, and believed that New England, "capable of powerful efforts," would rise to the crisis.

Burgoyne had pressed hard on St. Clair's retreat from Ticonderoga southward, and after severe fighting, with losses on both sides disproportionate to the small parties engaged, the British and Germans lay at Skenesboro (now Whitehall) at the head of Lake Champlain. St. Clair had got off to Rutland, Vermont. Burgoyne was forced to keep his camp for nearly three weeks while his Canadian woodsmen cleared the wagon track for his further progress toward the Hudson. Schuyler had had a thousand axmen felling trees across the way, tearing up bridges, and diverting streams to create swamps; at one place Burgoyne's men had to build a corduroy road two miles long. Finally, after a toilsome march (four days to cover twenty-three miles), Burgoyne reached Fort Edward, ten miles south of Lake George. He was tempted to give up and return to Ticonderoga, but Germain had said to go to Albany, so go he would. But to press forward he needed more horses. Major General Baron Friedrich Adolph von Riedesel, commanding the Germans, was insistent on mounts for his dragoons, who were almost as awkward afoot as knights in armor. Report was that plenty of horses, wagons, and cattle could be seized in nearby Vermont, particularly at Bennington where the Colonials had a depot of supplies.

Lieutenant Colonel Friedrich Baum, with 650 Germans, Tories, a few English troops, and an assortment of Canadians and Indians was dispatched on this errand (August 11). As Baum spoke no English, he took along a band of German musicians to serenade the countryside into submission. At Bennington the foraging expedition was astonished to encounter Brigadier General John Stark at the head of 2,000 farmers hastily mustered from New Hampshire, Vermont, and Massachusetts. Baum had time to fortify a 300-foot hilltop before, on August 16, he was assaulted on all sides. After a two-hour fight—"the hottest I ever saw in my life," Stark said—when Baum was killed, his men surrendered. The day was not over until the shirtsleeved countrymen had routed a similar force, which came up tardily to the relief of the first. In all, 207 of the invaders were killed and 700 captured; American casualties were 30 killed, 40 wounded. The byplay at Bennington weakened Burgoyne in troops, officers, weapons, and ammunition, and roused New England militia to resist his southward progress.

Burgoyne suffered another blow, to the west. He had ordered Lieutenant Colonel Barry St. Leger to set out from Oswego, on Lake Ontario, with a mixed force of Tories, German jaegers (rangers), and Indians to sweep through the Mohawk valley and join him on the Hudson. Starting July 26, 1777, St. Leger reached his first objective, Fort Stanwix (now Rome, New York) August 2. He was investing its garrison of 750 under Colonel Peter Gansevoort and Lieutenant Marinus Willett when he was obliged to interrupt the siege to meet 850 Tryon County militia advancing under command of Brigadier General Nicholas Herkimer to the relief of Stanwix. The Mohawk chief Captain Joseph Brant (otherwise Thayendanagea) laid an ambush for Herkimer in a ravine at Oriskany six miles south of Stanwix (August 6). In spite of a wounded leg Herkimer directed his men in bloody fighting that resulted in withdrawal of both sides with undetermined but heavy losses. General Schuyler sent General Benedict Arnold to resume Herkimer's task, Stanwix was defended, and Saint Leger returned to Oswego and thence to Canada.

Resolved to reach Albany, Burgoyne crossed the Hudson to Saratoga on the west side September 15. General Horatio Gates had reached Albany on August 19, superseded General Schuyler in command, and fortified Bemis Heights, between Saratoga on the north and Stillwater on the south. Gates had about seven thousand effective troops, a thousand more than Burgoyne. The first battle, at Freeman's Farm, was on September 19. Benedict Arnold begged Gates not to remain on the defensive in his entrenchments, but to carry the fight to the enemy in the woods where British artillery and bayonet charges could not come to bear against American small arms. But Gates would do no more than send Daniel Morgan's riflemen to resist a flanking movement on the left, Arnold's division to remain in reserve in that quarter. Arnold on his own initiative shifted to his right and attacked the British center. After a back-and-forth struggle in a clearing, Arnold appealed to Gates for reinforcements, with whose aid he could break through Burgoyne's lines and divide the enemy's forces. Gates's preference for prudence forbade. Arnold's opportunity was lost, for Riedesel, from the riverbank, brought his Germans to the rescue of the now-thinned British regiments. His attack, followed by grapeshot at close range, drove the Americans back. With the coming of darkness, the battle was over. British casualties were more than twice the American, but Burgoyne's forces held the field.

The armies lay facing each other until October 7 with no major move on either side. Burgoyne, in response to Sir Henry Clinton's conditional promise, begged for reinforcement from New York. His messengers did not get through before Sir Henry, at the head of four thousand troops, ascended the Hudson and (October 6) readily captured the undermanned forts Clinton and Montgomery, guarding the Highlands on the west side. He did not go farther, but trusted that this threat, plus the burning of Esopus (Kingston) by a detachment, would relieve Burgoyne by drawing off part of Gates's army. His courier to Burgoyne, with information of this limited design, was intercepted; Gates took no alarm, but Burgoyne clung to the hope that Clinton would come to his assistance. He fortified a line extending a thousand yards from the river, the strongest redoubt (held by the corps of Lieutenant Colonel Heinrich Breymann) on the western end, to prevent the flank being turned. Burgoyne was anxious. His troops, no more than five thousand, were on short rations, discouraged, and were deserting. General Benjamin Lincoln had recaptured all of the posts in his rear except Ticonderoga.

In contrast, New England and New York militia had increased Gates's force to eleven thousand, and Schuyler had sent more ammunition from Albany. Thus replenished, Gates was scornful of Arnold, whom most in the American army credited with what success had been achieved in the battle of September 19. In a bitter quarrel he refused Arnold any command, gave the left wing to Lincoln, recalled from the north. Gates excluded Arnold from headquarters and invited him to present his grievances to Congress. Arnold nevertheless hung on in camp.

Against the advice of Riedesel to withdraw, Burgoyne was set on a reconnaissance in force to discover whether he could get past the Americans' left, which he mistakenly believed remained unfortified. His movement brought on the battle of October 7 at Bemis Heights. Gates, in his headquarters well to the rear, gave but one order. This was to Daniel Morgan to circuit against the enemy's right while Brigadier General Enoch Poor's brigade assailed the left. Both attacks drove the British into their lines and captured their cannon. Burgoyne's order for a general retreat was not delivered, for his aide, taking the message, was shot down and made prisoner.

Brigadier General Ebenezer Learned was advancing his brigade against the unsupported Brunswickers in the center when Benedict Arnold, though forbidden the field, galloped to the head of the leading regiments. Gates sent Major John Armstrong to call him back, but the messenger could not catch Arnold, who was making rushes that forced the Germans to fall back. The British General Simon Fraser was frantically reforming the line when he was mortally wounded by one of Morgan's riflemen perched in a tree for that purpose. The British sought safety in their breastworks.

But Arnold was not content. He dashed through the crossfire to lead an assault on the defenses, captured and entered Breymann's redoubt before a musketball broke his thigh. Armstrong now arrived to call him off. Arnold's litter-bearers obeyed the order. Breymann had received a death wound, a feeble attempt to retake the redoubt failed, and darkness ended the battle.

The enterprise of Arnold and Morgan shamed the passivity of Gates, who nonetheless nominally had been in command of a victory.

The rest is quickly told. Burgoyne withdrew to Saratoga, where his beaten army was completely surrounded by the Americans. He and his officers agreed they must give up or continue the retreat in "a scene of carnage." Gates consented that Burgoyne's troops, on condition of "not serving again in North America during the present contest," should return to Europe when General Howe could furnish transports at Boston. The army of 5,722 surrendered, with the honors of war, October 17, 1777, in a meadow beside the Hudson.

Victorious troops from the north, or many of them, could now be drawn to Washington's army, confronting the enemy entrenched in Philadelphia. This was the decision of the commander in chief's council of five major generals and ten brigadiers in the camp at Whitpain, Pennsylvania, October 29. Hamilton took the minutes. It was supposed that the enemy numbered ten thousand fit for duty, the Americans a thousand more, but these would soon be reduced to nine thousand by expiration of militia enlistments. It was concluded that before General William Howe could be attacked, twenty regiments must be brought down from the Hudson, besides Morgan's riflemen, already on their march. The general should send one of his aides to procure the needed reinforcement. Washington notified Congress, in Hamilton's hand, that while he would not "frustrate any important plans [Gates] may have formed," he could not "conceive that there is any other object now remaining that demands our . . . most vigorous efforts so much as the destruction of the enemy in this quarter. Should we be able to effect this, we shall have little to fear in future."

Unspoken was the delicacy of Washington's posture vis-à-vis Gates. Following defeat at the Brandywine and Germantown, which permitted Howe to take Philadelphia, Washington stood in shadows now deepened by the brilliance of Gates's victory at Saratoga. What historians have called the "Conway cabal" against Washington's leadership was already building. The name comes from General Thomas Conway, of Irish birth and French military service. As brave as he was restless and discontented, he was more unguarded in his slurs on Washington in favor of Gates than others who were believed to share his animus. Among the latter, besides Gates himself, were General Thomas Mifflin, Dr. Benjamin Rush, and Adjutant General Joseph Reed, of Pennsylvania; the Adamses and James Lovell of Massachusetts, and two of the Lees of Virginia (Richard Henry and Francis Lightfoot). Some have thought that these military officers and members of Congress planned to displace Washington and install Gates as commander in chief. Gates was in fact made president of the Board of War. Hamilton viewed seriously the menace to Washington's leadership. Probably the anti-Washington, pro-Gates party never had cohesion or premeditation, was simply a passing irritation from the strains of war. But it was nonetheless divisive when it flared on the news of Burgoyne's surrender, which was more than a substantial relief to New England. The leaders of that section, in their triumph, forgot the need for defense of the continent in other quarters. It mattered not that the laurels of the hero of Saratoga had been won by Benedict Arnold and Daniel Morgan and, more distantly, by John Stark and Nicholas Herkimer. Nor was praise of Gates diminished because he gave the conquered overlenient terms. It was enough that Burgoyne's invaders, lately so menacing, were being marched under guard for expulsion from America.

An example of the adulation accorded Gates came to Hamilton from his patron in the West Indies, Dr. Hugh Knox. "We are now blessed," the clergyman wrote, "with . . . the glorious news of Burgoine's Surrender to the *Immortal Gates*; another bright Star in the Constellation of American Heroes." And he added, "we are momently Expecting to hear that Gen: Washington has done Something like the Same by Gen: Howe!—but wc

Yet tremble in Suspense." Others were franker in contrasting the exultant success of Gates with the anxious inaction of Washington. Should not Gates be put in position to save the continent as he had rescued New England? Gates's applauders were not put off by his nonmartial appearance and manner. What if he were unimpressive in build, myopic, and bespectacled, with thin graying hair, all becoming a man of the desk rather than of the battlefield? What if, like the Duke of Plaza-Toro, he "led his regiment from behind"? No superficial shortcomings could change the fact that he was victorious. Not all of his partisans were generously naïve, but from motives of personal ambition, military pique, or political clannishness were willing to see Washington disparaged.

These were the circumstances under which General Washington chose Alexander Hamilton for the ticklish mission to General Gates.

5

Succor from Saratoga

 Washington congratulated Gates on his victory over Burgoyne at Saratoga, but regretted that news of it had not been sent him by Gates immediately and directly. Gates, against the instructions of Washington, had relied on the president of Congress to relay reports to the commander in chief. In this instance Gates's messenger, his aide Wilkinson, had reached York, Pennsylvania, the meeting place of Congress after Philadelphia was captured, only tardily, due as much to loitering on the way as to illness. Gates's remissness was symptomatic of his neglect of Washington, to give his omission no worse name. Before he took time to preen himself and entertain chief officers among his prisoners, he should have got off the earliest possible express to the commander in chief, reciting not only the momentous fact of Burgoyne's surrender, but his own further plans.

Washington introduced his aide, Hamilton, to Gates; he was sent "by the advice of my Genl. Officers . . . to lay before you a full state of our situation, and that of the Enemy in this Quarter. He is well informed . . . and will deliver my Sentiments upon the plan of operations . . . now necessary." He did not enter into detail because—a reminder of Gates's error of silence—he was not "well advised how matters are circumstanced on the North River."

The next day, October 30, Hamilton received Washington's written instructions. He should at once set out for Albany, or nearby, where he would find General Gates, to "lay before him the State of this Army; and the Situation of the Enemy and . . . point out to him the many happy Consequences that will accrue from an immediate reinforcement being sent from the Northern Army." Repetition emphasized what Hamilton was "chiefly to attend to," namely, "point out in the Clearest and fullest manner to Genl: Gates the absolute necessity . . . for his detaching a very considerable part of the Army at present under his Command to the reinforcement of this." Such a measure "will in all probability reduce Genl: Howe to the same situation in which Genl: Burgoine now is should he attempt to remain in Philadelphia without being able to remove the obstructions in Delaware." (This was written after the Hessian attempt against Fort Mercer had failed, and ten days before the attack on Fort Mifflin commenced.)

It was expedient to draw down the three New Hampshire and fifteen Massachusetts regiments, with two of the sixteen additional Continental regiments, William R. Lee's and Henry Jackson's. However, if Gates had destined part of these troops to the capture or garrisoning of Ticonderoga, then let the complement required by Washington "be made up to the same Number out of other Corps." Relying on his aide's judgment, Washington vested Hamilton with discretionary power. If he found that Gates intended to employ his troops "upon some expedition by . . . which the common cause will be more benefitted than by their being sent . . . to reinforce this Army," Washington would not have that plan interrupted. But if what Gates designed was vague or trifling, then Washington's superior need must be insisted upon. This meant that Hamilton must decide, in effect, whether the war in the next months was to be conducted against Sir Henry Clinton at New York, or against Sir

William Howe on the Delaware. It was left to Hamilton to determine whether any eligible plan of Gates's was of sufficient promise to warrant disregard of the advice of Washington's war council.

Prompt action was an object. Perhaps if time had allowed, Washington would have had Hamilton refer critical questions to him, sending back expresses, but these would have taken at least a week each for the round trip. In any event, the commander in chief reposed remarkable confidence in the prudence and sagacity of his young aide. This was early evidence—Hamilton had been in his military family only eight months—of a trust that was preserved during the years of their association.

Further instructions were more specific. If Sir Henry Clinton (after his foray against forts in the Highlands) had returned down the Hudson with his whole force, then General Putnam, at Fishkill, would have no need for Nixon's and Glover's brigades, which Gates had sent him, and these should be dispatched "with the greatest expedition" to Washington's camp. Hamilton would likely meet Morgan's rifle corps on their way to join Washington; if so, hurry the riflemen along, though he would not have their health suffer "after their late fatigues" at Saratoga. Four regiments of General McDougall's division, already ordered forward, should be directed to proceed to Red Bank, New Jersey, i.e., to Fort Mercer, which yet held out. Hamilton must write Washington on reaching the Hudson and on his arrival at Albany.

Hamilton was accompanied by Captain Caleb Gibbs, of Washington's bodyguard; that he was a Massachusetts man may have suggested sending him along with the chief of mission, so to speak, known as a New Yorker. They rode hard. Leaving Whitpain probably not till afternoon of October 30, they crossed the Delaware at Coryell's Ferry (from New Hope, Pennsylvania, to Lambertville, New Jersey), had supper and spent the night nearby. The next day took them to Crossroads (between Burlington and Allentown), the next to Chester (something short of

Morristown), and by November 2 they had reached New Windsor, crossed the Hudson, and were in Fishkill. They covered 150 miles in three days, or on the average, 50 miles a day.[1]

From Fishkill, New York, on the west side of the river, Hamilton wrote his first report to Washington. Early that morning, leaving New Windsor, he had met Colonel Morgan, marching his corps for Washington's camp, and got his promise to hasten. (This was no empty assurance, for Morgan was famous for the swiftness of his movements.) Hamilton understood from Morgan "that all the Northern army were marching down on both sides the River, and would probably be to-morrow at New Windsor and this place [Fishkill]; . . . that General Putnam had held a council for the general disposition of them, in which it was resolved to send you 4000 men, and to keep the rest on this side the River." The welcome news that Gates had started all of his troops southward persuaded Hamilton that he could accomplish his errand "without going any farther; unless . . . to hasten the troops that were on their march." But on his arrival at Fishkill, this agreeable expectation was disappointed. There Hamilton learned from Lieutenant Peter Hughes, a former aide of Gates's, that Gates was keeping four Continental brigades—Patterson's, Glover's, Nixon's, "& Col. [Seth] Warners mountain boys"—with him in and about Albany, and was building barracks for them. This meant that Hamilton would be obliged to pursue his journey to Albany to inquire into Gates's reasons for retaining strong units, some of which, at least, were required by Washington.

Meantime, an interim expedient presented itself. General Enoch Poor's brigade was coming down the west shore to join Putnam, and would probably be at Fishkill next day. Brigadier General Ebenezer Learned's brigade (also Continental), General Jonathan Warner's brigade of Massachusetts militia,

---

[1] We have two memoranda of the itinerary. One, prepared in Washington's camp, is a table of distances to Albany; the other, more accurate as to route, is their expense account for the round trip, prepared by Captain Gibbs.

plus some regiments of New York militia, were expected soon. Hamilton, in Washington's name, directed General Putnam "to send forward with all dispatch" to Washington the two Continental brigades and the Massachusetts militia, though the latter had less than a month to serve. "Your instructions," the aide wrote to his superior, "did not comprehend any militia; but as there are . . . accounts here that most of [Sir Henry Clinton's] troops from New York are gone to reinforce General Howe [at Philadelphia], and as so large a proportion of the Continental troops have been detained at Albany, I concluded you would not disapprove of a measure calculated to strengthen you, though but for a small time." He did more on the same presumption. Learning from Putnam that General William Winds with seven hundred Jersey militia was at King's Ferry (Stony Point), ordered by Putnam to cross to Peekskill, Hamilton prevailed on Putnam "to relinquish that idea & send off an immediate order for them to march towards Red Bank" (that is, to Fort Mercer on the Delaware). This order would reach Winds at two removes from the commander in chief. Hamilton thought it possible that "unless your Excellency supports this order by an application from your self, [Winds] may march his men home instead of to the place he has been directed to repair to."

Hamilton was mindful that the council at Whitpain had specifically required that Lee's and Jackson's Continental regiments come there from Saratoga, and also that Washington wanted four regiments of McDougall's division to make for Red Bank. Hamilton had to report, however, that none of these troops had marched from Gates's command. "I have pressed their being sent, and an order has been dispatched for their instantly proceeding." Colonel Hugh Hughes, assistant quartermaster general —a partisan of Gates and later not so cooperative—was commandeering fresh horses for Hamilton. The moment they were ready, he would recross the river to fall in with the troops on the other side, and then "make all . . . haste . . . to Albany to get the three brigades there [Patterson's, Glover's, Nixon's] sent forward."

From "present circumstances and appearances," Hamilton expressed doubts of the need to leave at Fishkill the regiments Putnam proposed to keep there. However, the sense of the council at Whitpain forbade him to interfere. He added in a postscript that Poor's brigade had just arrived, and was joining Washington as quickly as possible. By now the aide, "strongly impressed with the importance of endeavoring to crush Mr. Howe," repeated his preference, council or no council, "to draw off all the Continental troops." Had this been determined, General Warner's sixteen hundred Massachusetts militia might have been left with Putnam.

Before describing Hamilton's encounter with Gates at Albany on the afternoon of November 5, that general's state of mind and what he considered to be the responsibilities of his command on the upper Hudson must be understood. While Burgoyne's invasion was causing anxious concern in New England, the Massachusetts Assembly had established frequent expresses to bring word of Gates's progress against the enemy. After the surrender, the people of the Northeast were thankful in proportion to their relief. They did not stop with proper gratitude to Gates, but drew comparisons reflecting on Washington. Thus James Lovell, member of Congress from Massachusetts, jittery at Howe's advance on Philadelphia, assured Gates that "Your army & the eastern militia are now strongly contrasted with those in the Middle State[s]. . . . It is said Howe would not have passed more than 70 Miles, from the Ships which landed him, in his whole Skin in Yr neighbourhood, or among Yankee Stone walls. . . . Our [hope?] springs all from the Northward, and about all our Confidence." Insinuating praise to Gates was not confined to politicians. Officers in Washington's camp wished the commander in chief would emulate the example of the conqueror of Burgoyne. Joseph Reed, congratulating Gates, regretted that "this Army . . . notwithstanding the

Labours . . . of our amiable Chief has yet gathered no Laurels."
Anthony Wayne, dissatisfied with Washington, was looking to
other leaders in his doubt about remaining in the service after
the present campaign; "there are Certain Generals—as *Lee—
Gates—Mifflin* &c. who will point out by their Conduct the
line which I shall follow." Shortly afterward Wayne was
blowing both hot and cold. Gates's success "Must eventually
save this (Otherwise) Devoted Country." However, in spite of
opportunities lost in the battles of Brandywine and Germantown, Wayne looked for better results "if our Worthy General
will but follow his own good Judgment without listning
[*sic*] too much to some Council." Colonel Walter Stewart
feared that General Mifflin would quit the army: "I can assure
you that we want a few such men as him with us, as Activity, and Enterprise seem to be almost banish'd our Camp." General Conway, who was negligent in his assignment to train
Washington's troops, was sending his plan for drill to Gates,
who presumably would know how to apply good advice. A
correspondent from Stonington, Connecticut, made belittling remarks about Schuyler, whom Gates had succeeded in the northern command; "tho' a polite man, [he] is no Soldier, and would
have made a much better Figure as an Assistant Dep[ut]y to
Genl. Mifflin in his Qr. Master Genls. Department than in the
exalted Rank the Congress mistakenly gave" him.

Congress called for a day of thanksgiving for Gates's victory,
and ordered for him a gold medal.

However, pleasing praise did not induce General Gates to
relax his vigilance as soon as he had overcome Burgoyne. The
enemy held Ticonderoga, and Sir Henry Clinton might extend
his destruction on the Hudson to an attack on Albany, with its
valuable army stores. Gates could not know that the enemy,
some time before, had abandoned Burgoyne to his fate. Even
now, instead of joining Burgoyne in Canada or sending his
troops to Howe on the Delaware, Sir Henry Clinton might
choose to retrieve the disaster at Saratoga by ravaging New Eng-

land. Gates was not so puffed up that he would risk letting pride go before a fall.

These apprehensions of danger were offered by General Gates in opposition to Hamilton's request for troops to be sent to reinforce the commander in chief. Gates was "inflexible in the opinion that two brigades at least of Continental troops should remain in and near this place." All of Hamilton's earnest argument, the aide reported to Washington on November 6, could not change this stand. Gates seemed to protest too much. Sir Henry Clinton might return up the river, and if Albany were left as bare of defense as Hamilton proposed, "expose the finest arsenal in America . . . to destruction." Until the roads froze, it would be impossible to remove the artillery and stores from Albany. The New England states would be left open to depredations. Depleting Gates's force would put it out of his power "to enterprise any thing against Ticonderoga."

These reasons struck Hamilton as unsubstantial. He pled Washington's superior need with all the information and fervor he was later to use in many a court of law. For all his exertion, a single brigade, in addition to those already sent down, was the most Gates would allow. Washington's young proxy was "infinitely embarrassed . . . in acting diametrically to the opinion of a Gentleman, whose successes have raised him into the highest importance." Hamilton, eager as he was to bring help to Washington, might in fact hurt him if he forced Gates to give ground. In that event Gates might stir political opposition, which would damage Washington's position and the prosecution of the war. "General Gates," he explained, "has won the intire confidence of the Eastern States; if disposed to do it by addressing himself to the prejudices of the people he would find no difficulty to render . . . odious" a measure plausibly held to subject them to unnecessary peril. Further, "General Gates has influence and interest elsewhere [in Congress]; he might use it, if he pleased, to discredit the measure there also." Should Gates by any chance suffer enemy attack, or miss the opportunity of a promising exploit, it would invite censure by persons looking for any pretext.

These cautions raced through Hamilton's mind as he urged his mission. They determined him "not to insist upon sending either of the other brigades remaining here." Perhaps Washington would disapprove, but he had done what he believed right. Also, he had sent on 2,000 militia that Washington had not expected. In addition, he had requested Putnam to forward to Washington 1,000 Continental troops in lieu of those retained by Gates. This last reinforcement would reach the main army faster from Peekskill than if it came from Albany. Gates was keeping ample troops to protect New England, and Putnam would still have enough to defend the Highlands. In sum, the troops gone and going to Washington were nearly 5,000 Continentals, rank and file, 2,500 Massachusetts and New Hampshire militia, and 700 Jersey militia. These totaled more than Washington had asked for, though not as many Continentals. Hamilton was troubled that the reinforcement was not composed "exactly in the way directed." However, he comforted himself with the reflection that the militia, according to General Lincoln, were excellent; when their enlistment expired, Washington might order to him the troops now remaining on the Hudson.

Vessels were preparing to take the brigade from Putnam to New Windsor on their way to Washington's camp. Hamilton himself was leaving Albany that afternoon on his return, and would press forward the troops on the road.

It soon developed that he could not carry out this intention, and was to remain on the Hudson seven weeks longer. Promptly after consenting that Gates should release to Washington a single brigade, Hamilton learned that the one proposed to be detached (Patterson's) "is, by far, the weakest of the three now here, and does not consist of more than about 600 rank and file fit for duty." In his letter to Gates, remonstrating, he took account of 200 militia in addition to the Continental troops, but pointed out that their enlistment would expire before they could reach Washington, "and to send them would be to fatigue the men to no purpose." [2]

Hamilton would not make this further concession, and used, courteously, his deputed authority.

I cannot consider it either as compatible with the good of the service or my instructions from His Excellency General Washington, to consent, that that brigade be selected from the three, to go to him; but I am under the necessity of requiring, by virtue of my orders from him, that one of the others be substituted instead of this; either General Nixons or General Glover's, and that you will be pleased to give immediate orders for its embarkation.

Spurred by what he considered a disingenuous act of Gates, Hamilton repeated his original contention that one brigade left at Albany, "in conjunction with the detached regiments in the neighbourhood of this place," would be sufficient. Evidently, after seeing Gates, he had been talking with officers on whose judgment and thorough knowledge he could rely. "Their opinion is, that one brigade with the regiments . . . mentioned would amply answer the purposes of this post." He repeated, in Washington's name, his demand for a stronger corps. While choosing, he would take the best: "As it may be conducive to dispatch, that Genl. Glovers brigade should be the one; if agreeable to you; you will give directions accordingly." He would take no further chances, and in a postscript said, "If you think proper to order Glovers brigade and will be pleased to send your orders to me, I will have them immediately forwarded."

[2] The general return of Gates's army a fortnight earlier, the day of Burgoyne's surrender, showed that Nixon's brigade numbered, fit for duty, 854 rank and file, all Continentals; Glover's had 1,362 fit for duty, of whom 444 were militia; Patterson's had 1,070 fit, of whom 338 were militia. Thus Patterson's, which Hamilton refused to accept, eliminating its militia, had 122 fit rank and file below Nixon's, and 630 below Glover's total. Two weeks later, when Hamilton complained to Gates against his selection of Patterson's brigade, the count had changed if Hamilton was correct in finding only 600 Continentals and 200 militia. Even so, Patterson's was 85 percent as strong as Nixon's in Continentals, not "little more than half as large," as Hamilton wrote. Patterson's Continentals numbered little more than half the usable troops of Glover's brigade.

As Hamilton waited in Albany to see the troops off—this actually took two days—his resolve to extract from Gates more reinforcement for Washington hardened. He wrote to the commander in chief: "Having given General Gates a little more time to recollect himself I renewed my remonstrances on the necessity and propriety of sending you more than one Brigade of the three he had detained with him, and finally prevailed upon him to give orders for Glover's in addition to Patterson's brigade to march . . . ." Evidently this was accomplished in a long face-to-face discussion, in which Hamilton had further armed himself for argument. The "necessity" of Gates's compliance (Washington's situation near Howe's army) was fully known to the aide; the "propriety" of Gates's parting with an additional brigade Hamilton could now better urge because he had used the time to inform himself of risks on the Hudson. He had probably inquired, among others, of Generals Lincoln and Schuyler, on whom he could rely, and was prepared to meet Gates's objections. Having procured the two brigades, he was busy at Albany collecting vessels to start the troops downriver, but could get only enough shipping for the smaller (Patterson's) corps. After delay by contrary winds this little fleet reached King's Ferry November 10, whence the brigade would take the shortest route to Washington's headquarters. Glover's brigade marched on the east side of the river, where the roads were better.

In Gates's letter to Washington the same day the troops departed (November 7), one reads—in the draft with the writer's revisions—of the contest between the reluctant general and the pertinacious young envoy, and sees how Gates belabored Washington over Hamilton's shoulder. Gates had hoped that after sending upward of five thousand men "to the Succour of the Southern Army," further reduction of the northern force would have been unnecessary. However, "Colonel Hamilton acquaints me that it was the unanimous Opinion of a Council of War that the whole of the Eastern Regits should march from hence & that Troops were only to be Station'd at peeks Kill, & in the Highlands for the defense of the Country this Way. [Crossed out: *I confess I want wisdom to discover the Motives that Influenced the Giving such an Opinion . . . I am astonished*]." Gates substituted a sentence which hardly softened his dissent: ". . . with the Greatest Defference to The Opinion of this Council of War, I must inform Your Excy that Troops posted at peeks Kill, or in the Highlands, cannot prevent the Enemy from Destroying this City [Albany], and Arsenal, whenever they please to make the attempt." He gave his reasons and continued: "Col. Hamilton After presenting me with Your Excellencys Letter Verbally Demanded that almost the whole of the Troops now in this Department should be ordered to proceed directly for New Windsor. I told the Colonel, that [crossed out: *whatever Orders he Gave in Your Excellency's Name in Writing*] Your Excellency's Orders should be obey'd; but that if my Opinion was to be taken . . . I was intirely Averse to more than One Brigade being sent from hence," since that would endanger Albany. He crossed out: *that all hopes of ever possessing Canada Vanishes with the Troops taken from hence;* he contented himself with "and of course every good Effect of the ruin of General Burgoyne's Army totaly lost, should The Enemy Succeed in an Attempt to possess this Town."

Gates, compelled against his will to accede to Hamilton's authority, yet questioned it, in a passage which, on second thought he struck out. It reads: "Although it is Customary & even Absolutely necessary to direct Implicit Obedience to be paid to the Verbal Orders of Aids de Camp in Action, or while upon the Spot—yet I believe it is never practiced to Delegate that Dictatorial power, to One Aid de Camp sent to an Army 300 Miles distant." In eliminating this slap at Washington, Gates doubtless realized that it was gratuitous and undeserved. He had failed to notify the commander in chief not only of Burgoyne's surrender but of his own posture following. Therefore Washington could not send him an outright order, but must make Gates's response conditional on his not having any important enterprise in prospect. Thus, and precisely because Gates was several hundred miles away, Washington must dispatch a confidential representative who could discuss the matter with Gates, and judge of comparative requirements on the Hudson and on the Delaware, before a conclusion was reached. Washington might have selected another emissary, but the whole episode exhibits the combined prudence and firmness with which Hamilton used his discretionary authority.

In the revised draft, betraying less hostility and chagrin, Gates ended simply: "Upon mature Consideration of all Circumstances, I have, nevertheless, ordered General Glover's Brigade to be added to General Patterson's, in Reinforcement of your Army, and they will march, immediately." Making up for earlier omission, he appended, "Col. Hamilton . . . will report everything that I wish to have you acquainted with, as well with Respect to the present State, as the future Operations this Way."

Gates promptly found that he could reduce danger to the Albany arsenal by sending thirty brass cannons and three thousand stands of arms to Springfield and Westbury, for which he asked Governor Trumbull of Connecticut to furnish him fifty ox teams and two hundred draft horses with a complement of drivers. Immediately afterward (November 10) he could inform Congress that the enemy had "evacuated every post on this side," would probably evacuate Ticonderoga within the month, and would have done so already had Gates been left with troops to threaten it.

When Hamilton had prevailed with General Gates at Albany, and was returning by way of New Windsor, he found his problems were not solved. He had ridden more than a hundred miles in something over two days to arrive at New Windsor headquarters the night of November 9. Fatigue heightened his disgust at General Israel Putnam's disregard of arrangements previously made with him. He immediately expressed his indignation in a letter to Putnam, who was across the river. "I cannot forbear Confessing that I am astonishd, and Alarm'd beyond measure, to find that all his Excellency's Views have been hitherto frustrated, and that no single step of those I mention'd to you has been taken to afford him the aid he absolutely stands in Need of, and by Delaying which the Cause of America is put to the Utmost conceivable Hazard." He had so fully explained the commander in chief's exigency that he had been sure Putnam would give the destined reinforcement his first attention. But Washington "will have too much Reason to think other Objects, in Comparison with that Insignificant, have been Uppermost. I speak freely, and emphatically, because I tremble at the Consequences of the Delay . . . General Clintons Reinforcement is probably by this time with Mr. Howe; this will give him a Decicive superiority over our Army." He acknowledged the warmth of his words, but they proceeded "from the overflowing of my heart in a matter where I conceive this Continent essentially Interested." He added that he had written from Albany, wishing Putnam to send down a thousand Continental troops first proposed to be left with him. "This I Understand has not been done; how the Non Complyance can be answered to Genl. Washington you can best Determine."

"Old Put," as he was affectionately called, was fifty-nine, almost thrice Hamilton's age, but the young aide was through with deference that might bring further mischances: "I now Sir, in the most explicit terms, by his Excellency's Authority, give it as a positive Order from him, that all the Continental Troops under your Command may be Immediately marched to Kings Ferry, there to Cross the River and hasten to Reinforce the Army under him." The Massachusetts militia would be detained until troops arriving from the north could replace the Continentals Putnam was sending off. Washington's idea of keeping troops with Putnam "does not extend further than Covering the Country from any little eruptions of Small parties and carrying on the Works Necessary for the Security of the River." Attacking New York was out of the question, though a diversion in that direction might be attempted, could men be spared from better objects.

Next day, still at New Windsor, Hamilton recited the situation at greater length for Washington. "I am pained beyond expression to inform your Excellency that on my arrival here I find everything has been . . . deranged by General Putnam." The brigades of Poor and Learned remained at New Windsor and at Fishkill. "Col: Warner's Militia, I am told, have been drawn to Peeks-Kill to aid in an expedition against New York which it seems at this time is the Hobby horse with General Putnam. Not the least attention has been paid to my order in your name for a detachment of one thousand men from the troops hitherto stationed at this post. Every thing is sacrificed to the whim of taking New York."

Want of proper management of difficulties in Poor's and Learned's brigades had stopped these troops from marching. The men refused to go unless they were given money and necessaries, several regiments having had no pay for six or eight months. A "nigh mutiny" on this account in Poor's brigade resulted in a captain killing a soldier, and the officer was then shot by the dead man's comrade. Only Governor Clinton had coped with the situation, but from lack of Putnam's cooperation could do no more than prevail on Learned's brigade to march to Goshen, in hopes that once on the go they would continue.

As soon as Hamilton arrived, he took hold. Governor Clinton borrowed for him five or six thousand dollars, which Colonel John Bailey, commanding Learned's corps, believed would keep his men in humor till they joined Washington. Hamilton saw them march toward Goshen. He would do all in his power to get General Poor along. It was now too late to send Warner's militia, as by the time they reached Washington, their term of enlistment would have expired. Therefore he had directed General Putnam to keep the militia and forward all of his Continental troops. Governor Clinton, who cooperated with Hamilton in several ways, would beat up more militia for Putnam when Warner's left. It was necessary to retrieve Putnam's Continentals from Tarrytown, where he had marched them in preparation for "a farcical parade against New York."

If Washington agreed, he would do well to support Hamilton's directions to Putnam with instant orders of his own. Putnam would probably not obey Hamilton, who in exasperation wished "General Putnam was recalled from the command of this post, and Governor Clinton would accept it. The blunders and caprices of [Putnam] are endless." (The fact was that Congress five days earlier, though not yet known to Hamilton or Putnam, had relieved the latter and ordered him to Washington's camp.) Hamilton was "very unwell," but would not spare himself "to get things immediately in a proper train." As soon as he could get Poor's brigade in march, he would proceed to Putnam at Peekskill.

But Hamilton was detained two days at New Windsor "by a fever and violent rheumatic pains" throughout his body. Thus disabled, he was glad of Governor Clinton's help in executing his mission. The aide wrote to General Washington from his sickroom. General Poor would march at once, and would have done so sooner except that his men had been "under an operation for the itch" and could not take the road until effects of the treatment were over. Washington could expect the brigades of Parsons and Learned in five or six days. Glover's men should be at Fishkill this night, but were objecting, officers included, to joining Washington. They were complaining that they had done their part in the campaign, were unpaid, and should not be put to a long march in cold weather. A letter from the commander in chief to Putnam (of November 9) was brought to Hamilton, who took the liberty of reading it before forwarding. If Putnam had been attentive to Hamilton's directions, Washington's orders (to send forward most of his Continental troops) could have been promptly executed. But, Hamilton reported, "Every part of this Gentleman's conduct is marked with blunders and negligence, and gives general disgust." The aide had received no response to his last applications to Putnam, who, Governor Clinton learned, had gone down to White Plains, eyeing New York.

Hamilton informed General Washington that the "enemy appear to have stripped New York very bare," throwing the Tories in that city into "a very great fright." Reports that troops were being sent from New York to reinforce Howe gave Hamilton additional anxiety that as many troops as possible from the Hudson should strengthen Washington. The aide had written Gates that Howe's army was being increased beyond what was first expected; perhaps this news would "extort" from Gates further assistance to Washington. (Hamilton's report of troops drawn off from New York to Philadelphia was accurate. Sir Henry Clinton on October 18 received Howe's orders to send him "*without delay* the Seventh, Twenty-sixth, and Sixty-third Regiments, two battalions of Anspach, and [the] Seventeenth Dragoons, together with . . . the Jaegers and artillerymen which came by the English fleet," besides some other contingents. Sir Henry complained that he was thus "left . . . in a most starved defensive . . . 6142 rank and file fit for duty," and he renewed his efforts to be allowed to return to England.)

In spite of the increased menace to Washington, Hamilton expected no more help from General Gates, "as he pretends to have in view an expedition against Ticonderoga . . . in the Winter . . . calculated to catch the [applause of] the Eastern people" and afford excuse for keeping troops at Albany. However, Hamilton wrote Gates that without doubt more troops, six or seven thousand, had gone from New York to Howe than had gone from the Hudson posts to Washington. Since the British would obviously attempt nothing up the river this season, perhaps Gates could afford more aid to Washington.

The young colonel's physical exertion and anxiety over sending reinforcements to the commander in chief had laid him low for two days at Governor Clinton's house at New Windsor. Imagining he had got the better of his complaints, and eager to attend to the march of the troops, he crossed to Peekskill November 13, but soon had a relapse and was seriously ill at the home of Dennis Kennedy on the King's Ferry road between Montrose and Verplanck's Point. He wrote to Washington the day after his arrival on the east side of the river, but there is nothing more from his pen for five weeks, until December 22, when he wrote that he hoped he would be well enough to start his homeward journey next day. At intervals during his military service Hamilton was taken sick, but never again so gravely or for so long a period as on his mission to the Hudson posts. Though erect and active, he was never as strong in body as in mind and nerve.[3]

Before he was unable to write further, he had explained to General Washington that Glover's brigade would be at King's Ferry that night and that wagons were provided on the west side for the movement to White Marsh headquarters. Poor's troops had crossed the river two days earlier, accompanied by two New York regiments. Putnam had detached a Connecticut regiment to join Washington, but was keeping others with him, complaining that the men lacked shoes and stockings for marching.

Governor Clinton and Captain Gibbs were attentive during Hamilton's illness. When he seemed worse after a week abed at Kennedy's house, Clinton sent in alarm for Dr. John Jones at Bellemont, but the physician was himself ill and could only re-

---

[3] He had more than the usual layman's knowledge of medicine. His interest in the subject had been aroused by Hugh Knox in Saint Croix, for that clergyman, like many in remote communities, ministered to bodies as well as souls of his parishioners. At King's College, having "originally destined himself for the Science of Physic . . . he was regular in attending the anatomical lectures . . . by Dr. [Samuel] Clossy." He learned also from his lifelong friend Dr. Edward Stevens, who pulled him through an attack of yellow fever in Philadelphia in 1793. Later in life he consulted another physician-friend, Dr. James McHenry, concerning diet. When shot by Burr in the duel, he had just strength to say to Dr. David Hosack, "This is a mortal wound."

turn the messenger with directions for treatment. This did not serve, for two days later the patient "seem'd . . . to be drawing nigh his last." He improved somewhat, but after two days more "the Coldness came on again, and encreased (he was then cold as high as the knees)." The doctor had finally reached him, but "thought he could not survive." The physician, on the spot, must have exerted himself, for after four hours Hamilton's fever went down, and he was soon pronounced on the mend. Gibbs noted in their expense account payments for special foods prescribed for his friend's convalescence—mutton first but soon changing to nourishing delicacies, such as chicken, eggs, quail, partridge, and shrub (sweetened fruit juice with spirits). Gibbs paid Dr. Jones six shillings, and bought for Hamilton, for forty-five shillings, a bed, evidently more comfortable than an army cot. Apparently Hamilton had suffered an attack of acute rheumatic fever.

The aide must have been cheered in the early stage of his sickness by a letter from Washington (from White Marsh, November 15). The commander in chief had received Hamilton's reports through the twelfth, and assured him, "I approve intirely all the Steps you have taken, and have only to wish that the exertions of those you have had to deal with had kept pace with your Zeal and good intentions." Hamilton surely appreciated Washington's solicitude for his health, and wished that he were able, as Washington hoped, "to push on the rear of the whole reinforcement beyond New Windsor." This was the more necessary because, the general informed him, British ships with troops had arrived in the Delaware. "The Enemy have lately damaged Fort Mifflin considerably, but our people keep possession and seem determined to do so to the last extremity."

When convalescent, irked at not being on his feet, Hamilton must have shown his irritation, for Colonel Hugh Hughes informed Gates (December 5), "Colonel Hamilton, who has been very ill of a nervous Disorder, at Peekskill, is out of Danger, unless it be from his own sweet Temper." Hamilton and Gibbs left Peekskill December 23 and, evidently for the sake of the former's health, made a slow return to Washington's camp, reached not before January 20, 1778. Even then he seems to have been obliged to recuperate a week or more before commencing his regular duties at headquarters, which had now been established at Valley Forge.

Had the assiduous young aide not fallen sick as soon as he had started troops from the northern army, he would surely have obeyed the command to push on the reinforcement to Washington. In any case they could not have arrived in time to relieve Fort Mifflin, but they would have relieved the anxiety of the American camp for the near future. General St. Clair wrote to Gates (November 21), "it is certain our Discipline and . . . Numbers . . . are inferior to theirs, but when your victorious Troops arrive, they will make our Scale preponderate but what can delay them so—Morgan has been arrived above a Fortnight." The day previous Major General John Armstrong confided to Gates: "We are ill Cloathed, the Winter is on, to Hutt near the Enemy will be as arduous as dangerous, to retire back for Quarters & thereby leave the Country Open appears to be intolerable. . . . Our troops express their wishes for another tryal and must be greatly animated by the arrival of yours."

Certain officers and politicians were soon animated by the arrival in Pennsylvania of Gates himself to be president of the new Board of War. The confidence of Congress in the conqueror of Burgoyne was expressed by Henry Laurens in notifying him of his appointment to a trust on which "the safety & Interest of the United States eminently depend." James Lovell, a delegate in Congress from Massachusetts, had plainly lost faith in Washington when he cried to Gates, "We want you most near Germantown. Good God! What a Situation we are in! . . . Come to the Board of War if only for a Short Season." Gates was to remain in uniform, to be recalled to field command if required. Placing Gates, in more than a titular sense, in direction of the war came now as close as his partisans could contrive to giving him preference above Washington.

A sequel to Hamilton's extraction of troops from Gates was

the beginning of discredit of the "Conway cabal" against Washington. An actor in the scene, on the side of Washington's critics, besides Conway and Gates, was Gates's adjutant, Colonel James Wilkinson. Washington's supporters included Lord Stirling and Stirling's aide, Major William McWilliams, Hamilton, and, incidentally, Hamilton's friend from college days, Major Robert Troup, then an aide to Gates.

While Hamilton was yet in the Highlands of the Hudson, Washington pricked the bubble with the point of his pen. This was in a terse note of accusation to Conway: "Sir: A Letter which I received last Night, contained the following paragraph. In a Letter from Genl. Conway to Genl. Gates he says: 'Heaven has been determined to save your Country; or a weak General and bad Councellors would have ruind it.'"

This thrust of Conway had been disclosed, as it later transpired, by Wilkinson. On his leisurely journey from Albany to Congress at York to announce victory and justify the terms of surrender given to Burgoyne, Wilkinson had spent a convivial day with Stirling and his lordship's military family at Reading, Pennsylvania. Gates had dispatched his messenger with the endorsement, "I have not met with a more promising Military Genious than Col. Wilkinson . . . whose services have been of the last importance to this Army." Wilkinson, thus in Gates's confidence, as Troup reported, "became acquainted with the correspondence, passing between General Conway, and General Gates, to the prejudice of General Washington's military character." Wilkinson's "promising Genious" forsook him in his cups at Reading. As he described the occasion, to cover his indiscretion, the conversation at Stirling's headquarters "became general, unreserved and copious . . . and the nature of our situation [all tipsy] made it confidential." Just what passed he could not recall, but would "acknowledge it is possible in the warmth of social intercourse, when the mind is relaxed and the tongue is unguarded, that observations may have elapsed which have not since occurred to me."

One of his loose-tongued observations was recalled to him when he reached Washington's camp at White Marsh, by the discomfited Conway. That officer "had been charged by General Washington, with writing a letter to Major General Gates which reflected on the General [Washington] and on the army." Conway taxed Wilkinson with the disclosure. Lord Stirling had had the tale from his aide, McWilliams, and felt duty bound to inform Washington of "such wicked duplicity of conduct" on the part of Conway. Mifflin, at Reading, tipped off his friend Gates to Wilkinson's lapse, and was plainly afraid that he himself would come under the commander in chief's censure. "An extract from General Conway's letter to you," Mifflin wrote, "has been procured and sent to head quarters." The comment of Conway, quoted back to him by Washington, was "such as should not have been entrusted to any of your Family. My dear General, take Care of your Generosity & Frank Disposition; they . . . may injure some of your best friends."

Thus warned of unpleasant consequences, Gates wrote anxiously to Conway, "I intreat you . . . to let me know which of the letters was copied off. [Evidently more than one may have given Washington umbrage.] It is of the greatest importance, that I should detect the person who has been guilty of that act of infidelity: I cannot trace him out, unless I have your assistance."

Meantime Gates put himself on a false scent. When Wilkinson returned to Albany, his general exclaimed, "I have had a spy in my camp since you left me!"

"I did not comprehend the allusion," Wilkinson recorded, "and he explained by informing me, 'Colonel Hamilton had been sent up to him by General Washington; and would you believe it, he purloined the copy of a letter out of that closet,' pointing to one in the room. I answered him that I conceived it impossible," only to have Gates continue with his deduction. He said, according to Wilkinson, that when his aides were called out on business, " 'Colonel Hamilton was left alone an hour in this room, during which time, he took Conway's letter out of that closet and copied it, and the copy has been furnished to Washington.' "

Suspicion of someone other than himself seemed to Wilkinson a lead to be encouraged. Gates knew the intimacy between Troup and Hamilton, for the two had sought each other's company during Hamilton's recent visit to Albany. Likely Troup had confided Conway's slur on Washington to his friend Hamilton, who had repeated it to the commander in chief. But Gates dismissed such indirection. Hamilton was the miscreant; Gates had a plan " 'which would compel General Washington to give him up, and . . . the receiver and the thief would be alike disgraced.' " The prospect of an attempt to fasten on Washington complicity in the shameful act of going behind Gates's back set Wilkinson to preparing his own defense, for plainly the blame would soon be put on him. Surely, he expostulated in his later account of the contretemps, Gates had not held Conway's letter confidential, "because he had read it *publicly* in my presence, as matter of information from the grand army . . . and therefore I did not dream of the foul imputations it was destined to draw upon me."

Gates, in an insinuating plea to Washington, all but named Hamilton as the culprit:

I conjure your excellency, to give me all the assistance you can, in tracing out the author of the infidelity which put extracts from General Conway's letters to me into your hands. These letters have been *stealingly copied* . . . It is . . . *in your* . . . *power* to do me and the United States a very important service, by detecting a wretch who may betray me, and capitally injure the *very operations under your immediate direction.*

As though to say Washington's zeal in running the villain to earth might not be sufficient, Gates was sending a copy of his letter to the president of Congress.

Washington's reply set Gates back on his heels and made him wish he had not been so forward. Ignoring the imputations against Hamilton, Washington recited that Stirling, "from motives of friendship," had conveyed what Wilkinson, Gates's man, had babbled at Reading. Washington ended with a stinging reprimand for Gates. When first told of the aspersion upon himself, and before he discovered Gates in pursuit of a traitorous telltale, he had supposed that Gates had meant to warn him against "a dangerous incendiary . . . Genl. Conway. But, in this, as in other matters of late, I have found myself mistaken."

Gates answered from York, where he had gone to be head of the Board of War. Contradicting his previous admissions, he now said the paragraph quoted to Washington was "spurious . . . a wicked forgery." Conway's letter mentioned neither the weakness of any general nor bad counselors. In a further about-face, Gates now disowned suspecting Hamilton, and arraigned the faithless Wilkinson, who he said should be punished. Doubtless Hamilton, having been meanly accused, applauded when Washington discredited Gates's argument. Gates at first accepted the authenticity of a stricture, the existence of which he then denied. If Conway's letters were innocent, why had Gates not produced them? By his silence under Washington's indictment, Conway had practically admitted his authorship of the offensive passage. However, Washington was through with the topic, and willing, "as far as future events will permit," to bury the episode in oblivion.

The denouement of this little drama was semicomic. Returning from Albany to York, Wilkinson learned that Gates had denounced him "in the grossest language." Protesting his innocence and rehearsing his sacrifices in the service of Gates, he demanded that Gates meet him behind the English church prepared to shoot it out. Gates accepted the challenge, but at the last minute sent a request for an explanation. As they walked in a back street, Gates burst into tears, and Wilkinson's resentment was appeased. He had similarly vowed vengeance on Stirling, but was quicker, on the latter's dignified reply, to cry quits. The mutterers—perhaps schemers—against Washington lost face.

The talkative Wilkinson resigned his undeserved commission as brigadier general and his appointment as secretary of the Board of War. Gates stepped down as president of the Board of War when assigned to command the garrison of Ticonderoga. Mifflin, under embarrassing though unproved charges, ended his duties as quartermaster general, later placed in the capable hands of Nathanael Greene. The subsequent history of each of them was checkered.

After his mission to Gates, Hamilton had been back in camp at Valley Forge six weeks when he began preparing for a more formal diplomatic assignment. Together with Colonel William Grayson, Elias Boudinot, the commissary general for prisoners, and his fellow aide Robert H. Harrison, he was to meet with officers assigned by Sir William Howe "to fix the exchange . . . of Prisoners of War, upon a more certain, liberal, and ample foundation." Unfortunately the agreement reached by Washington and Howe in the summer of 1776, stipulating an exchange of "officer for officer of equal rank, soldier for soldier and citizen for citizen" had proved unworkable. It did not anticipate the complications that arose, chiefly as a result of the capture of General Charles Lee, who was held by the British under threat of trial as a traitor, since he had quit the king's army to join that of the Colonies. Until it was established that Lee would be treated as an ordinary prisoner of war, Washington would not permit exchanges to proceed under the agreement. Lee was finally released in return for Major General Richard Prescott.

With a suitable escort of dragoons—stipulated by Hamilton to be "picked men and horses [to] make the best possible appearance"—the American commissioners began meetings at Germantown (March 31, 1778) with their British counterparts, Colonels Charles O'Hara and Humphrey Stephens, and Captain Richard FitzPatrick. Immediately two procedural difficulties interposed. Though Hamilton and his colleagues were clothed with full powers from Congress and the commander in chief to fix upon "a Treaty and Convention for the Exchange of Prisoners of War," the British commissioners acted on authority of General Howe alone. If another succeeded to command, he could disavow Howe's agreement. In the second place, the British demanded that both parties of negotiators should retire within their own lines daily. The Americans protested that this would impede progress, and that their round trip, Valley Forge to Germantown, thirty-four miles, imposed on them the greater hardship.

During an adjournment, however, the Americans discussed the many contingencies that had to be provided for in a permanent, general cartel, and Hamilton embodied these in a proposed agreement. The fourteen articles covered in detail the many problems, civil as well as military, which experience had revealed. Hamilton took no stock in the contention of some American politicians that it was not to the interest of the revolutionaries to exchange prisoners, since to hold captives would weaken the enemy, distant from the sources of reinforcement. "I have so much of the milk of humanity in me," he told Governor Clinton, "that I abhor such *Neronian* maxims." "The prospect of hopeless captivity" would discourage "men constantly exposed to the chance of it." It would slow recruiting, and, once taken prisoner, troops would be tempted to enlist with the enemy. The dreadful sufferings of Americans in the hands of the British were certainly known to Hamilton, either through first-hand reports or from Boudinot, and he had compassion for those immured for months in hulks in Wallabout Bay or in the old sugar house in New York City.

The conferees never acted on substantive matters, for the Americans could not accept Howe's insistence that any agreement on the British side be a personal compact rather than a public treaty.

The effort at a formal binding contract, thus collapsed, was resumed by General Sir Henry Clinton, who succeeded Howe, eight months later (December 1778). His proposal, accepted by Congress and Washington, was to exchange officers of the American army in his hands for officers and men of the "convention troops," those taken prisoner at Burgoyne's capitulation at Saratoga. This time Hamilton and Harrison were duly authorized to meet Colonels Charles O'Hara and West Hyde at Amboy, New Jersey (December 11, 1778). But again the commissioners could not agree. The Americans considered that the British had consented to exchange officers for officers, whether or not of equal rank or in customary proportions according to differences in rank. Private soldiers, as the Americans understood the proposal, would not be exchanged for officers, in any proportion, unless one side was deficient in officers held prisoner. The British contended that they had not so understood the plan. "Every Sense of Honour, Justice and Humanity," they declared, "make it impossible to acquiesce in a Proposal, which might . . . separate the Officers from the Private Soldiers, by exchanging the former, and suffering the latter to remain in Captivity. Companions in their more fortunate Hours, they must be equally Sharers of Affliction." They wanted privates exchanged for officers—since at Saratoga the enlisted men had been surrendered wholesale. Hamilton and Harrison, in obedience to the preliminary proposal, would not consent to this demand. They did make one concession: exchange of officers of equal rank, so far as numbers would extend. This would leave some British officers with their troops, though, to be sure, as prisoners. In spite of Hamilton's argument, which in fidelity to the preparatory agreement was unimpeachable, the British commissioners broke off the negotiation after one sitting.

Some exchanges of prisoners, of course, did take place, before and after these abortive attempts at a general cartel, occasionally a few individuals at a time, oftener in batches, but such exchanges were by special arrangement. No mutually accepted system, to be automatically applied, was ever in force during the war.

During this period Hamilton tried to promote the proposal of his friend John Laurens for the enlistment of slaves in the Revolutionary army. The great contradiction of the war was that the Americans were fighting for liberty and proclaiming the rights of man while holding Negroes in slavery. Of course this grossest form of oppression, damaging to the community as well as to persons of both races, had abundant white apologists, on practical, political, and even moral grounds. A favorite rationalization, so incessantly repeated that it became widely accepted, was that the African was a lower order of being. To be sure, in God's providence, he possessed a soul, but he was by nature inferior in the qualities of courage, intellect, self-respect, and responsibility. The foundation for all justifications, or excuses, for slavery was the supposed private interest of the owners. The Society of Friends, the Moravians, certain other religious groups, and conscientious, enlightened individuals accused the majority of perpetrating a social wrong. At times and in particular places sentiment was strong for prohibiting the importation of slaves, and for manumission. But for some years during the Revolution every state tolerated the institution, including Rhode Island, the creation of Roger Williams; Pennsylvania, the commonwealth of brotherly love; not to speak of Virginia, the home of the author of the Declaration of Independence.

Among the opponents of slavery, Alexander Hamilton and his fast friend John Laurens were conspicuous for efforts to include Negro slaves in the Revolutionary army, with "the promise of their freedom with their swords." Both Hamilton and Laurens spent their boyhoods in slave societies—Hamilton in the West Indies, Laurens in the low country of South Carolina, and the two places differed little in the high proportion of blacks to whites. Hamilton was an early member, with John Jay and Hamilton's patron Hercules Mulligan, of the Society for Promoting the Manumission of Slaves, and paid solicitous visits to freedmen in New York. In the New York Assembly he supported a bill for gradual emancipation, vigorously espoused, to his honor, by Aaron Burr. Hamilton's record condemning slavery is clear, with the single exception that he apparently purchased a Negro woman as a servant for Mrs. Hamilton. John Laurens, when his father, Henry Laurens, proposed to free his many slaves, was glad to surrender this portion of his patrimony.

The most laudable feature of the antislavery advocacy of these young officers was that it proceeded not simply from noblesse oblige and a sense of fairness, but from the insistence that Negro slaves had normal capacities for development and achievement if freed from their degraded condition.

Negro freedmen, including those liberated for that purpose, served as soldiers in the Continental army.[4] In August 1778 seven brigades had an average of fifty-four in each. Slaves, employed from their masters, were laborers for the army on many occasions.

John Laurens inherited his emancipation sentiments from his father, Henry Laurens, who, though sometimes equivocal in the matter, had derived antislavery views from his father. In 1776 Henry Laurens wrote to John,

I abhor slavery. . . . The day I hope is approaching when from principles of gratitude and justice every man will strive to be foremost in complying with the golden rule. £20,000 sterling would my negroes produce if sold at auction tomorrow. . . . Nevertheless I am devising means of manumitting many of them and for cutting off the entail of slavery. [This last meant that the children of those remaining slaves would be free.] Great powers oppose me: the laws and customs of my country, my own and the avarice of my countrymen.

4 For an excellent short summary, see Charles Knowles Bolton, *The Private Soldier under Washington* (London, George Newnes, Ltd., 1902) pp. 20–25. Lord Dunmore's proclamation (November 1775) freeing all indentured servants and slaves willing to join the British army may have induced Washington the following month to allow recruiting officers to enlist free Negroes. Rhode Island purchased the freedom of slaves before enrolling them in the army, the men presumably willing, and looked to the Continental Congress for repayment. General William Heath in June 1780 spoke to Colonel Christopher Greene's regiment "of blacks" from Rhode Island. Henry Laurens, when he knew that Charleston would be surrendered (May 1780), declared that the state could have been saved had his plan of enlisting Negroes for its defense been followed.

John Laurens in reply saw through the disingenuous arguments his fellow Southerners used in support of slavery—" 'Without slaves how is it possible for us to be rich?' " He had for some time been agitating against "the complete mischief occasioned by our usurpation—we have sunk the African[s] and their descendants below the standard of humanity, and almost render'd them incapable of that blessing which equal Heaven bestow'd upon all." Still, there would be "danger in advancing men suddenly from the state of slavery," and he was pondering by what "shades and degrees" slaves might be enabled to enjoy freedom.

Early in 1778 John was eager to raise and command a regiment of freed slaves. His father now drew back, and scolded. Your "whole mind is enveloped in the cloud of that project," the elder Laurens remonstrated. "Your own good sense will direct you to proceed warily in opposing the opinions of whole nations, lest, without effecting any good, you become a bye word, and be so transmitted to your children's children." But John was not budged from his determination, declaring "it will be my duty and my pride to transform the timid slave into a firm defender of liberty & render him worthy to enjoy it himself." As a soldier, as a citizen, as a man, he was "interested to engage in this work."

The perilous condition of South Carolina and neighboring states in 1779, when the British resolved to carry the war to that quarter, hastened the governor to send General Isaac Huger to Philadelphia for aid; Huger, William H. Drayton, and Henry Laurens in the emergency espoused black regiments. Laurens (mid-March 1779) wrote Washington, "Had we arms for three thousand such black men as I could select in Carolina, I should have no doubt of success in driving the British out of Georgia and subduing East Florida before the end of July." Washington objected that the enemy could arm a larger Negro force, and that those left in slavery would be restless. Congress was not put off, and, on the plea of John Laurens, among others, recommended to South Carolina and Georgia that they raise three thousand Negro troops, under white officers. All the slaves who served to the end of the war would be freed, and Congress would recompense their owners.

One who assisted this resolve was Alexander Hamilton. Enthusiastic for John Laurens' proposal, Hamilton sent by him a letter to John Jay, president of Congress, already likely to be favorable. In "the present situation of affairs" in South Carolina, he said, the project of recruiting several battalions of Negroes deserves "every kind of support." The idea was that Congress should recommend the plan, that the South Carolina legislature should comply, and that owners should be obliged to contribute slaves in proportion to the numbers they possessed. Congress was to take the battalions into Continental pay. Hamilton boldly suggested that the white militia of North Carolina and Virginia be drafted for a year, while South Carolina, "being very weak in her population of whites," should furnish the black battalions instead.

I have not the least doubt that the negroes will make very excellent soldiers. . . . I have frequently heard it objected to the scheme of embodying negroes, that they are too stupid to make soldiers. This is so far from appearing to me . . . valid . . . that I think their want of cultivation (for their natural faculties are as good as ours), joined to that habit of subordination which they acquire from a life of servitude, will enable them sooner to become soldiers than our white inhabitants. Let officers be men of sense and sentiment; and the nearer the soldiers approach to machines, perhaps the better.

He foresaw the inevitable opposition to the proposal. Only one familiar with a slave society and who had risen above its prejudices could have written Hamilton's next sentence: "The contempt we have been taught to entertain for the blacks, makes us fancy many things that are founded neither in reason or experience." Unwillingness to part with valuable property "will furnish a thousand arguments to show the impracticability, or pernicious tendency, of a scheme which requires such sacrifices." Freeing the slaves on enlistment, he believed, would secure their fidelity, animate their courage, and give others the hope of emancipation.

Hamilton has been typed as aristocratic, disdainful of the body of the people. The inaccuracy of this stamp appears in his remark that he wished the success of recruiting slaves to be free soldiers, because "the dictates of humanity, and true policy, equally interest me in favor of this unfortunate class of men."

John Laurens, headed south to the defense, was to deliver the resolve of Congress, which precisely reinforced his proposal in the legislature of his own state, of which he was a member. He urged his plan whenever lulls in the fighting permitted him to attend legislative sessions. But South Carolina would not save herself by such means. John, for his pains, got only a few favoring votes. His father announced to him, "Your black regiment is blown up with contemptuous huzzas," but no longer scolded his son for his activities. "You have encountered rooted habits and prejudices, than which there is not in the history of man . . . a more arduous engagement. If you succeed"—he knew his son's persistence—"your name will be honorably . . . transmitted to posterity. . . . The work will at a future day be efficaciously taken up, and then it will be remembered who began it in South Carolina." [5]

John Laurens was made prisoner at the surrender of Charleston, was paroled, and later was exchanged. After playing a valiant part, with Hamilton, in capture of the last enemy redoubt at Yorktown, and helping to settle the terms of Cornwallis' capitulation, he returned to South Carolina. To aid in expulsion of

[5] David D. Wallace, *The Life of Henry Laurens* (New York, G. P. Putnam's Sons, 1915), p. 450, observes, "The whole incident exercised a strong alienating influence towards the central government. South Carolina felt herself not only abandoned, but mocked and insulted—a frame of mind which doubtless [helped lead] Governor Rutledge to propose when the triumph of the British a few weeks later seemed inevitable that the State should withdraw from the contest and remain neutral to the end of the war." A voluntary beginning in emancipation at this relatively early date, besides military benefits, might have saved much grief later, but South Carolina refused to repent, even with the British at hand.

the British, he renewed his appeal to the legislature in 1782 for his black regiment. He received more support than before, but not enough.

In a volunteer attempt to intercept with fifty troops a British foraging party three times as large, he dashed to the attack, but was killed at the first fire (August 27, 1782).

A fortnight earlier, about to enter Congress, Hamilton had written Laurens a summons which his friend probably never received. "Peace made . . . a new scene opens. The object then will be to make our independence a blessing. . . . Quit your sword . . . put on the toga. Come to Congress. We know each other's sentiments; our views are the same. We have fought side by side to make America free; let us hand in hand struggle to make her happy."

Hamilton suffered "the deepest affliction" at learning, through General Greene, of the death of Laurens, "a citizen whose heart realized that patriotism of which others only talk. I shall feel the loss of a friend I truly . . . loved." Others—Greene, Washington, John Adams, even the Charleston *Royal Gazette*— were similarly sorrowful.

It may be reasonably supposed that had John Laurens survived to play the role in civil life for which he was fitted by talents and prestige, he would have been an eager teammate in Hamilton's achievements. Their companionship in the army, and mutual understanding, would have led to results in the public forum. Had John Laurens been in the Constitutional Convention, his national loyalty would have been thrown against the proslavery reservations of his far-south compatriots. In any event, Laurens and Hamilton, from different and often antagonistic sections, would have assisted each other in the struggle for a united country.

6

Prussian Discipline with a Difference

 Early on mid-March mornings in 1778 an imposing personage could have been seen posting to the parade ground at Valley Forge. His hair was carefully dressed; he wore a blazing decoration over his heart; and he carried his pistols in enormous holsters over the pommel of his saddle. Two men rode in that saddle, one a fiction, but the other exceedingly genuine. The make-believe one was a lieutenant general in the army of Frederick the Great. The true soldier was Baron Friedrich Wilhelm von Steuben, serving as a volunteer under Washington, and now about to commence the training of America's troops.

The lieutenant general was the product of Benjamin Franklin's gift for public relations. Urged by Claude Louis de Saint-Germain, the French minister of war, Franklin had dispatched Steuben to the rebelling Colonies with flattering letters to Congress and to the commander in chief. Steuben, knowing scarcely any English, could not read Franklin's extravagances, but as far as he understood them, he acquiesced in the praise. Rarely have fraudulent representations proved more fortunate in the out-

131

come. The false entitlements bestowed by Franklin insured Steuben prestige that overcame ready jealousies. The puffs of the diplomat were confirmed by the modesty, unexampled among foreign officers, with which Steuben offered himself to Congress and commander. He made no stipulation for rank or pay, simply declaring his desire to serve the cause of American independence. Explaining his policy to Hamilton, he said, "From the information I received . . . that the preferment of foreigners to military employments had been the cause of discontent in the American army, I foresaw the necessity of pursuing a different course from that . . . adopted by my predecessors. . . ." Steuben was confident of his ability; the problem was to be given the opportunity to prove himself. "Any conditions proposed by me, under these circumstances, tending to insure me a recompense proportioned by my sacrifices and my services, would have rendered all my negotiations abortive." This generosity on the baron's part was politic at the moment, but soon rose to plague him and Congress. Unquestionably, Steuben's contribution had to be recognized in rank, pay, and ultimately, indemnification for his losses—if any—in coming to America. It was a dispute over this last item, the value of his "sacrifices," that was to engage the intercessions of Hamilton in his behalf.

Then forty-eight, a soldier since the age of sixteen, he had never been more than a captain in European armies. His title of baron had been honestly conferred by the prince of Hohenzollern-Hechingen, and he was also a knight of the Order of Fidelity (hence that jeweled star he invariably wore) due to the intercession of Princess Frederica of Württemberg. More important, he had fought through the Seven Years' War under Frederick the Great and, as a member of his staff, had been selected to receive the general's special training in the military art. Of greatest consequence were his intelligence, industry, devotion, and personal magnetism.

The American army had suffered, in morale as well as in battle, from lack of drill and discipline. This was inevitable because the troops were recruited, often tardily, by the states separately, on one-year enlistments, and except for the few men who chose to remain, a new force had to be collected for every campaign. Methods of drill, where any were practiced, followed different forms—English, French, or German. Few American officers knew the manual of arms, let alone how to conduct field maneuvers, how to dress a line when the poor fellows in it were half clad, or how to induce them to precision of movements when their bellies craved food. The Americans had borrowed too much from Indian warfare, in which it was each man for himself. Marches were in single file, which delayed massing troops to make or meet attack. The very idea of systematized action under orders of command seemed uncongenial to the habit of the country.

Washington, aware of his army's deficiencies, had made an attempt to standardize training procedures prior to Steuben's arrival in camp. In the fall of 1777 he asked the general officers at Valley Forge to submit their ideas for reform of army regulations. Hamilton worked up their replies, probably including some suggestions of his own, into a report of the commander in chief, which was submitted January 29, 1778, to the committee of Congress then in camp. The report included a recommendation by Washington that a uniform system of training be established under the supervision of an inspector general, who would report directly to Washington himself. Solutions were also proposed for a number of other pressing problems. To restore the morale of officers, a plan of half pay or pension on retirement was recommended. An annual draft of troops, with bounty payments limited to re-enlistments, was urged. The report also recommended that weak regiments be consolidated; that cases of faulty bestowal of rank be rectified; that the cavalry and inspector general's department be expanded; that contracts be assigned to the French government to provide sufficient clothing for the army; and that the military hospitals be enlarged and better supplied. The report warned that unless remedies for sufferings and discontents in the army were applied at once, "the most alarming . . . consequences" would follow.

Apparently, earlier, Hamilton had voluntarily addressed to Washington a catalogue of improvements for the service. "There are still existing in the army so many abuses," he declared, "absolutely contrary to the military constitution, that, without a speedy stop be put to them, it will be impossible . . . to establish any order or discipline among the troops." He laid down corrections for officers overstaying their leaves, taking too many soldiers as servants, or demanding standing guards, and he proposed that arms and ammunition not be issued to noncombatants. He gave detailed directions for sentries to protect advanced posts against surprise and suggested that each regiment be held accountable for the arms and accoutrements in its possession. He further proposed that absences due to sickness, whether the men were in the hospital or in private houses in the country, be reported regularly, and that men on furlough or away from camp on special duty be recalled within a reasonable time. The provost corps, he suggested, not answering the purpose for which it was raised, should be used instead for limited courier service.

Despite headquarters' efforts, the Board of War, at this time hostile to Washington, preferred a plan of Brigadier General Thomas Conway, and they appointed Conway inspector general, to be responsible not to the commander in chief but directly to the board. This provision undercut Washington in both aims and authority. Conway had been correctly but not cordially received by Washington in camp, had incurred the displeasure of the field officers, had accomplished nothing, and had betaken himself to other posts when Steuben arrived at Valley Forge in late February 1778. Washington found Steuben all that Conway was not, invited his acquaintance with existing needs, approved his proposals for remedy, in which the baron was assisted by Greene and Hamilton, and appointed him acting inspector general for the main army. Washington, taught by previous experience with foreign officers of spurious pretensions, was cautious in even this informal assignment of the newcomer. The jealousy of commanders for the drill of troops whom they must lead in battle should not be aroused. But the baron, in spite of, or perhaps because of, his lack of English, by his ingenuous manner won general confidence. Greene, Wayne, and other principal officers confirmed Washington's approval. Of no less importance, Hamilton and John Laurens, of the headquarters staff, became Steuben's interpreters as well as his enthusiastic supporters. His young secretary, Duponceau, who came over with him, could turn the baron's French into English, but he lacked the military knowledge and the native character that Hamilton and Laurens supplied to make the stranger understood and accepted.

Steuben was a bundle of contradictions. Generous to a fault and improvident in his personal finances, his system of inspection, which demanded both efficiency and accountability, notably reduced public expenses. Trained in the highest school of military perfection, he reduced his goals for the raw American troops to the feasible rudiments. Devoted to honors and display, he was proud to begin his reforms by taking musket in hand and drilling a squad. His explosive curses in German and French, sprinkled with a few words in English, endeared him to his awkward pupils instead of angering them. Actually, his displays of rage and profanity were often put on for the troops' satisfaction.

With picked men added to Washington's bodyguard for the purpose, the baron began his instruction. All was by demonstration—the posture of the soldier, the quick and slow step, the halt, the motions of each foot in the about-face. His sub-inspectors for brigades and divisions, together with the junior officers who were to conduct drill in their own units, were commanded to be present at his daily exercises. Every night he dictated to Duponceau exactly what was to be performed in the next lesson, Duponceau translated the French into English, then

Hamilton and Laurens translated Duponceau's English into American military language. These directions, copied as swiftly as possible by every officer who must use them, were disseminated by word and action throughout the camp. The baron himself learned to give the chief commands in English, and supplemented them with sign language. As soon as his single squad could execute his orders perfectly, he assigned its members to teach other squads, until he could begin drilling by platoons, then companies, battalions, and finally regiments.

At the end of April 1778 Conway resigned the inspectorship in a pet. Washington was now ready to recommend to Congress that Steuben be appointed, with the rank and pay of major general. The brigadiers, in Steuben's case, made no objection to the advancement of a foreign officer above them. Now, after Valley Forge's bitter winter, spring brought bright prospects. The new levies came in fast, and the baron's cadre of instructors was prepared to train them. The rivalries against Washington broke down; his critics in Congress were silenced by the majority, which also dispersed his enemies in the Board of War; Conway, discredited, departed the country. The influx of recruits was matched by supplies to feed and clothe them, for Nathanael Greene replaced the incapable Mifflin as quartermaster general, while Jeremiah Wadsworth invigorated the commissary.

When the splendid news of the French alliance was sped to Washington on May 1, he called on Steuben to arrange a grand review on the fifth in celebration. Who would have supposed that the camp of scarecrows of a few months earlier could now present the spectacle of the whole army in exact maneuvers, capped by the feat of the *feu de joie,* the successive firing of muskets up and down the ranks, thrice repeated "in honour of the King of France, the friendly European powers, and the United American States"? On the same day Congress commissioned Steuben major general and inspector general of the armies; and Washington got word in time to announce the action to the officers and their ladies assembled for a "cold collation" after the ceremonies. A couple of days afterward Washington congratulated the troops on their proof of "progress . . . in Military Improvement," and gave special thanks "to Baron Steuben & the gentlemen under him for their Indefatigable Exertions" to this end.

The baron by this time had acquired two aides, proficient in French, who became his lifelong protégés, Benjamin Walker and William North. (Medallions acknowledging their devoted help appear on the Steuben monument in the national capital.) Except for letters that the baron penned in French to friends, including Hamilton, and private petitions to Congress, composed for him by Hamilton, the inspector general's correspondence and reports were translations by North and Walker, or were written by them at his direction. Later Steuben acquired a bastard English, amusing in itself and enlivened by the baron's humor.

Though Steuben was duly appointed to the office, the scope of the inspectorship remained to be defined by Congress. Commanders in camp praised the baron's success in training the troops, which training was soon demonstrated in the orderly extrication of a corps of 2,800 under Lafayette when they were suddenly almost surrounded by British attackers at Barren Hill across the Schuylkill. But field officers were alarmed lest Steuben stretch his authority to encroach on their prerogatives of control over the men under them. For instance, Steuben ordered adjutants to report directly to him, instead of passing this information through their superiors in the line. Brigadier General James M. Varnum complained to Washington: "If the Baron by his Aids and Inspectors can manage my Brigade without my Orders, his Power is directly in Opposition to Your Excellency's, and there are two Commanders in Chief at the same time."

The loudest protestant of those who felt the baron stepping on their toes was General Charles Lee, who had returned from his captivity May 20, 1778. As a biographer of Steuben points out, Lee found drill and discipline in the army so much improved by the baron's efforts that he feared his own reputation as chief professional expert would be injured. Furthermore, the treasonable plan Lee had submitted to General Howe for British victory would be overthrown if American troops were taught to respond efficiently to commands. Steuben, with the help of Richard Peters of the Board of War, drew a plan for the duties and powers of his office, to be presented to Congress. In several respects it poached on the preserves of field commanders, provoking their vigorous resentment. Washington, pending action by Congress, met the conflicting contentions with a general order, which quieted controversy. The inspector general's functions were those of staff, not of line. His regulations, when approved by the commander in chief, would be issued by the adjutant general, and must be carried into effect by commanders. Those among the latter who had cried that the baron took too much on himself were now hushed, not least because they must now make themselves competent to carry his system into effect.

Steuben, ambitious as he was zealous, was restive under this solution. He thanked Washington for his "wise step . . . to engage the General Officers and Field Officers of Regiments to take command of the troops in our daily Exercise," a toilsome duty of which he had been willing to relieve them. But as they would require some days to become familiar with his instructions, now promulgated by the commander in chief, Steuben begged permission to visit York, Pennsylvania, at that time the seat of government, ostensibly to take leave of a friend who was going to South Carolina. Washington knew—in fact, from the baron himself—that a purpose of his journey was "to get the duties and powers of his office minutely defined and settled" by Congress. Washington sent by Steuben his own general orders, provisionally governing the inspectorship. He agreed to the baron's trip, but knowing that it might stir serious mischief, the commander in chief embraced confidence and caution in a single sentence. He was persuaded, he told Steuben, "that after having seen the difficulties which opposed the establishment of the inspectorship according to your first ideas, you will, from a desire to promote the service, lay before Congress such a Plan as will be most likely to obviate the causes of disagreement, and comprehend all the essential duties of your office."

Washington, despite his parting words to Steuben, was apparently not content to leave so important a matter in the inspector general's hands. The lawmakers, who had been disgusted with Conway and were correspondingly receptive to his successor, must be pointedly warned against his blandishments. For this purpose Hamilton wrote on June 18 to New York delegate William Duer, no doubt at General Washington's inspiration. Hamilton said he would trouble Duer

with a few hints on a matter of some importance. Baron von Steuben, who will be the bearer of this, waits on Congress to have his office arranged upon some decisive and permanent footing. It will not be amiss to be on your guard. The Baron is a Gentleman for whom, I have a particular esteem, and whose real intelligence and success . . . intitle him to the greatest credit. But I am apprehensive, with all his good qualities, a fondness for power and importance natural to every man may lead him to wish for more extensive prerogatives in his department, than it will be for the good of the service to grant. . . . In the first institution of his office, the General allowed him to exercise more ample powers, than would be proper for a continuance. They were necessary in the commencement, to put things in a train with a degree of dispatch, which the exigency of our affairs required. The novelty of the office excited questions about its boundaries. The extent of its operation alarmed the officers of every rank for their own rights. Their jealousies and discontents were rising fast to a height that threatened to over turn the whole plan. It became necessary to apply a remedy.

Washington's order covering the functions of the inspectorship, which was being sent to Congress, was "good and satisfactory, to the army in general," and "it will be unsafe to deviate essenially from it."

Hamilton, surely in Washington's behalf, suggested that Congress curb itself as well as Steuben. With all deference to the legislature, the commander in chief, on the spot and knowing the need for piecemeal reform, must be allowed leeway. Congress could confirm or reject his decisions afterward. The plan established by Congress when Conway was appointed was objectionable, principally in making the inspector independent of the commander in chief. That misconceived scheme was "a brat of faction, and . . . ought to be renounced."

Steuben, collaborating with Richard Peters, had proposed that the inspector general and his assistants be authorized to refer infractions of discipline, by officers as well as men, to courts-martial. This, "which the Baron has much at heart," Hamilton cautioned, "in good policy he can by no means be indulged in." This power of enforcing obedience to orders "can only be properly lodged with the commander in chief, and would inflame the whole army if put into other hands. Each Captain is vested with it in his company, each Colonel in his Regiment, each General in his particular command, and The Commander in Chief in the whole."

As an afterthought Hamilton proposed what was later called "incorporation of regiments," or reduction of their number so as to have each one, and all of its component parts, filled, with the proper strength of troops and no more than the needed complement of officers. He stressed and illustrated the advantages of having "complete corps." "Ten thousand men distributed into 20 imperfect regiments will not have half the efficiency of the same number in half the number of regiments. The fact is, with respect to the American army, that the want of discipline and other defects we labour under are as much owing to the skeleton state of our regiments as to any other cause." (Steuben had reported finding one company that was reduced to a single enlisted man, one regiment that contained only thirty privates, and all of the regiments in merely nominal strength. For purposes of effective daily drills, the baron formed battalions of 112 privates each, superfluous officers watching the exercises or taking their turns directing them.) The expected recruits had arrived, and still there were not enough men to fill the ranks of the existing regiments. The answer was to combine units and dispense with superfluous officers, perhaps contenting them with half pay for a time. Hamilton hoped this reform could be adopted at once. This was June 18, 1778. Exactly seven months later, January 1779, still confronted by the same difficulty, Washington deputed Steuben to discuss military legislation with Congress. Some favored the merging of regiments, such as Hamilton had proposed, since voluntary enlistment did not fill those authorized, and Washington's recommendation of a compulsory draft proved politically impossible. Steuben endorsed the scheme in principle, but urged that such a reorganization of the army be deferred until the following autumn. To attempt it then, with the new campaign impending, would give no time for the thorough preparation needed. Immediate discharge of a large number of faithful officers would be unjust. His only present concession was internal to the existing regiments—that is, form each company of the small number of thirty-six men.

The baron's intended sortie upon Congress in June 1778 was prevented by the enemy's evacuation of Philadelphia on June 18, the same day Hamilton had written Duer about the proposed trip. Steuben joined the army in its chase after Clinton across New Jersey. His participation in councils of war, his ordering of troops in the emergency at Monmouth, and his temporary assignment to lead a division in the march from New Brunswick to White Plains had all seemed to open the way to his ambition for line command in addition to the inspectorship. Sharply disappointed when Washington returned him to his staff duties, he threatened to resign. Not even his powers as inspector general had been settled by Congress, and Noirmont de la Neuville, the inspector in Gates's army, refused to obey the baron's orders. So he hied himself to Philadelphia, where the legislators had been warned by Washington that his aim for field command must by no means be gratified. Hamilton, to whom Steuben had confided his discontent, wrote to Elias Boudinot (for the ear of Congress), expressing admiration of the baron's contribution as inspector and hoping that he might be reconciled to that assignment. "Perhaps . . . the objects of the Inspectorship [may be] enlarged, so as to render it a more important employment. Perhaps a resolution of Congress giving the Baron a right to be employed on detachments, might, for the present, compensate for the want of a permanent command in the line, and might not be disagreeable to the officers."

However, on his journey Steuben thought better of his intended demands, realized that his future lay in this country in the fullest possible discharge of his office of inspector general. He returned to the army, and without waiting for the authorization by Congress a month later (August 1778), he resumed his staff duties and extended them far beyond mere drills to promoting efficient administration in every military department. Renouncing his former personal ambition, he performed the unique service for which he is famous. As Washington's trusted adviser he exercised wider influence than he had ever expected.

The winter of 1778–79 Steuben spent in Philadelphia preparing his *Regulations for the Order and Discipline of the Troops of the United States*. He had the assistance of Lieutenant Colonel Fleury, Duponceau, and Walker as translators from the French, and Captain Pierre Charles L'Enfant in drawing the diagrams. Approved by Congress, the "Blue Book," as it was familiarly known from its cover, remained the official army manual until the War of 1812, and in transmuted form has effect to this day. The success of his rules, and of their author in America altogether, lay in his observation to a European officer: "the genius of this nation is not in the least to be compared to that of the Prussians, Austrians or French. You say to your soldier, 'Do this, and he doeth it'; but I am obliged to say, 'This is the reason why you ought to do that: and then he does it.' "

Hamilton's friendship for Steuben made him a chief pleader for compensation by Congress for the baron's sacrifices in coming to America and his services in the winning of independence. The baron's understanding with a committee of Congress on his arrival had been oral; he was to be paid his expenses in the army, and if he contributed to success in the war, he should be indemnified for his loss of income in Europe, plus "such marks of . . . generosity, as the justice of the United States should dictate." The baron's penchant for overstating his claims cast doubt in legislative minds on the accuracy of the sums he included. Hamilton was chief private lender to Steuben; the total stood in 1790 at £704 New York money. Hamilton wrote to Washington (November 25, 1785): "The poor *Baron* is still soliciting Congress, and has every prospect of Indigence before him. He has his imprudencies, but . . . his merits and the reputation of the Country alike demand that he should not be left to suffer want." And again, "Our reputation abroad is not at present too high. To dismiss an old soldier empty and hungry . . . to complain of . . . violated engagements will . . . not tend to raise it." Washington responded cordially in letters to Congress, to the baron, and to Hamilton.

The new Congress under the Constitution (1789) referred Steuben's memorial to Secretary of the Treasury Hamilton for a report. After full review Hamilton recommended a lump-sum payment of $7,396 plus a yearly pension of 580 guineas for life. Congress slightly reduced both sums. In spite of these grants, Steuben's borrowings continued until his death in 1794 on his frontier farm near the present Utica, New York. The attachment between Steuben and Hamilton is remembered in Hamilton College, the cornerstone of which (as Hamilton-Oneida Academy) the baron laid a few months before his death.

7

March to Monmouth

   The surrender of Burgoyne at Saratoga pro-
duced the open, formal alliance of France with the rebelling Col-
onies (February 6, 1778), which determined the issue of the
contest. Not at once, for the fighting had yet nearly four years to
run, but the promise of military, financial, and above all naval assistance decisively brightened the prospect for America. Britain,
faced with a new enemy, soon joined by Spain and Holland, sent
peace commissioners empowered to yield on every demand of
the Colonies save political independence. Sir Henry Clinton,
who relieved Sir William Howe in supreme command in April
1778, approached his duty without enthusiasm. He confessed
that the "great change which public affairs had undergone, in
Europe as well as America . . . had so clouded every prospect of
a successful issue of the unfortunate contest we were engaged in
that no officer who had the least . . . regard for his professional
fame would court a charge so hopeless as this now appeared
likely to be." He was ordered to detach five thousand troops to
the West Indies and send another three thousand to Saint Augustine and West Florida. If the attempted negotiation failed,
and his weakened force was in danger of being overwhelmed, he
was to withdraw the army (except for a garrison in Rhode Is-
and) to Canada.

Sir Henry Clinton reached Philadelphia May 8 to relieve Sir William Howe, who returned to England. The change of commanders signaled a change of policy, for Clinton had orders to evacuate the American capital. Philadelphia never had the military importance attributed to it by Howe. In European warfare the capture of the enemy capital was a stroke, but Philadelphia was not the nerve center of American life, and the government —Congress and the Board of War—functioned as well after moving elsewhere. If Clinton were to occupy both New York and Philadelphia, maintaining communication between the two forces would be difficult, whether across the disputed hundred miles of New Jersey or a distance three times as great by water.

Sir Henry's immediate problem, on evacuating Philadelphia on June 18, was to march all of his troops across New Jersey to New York, since Lord Howe had not transports to take by water more than certain stores and the Loyalists who were afraid to be left behind. Clinton could cope with obstructions sure to be placed in his way (the filling of wells, breaking down of bridges, tearing up of causeways); he even hoped that by drawing his enemy down from the hilly country "an opportunity might offer of getting a fair stroke at him before I finally took my leave." However, this expectation faded as his cumbersome twelve-mile-long train passed Mount Holly, proceeded by easy stages to Allentown, and thence to Cranbury, while Washington "still observed his usual caution." Having chosen to make for Sandy Hook rather than encounter the difficult crossing of the Raritan, at Freehold he "relinquished every idea of a decisive action." He "could not entertain so bad an opinion of Mr. Washington's military abilities" as to suppose he would risk a fight where he must penetrate "so many . . . boggy bottoms . . . at single narrow defiles." At Freehold Clinton determined to halt for a day. Obviously the British commander was unprepared for the approaching Battle of Monmouth (Monmouth Court House and Freehold being different names for the same village).

The evacuation of Philadelphia had begun on June 17, when

contingents of Clinton's army crossed the Delaware. From the stripping of the batteries, it was plain to the Americans that all would promptly follow. That day, at Valley Forge, Hamilton prepared a statement for Washington to present at a council of general officers about the relative strengths of American and enemy forces, including queries concerning the course of action to be followed. The crucial point on which opinions were asked was: "In case . . . this army . . . overtake the enemy on their march, will it be prudent, with the aid which may reasonably be expected from the Jersey militia, to make an attack upon them, and ought it to be a partial or a general one?" Lee, Steuben, and DuPortail were against hazarding a general engagement. Wayne, Cadwalader, Lafayette, and Greene were, in different degrees, for an attack, more than mere harassment; Greene urged that if a stroke by an advance party brought on a full-fledged battle, so be it. Washington's army that crossed the Delaware at Coryell's Ferry (from New Hope, Pennsylvania, to Lambertville, New Jersey) numbered between eleven and twelve thousand of all ranks fit for duty, and they were fitter, too, than had seemed possible in the desperate winter months at Valley Forge, for Wadsworth, commissary general, had fed them; Greene, as quartermaster, had equipped them; and Steuben, as drillmaster, had disciplined them. Besides these, Maxwell's brigade of thirteen hundred and Dickinson's militia, eight hundred, were already in New Jersey. Clinton's army was estimated at ten thousand, superior in cavalry, but at a disadvantage because retreating with every sort of impedimenta, including fifteen hundred wagons and a flock of unruly camp followers. Clinton declared that "though the principle of my march was unquestionably retreat, I wished to avoid every appearance of a precipitate one." Oppressive heat and drenching rains assisted this design, for he took six days to cover the thirty-four miles to Allentown. Washington's army, notably less burdened in pursuit, was ordered to begin "every day's march . . . at 4 o'clock A.M. at farthest," in order to avoid the worst heat and permit the men time to cook for the morrow.

General Lee went ahead, on short notice for once, June 18;

Washington, in immediate command of the main body, left Valley Forge next day, Hamilton with him, and the entire American force was in New Jersey by the twenty-third. In no other campaign was Hamilton active in so many roles as in this of Monmouth. He was long hours in the saddle seeking news of the enemy's whereabouts and intentions; he served as liaison between the various advance units and between these and the commander in chief; he kept minutes of councils of war; and wrote for Washington the final orders to General Lee. He was on the battlefield in both stages of the engagement. In the early, abortive maneuvers of Lee he exerted himself to stem the American retreat. He was at Washington's side in the later repulse of the British attack, until disabled by a fall from his wounded horse. In the sequel he was a principal witness at Lee's court-martial, and was a second for his fellow aide John Laurens in that officer's duel with Lee. If others were in doubt about the wisdom and firmness of Washington that day, not Hamilton, whose description of the battle has helped to fix in history the commander in chief's noble performance.

James McHenry kept a lighthearted diary of the march, which gives sportive glimpses of Hamilton before the business became too serious for banter. The first stop of the staff was "8 miles from Moors & 25 from Philadª Head quarters at . . . Jonatⁿ Fells [Doylestown]. A raining evening." The "Company . . . within Doors" included "a pretty, Fullfaced, youthfull, playfull Lass," from whom Hamilton was covetously warned away, perhaps unnecessarily, as he was occupied that evening in writing Washington's instructions to Benedict Arnold to take command in Philadelphia. The next day, Saturday, June 20, brought "A Rapid Mornings March" in weather so "excessive hot" that "Some of the soldiers die suddenly." Thus commenced a week of high temperatures culminating in 96 degrees on the day of battle. Both armies lost men from sunstroke and exhaustion; the Hessians, especially, suffered due to heavy clothing and the burden of full packs.

Hamilton doubtless was with Washington when the general

crossed Coryell's Ferry at noon on Sunday the twenty-first and took quarters at Holcombe's house. "Here are some charming Girls," the sociable McHenry recorded, "but one of the Drums of the General's Guard more a favorite than Hamilton." Again the aide's advances must have been hindered by the general's assignment to him to inform Gates, who commanded at Peekskill, that the enemy had moved to Moore's Town and Mount Holly. Obviously Clinton would "traverse the Jerseys," but whether he would point to the Raritan or to Sandy Hook was yet a mystery, which puzzled Washington in spite of the bold spying of Captain Allen McLane in Clinton's camp at Haddonfield. Hamilton was soon detailed for scouting, and diligently reported the intelligence he gathered.

The question whether or not to launch a major attack on the British, assuming the Americans could catch up with them, also had yet to be resolved. If Sir Henry Clinton could be defeated as decisively as Burgoyne, the war might be ended. On the other hand, it might be wiser not to hazard a strike at Clinton right away, but to wait for the promised aid from France to American arms. This second course would require patience and would prolong the struggle. And when the French did arrive, would another chance of catching the enemy at such a disadvantage present itself? Now that Washington had Clinton on the run, should he prefer the bird in hand?

The American army halted on June 23 at Hopewell Township, a few miles northwest of Princeton, the British being at Allentown some twenty miles to the south. Hamilton, acting for Washington, tried to discover whether the enemy's dilatory advance was from choice, in which case the object was to tempt Washington into a battle. In this state of doubt, orders for "a march or Action very early in the morning" of June 24 were canceled; the army discarded heavy baggage, cooked rations, cleaned muskets, and rested. The commander in chief called a council of war to determine whether he should hazard a general action, and if so, how, and if not, what the best means were of hampering

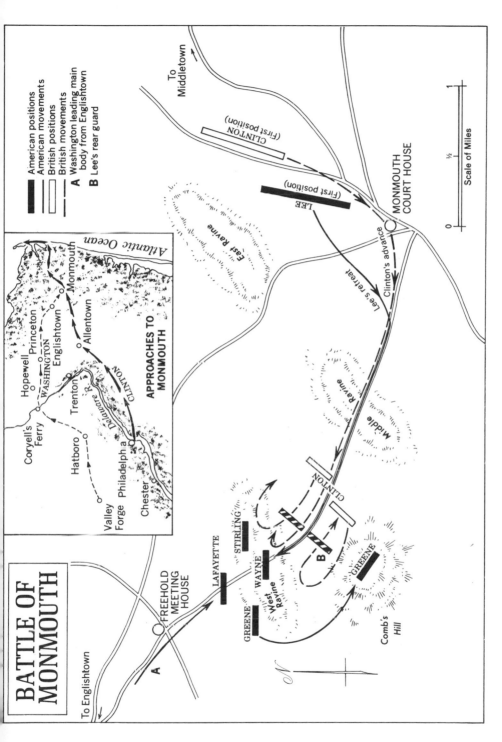

BATTLE OF MONMOUTH

Legend:
- American positions
- American movements
- British positions
- British movements
- A Washington leading main body from Englishtown
- B Lee's rear guard

FREEHOLD MEETING HOUSE

To Englishtown

A

LAFAYETTE

STIRLING

GREENE

WAYNE

West Ravine

GREENE

Comb's Hill

CLINTON

B

Middle Ravine

East Ravine

LEE (First position)

Lee's retreat

Clinton's advance

MONMOUTH COURT HOUSE

CLINTON (First position)

To Middletown

Scale of Miles

0   ½   1

APPROACHES TO MONMOUTH

Atlantic Ocean

Monmouth

Princeton

Hopewell

Englishtown

WASHINGTON

Allentown

Coryell's Ferry

Trenton

CLINTON

Delaware R.

Hatboro

Valley Forge

Philadelphia

Chester

149

the enemy's march. General Charles Lee was most persuasive with his argument that Clinton should be allowed to cross New Jersey unhampered; equal numbers of Americans could not match the prowess of trained European soldiers (a frequent refrain with him). Trust to the aid of the French for eventual victory, said Lee. His authority as a professional soldier of long and varied experience was powerful; the satisfaction at his return from captivity was not yet dispelled by his later behavior. Others, including Knox and Stirling, unwilling to allow the enemy free passage, were for advancing fifteen hundred troops, in addition to the detachments already harassing Clinton's left flank and rear, while the main army remained watchful, awaiting events. Hamilton recorded this decision, signed by all but Wayne, who was for bringing on a battle, regardless. Hamilton, only an absorbed bystander, wished that the council had not been called to produce a result that "would have done honor to the most honorable society of midwives, and to them only. The purport was, that we should keep at a comfortable distance from the enemy," content with "a vain parade of annoying them by detachment." Lafayette and Greene, who had gone along hesitantly with the majority, and Wayne, who needed no second thoughts, after the council individually wrote to Washington urging that he should not be governed by timid advice.

A story that Hamilton besought Greene to go with him to beg Washington to give battle, that the commander in chief agreed, and that thus "the attack was decided" is improbable. The young aide doubtless supported his friend Greene in the latter's efforts to produce a major strike. A dozen years afterward, in his eulogy of Greene, Hamilton stigmatized

those impotent Councils, which by a formal vote had decreed an undisturbed passage to an enemy retiring from the fairest fruits of his victories to seek an asylum from impending danger, disheartened by retreat, dispirited by desertion, broken by fatigue, retiring through woods, defiles, and morasses in which his discipline was useless, in the face of an army superior in numbers, elated by pursuit and ardent to signalize their courage. 'Tis enough for the honor of Greene to say that he left nothing unessayed to avert and to frustrate so degrading a resolution.

In accordance with the recommendation of the council of officers, Hamilton penned Washington's order sending Brigadier General Charles Scott forward with fifteen hundred troops to co-operate with other detachments "to gall the enemy's left flank and rear." He had already sent Colonel Daniel Morgan to aid General Dickinson in similar harassment of the right flank, and small parties of foot under General Cadwalader and of horse under Lieutenant Colonel Anthony White would be joining them.

Then Washington began to overrule his general officers. From Kingston, four miles northeast of Princeton (June 25), Lafayette with one thousand additional troops under Wayne was advanced to the vicinity of the enemy, where the marquis would take command of all American detachments, amounting to some four thousand men, whom he was empowered to commit in an attack. Washington now saw that Clinton was taking the shortest route to the sea, by Monmouth Court House, and would shortly escape him unless prompt measures were used. Both Lafayette and Wayne were spirited leaders primed for action, which was Washington's purpose. He had felt obliged, before giving command to the marquis, to get the consent of Charles Lee to yield his claim as senior major general. This Lee did, with the disdainful remark that the assignment was "a more proper business of a young volunteering general, than of the second in command of the army." Hamilton described the subsequent farcical switches, due to Lee's vanity, which prefaced later misfortune.

General Lee's conduct . . . was truly childish. According to the incorrect notions of our army, his seniority . . . entitled him to the command of the advanced corps; but he in the first instance declined it in favor of the marquis. Some of his friends having blamed him for doing it, and Lord Stirling having shown a disposition to interpose his claim, General Lee . . . inconsistently reasserted his pretensions.

The matter was a second time accommodated, General Lee and Lord Stirling agreed to let the marquis command. General Lee, a little time after, recanted again and became very importunate. The general [Washington], who had all along observed the greatest candor in the matter, grew tired of such fickle behavior, and ordered the marquis to proceed.

This was not the end of it. When Lee saw that a third of the army was to be turned over to the Frenchman on a coveted mission, he reversed himself once more and demanded the honor. After all of Lee's wavering, Washington would have been justified in refusing his latest insistence. Lee confidently played on the indecision that he knew was his superior's failing at times—a failing Lee had previously condemned. Washington finally put Lee, with additional brigades, in command of the whole forward body, but with the reservation that Lee was to aid any design that Lafayette as his subordinate adopted. The marquis, who was for fighting the enemy and forgetting internal quarrels, loyally accepted this compromise.

Hamilton, much to his liking, was detailed to Lafayette as liaison officer, and on June 25 went ahead of the marquis to Cranbury. Here he was equidistant, a dozen miles, from Washington at Kingston on the north, from Clinton's moving column about Allentown on the south, and from the future camp of the American main army at Englishtown on the east. He was to spur over the sandy roads in the wooded country, collect intelligence, keep Lafayette and Washington informed of all developments, and prepare for concentration of the scattered detachments for attack.

After a busy day Hamilton's message to Lafayette, at nine o'clock that night from Dr. Hezekiah Stiles' house at Cranbury, told that the enemy had all filed off from Allentown on the Monmouth road, their rear guard straggling over a five-mile distance. The British vanguard was approaching Lawrence Taylor's tavern. General Maxwell was at Hyde's Town (Hightstown), three miles southwest of Cranbury. General Philemon Dickinson with his Jersey militiamen was said to be on the enemy's right flank, but just where, Hamilton could not discover. Nor did he know anything certain of General Charles Scott, but circumstances placed him at Allentown. Colonel Daniel Morgan had had a skirmish with the British right flank that morning at Robert Montgomery's on the Monmouth road. "We shall[,] agreeable to your request," Hamilton informed Lafayette, "consider and appoint some proper place of rendezvous, for the union of our force, which we shall communicate to General Maxwell & Scot and to yourself. In the mean time, I would recommend to you to move towards this place [Cranbury] as soon as the convenience of your men will permit." Hamilton said he was setting off immediately to see Maxwell, after which he would write further. The present message should be sent on to Washington.

That night (June 25) the commander in chief marched to Cranbury, where he halted in a heavy rain. This Hamilton did not know when he wrote to the general at noon next day from a point eight miles east of Allentown, where he was with both Lafayette and Wayne. The enemy by last reports were four miles distant, and their rear had passed the road that turned off to Amboy, "which determines their route toward Shrewsbury." (This meant they were making for the sea at some place south of Raritan Bay.) Lafayette was eager to press on in pursuit, but was compelled to halt because of "extreme distress of the troops for want of provisions. General Wayne's detachment is almost starving," Hamilton reported, "and seem both unwilling and unable to march further 'till they are supplied. If we do not receive an immediate supply, the whole purpose of our detachment may be frustrated." Other discouragements were lack of horsemen near the enemy, and by the time Hamilton could send out parties, the king's troops were marching so briskly that the American advance corps could not come up with them that day, even had the needed food been available. Furthermore, Lafayette was ignorant of the location of Washington's force; "if the army is wholly out of supporting distance, we risk the total loss of the detachment in making an attack," but if the main body was at hand "something clever" could be accomplished. "It is evident the enemy wish to avoid, not to engage us." A postscript added that a hard-riding officer had just come in to report the enemy's rear five miles off. Clinton had put three brigades behind his baggage—which of course was a precaution against American attack, and was more reason for Hamilton's assurance to Washington that eagerness to strike the foe would not overcome prudence. To be surer of Clinton's route, Hamilton had ordered a fresh party to reconnoiter the head of the column. Lafayette added (7:15 P.M., June 26) that Hamilton had ridden the whole of the night before, without finding anybody who could give him reliable information. However, the marquis learned from another source of conflicting information that the enemy were only six or seven miles away, and he was preparing to strike them if they did not elude him in the night, "which I much fear, as our intelligence are not the best ones." He repeated Hamilton's hope of delivering a blow if Washington could come up.

Washington's prompt replies that day stressed caution, lest the eagerness of Lafayette, seconded by Hamilton, should precipitate a premature assault. The troops should not be pressed in the heat. Food was on the way, but his own army was halted for the want of it.

Later on the twenty-sixth Hamilton dispatched to Washington a report that the enemy had encamped, with the van beyond Monmouth Court House and the rear at Manapan, halfway back to Hightstown. He emphasized again Clinton's new disposition on his quickened march; he had placed his baggage in front, his "flying army in the rear, with a rear guard of 1000 men about 400 paces from the main body." For the detachment to attack them without support would be "folly in the extreme." But if Washington chose to move to a position on the British left flank, the enemy would be in an awkward situation, with Lafayette's sizable body in their rear.

Hamilton had written thus far, when Lafayette received an

order from Washington at Cranbury to march to Englishtown, where the main army could better reinforce his attack or cover his retreat. Accordingly the detachment would march next morning at three o'clock to Englishtown. Lafayette replied separately that in consequence of Washington's instructions he had deferred the project of attacking. He would join Lee, marching at two the next morning. He could not resist expressing his disappointment at not being allowed to act independently of Lee, whose reluctance he accurately estimated. "I do not believe General Lee intends to make any attack tomorrow, for then I would have been directed to fall immediately upon them without making eleven miles entirely out of the way. I am here as near as I would be at Englishtown." However, Hamilton continued to prepare for a possible attack. Before dawn of June 27 he dashed off a dispatch to Brigadier Scott: "This part of the troops marches instantly. We are to join in the Monmouth road one mile this side of Taylor's tavern. You will govern yourself accordingly. If you can find Morgan let him be desired again to keep close to the enemy and attack when we attack." At Englishtown Hamilton and Lafayette were reunited with the main army under Washington.

The Monmouth battlefield was roughly the size and shape of New York's Central Park, 3 miles long and less than 1 mile wide. Across it at unequal intervals lay three marshy depressions (referred to as "ravines," but hardly such). Artillery could cross two of these depressions only by a narrow bridge over the western one and a causeway over the middle one. The British were camped near Freehold village, then called Monmouth Court House, in a flat area. At the opposite (western) end of the battleground are hills forming an extensive amphitheater sloping to the level ground—that is, level except for the boggy hollows. The easternmost marsh lay well to the north of Monmouth Court House and was avoided by both sides in the minor fighting that took place at that end of the field. The scene is changed today in two respects; the marshes are dried, and the woods that bordered the plain have been cut. However, at the western end, on the commanding height, still stands the Tennent Church (named for a noted pastor but referred to in battle accounts as Freehold Meeting House). Here some of the American wounded were brought, and one of the old pews yet shows, so it is claimed, the dark stains of blood.

General Washington, accompanied by his aides Tench Tilghman and Robert H. Harrison, was bringing the army from Englishtown to Monmouth. Hamilton had arrived shortly before and "told him he had come from our advance corps, and that he imagined from the situation he had left our van and the enemy's rear in, they would soon engage." Hamilton (Tilghman the narrator) "advised General Washington to throw the right wing of the army round by the right and follow with the left wing directly in General Lee's rear to support him. He gave reasons for this disposition, which were thought good. While order was given to make the disposition, a countryman rode up . . . he said he heard our people were retreating, and that that man, pointing to a fifer, had told him so."

According to the account of Harrison, a most reliable witness,

. . . we met a fifer, who appeared to be a good deal frightened. The General asked him whether he was a soldier belonging to the army, and the cause of his returning that way; he answered, that he was a soldier, and that the Continental troops who had been advanced were retreating. On this answer the General seemed to be exceedingly surprised, and rather more exasperated, appearing to discredit the account, and threatened the man, if he mentioned a thing of this sort, he would have him whipped. He then moved on a few paces . . . (perhaps about fifty yards,) where we met two or three persons more on that road.

One was a soldier who gave news "that all the troops that had been advanced, the whole of them, were retreating. His Excellency appeared to discredit the account, having not heard any firing except a few cannon a considerable time before." However, as the report came from different persons, it could not be disregarded, and Harrison and Fitzgerald spurred ahead to discover the truth. After riding the short distance to the bridge over the first depression they met an officer of William Grayson's regiment, who told them many more were retreating. Another didn't know why they retreated, "that they had lost but one man." Colonel Ogden, farther back in the line, exclaimed, "By God! They are flying from a shadow." No officer seemed to know the cause, but after a short time "the enemy's light infantry and grenadiers came issuing out of the woods, pressing very hard upon us" at a few hundred yards' distance.

The aides galloped back to tell Washington the enemy would be upon him in fifteen minutes. Astonished and indignant at encountering the American troops in flight, Washington had angry words for Lee when the two met at a point a short distance east of the cup of hills. After the last of the retreaters had arrived, Washington and Wayne thought the place where they stood "appeared to be an advantageous spot to give the enemy the first check." Hamilton described the scene when Washington reversed Lee's retreat:

. . . the General rode forward and found the troops retiring in the greatest disorder and the enemy pressing upon their rear. I never saw the general to so much advantage. His coolness and firmness were admirable. He instantly took measures for checking the enemy's advance, and giving time for the army, which was very near, to form and make a proper disposition. He then rode back and had the troops formed on a very advantageous piece of ground, in which and in other transactions of the day General Greene & Lord Stirling rendered very essential service, and did themselves great honor. The sequel is, we beat the enemy and killed and wounded at least a thousand of their best troops. America owes a great deal to General Washington for this day's work; a general rout, dismay, and disgrace would have attended the whole army in any other hands but his. By his own good sense and fortitude he turned the fate of the day. Other officers have great merit in performing their parts well, but he directed the whole with the skill of a Master workman . . . he brought order out of confusion, animated his troops and led them to success.

The first check to the enemy's pursuit was east of the ravine below the hills, where Washington faced about the regiments of Nathaniel Ramsay, Walter Stewart, James M. Varnum, and Henry Beekman Livingston, reinforced by ten guns under Knox. This resistance gave time for Washington, mounted on his great white horse, to gallop back over the bridge to his main force, which was pressing forward. He posted them on the "very advantageous piece of ground," the amphitheater of hills, with Stirling on the left, Greene on the right, and himself in the center. Wayne was nearest the ravine in front, Lafayette drew up the second line on the central hillside toward the church. It was now that Steuben's training of the troops enabled them to wheel into line with calm precision, under heavy fire, to meet the attack of the finest British regiments against Stirling's position. Steuben rode back and forth with Washington and Stirling, encouraging the defenders.

The battle of Monmouth was in three phases. The first phase consisted of attacks by the British on American advanced units north of Monmouth Court House, which drove some of Lee's force into the woods while others of his troops took to flight without firing a shot. The second stage was Lee's retreat, pursued by the enemy the whole length of the field. The fiercest fighting was in the third period, in the western portion of the ground, between the middle ravine and the hills that rose to Tennent Church. Once the Americans rallied, they not only stopped the enemy pursuit but forced back the veteran enemy regiments deep into the plain over which Lee's force had retreated. The American artillery, planted on the hills—Stirling to the left, Greene on the right—had much the advantage of the British guns, both because of height and because they could enfilade the enemy columns. Wayne's infantry protected the bridge over the west ravine, while Lafayette's men, between and behind the American cannon, were in reserve. The battle swayed chiefly in the level ground west of the middle ravine. Here American units, infantry and artillery, under Stewart, Ramsay, Varnum, Livingston, Knox, and Wayne withstood the charges of enemy dragoons, grenadiers, and guards commanded by Cornwallis. Late in the afternoon, near six o'clock, the enemy musket fire ceased. Wayne, in a valiant advance, pushed the last of the British and Germans across the middle ravine. Then darkness descended, preventing further conflict.

Hamilton had no part in the portion of the battle in which the Americans took the offensive, for he had been hurt when thrown from his wounded horse; this was in the course of the withdrawal when he urged Lee to make a stand. The fight had not only its heroes, but its heroine, "Molly Pitcher." She was Mary McCauley, the wife of an American gunner, who repeatedly fetched water—not from the well now shown to visitors, which was dug later—for the exhausted troops that blistering day; then when her husband fell at his post, she continued to "man" his cannon.

Monmouth, the longest engagement of the war and the last of major importance in the North, was a drawn battle. After the fighting, the Americans occupied the field, Clinton having withdrawn that night to resume his march to Sandy Hook. Hamilton, citing a thousand casualties, may have exaggerated enemy losses; Washington reported that his detail buried 249, and that the enemy had buried some of their dead themselves; he did not know the number of the king's troops wounded. The Americans had 69 killed, 162 wounded, and 131 missing; of these last, many dropped from fatigue and came in later, as the army, next day, withdrew to New Brunswick. The real victory of the Americans was in retrieving a retreat that looked disastrous, and throwing back the most formidable British and Hessian attackers.

After the battle General Charles Lee, smarting under Washington's reprimand when he met Lee retreating, wrote the commander in chief two insulting letters. He demanded opportunity to justify himself, which Washington at once afforded him by ordering his court-martial, with Lord Stirling as president. The charges were disobedience of orders to attack, making a shameful retreat, and afterward writing disrespectfully to the commander in chief. The court sat first at New Brunswick July 4 and thereafter at Paramus, North Castle, and Peekskill, as the army moved to the Hudson. The trial did not conclude until August 9.[1] The details of Lee's retreat and Hamilton's efforts to stem it were presented in evidence before the court. Hamilton testified on the opening day and on July 13 at Paramus. His initial evidence concerning Washington's orders to Lee was of crucial importance.

In answer to the question, "Did you deliver General Lee any orders from General Washington the 27th or 28th of June respecting attacking the enemy?" the aide replied:

I wrote General Lee a letter the evening of the 27th June, by General Washington's order, a copy of which I have not; but it was conceived in the spirit, as I understood, of former orders that had been given by him to General Lee, and was occasioned by an apprehension (as declared to me by General Washington) that the enemy might move off either at night or very early in the morning, and get out of our reach, so that the purpose of an attack might be frustrated. To remedy this the order directed that General Lee should detach a party of 600 or 800 men to lie very near the enemy as a party of observation, in case of their moving off to give the earliest intelligence of it, and to skirmish with them so as to produce some delay, and give time for the rest of the troops to come up. It also directed that he should write to Colonel Morgan, desiring him (in case of the enemy being in their march) to make an attack on them in such a manner as might also tend to produce delay, and yet not so as to endanger a general rout of his party, and disqualify them from acting in concert with the other troops when a serious attack should be made. This, I understood from General Washington, was in pursuance of his intention to have the enemy attacked, and conformable to the spirit of previous orders he had given General Lee for that purpose. This let-

[1] At New Brunswick the sessions were doubtless held at Washington's headquarters in Ross Hall, the commodious Dutch-style home fronting the Raritan River near the point where Captain Hamilton's battery had fired on Cornwallis' advance two years before. On the route to Paramus, Washington and his aides stopped for a picnic lunch at "the falls of Passaic," which may have given Hamilton his first view of the site where a dozen years later he and his friends of the Society for Useful Manufactures founded the town of Paterson.

ter was sent off by a lighthorseman, and the foregoing is the purport of it to the best of my recollection.

Doubts that constantly obtruded during the trial would have been removed had Hamilton kept a copy of this letter. It was written, as he said, "late in the evening. I went to bed soon after." General Lee, if he retained the letter, did not produce it, but two of his aides testified that Lee had received it. Major John Francis Mercer said "past one o'clock in the morning" of the twenty-eighth; Captain Evan Edwards said "near two o'clock by the watch," and added, "I then immediately wrote to Colonel Morgan, General Dickinson and Colonel Grayson to comply with the contents of the letter that General Lee received from Colonel Hamilton, and sent off the lighthorseman to them."

As Lee's disobedience to command—as charged—hinged on Hamilton's wording of it, the court sought further clarification with the query, "Did you conceive General Washington's orders, or the spirit of them, to General Lee, were to attack the enemy at all events?" The reply, "I did not," though frankly given, suffered in interpretation from absence of the letter. Hamilton continued

I can't conceive that General Washington could mean to give orders so extremely positive, but that circumstances, which had been unforeseen, might arise, to leave the officer, who had the execution of them, liberty to deviate; but, from everything I knew of the affair, General Washington's intention was fully to have the enemy attacked on their march, and that the circumstances must be very extraordinary and unforeseen, which, consistent with his wish, could justify his not doing it.

General Lee immediately exploited this opening. "Did you," he asked Hamilton, "either by letter to me, or in conversation with me, communicate this idea of General Washington's intentions as fully and clearly as you have done it to the Court?" Hamilton's admission was, "I do not recollect that I ever did." Lee pressed on, citing the formidable appearance of the enemy he had faced: "Was your idea of General Washington's intention that I should attack the enemy, had I found them in the situation which General Dickinson's intelligence assured me they were; that is, the whole arranged in order of battle, at or near the Court-house?" To this Hamilton responded: "I knew nothing of General Dickinson's intelligence; but were the enemy's whole army drawn up in order of battle near the Court-house, I do not conceive it was General Washington's intention to have them attacked by your detachment."

The testimony of Hamilton's fellow aides Meade and Laurens was briefer and less qualified. The former witnessed no steps of Lee to put his troops in order, though they were in confusion and but a mile from the enemy. When Lee, his men in retreat, met Washington, Meade said, he protested that he was averse to an attack or a general engagement and that "while the enemy were so superior in cavalry we could not oppose them." Laurens vouchsafed that Lee in his hearing gave no orders to attack except a direction to General David Forman to cut off some of the enemy who were retreating. Laurens had brought a message from Washington saying that the commander in chief was ready to support with his whole army. Twice asked by Laurens for his reply, Lee "answered that he really did not know what to say." When part of Lee's detachment fell back, and the enemy, 150 or 200 at most, pursued, he "ordered the whole of our troops to retreat." Lee's directions were given indistinctly; Laurens attributed his embarrassment "to want of presence of mind." This stung. Lee disparagingly asked Laurens, "Were you ever in an action before?" Laurens heaped coals of fire: "I have been in several actions; I did not call that an action, as there was no action previous to the retreat." ·

In his testimony on July 13, Hamilton recalled that the day of the battle Lee had under his immediate command about five thousand rank and file, and that six hundred under Morgan and eight hundred under Dickinson were subject to Lee's orders. Hamilton also told of his own efforts to assist when sent by Washington to bring back word of Lee's situation. Volunteering to ride to the front of some of Lee's columns as they advanced through a woods near Monmouth Court House, Hamilton observed enemy cavalry filing off "as if . . . to attempt something on the right of General Lee's troops; this I informed him of, and submitted to him whether it would not be proper to send some troops to counteract that manoeuvre . . . and turn their flank; he approved . . . and authorized me to give orders for that purpose." Hamilton, accordingly, gave the indicated order to Lafayette. Lee's position was on open ground slightly lower than that of the enemy, but the difference could not make "any considerable impediment to an attack, and the distance . . . was such, that it appeared to be extremely dangerous [to make] a retrograde movement in the face of the enemy," who numbered about eight hundred infantry and cavalry. Aside from directing attacks on the enemy's flanks, Hamilton did not see Lee order "any general disposition of the remaining troops." Returning to report to Washington, Hamilton fell in with Lee's retreating troops, "a little time before the stand was made, by which the enemy received their first check"—that is, just before Washington, coming from Englishtown, met Lee leaving the field. "I heard General Washington say to General Lee, that it would be necessary for him (General Washington) to . . . form the main body of the army, while . . . he recommended to General Lee to remain there, and take measures for checking the advance of the enemy." Lee declared he would obey orders, but Hamilton did not see him do anything to the purpose. Instead, when Wayne took an advantageous position, it was at the direction of Washington.

When Hamilton saw some artillery requiring infantry support, he got Lee to order that. Riding toward the rear, Hamilton found Colonel Olney retreating; knowing, as Olney did not, that Washington had reversed the withdrawal, he urged Olney to form his troops along a fence, "which he immediately performed, and had a smart conflict with the enemy. These were all the measures I knew of, taken by any part of the advanced corps

163

[Lee's] to check the progress of the enemy." As nearly as he could tell, there seemed to be no plan for the retreat, such as a covering body in the rear, nor did Lee, to his knowledge, advise Washington of his retreat. Asked whether Lee gave orders "distinct and clear," Hamilton thought "he seemed to be under a hurry of mind." Since Hamilton was hurt by his fall when his horse was wounded during Olney's action, he was obliged to retire and did not witness the rest of the action in which Lee's corps was involved.

Lee resented Hamilton's testimony, which coincided with Laurens' description of his apparent confusion during the battle. He cross-questioned Hamilton, "Did you not express in the field an idea diametrically [the] reverse of my state of mind, from what you . . . mentioned in your testimony?" Not so, Hamilton replied. He had not meant in his present evidence to insinuate that Lee showed any personal fear, but rather "a certain hurry of spirits, which may proceed from a temper not so calm and steady as is necessary to support a man in such critical circumstances." Meade, recalled to the stand, confirmed this; he said that Lee, when asked for a report for Washington on how matters stood, answered "they were all in confusion." Washington's secretary, Harrison, testified that he saw Hamilton and Lee, on the field, having a difference of some sort. Lee was asking, "Do I appear to have lost my senses?"

8

Testimony at a Trial

The story has come down that Washington became enraged when he met the retreating Lee and reviled him for his actions. Lee himself, in testimony and in a letter to Washington, described Washington's language in a fashion to encourage this idea. Nothing in the testimony at the court-martial, though several described the encounter, hinted that Washington was abusive, much less that he cursed Lee. Washington was probably too occupied in turning flight into fight to waste words in vituperation. Hamilton in his account of the confrontation simply quoted Washington as urging Lee to make an about-face. James McHenry, another aide, reported that Washington wanted to know the cause of the retreat. "General Lee hesitatingly replied, sir—sir. General Washington then repeated the question. . . . I did not clearly understand General Lee's reply to him, but can just remember the words confusion[,] contradictory information, and some other words of the same import . . . General Lee seemed under an embarrassment in giving the answer." Tilghman similarly referred to Lee's hesitant answers. Later, back at Englishtown, McHenry had found Lee justifying his retreat, telling those around him that "to make attempts against the enemy where they possessed so great a superiority in cavalry" was "mere folly." Years afterward Hamilton answered the question whether the commander in chief had cursed Lee at Monmouth. No, he said, "Washington was modest. He was careful of his words. He had not time to curse. He had to retrieve the day."

Brigadier General Henry Knox, at North Castle on July 24, 1778, gave testimony favorable to Lee, whose conduct, however, he had not witnessed until Lee in his withdrawal met Washington. Knox said "his Excellency expressed much displeasure to General Lee at the situation of affairs." While Washington galloped to the rear to form the main army, Lee, as ordered, took command of the troops who had arrived in the retreat and declared he would "be one of the last men off the field." He directed Knox to an advantageous hill for the cannon. Lee interrupted to ask, "Did you think whenever you saw me, that I was perfectly master of myself, and not in the least discomposed?" Knox answered, "I thought you perfectly master of yourself; the circumstance of pointing out the knoll, I thought a very good proof of it, though not the only one." Lee observed of Brigadier General Anthony Wayne's testimony, "I have no doubt that had he been well informed of the whole circumstances of the day, I should, instead of a prosecutor, have found in him a friend and advocate."

When witnesses had finished, Lee defended himself with skill and plausibility, though he would doubtless have done better to refrain from sarcasm at the expense of those who had testified against him. He laid his groundwork by asserting that the orders he received from the commander in chief "were by no means precise and positive, but in a great measure discretionary." The councils of war had disapproved risking a general engagement, only recommending "some important but partial blow." Granted that he must obey Washington's command, "No letter I received, or conversation I ever had with him, indicated an intention . . . to court a general engagement." Here his reliance must have been on the instructions drafted by Hamilton, the last to reach him before the battle, as well as on less definable oral directions. Perhaps Washington did not scan the message before it was handed to the lighthorseman for delivery. Whether Hamilton put it plainly or not, it is clear that Washington intended that Lee should attack. Because Washington brought up the main body of the army from Englishtown before he knew the result of Lee's stroke at Monmouth, one can conclude that Washington meant to mount a major assault on Clinton's force. This purpose was in spite of Hamilton's information, a day and a half in advance, that Clinton had shifted his best troops to the vulnerable rear of his long marching columns.

Lee recounted circumstantially Washington's remonstrance when they met, going in opposite directions, on the field: "When I arrived first in his presence . . . I was disconcerted, astonished and confounded by the words and manner in which his Excellency accosted me. . . . The terms . . . were these—'I desire to know, sir, what is the reason—whence arises this disorder and confusion?' The manner in which he expressed them was much stronger and more severe than the expressions themselves." Lee explained to the court that "the retreat, in the first instance, was contrary to my intentions, contrary to my orders, and contrary to my wishes." However, following this initial falling back, the general withdrawal had been his own choice. The enemy had been too strong to be successfully attacked by his corps. The body of the army had been eight miles away, too far to come soon to his support. If beaten, as he would have been, he said, he could not have extricated his troops through three marshes, with only narrow crossing places, that lay behind him. His only chance had been to get back while there was still time to save his detachment. Actually he had tried to slow the retreat at one point, when urged by Hamilton, but had given it up because the enemy was on higher ground and it would be unpardonable "to risk anything further than the troops then halted" on his indefensible ridge. His retreat through two and a half miles of hazardous terrain had taken three hours, and had been accomplished with no loss of men or artillery. "So far . . . from considering ourselves as beaten or disgraced," he protested,

I really thought, taking into consideration . . . the various contradictory and false intelligence, disobedience or mistakes in some officers, precipitancy in others, ignorance of the ground, want of cavalry, that it was the flower of the British army that we had to deal with. . . . I really thought the troops entitled to the highest honor; and that I myself, instead of the thundering charges brought against me, had merited some degree of applause from the General and from the public.[1]

He excused the tone of his letters to Washington by his surprise and resentment at reproof for having done his duty.

Lee could not resist countering some of Hamilton's testimony with a thrust at the aide's extravagant behavior. Hamilton's remarks about Lee's lack of self-possession had impeached Lee's qualifications as an officer; this "has hurt me the more, as it comes from a man of esteemed sense, and whose valor I was myself a witness of." But Hamilton's valor, said Lee, needed control. After Washington asked Lee whether he would turn about and meet the pursuing enemy,

I had answered [Lee related] that I undoubtedly would. . . . Colonel Hamilton flourishing his sword, immediately exclaimed: That's right, my dear General, and I will stay, and we will all die here on this spot. . . . I could but be surprised at his expression, but observing him much flustered and in a sort of frenzy of valor, I calmly requested him to observe me well and to tell me if I did not appear tranquil and master of my faculties; his answer was, that he must

---

[1] It is not surprising that Sir Henry Clinton, commanding the enemy forces, pronounced General Lee's discretion in retreating the better part of valor. His whole corps, said Clinton, "would probably have fallen into the power of the King's army if he had . . . not retreated with the precipitancy he did. For my rear guard and the other troops then up were at that time nearly fresh, my cavalry was infinitely . . . superior . . . to his, and the quality of all my corps so far exceeded anything he had to oppose them that there cannot be the smallest doubt but they would . . . have obtained the completest success in ground so greatly in their favor—especially as the affair must have been finished long before Mr. Washington's main army could possibly be near enough to support him."

own that I was entirely possessed of myself; well, then (said I), you must allow me to be a proper judge of what I ought to do.

With that Lee declined to make a stand there because the enemy had the advantage of a higher hill.

It has been offered in Lee's defense, by him and others, that he fell back from the vicinity of the court house because the main American army was too far away to support him and because he wished to draw the enemy through the ravines after him, so they could be attacked by Washington's force on ground advantageous to the Americans. Lee set forth these justifications some months after the battle. Writing to his friend Dr. Benjamin Rush on September 29, 1778, Lee said he resented the implication that he had blundered. "If I did I am incorrigible," he wrote, "for I declare solemnly if the transactions of that day were to be done over again I wou'd do just the same, and I aver that my conduct was in every respect irreproachable." He acknowledged that the backward movement, so desirable, did not originate with him. ". . . this retreat tho' necessary was fortunately brought about contrary to my orders, contrary to my intention, by an accident, and if anything can deduct from my credit it is that I did not order the retreat which was so necessary."

On the second argument—that he had presented Washington with the opportunity of counterattack—Lee said in his published vindication that, once the retreat had commenced, he had rightly rejected Hamilton's plea to halt it midway. In the second position to which he had fallen back, on "the hill which Colonel Hamilton was so strongly prepossessed in favor of," he could not have annoyed the enemy. The best plan had been to let his pursuers pass the final ravine and be opposed by fresh American troops, arriving from Englishtown, on the superior heights enclosing the end of the field. This position had been "A sort of natural glacis, extending itself in our front, from the crest of the eminence quite down to the [westernmost] ravine, over which

Among the distinguished foreigners who fought under Washington, the Marquis de Lafayette is held in particular affection by the American people. Young, spirited, wealthy, he devoted himself enthusiastically to winning this country's independence. His rank of major general was bestowed from political considerations, but he justified his title by military performance. Of the same age, animation, and loyalties, Lafayette and Hamilton were always fast friends. (*Engraving by Hopwood, Prints Division, New York Public Library*)

During the winter of 1779–1780 General Washington used this room in the Jacob Ford mansion at Morristown, New Jersey, as his office. Here he met with his commanders and staff officers. His aides-de-camp, of whom Hamilton was by this time the chief, wrote in a room behind the one here shown, and had crowded sleeping quarters on the second floor. (*Courtesy of National Park Service, Morristown National Historical Park*)

No member of Washington's "military family" (headquarters staff) was more selflessly committed than Tench Tilghman of Maryland. Early in the war he volunteered to act as secretary and aide without rank or pay. In recognition of faithful service he was deputed to take to Congress the news of Cornwallis' surrender. He stood at Washington's side when the commander in chief resigned his commission at Annapolis in 1783. (*Etching by H. B. Hall, Prints Division, New York Public Library*)

During the Revolution a special friendship existed between Lieutenant Colonel John Laurens and Alexander Hamilton, both of them aides to Washington. Had Laurens survived the war, a brilliant public career would doubtless have been the sequel to his admirable military contribution. Indeed, as emissary of Congress to France to secure the assistance of funds and fleet (1780–1781), he had already shown his civil talents. (*Etching by H. B. Hall, Prints Division, New York Public Library*)

This house at New Windsor, New York (south of Newburgh), no longer standing, was General Washington's headquarters in the winter of 1780–1781. Here occurred the tiff between the commander in chief and his aide, Hamilton, which was their only difference in a close association of twenty-two years. (*Washington's Headquarters, Newburgh, New York*)

Major General Nathanael Greene is esteemed by many military judges to have been the ablest soldier who fought under Washington. His defeats at the hands of Cornwallis in the Carolinas in 1780–1781 were in effect American victories, because they wore down enemy initiative. Hamilton pronounced a notable eulogy when Greene died in 1786. (*Emmet Collection, New York Public Library*)

CHARLES EARL CORNWALLIS. 1783.

After serving with distinction under Generals Howe and Clinton in New York, New Jersey, and Pennsylvania, Major General Charles Cornwallis was given independent command in the South in 1780–1781, the last phase of the fighting war. At the siege of Yorktown, Virginia, Hamilton's brilliant capture of a forward redoubt helped to compel Cornwallis' surrender, which practically ended British resistance in the Revolution. (*Portrait by Gainsborough, National Portrait Gallery, London*)

Lieutenant Colonel Francis Barber had been Hamilton's teacher in the Elizabethtown, New Jersey, academy. He was wounded at Yorktown in the assault commanded by his former pupil. After surviving many battle dangers, Barber was killed by the felling of a tree in the camp near Newburgh, New York. (*Engraving by Stephen Cimber from a painting by James Herring from a sketch by a fellow officer, Prints Division, New York Public Library*)

Alexander Hamilton died in the Bayard House, in what is now Jane Street, New York City, on July 12, 1804. He had been mortally wounded the previous day in a duel with Aaron Burr. (*Prints Division, New York Public Library*)

Elizabeth Hamilton, daughter of General Philip and Catherine Schuyler, was beautiful, intelligent, and the very pattern of loyal wife to a man of genius. Hamilton and Elizabeth were married in the Schuyler mansion at Albany in December 1780. During her widowhood of fifty years (she lived to the age of 94), she assiduously collected Hamilton's papers, most of them now in the Library of Congress, in order to document and preserve her husband's fame. (*Portrait by Ralph Earl, courtesy of Museum of the City of New York*)

there was only one narrow pass, the plain so narrowed as to give no play to the manoeuvres of their cavalry." Here, to assist Washington's force, he would have rallied his own troops. "I proposed to the General to form them" on the hill, "but was precipitately ordered (and . . . in a manner that extremely ruffled me) to three miles distance in the rear."

The opinion of charitable observers was that of Major Samuel Shaw, aide to General Knox, given to a friend a few days after the battle. He recited that the main army, from a distance of six or eight miles, had been advancing to what was expected to become a general engagement, "but our [forward] detachments were ordered to retire. I will not presume to judge of the propriety or impropriety of this measure; it is a nice point, and something difficult to draw proper conclusions."

Hamilton, on the other hand, was never in doubt about Lee's fault. The court-martial had barely begun when he reviewed the battle for Elias Boudinot. "American arms gained very signal advantages," he declared, but

I can hardly persuade myself to be in good humour with success so far inferior to what we, in all probability, should have had, had not the finest opportunity America ever possessed been fooled away by a man, in whom she has placed a large share of the most ill judged confidence. You will . . . know that I mean General Lee. This man is either a driveler in the business of soldiership or something much worse. . . . Whatever a court Martial may decide, I shall continue to believe and say his conduct was monstrous and unpardonable.

The court-martial tried Lee on three charges: "First: For disobedience of orders in not attacking the enemy . . . agreeable to repeated instructions. Secondly: For Misbehaviour before the Enemy . . . by making an unnecessary, disorderly, and shameful retreat . . . . Thirdly: For disrespectful behaviour to the Commander-in-chief in two letters . . . ." On the first count the court found Lee guilty as charged. On the second count the verdict was similar, but the language was qualified: "he is guilty of misbehaviour before the enemy . . . by making an unnecessary and, in some instances, a Disorderly retreat." On the third count, of disrespect toward Washington, Lee was pronounced guilty as charged. He was sentenced to be suspended from any command in the armies of the United States for the term of twelve months. Rejecting Lee's appeal, Congress confirmed the verdict and sentence.

The question of Lee's conduct at Monmouth may be judged in the light of his behavior on other occasions during the war. He was fully persuaded of his own military skill, contemptuous of Washington's, and therefore disposed to slight the latter's authority. While a prisoner of the British, his proposal to Congress to send peace commissioners to Sir William Howe having been rejected, he drew up for Howe a military campaign plan,[2] which he believed would restore the Colonies to the empire. The biographer who has put the most favorable interpretation on his character and actions (John Richard Alden, *General Charles Lee, Traitor or Patriot?*) concludes, "Had his plan fallen into American hands when he could be brought before a military court, it is not unlikely that he would have been found guilty of treachery and sentenced to death."

The court-martial verdict by no means ended the Lee affair. Military men in the eighteenth century were especially touchy about their "honor," and were quick to seek vindication with weapons, even when the provocation was slight. The angry testimony at Lee's trial provided grounds for duels; one actually was fought, with Hamilton participating as a second, and other "interviews" were threatened.

Steuben, for example, sent Lee a challenge after reading the belittling remarks Lee had made about him during the trial. Lee, in turn, had particularly resented Steuben's testimony, perhaps because the discipline the baron instilled in the troops so contrasted with the confusion of his own retreat. Defending himself before the court, Lee had taunts for Steuben, declaring:

[2] Not signed, but in Lee's hand and otherwise identified, the paper was not known to Americans until many years later. Lee was dismissed from the American army in 1780, suffered declining fortunes, and died in 1782 in disgrace with all but a few.

Of all the very distant spectators of the manoeuvres of this day, and those a very trifling part of them, the Baron Steuben is . . . the only gentleman who has stepped forth to prove their demerits; he has certainly shown a very laudable zeal for bringing a criminal officer to condign punishment; but the next time he takes the field of prosecution . . . I hope his prudence will dictate to him the necessity of being furnished with a better apparatus.

Steuben was incensed by Lee's characterization of him as a "distant spectator." True, he had not actually witnessed Lee's early maneuvers, but this had not been for any lack of courage on his part. He had not reached the field until Washington arrived with the main army from Englishtown, and after helping organize the counterattack, he had been ordered back to try to form Lee's still-retreating troops. When Steuben's aide, Captain Benjamin Walker, brought the baron's challenge to Lee, the latter backed off. He replied that he had not questioned Steuben's courage, but objected to his "forwardness" in testifying for the prosecution. He would make this statement publicly, but "If you found that I have not dealt honestly, I am ready to satisfy you in the manner you desire." Steuben accepted this explanation as sufficient.

Steuben was probably extrasensitive to the implications of Lee's taunts because, as inspector general, he had been denied a command in the line. His young friend Hamilton, who had tried to promote his cause, wrote the baron sympathetically, and added: "I have read your letter to Lee, with pleasure—it was conceived in terms, which the offence merited . . . . Considering the pointedness and severity of your expressions, his answer was certainly a very modest one and proved that he had not a violent appetite, for so close a *tête à tête* as you seemed disposed to insist upon. His evasions, if known to the world, would do him very little honor."

The duel that actually came off resulted from John Laurens' challenge to Lee because, as Hamilton wrote, "he had been informed[on] good authority, that General Lee had spoken of

General Washington in the grossest and most opprobrious terms of personal abuse, which . . . Col. Laurens thought himself bound to resent, as well on account of the relation he bore to General Washington [as aide], as from motives of personal friendship, and respect for his character."

Two days after the battle, John Laurens had written to his father, then president of Congress, what he learned from his headquarters intimacy, that "Genl Lee, I think, must be tried for misconduct." But he properly added, "However, as this is a matter not generally known, tho' it seems almost universally wished for, I would beg you, my dear father, to say nothing of it." And shortly after, when the court-martial had been ordered, he imparted further to Henry Laurens, "Mr. Clinton's whole flying army would have fallen into our hands, but for a defect of abilities or good will in the commanding officer of our advanced corps. His precipitate retreat spread a baneful influence everywhere." His reference to Lee's possible "defect of . . . good will" imputed what others suggested: a treacherous intent to obstruct Washington's orders. According to Major Shaw, when Lee's case came before Congress, Henry Laurens on the floor made statements that provoked a challenge from John Penn of North Carolina, a Lee supporter, and the two exchanged harmless shots. Shaw went on to observe that in Philadelphia "duels are now exceedingly in vogue, though fortunately seldom attended with fatal consequences."

By this time, almost six months after the event, Congress had agreed with the court's verdict that Lee had been guilty of "disrespectful behaviour to the Commander-in-Chief." Perhaps for this reason and perhaps because, having mollified Steuben, he did not want to seem to avoid a second challenge, Lee decided to satisfy Laurens' quixotic demand.[3] Prefacing his reply with

---

[3] Samuel Shaw, alluding to Laurens' vindication of Washington's honor, suggested that the challenge might have been issued in accordance with the ancient knightly custom of *pro vidua*, by which "Monks, old women, and widows were allowed a champion."

the statement that he was sorry that his affairs (pleading his cause with Congress) had delayed him, Lee said "I will do myself the Honour of meeting you attended by a Friend with a brace of pistols to-morrow [Dec. 22, 1778] ½ past 3. P.M. I would willingly bring a small sword at the same time, but from the effects of my fall and the quantity of Physick I have taken to baffle a fit of the Gout which I apprehended I do not think myself sufficiently strong on my legs." Though thus hampered, he went on to designate "a very convenient piece of wood . . . on the point no point road, to the left hand a little on the Philad. side of the four mile stone," where, "unless it should rain" he would present himself.

Lee was there promptly with his aide Major Evan Edwards as second, but they had to wait a while for Laurens, with Hamilton as his friend, to appear. It was agreed that the combatants, provided with two pistols apiece, should advance toward each other, firing when they chose. At five or six paces they shot almost simultaneously. Laurens was preparing for a second shot when Lee said he was wounded. Laurens and the two seconds immediately went to help him, but he protested that his hurt was trifling, and that he, too, wanted another crack at his opponent. Both Hamilton and Edwards insisted that all requirements of honor had been fully satisfied, and that the encounter must end without more ado. While the seconds conferred, Laurens restated his grievance, and Lee acknowledged that he had given an opinion of Washington's military character to his close friends and might do so again. Lee declared, however, that he had never spoken of Washington in the terms alleged, and said that he esteemed him as a man.

The seconds published a report of the event, pronouncing that after the two gentlemen met, "their conduct was strongly marked by all the politeness, generosity, coolness, and firmness, that ought to characterize a transaction of this nature." Lee is reported to have said later of Laurens, "I could have hugged the noble boy, he pleased me so."

General Anthony Wayne, chancing to meet General Lee at Elizabethtown a fortnight later, accused him ot trying "to injure my military character in the eye of the world," and asked satisfaction for being disparaged "in so tender a point." Lee said he would accept the invitation to a duel if Wayne insisted, but Wayne thought Lee's explanation sufficient, and withdrew the challenge.

Hamilton figured in another sequel to Monmouth. Describing the battle in a letter to his old friend and patron Elias Boudinot, Hamilton praised Washington's prowess in retrieving the day and roundly criticized Lee's conduct, suggesting that perhaps he meant to forfeit the battle. Boudinot, in reply, agreed with the last intimation, condemning those "capable of betraying America." He was thankful, said Boudinot, that the "Supreme Disposer of human events" baffled "not only the formidable & open force of our enemies, but also the more dangerous & secret efforts of false or lukewarm friends." In this mood of prosecution, Boudinot published part of Hamilton's strictures, without signature, in the Pennsylvania *Packet* of July 16. Six months later, after Lee had been convicted by both court-martial and Congress, Boudinot did worse, sending to the New Jersey *Gazette* an excoriation of Lee as a villain, traitor, and profligate. The piece was by a Tory, resentful of Lee's defection to the American cause, and had been printed earlier in the war. Now Boudinot prefaced it with sentiments of his own, signed only with initials, and false ones at that. Boudinot and Charles Lee were completely antithetical personalities. The eccentric Lee, free in his moral conduct, would have accurately called Boudinot, in modern phrase, a "square." Learning that Boudinot was responsible for the publication, Lee besought Governor Livingston to remove him as commissary of prisoners for New Jersey. This Livingston would not do, but he advised the offended general to sue his defamer for libel. Isaac Collins, editor of the newspaper, did print, soon after, a rejoinder by Lee's aide Evan Edwards, despising the "rancorous villain . . . capable of composing, or instrumental in publishing such . . . dastardly . . . calumny." The best thing Boudinot was ever able to say of Lee was that he "had considerable military knowledge & did very well on a small scale, but . . . whenever anything on a very large scale struck him"—as on the field of Monmouth—"a partial Lunacy took place."

9

Trough of the War

 Hamilton was with Washington in Philadel-
phia from late December 1778 to early February of the new
year. The war, on America's part, was at more than the usual
winter pause. The alternatives for the 1779 campaign were presented in a series of questions, framed by Hamilton, to a committee of Congress of which Duane was chairman and Gouverneur Morris was a member. The argument for defensive operations was strong:

Will not the situation of our affairs, on account of the depreciated
condition of our Money, deficiency of Bread, scarcity of Forage, the
exhausted state of our resources in the Middle department, and the
General distress of the Inhabitants render it advisable for the main
body of the Army to lye quiet in some favourable position for confin-
ing . . . the enemy in their present posts . . . in order to save expenses, avoid New Emissions, recruit our finances, and give a proper
tone to our Money for more vigorous measures hereafter?

The congressional committee agreed that the new nation
would do best to conserve its slender resources while awaiting
aid from France. It simply wasn't possible to mount a campaign
during the coming year that would be strong enough to expel
the enemy from Rhode Island and New York. Along the fron-

tier, however, the British and their Indian allies appeared more vulnerable. An expedition against the Iroquois tribes in the northwest country was appealing on at least four counts: It would relieve a distressed district, which had been left for too long to defend itself against savage raids; it would drive the Indians back, hungry and homeless, to burden their British friends; it could be carried out with relatively small expense by detachments that traveled light; and it would permit the rebels to avoid the discredit of total passivity during the 1779 campaigning season.

Washington favored the plan and invited Gates (in a letter penned by Hamilton) to command the punitive foray in the Mohawk valley. But Gates declined on account of decrepitude. "The Man who undertakes the Indian Service," he replied, "should enjoy Youth and Strength, requisites I do not possess," adding sourly that "it . . . Grieves me that Your Excellency should Offer me The only Command to which I am intirely unequal." Hamilton then took special satisfaction in Washington's order to shift the assignment to his friend General John Sullivan.

Hamilton undoubtedly realized that the appointment to lead the expedition against the Six Nations would repair Sullivan's feelings after a reproof that Washington had been obliged to administer. A few months before (August 1778) Sullivan's Irish ire had thrown him into a serious indiscretion. A planned combined attack on Rhode Island had been forfeited when Count D'Estaing took his fleet from Newport to intercept that of Lord Howe. The only enemy he met was a storm, and he limped back with crippled ships. Sullivan and Greene, impatient for his return, were left in a dangerous position when the admiral insisted on sailing to Boston for repairs. Warned by Washington that enemy reinforcements were on the way, Sullivan saved his army by a skillful retreat. However, another warning from Washington, conveyed in Hamilton's words, did not arrive in time. Fearing that American disgust might cause a rupture in relations with France, Washington cautioned: "Should the expedition fail, thro' the abandonment of the French fleet, the [American] Officers . . . will be apt to complain loudly. But prudence dictates that we should put the best face upon the matter and, to the World, attribute the removal to Boston, to necessity." Instead, Sullivan issued general orders in which he said he hoped "the event will prove America able to procure that by her own arms, which her allies refuse to assist her in obtaining."

As always when tactless affront was given the French, Lafayette, on the Rhode Island scene, was quick to regret the slip. Others also gave the alarm to Washington. Since Sullivan was admired by Americans for his feat of extricating his troops when left in the lurch, it was not advisable to give him the official reprimand that French umbrage desired. Instead, Washington employed Hamilton to deliver a soft impeachment to the outspoken general: "The disagreement between the army under your command and the fleet," it ran, "has given me . . . singular uneasiness. The continent at large is concerned in our cordiality . . . . In our conduct towards [the French] we should remember that they are a people old in war, very strict in military etiquette and apt to take fire where others scarcely seem warmed. Permit me to recommend in the most particular manner, the cultivation of harmony and good agreement." Hamilton also penned a soothing letter from Washington to D'Estaing.

Hamilton in a semipublic letter to Boudinot in Congress at once condemned Sullivan's tactless remark as "the summit of folly" and an "absurdity without parallel," while praising the courage of a French major who had lost an arm in a solo charge against a British field-piece. This letter satisfied the French; it issued from the American headquarters, though it was not signed by the commander in chief. Congress avoided all negatives by thanking Sullivan and his army and declaring the French admiral and his officers "fully entitled to the regards of the friends of America."

After the circumlocution occasioned by Sullivan's lapse, Hamilton must have found pleasure in wording the commander in chief's instructions for decimating the Indian towns. Sullivan was to copy the red men's method of fighting, not omitting the war whoop; to "make . . . attacks . . . with as much impetuosity . . . and noise as possible"; his troops were to "act in as loose and dispersed a way as is consistent with . . . mutual support." Shades of Braddock's disaster informed Washington's directions. Following the advice of Schuyler and others who knew that frontier region, Sullivan should assemble his main force at Wyoming on the Susquehanna (midway between present Scranton and Wilkes-Barre, Pennsylvania), and then march northwest to Tioga (just below the New York border), from where he would penetrate deeper into the interior. General James Clinton's brigade would rendezvous at Canajoharie and, as later developed, would join Sullivan on the Susquehanna by way of Otsego Lake. A table of distances between potential camping places all the way to "Chenise Castle" (the castle of Chenesee, principal Seneca Indian settlement near present Geneva, New York) was furnished.

General Sullivan complained of lack of clothing and other supplies for the expedition, and of wagons to move what he had. He too far disregarded Washington's advice to "disencumber yourself of every article of baggage and stores which is not necessary to the expedition. Not only its success but its execution at all depends on this." Both officers and men

must not . . . expect to carry the same apparatus which is customary in other operations . . . if you do not lighten yourself to the greatest possible degree, you will not only immediately hazard a defeat, but you will never be able to penetrate any distance into the Indian Country—The Greater part of your provisions will be consumed in preparation, and the remainder in the first stages of a tedious and laborious march.

Following his general instructions, Washington repeated to Sullivan, for emphasis, the two purposes of the expedition:

"The one is, the necessity of pushing the Indians to the greatest practicable distance, from their own settlements, and our frontiers . . . throwing them wholly on the British enemy.—The other is, the . . . destruction of their settlements so final and complete, as to put it out of their power to derive the smallest succour from them, in case they should attempt to return this season."

In spite of delays and other mischances, Sullivan's army produced thorough ruin where it passed, and he sent out detachments along trail and creek to demolish even the smallest cluster of houses and crops. "I flatter myself," Sullivan reported to Congress from Tioga (September 30, 1779), "that the orders with which I was entrusted are fully executed, as we have not left a single settlement or field of corn in the Country of the Five Nations, or is there even the appearance of an Indian on this side of Niagara." With rations of fifteen days more he would have routed the starving Indians and trembling British from Niagara. "The number of Towns destroyed . . . amounts to 40, besides scattering houses. The quantity of Corn destroyed . . . must amount to 160,000 bushels, with a vast quantity of vegetables of every kind." The main "castle" of "Chenesee" had been deserted two days before; it "consisted of one hundred & twenty eight houses, mostly very large and elegant [some framed, and with chimneys]. The town was beautifully situated . . . encircled with a clear flat . . . for a number of miles, where [were] the most extensive fields of corn and every kind of vegetable. The whole army was immediately engaged in destroying the crops. The corn was collected & burned in houses." At another town 1,500 fruit trees, many of them old, showing long habitation, were chopped down. The depredations of the Indians on the frontier communities, cruel as they had been, were spasmodic and small-scale compared with the massive vengeful sweep of the army of 2,700 against the hostile tribes.

Except for the stand the Indians and British rangers made at Newtown (near present Elmira, New York), in which Sullivan's loss was only three killed and thirty-nine wounded, the savages and their allies generally had fled before the approaching army. They took fearful retaliation on Lieutenant Thomas Boyd and his only surviving companion of a scouting detachment near their main castle. Sullivan reported

the unparalleled tortures they inflicted upon the brave . . . Boid, whose body with that of his equally unfortunate companion we found at Chenesee . . . they had whipped them in the most cruel manner, pulled out Mr. Boid's nails, cut off his nose, plucked out one of his eyes, cut out his tongue, stabbed him with spears . . . & inflicted other tortures which decency will not permit me to mention; lastly cut off his head.

During the next eighteen months Hamilton shared with the commander in chief a few bright moments but far more of frustration and grief. The feeble support that was all that could be sent to General Benjamin Lincoln in the South doomed to failure the effort to retake Savannah and to hold Charleston. General Horatio Gates's discreditable defeat at Camden was the preliminary to Lord Cornwallis' sweeping campaign in the Carolinas. In the North several principal officers were incapacitated by illness or wounds, others quit in resentment at their treatment by Congress. A group of officers of the New Jersey line refused to command their troops until their (the officers') grievances were remedied, and a larger number of the New York line prepared to petition for retirement. Anthony Wayne's daring capture of Stony Point, New York, was a brilliant stroke, but the position could not be held, and the chief benefit to the Americans was negative; the British were compelled to divert materials and men to rebuilding the stronghold. Major Henry Lee's surprise attack on Paulus Hook (Jersey City) was a combination of heroism and luck that cheered American spirits but had no military effect.

The winter encampment at Morristown, New Jersey (1779–1780), was the bitterest of the war for cold and hunger —worse than Valley Forge. Amidst the snows the freezing sol-

diers toiled at felling hardwood trees to hut themselves. Of one
brigade, Steuben said the men "exhibited the most shocking picture of misery I have ever seen, scarce a man having where-
withal to cover his nakedness, and a great number very bad with
the itch." Another officer wrote, "many a good lad [had] nothing to cover him from his hips to his toes, save his blanket."
Some had no blanket; shoes were unprocurable. Nathanael
Greene, the quartermaster general, declared, "there never was a
darker hour in American prospects than this. . . . Our treasury
is dry and magazines empty; how we are to support the war is
beyond my conception. Shillings cannot be had where pounds
are wanting." Washington warned a negligent Congress that
the army was on the point of disbandment. In Hamilton's words
the commander in chief unburdened himself (May 31, 1780) to
President Joseph Reed of Pennsylvania: "All our . . . operations
are at a stand and unless a system very different . . . be immediately adopted throughout the states our affairs must soon become
desperate beyond the possibility of recovery. . . . Indeed I have
almost ceased to hope."

Congress at last, in March 1780, quit the farce of exhorting the
people to accept the outstanding Continental currency at face
value, and offered to receive the existing paper money at the rate
of forty dollars for one dollar of a "new tenor" restricted issue.
This repudiation furnished only temporary check to the soaring
inflation, since the new issue notes depreciated with the old.
Having no media with which to buy, the commissaries and
quartermasters resorted to impressment of food and forage and
gave receipts of doubtful value at a distant day in the future.

The ranks of enlisted men were thinned by desertions among
those with enough clothing to permit them to brave a winter
escape. Many on "sick leave" were struck from the rolls, as it
was ruefully recognized that they would never return. In face
of the misery in camp it was next to impossible to persuade
men whose terms expired to re-enlist, in spite of promised bo-
nuses in pay and generous furloughs. Too many general and regi-

mental officers had received permission to be absent from camp. This threw additional burdens of administration on the commander in chief, and increased the duties of Hamilton as principal aide.

The war, on the American side, was primarily a problem of organization and public support; political and economic competence were basic if an army was to be kept in the field. As in other instances in history, reaching to our own time, it was easier to rouse people to revolt than to form an efficient government and economy to maintain the fight. Deliberation and reconciliation of divergent interests were impossible in the crisis of violence. The establishment of the Constitution, not until six years after the peace, was properly called the second American revolution. The war was fought under emergency auspices. Congress was an ad hoc body, the outgrowth of trade conventions. Until the Articles of Confederation were approved in 1781, the central power acted on sufferance. Thereafter the Continental Congress, while possessing legal sanction, was beset with weaknesses. The country was still a collection of ex-colonies, differing in institutions and interests. Cohesion required time and experience, extending actually seventy-five years until the end of the Civil War.

George Washington's career was unique in that he presided over both war and peace; the stability he achieved as President was through democratic consent rather than military dictatorship.

Throughout the war the commander in chief's battle was to summon ways and means, while being deferential to confused and often incapable civil authority. Hamilton, as aide and on his own initiative, was constantly active in this effort. In fact, he went beyond Washington in outlining and urging needed reforms. This he did in his private capacity, though his proposals surely had the unspoken approval of his superior. The future statesman, who would help to devise the Constitution and set the United States Treasury on a prosperous course, began his services in uniform. His political and economic preachments sprang from lessons of the war.

Washington's worries over sinking resources and morale, which threatened dissolution of the army and extinction of the very desire for independence, were echoed in notable personal letters of Hamilton urging imperative reforms.

It was probably in the spring of 1777, after he joined Washington's staff, that Hamilton turned to "some reading on the subjects of commerce and finance." Notes taken from such works as Postlethwayt's *Universal Dictionary of Trade and Commerce* occupy the otherwise unused pages at the back of his artillery company paybook, indicating that he entered the memoranda shortly after giving up his field command. This reading, combined with his "reflexions on our particular situation," produced the first of his letters analyzing the plight of the army and of the country's economy as a result of depreciation of the paper currency. It was written from Morristown some time between December 1779 and the following March, to whom is uncertain, except that he addressed one able to help "to extricate us from our embarrassments." (Robert Morris, John Sullivan, and Philip Schuyler, for various reasons, have been suggested.)

"The war," he declared, "[has] required exertions . . . to which neither our population nor riches were equal. We have the fullest proof of this in the constant thinness of our armies, the impossibility, at this time, of recruiting them otherwise than by compulsion . . . the decrease of our staple commodities and the difficulty of every species of supply." Lacking internal financial resources, "artificial revenues" (paper money, which fell in value as its quantity multiplied) became the resort, with the evil consequences of inflation. "There was but one remedy, a foreign loan," such as even the most opulent countries in time of war were obliged to employ. "Could a loan have been obtained and judiciously applied, assisted by a vigorous system of taxation, we might have avoided that excess of emissions which has ruined the paper." A foreign loan of two million pounds, he felt, should now be sought, and used, not to import army supplies, but to form the government's contribution to the capital of a Bank of the United States established by Congress. Thus encouraged, men of means could be induced to invest an equal amount in real value, guaranteed by government to be returned to them in Spanish milled dollars at dissolution of the bank. Only such a plan "that will make it the *immediate* interest of the monied men to cooperate with government" could "preserve the currency."

Preserving the currency meant eliminating its excess. Increased taxes, in paper money, would aid this object; the remaining paper should be called in, at the option of the possessor, and bank notes be given in lieu, at the rate of one dollar sterling for sixty dollars paper, the sterling notes to bear interest of 2 percent per annum. The bank should lend government two million pounds annually in its notes, for three years, at 4 percent interest.

The bank notes, got into circulation by these and other means, including private loans, would have superior value and combat inflation. However, because purchasing power of the paper money had been practically destroyed, a tax in kind "ought instantly to begin throughout the states."

Hamilton strongly urged improvement of administration by substituting competent individuals to head public departments in place of committees of Congress. "We want a Minister of War, a Minister for Foreign Affairs, a Minister of Finance and a Minister of Marine. There is always more decision, more dispatch, more secrecy, more responsibility where single men, than when bodies are concerned." Especially necessary was a minister of finance capable of persuading monied men of the utility of the bank project.

Here in embryo were proposals that figured in Hamilton's program from that time forth. The need of the army and of the country for remedies had not lessened when (September 3, 1780) he appealed to the influence of James Duane, member of

Congress from New York, with whom Hamilton was often in friendly communication. Duane had asked for Hamilton's "ideas of the defects of our present system, and the changes necessary to save us from ruin."

Hamilton's emphasis now was political. "The fundamental defect is a want of power in Congress." Causes were three: insistence of the individual states on their superior authority, diffidence of Congress in discharging its functions, and inability of Congress to command revenue equal to its responsibilities. The result was that Congress had lost credit with the army, which was obliged to depend on the separate states. (Congress could not lay and collect taxes, could only apply to the states to furnish funds.) Congress had given too narrow an interpretation to its role, should have considered itself "vested with full power *to preserve the republic from harm.*" He stated what later became a famous doctrine with him and other Federalists: "Undefined powers are discretionary powers, limited only by the object for which they were given—in the present case, the independence and freedom of America." The Confederation, though not yet adopted, required to be altered; "it is neither fit for war, nor peace. The idea of an uncontrolable sovereignty in each state, over its internal police, will defeat the . . . powers given to Congress, and make our union feeble and precarious." The states should have nothing to do with the army.

The entire formation and disposal of our military forces ought to belong to Congress. [The army] is an essential cement of the union; and it ought to be the policy of Congress to . . . make it look up wholly to them. For this purpose all appointments, promotions, and provisions whatsoever ought to be made by them . . . . Already some of the lines of the army would obey their states in opposition to Congress. . . .

He lamented "the want of a proper executive" (the closest thing was an annually elected president of Congress). He repeated his preference for able individuals to administer departments, relieving Congress of detail. Without a speedy change, the army, depending on short enlistments, "must dissolve; it is now a mob, rather than an army, without cloathing, without pay . . . without morals, without discipline. We begin to hate the country for its neglect of us; the country begins to hate us for our oppressions of them."

Since Congress would not exercise its discretionary powers, a convention of all the states should be called, the sooner the better, to devise "a solid coercive union . . . . Congress should have complete sovereignty in all that relates to war, peace, trade, finance, and to the management of foreign affairs," reserving to state legislatures their internal concerns. An army should be recruited for the war, or at least for three years; officers should be promised half pay for life. Again he begged for "a foreign loan, heavy pecuniary taxes, a tax in kind, a bank founded on public and private credit." Finally, "In what Congress have at any time done for the army, they have . . . seemed to yield to importunity rather than to sentiments of justice or to a regard to the accommodation of their troops." The "progress of the present discontents" was due in large measure to this mean spirit.

Hamilton was not giving counsel of perfection. He wished to repair demonstrable weaknesses that threatened success in the war. Moreover, the corrections defined by this young soldier (he was twenty-five at the time) were accomplished a decade later, not a little by his own efforts.

Some mistook his views of the incompetence of existing government to make him a would-be Caesar or a Cromwell. He blasted a report stating he had declared in a Philadelphia public house that "it was high time for the people to rise, join General Washington & turn Congress out of Doors." He immediately traced this gossip to Reverend William Gordon, as he believed, and was "running the [old Jesuit] pretty hard." Others, since, while not attributing to him dictatorial ambitions, have thought him too much the advocate of centralized authority. This is not the place to refute that contention; it is simply remarked that American history since his day has assigned a progressively larger role to his concept of the national government.

The third in this group of letters suggesting remedies for the country's distresses was to Robert Morris, who, Hamilton devoutly hoped, would accept his recent appointment by Congress as superintendent of finance. Hamilton had left Washington's staff shortly before, and wrote (April 30, 1781) from De-Peyster's Point, near Beacon, across the Hudson from New Windsor headquarters, where he and his wife were living until he could return to the army in a field command. This interval of leisure, coupled with the expectation that Morris might make practical use of his proposals, explains the greater length of the paper he now prepared. He had asked Timothy Pickering to lend him, if possible, works of Richard Price, David Hume, Malachy Postlethwayt, and Wyndham Beawes, bearing on finance and commerce, with which Hamilton was already familiar. Hamilton himself had been considered, probably without his knowledge, by John Sullivan and others for the important post to which Robert Morris was named. At this stage Morris was the right choice, but in his discussion of the problem Hamilton gave striking evidence of his fitness for later responsibility, as Morris cheerfully acknowledged.

"'Tis by introducing order into our finances," Hamilton declared, "by restoring public credit—not by gaining battles, that we are finally to gain our object. 'Tis by putting ourselves in a condition to continue the war not by temporary, violent and unnatural efforts to bring it to a decisive issue, that we shall in reality bring it to a speedy and successful one."

After exploring the deficiency of other means of prosecuting the war, he, as before, centered on "the institution of a National Bank. This I regard . . . as an expedient essential to our safety and success. . . . There is no other that can give to government that extensive and systematic credit, which the defect of our revenues makes indispensably necessary to its operations." The bank, which he described in detail, would unite public and private resources and interests, give power to the state, and multiply commerce, agriculture, and manufactures.

The rigors of the Morristown winter were relieved for Alexander Hamilton by the presence at headquarters of Elizabeth

Schuyler, the second daughter of General Philip Schuyler and his wife Catherine. Elizabeth, then just over twenty-two, accompanied by her older sister, Angelica, came to Morristown in November 1779 to visit their aunt, Mrs. John Cochran, wife of the surgeon general of the Middle Department. Their parents, with the younger Schuyler daughters, had gone to Philadelphia, where General Schuyler took his seat in Congress. Alexander's wooing was ardent. One night in his absorption he forgot the password, and when he returned to the Ford mansion, Washington's headquarters, he was refused admission by the sentry; fortunately Mrs. Ford's little son, playing outside, whispered the open sesame in time to prevent embarrassment. "Hamilton is a gone man," Tilghman pronounced. So it was, for Alexander and Betsey were already engaged when the Schuylers arrived from Philadelphia in March 1780. General Schuyler was a member of the committee of Congress sent to camp to concert plans for the coming campaign. As prospective son-in-law, Hamilton's dealings with him were all the closer.

Alexander Hamilton and Elizabeth Schuyler were married in the Schuyler family mansion at Albany, December 14, 1780. They had wanted the wedding to be earlier, at headquarters at Morristown, but the bride's parents insisted on delay until the ceremony could take place at their own home. "Mrs. Schuyler did not see her eldest daughter married," the general wrote; "that also gave me pain, and we wish not to experience It a Second time." (Angelica and John Barker Church had eloped.) Hamilton's fellow aide, James McHenry, was a wedding guest, and celebrated the occasion with a graceful ode. The honeymoon, over the holidays, was spent at Albany, after which the young couple repaired to headquarters at New Windsor, New York. Hamilton's marriage into a wealthy and influential family was for love, not from social ambition, nor could he have been more cordially received by the Schuylers. The union resulted not only in familial affection, but in enduring political partnership between Hamilton and Philip Schuyler.

10

Chase After Arnold, Compassion for André

 Benedict Arnold importuned Washington to give him command of the chief American fortress on the Hudson, at West Point, New York. His plea was that his wound received at Saratoga incapacitated him for more active duty. Only after his second pressing application did Washington yield. Arnold's "extreme solicitude," as Hamilton observed, "to get possession of the post would have led to a suspicion of treachery, had it been possible from his past conduct to have supposed him capable of it."

Shortly after this (September 17, 1780), Washington and his companions—Lafayette, Knox, and their aides—set out from New Bridge, New Jersey, for Hartford for a conference with General Rochambeau and Admiral Charles Louis d'Arsac De-Ternay. Nearing King's Ferry (Stony Point, New York), they dined and lodged at the home of Joshua Hett Smith. Though he was the brother of William Smith, royal chief justice of New York, he was held to be so much the patriot that he had been employed by the American General Robert Howe to gather information of the enemy.

General Arnold was a dinner guest. He consulted Washington about letters received that day from Colonel Beverley Robinson on the *Vulture*, lying off Teller's Point (Croton Point, six miles below King's Ferry). Robinson was a Tory, commanding a regiment of Royal Americans. His letter to Arnold enclosed one to General Israel Putnam, asking for an interview on a private matter. However, if Putnam was not in reach, could Robinson see Arnold? Washington said no, that Robinson should be referred to the civil authority.

Washington's negative, as Hamilton later observed, "fortunately deranged the plan, and was the first link in the chain of events that led to the detection" of Arnold's treasonable intent. "The interview could no longer take place in the form of a flag, but was obliged to be managed in a secret manner."

Washington and his party went on to meet the French at Hartford. There Lafayette and Hamilton served as interpreters and translators of queries and answers. The import of all this was that the next campaign must depend on additional French support, especially at sea, but on land also. If this aid arrived by October, the siege of New York would be the object; if later, operations would be to the south.

On his return, Washington was delayed at Fishkill, where Joshua Hett Smith was again at dinner. The general and his entourage left next morning, September 25, before breakfast for Arnold's headquarters (in the former home of Beverley Robinson, almost opposite West Point), and an inspection of the fort. Hamilton remained with Washington and the other generals when they turned off to examine redoubts at the riverbank. Major James McHenry and Captain Samuel Shaw, aides of Lafayette and Knox, posted ahead to give notice to Arnold's household that Washington would be along for breakfast. On arrival Washington was told by Arnold's aides that the latter had been called to West Point but would return within the hour. Colonel Richard Varick had risen from a sickbed to receive the commander in chief in Arnold's absence.

Following breakfast, Washington, Lafayette, and Knox crossed to West Point, expecting to find Arnold there. Hamilton remained at Robinson's. After an hour he was called to Mrs. Arnold's bedside by her "hysterics and utter frenzy." She raved deliriously of hot irons on her head and charged that Varick had ordered her infant killed. The aides summoned Dr. William Eustis, but the attempts of all to quiet her and assure her that her husband would soon return were met with her cries of "No, no, he is gone forever!" While her hysterics continued, Hamilton learned that at breakfast, shortly before Washington arrived, an officer had brought Arnold two letters. Arnold had glanced at them and gone to his wife's room. Then, when his aide Major David Franks reported that Washington was expected at any minute, Arnold "came down in great confusion, and, ordering a horse to be saddled, mounted," and told an aide "to inform his Excellency that he was gone over to West Point."

While Hamilton was sorting out the events that preceded the party's arrival at the Robinson house, Captain Jeronimus Hoogland, courier for Lieutenant Colonel John Jameson, commanding at the outpost of North Castle, brought a packet for Washington. In the general's absence, the packet was given to Hamilton, who did not open it. Delivered to Washington on the latter's return in midafternoon, the shocking contents instantly solved the mystery of his not finding Arnold at West Point, where every precaution for defense had been neglected. Revealed were a pass in Arnold's hand for a John Anderson; a plan of the fortifications at West Point; a roster of garrison; inventories of ordnance and stores; and a copy of the minutes of a council of war held by Washington three weeks before. The covering letter of Jameson explained that these documents had been taken from the stocking feet of a traveler bound for New York, arrested by militiamen at Tarrytown that morning. If all of this, coupled with an earlier report that Arnold's barge had been seen headed downriver, did not betray the plot, the enclosed letter of the prisoner to Washington was conclusive. Identifying himself as Major John André, adjutant general of the British army, the prisoner said that he had come ashore from the *Vulture*, seeking military intelligence, and that he had been forced against his will to enter the American lines and disguise himself as a civilian. By this explanation he wanted to acquit himself of "an imputation of having assumed a mean character for treacherous purposes." He did not name Arnold as his confederate, but the connection was all too plain.

Hamilton and McHenry were immediately dispatched to ride the dozen miles to Verplanck's Point in hope of intercepting Arnold. This mission failed, but Hamilton at once did all possible to protect West Point. He got off an express to Washington, saying,

we are too late. Arnold went by water to the Vulture. I shall write to General Greene [whom Washington had left in command at Tappan] advising him . . . to be in readiness to march and even to detach a Brigade this way, for though I do not believe the project will go on, it is possible Arnold has made such dispositions with the Garrison as may tempt the enemy in its present weakness to make the stroke this night. I shall endeavour to find [Colonel] Meigs [whose Connecticut regiment was on the east side of the Hudson] and request him to march to the Garrison, and shall make some arrangements here.

He hoped Washington would approve these steps, "as there may be no time to be lost."

He enclosed a letter for Washington from Arnold, written on board the *Vulture* and sent ashore. It was a plea in self-defense and exculpation of Mrs. Arnold and his aides. "I have ever acted from a Principle of Love to my Country, since the Commencement of the present unhappy Contest . . . the same principle of Love to my Country Actuates my present Conduct, however it may appear Inconsistent to the World." He begged Washington's protection for "Mrs. Arnold from every Insult and Injury that the mistaken Vengeance of my Country may expose Her to. . . .

She is . . . as Innocent as an Angel, and . . . Incapable of doing wrong." Likewise, said Arnold, Colonel Varick, Major Franks, and Joshua Hett Smith were "totally Ignorant" of his plans.

Other enclosures were a letter from Beverley Robinson to Washington with what Hamilton called the "frivolous" pretense that André was covered by a flag of truce, and a letter from Arnold to his wife, which Washington delivered to her unopened.

Hamilton, dashing in pursuit of Arnold, missed dinner at the Robinson house. Accounts of the order of events there are conflicting. Washington did not yet know that Hamilton was too late in his errand. According to Varick, who in spite of his high fever presided at table, only Washington behaved as if nothing were awry. This may mean that he had not at once believed, as did Lafayette and Knox, the evidence of Arnold's treason. However, suspicion was rife. The other generals had seen the disorder at West Point, knew that Arnold was unaccountably absent, and that Hamilton and McHenry had hurried south, the direction Arnold's barge had been seen moving. Mrs. Arnold kept up her ravings. At some point Washington was taken up to see her, only to be "upbraided . . . with being in a plot to murder her child." The general's promise that she would not be harmed could not calm her.

When Hamilton got back from Verplanck's Point—and he must have ridden as hard on the return as going, for he reached Robinson's about seven o'clock—Peggy Arnold was still hysterical. That night, busy as it was, he found time to write to his fiancée, Elizabeth Schuyler, noting his compasion for

an amiable woman frantic with distress for the loss of a husband she tenderly loved—a traitor to his country . . . one moment she raved; another she melted into tears; sometimes she pressed her infant to her bosom and lamented its fate . . . in a manner that would have pierced insensibility itself. All the sweetness of beauty, all the loveliness of innocence . . . showed themselves in her appearance and conduct. We have every reason to believe she was intirely unacquainted with the plan. . . .

Hamilton could not linger over the distresses of Mrs. Arnold, for he had to help his chief prepare orders for the safety of West Point. First, Hamilton's message to Greene from Verplanck's Point was confirmed; Greene must put his left division in march to King's Ferry, and hold other troops in instant readiness. Wayne was to bring his brigade to West Point. Directions to Colonel Nathaniel Wade, on whom the command at West Point devolved, for placing that fort and its dependencies in a condition of defense were not completed until two o'clock the next morning, September 26. Meantime, André was to be brought to West Point. When André was captured, Jameson at first had ordered that he be taken to Arnold, but on realizing that Arnold was probably guilty, he decided to confine the British officer at Old Salem. Also during the night, Lieutenant Colonel Jean Baptiste Gouvion set off for Fishkill to apprehend Joshua Smith, whom Arnold had sought to exculpate.

The following day (Tuesday, September 26) held no rest for the weary officers at Robinson's house. Smith arrived under guard before eight o'clock that morning, and was given a preliminary interrogation by Washington in the presence of Lafayette, Knox, Hamilton, and Harrison. The prisoner's bold features under his unpowdered wig must have shown his agitation as he was questioned by Washington "with some warmth." But in spite of sudden arrest, night ride, and chills from which he said he was suffering, Smith kept himself in hand. Hamilton a week later, at Smith's civilian trial, reviewed what passed.

Smith began by declaring himself a patriot, saying that he had been previously employed by Major Generals Howe and Arnold "for the purpose of procuring intelligence from the enemy." On the night in question (September 21) "General Arnold informed him of an interview he was to have with Colonel Robinson of the British army, in which . . . he expected to derive information of importance, and wished to engage Mr. Smith to go on board the *Vulture*, sloop-of-war, then lying in the North-river, to bring Colonel Robinson on shore for the purpose of that interview." Arnold gave him an order for a boat, in which "he went secretly and in the night on board the *Vulture* . . . with a note from General Arnold to Colonel Robinson . . . that instead of Colonel Robinson, a person under the name of John Anderson came on shore with him." Smith then said, according to Hamilton, that "General Arnold and Anderson were that night and the next day at his . . . house," but that he was "an absolute stranger to the business they transacted." Smith detailed his further actions. Because he had the fever and ague, he was not able to return Anderson to the ship, but "took a different mode, and proceeded with him by King's Ferry towards the White Plains," then left Anderson on the road. Smith had "assisted Mr. Anderson to exchange the clothes he had [his regimentals] for others . . . at the desire of General Arnold." Smith, before he went to the *Vulture*, understood that Arnold hoped to get intelligence from Colonel Robinson in return for Arnold's assistance in obtaining the safety of Robinson's estate.

Thus far Smith had been offering what Hamilton called his "Confession," his own statement of his doings. He was pressed to say how he could give credence to Arnold's commission to him. Since Robinson came up in a king's vessel, necessarily with the knowledge of Sir Henry Clinton, and was willing to entrust his business to a third person (Anderson), his errand "must have been for promoting the interests of the enemy." "Mr. Smith," Hamilton testified, "appeared at first a good deal embarrassed, but finally replied that he acted from the perfect confidence he had in General Arnold, whose rank and services to the country would not suffer him to entertain the least suspicion of his being capable of entering into a treasonable combination." Asked whether the person he brought on shore was dressed in a uniform, Smith answered that "he could not perfectly distinguish whether he wore a uniform or not, but that he had on a red coat, with a blue surtout" (overcoat). Smith acknowledged "that he had carried a pass on board the *Vulture*, for John Anderson from General Arnold." Hamilton testified that "this

John Anderson proves to be Major Andre, adjutant-general of the British army."

At his trial Smith said that he did not board the *Vulture* with the privity of the officers. Hamilton's recollection was that Smith, when first interrogated by Washington, said he was challenged by the watch, but that he "complained of no rude treatment by the other officers," who knew he had business with Colonel Robinson, and were likewise acquainted with John Anderson whom he took off. Smith declared he had told earlier how he came to supply Anderson (André) with a civilian cloak to go over his uniform. This was because Arnold explained that Anderson "was only a merchant, and from pride had borrowed a [military] coat from an officer in New York." Hamilton had no recollection of Smith's having given this reason for furnishing André with his disguise. (André, a British officer within the American lines, not under a flag of truce, was vulnerable in any case. When he donned Smith's civilian cloak to hide his uniform, he proclaimed himself a spy, that is, if he were stopped and searched.)

Smith appealed to Hamilton: "Was not my character in New York always esteemed as a warm friend to the cause of America, before we quit the city, as far as came to your knowledge?" Hamilton replied that many persons esteemed Smith "as a zealot on the popular side"; there were doubts of him because of his Loyalist family, but not from Smith's own political conduct. Smith was eager to establish through Hamilton that he had shown much surprise at learning from Washington that Arnold had gone off to the enemy, and that the person Smith brought on shore was the adjutant general of the British army. But Hamilton did not "exactly recollect [Smith's] appearance at the time."

The same morning that Smith was brought to Robinson's, Hamilton paid another visit to Mrs. Arnold; she was more composed than the day before, but could not be dissuaded from her fear that "the resentment of her country would fall upon her (who is only unfortunate) for the guilt of her husband. . . . Her sufferings were so eloquent that I wished myself her brother, to have a right to become her defender."

Hamilton, for Washington's signature, wrote Governor George Clinton details of Arnold's plot, and similarly gave the distressing news to General Rochambeau. Two days later he accompanied the commander in chief to Tappan, New York. There he wrote, at Washington's direction, to Brigadier General Wayne, who was near Haverstraw, to send a party of fifty men as additional guards for the prisoners, André and Smith, who were being brought from Robinson's house to headquarters at Tappan.

Those were the events to the extent that they became known to Hamilton. By the time he wrote his narrative for John Laurens, a fortnight later, he was able to relate what has thus far been omitted. Joshua Hett Smith, with some difficulty, persuaded two farm hands, the Cahoon (or Colquhoun) brothers to row him to the *Vulture* to fetch, as he thought, Colonel Robinson, though it was André, pretending to be John Anderson, whom he brought off. Smith carried no flag of truce; the trip was secret, at night, and in silence, the oars muffled with sheepskins. The party landed at the foot of Long Clove mountain, two miles below Haverstraw, near where Arnold said he would be waiting with a spare horse. Smith's passenger climbed the bank and was for some time in conversation with Arnold in the dense growth of firs. When André was ready to return, the boatmen, already tired and irked by the long delay, refused to row him back. Dawn was approaching, and they were afraid of attack by American guard boats if they approached the British warship in daylight. Arnold and André therefore rode, passing an American picket, to Smith's house, where they remained through the day. Without Arnold's knowledge the commanding officer at Verplanck's Point had run out a couple of fieldpieces and fired on the *Vulture*, hitting her hull "between wind and water," and tearing her rigging. She dropped down the river out of range, so far that André could not be sent aboard her the second night.

André and Arnold could not risk staying any longer at Smith's house. Arnold insisted that André should cross the river by King's Ferry, from nearby Stony Point, and return to New York by land. This necessitated his disguise. Since he was within the American lines, André "remonstrated warmly against this new and dangerous expedient," but "at length reluctantly yielded," when Smith, at Arnold's direction, furnished a loose coat to cover his uniform. Smith accompanied André across the ferry and south to Crompond. Here a militia officer let them pass; to avert any suspicion, they accepted the officer's suggestion that they spend the remainder of the night at a farmhouse. Before sunrise they started again and rode seven miles before breakfast. A little beyond Pine's Bridge over Croton River Smith turned back. André, persuaded that he was on a road less haunted than others by parties of American irregulars, had got as far as Tarrytown "when he was taken up by three militia men, who rushed out of the woods and seized his horse."

Hamilton described the famous occurrence that exploded the plot. "At this critical moment [André's] presence of mind forsook him. Instead of producing his pass which would have extricated him from our parties and could have done him no harm with his own, he asked the militia men, if they were of the *upper* or *lower* party. . . ." (In this neutral district small bands of patriot "Skinners" and Loyalist "Cowboys," bent as much on booty as on duty, stopped travelers. Though the groups sometimes worked in collusion, the Skinners generally operated north of Croton and hence were known as the upper party, while the Cowboys operated south of that point and were known as the lower party. The three who pounced on André were Skinners, operating outside their usual territory.)

The militiamen replied they were of the lower party; upon which he told them he was a British officer and pressed them not to detain him, as he was upon urgent business. This confession removed all doubt; and it was in vain he afterwards produced his pass. He was instantly forced off to a place of greater security; where after a careful search there were found concealed in the feet of his stockings several papers of importance delivered to him by Arnold. . . . He tempted [his captors] with the offer of his watch, his horse and any sum of money they should name. They rejected his offers with indignation; and the gold, that could seduce a man high in the esteem and confidence of his country . . . had no charm for three simple peasants, leaning only on their virtue and an honest sense of their duty. While Arnold is handed down with execration to future times, posterity will repeat with reverence the names of Van Wart, Paulding and Williams! [1]

During the week that André, after several moves, was imprisoned at Tappan, [2] Hamilton solicitously visited him several times, and was the bearer of his request to General Washington to be allowed to send an open letter to Sir Henry Clinton. He used to Hamilton substantially the words Hamilton wrote to his chief:

I foresee my fate (said he) and though I pretend not to play the hero, or to be indifferent about life; yet I am reconciled to whatever may happen, conscious that misfortune, not guilt, has brought it upon me. There is only one thing that disturbs my tranquillity—Sir Henry Clinton had been too good to me . . . I am bound to him by too many obligations and love him too well to bear the thought, that he should reproach himself . . . on the supposition of my having conceived myself obliged by his instructions to run the risk I did. I would not for the world leave a sting in his mind. . . .

André burst into tears, but controlled himself to add, "I wish to . . . assure him, I . . . submitted to a necessity imposed upon me as contrary to my own inclination as to his orders."

A special sympathy immediately sprang up between the aide of the American commander and the doomed British adjutant. They were much of an age and of similar deportment and tal-

---

[1] A monument to Isaac Van Wart, John Paulding, and David Williams now stands on the site of André's capture. Later, as a reward, they were given André's horse, watch, and money.

[2] The stone house, then an inn, is yet standing, as is the dwelling that was Washington's headquarters. Both are in the Dutch style.

ents. Hamilton's description of him helped to fix André in the compassionate memory of his enemies: "To an excellent understanding well improved by education . . . he united a peculiar elegance of mind and manners, and the advantage of a pleasing person. . . . His sentiments were elevated, and inspired esteem; they had a softness that conciliated affection. His elocution was handsome; his address easy, polite and insinuating. By his merit he had acquired the unlimited confidence of his general."

Surely Hamilton was among the American officers who drew the captive's thanks for courtesies shown him. Lafayette remembered that "Col. Hamilton . . . was one of those who were daily searching for some way to save him." It is not known whether Hamilton had a part in prompting an offer of Washington to Sir Henry Clinton to release André in return for Arnold. Captain Aaron Ogden, at Tappan, was ordered to headquarters at eight o'clock the morning of September 30, 1780. He was met by Washington alone, who gave him a packet addressed to Sir Henry Clinton. Ogden took the packet under a flag of truce to Paulus Hook (Jersey City), the nearest enemy post, intentionally planning his arrival so late in the evening that he had to spend the night. In order to speed the message on to Clinton, Ogden intimated the nature of the dispatch to the post commander. However, that officer returned in two hours from British headquarters with the message "that a deserter was never given up," and that Captain Ogden's horse would be ready for him in the morning. This abortive attempt may have been inspired by the conjecture of some that, as Hamilton said, "Arnold had taken his measures in such a manner, that if the interview had been discovered in the act it might have been in his power to sacrifice André to his own security. This surmise of double treachery made them imagine Clinton might be induced to give up Arnold for André."

Several historians have attributed to Hamilton an appeal to Clinton to this effect. The letter is dated September 30, 1780, and is signed "A B." It recites that

Major André . . . was captured in such a way as will according to the laws of war justly affect his life. Though an enemy his virtues and his accomplishments are admired. Perhaps he might be released for General Arnold, delivered up without restriction or condition . . . . Arnold appears to have been the guilty author of the mischief, and ought more properly to be the victim, as there is great reason to believe he meditated a double treachery, and had arranged . . . that if discovered in the first instance, he might have it in his power to sacrifice Major André to his own safety.

And in a postscript, "No time is to be lost."

The letter was endorsed by Sir Henry Clinton in a sketchy fashion: "Hamilton Was [or possibly "W's," meaning Washington's] aide de camp[;] received after A [André's] death."

Lieutenant Colonel John Graves Simcoe, commander of the Queen's Rangers, who had appealed to Henry Lee in André's behalf, recorded that "Amongst some letters which passed [from American to British headquarters] on this unfortunate event, a paper was slid in without signature, but in the handwriting of Hamilton, Washington's secretary, saying that the only way to save André was to give up Arnold." If this paper was "slid in" it may have been on October 1, when Clinton sent commissioners in the *Greyhound* to Dobbs Ferry to make an oral plea to General Washington to rescind André's death sentence. When the vessel anchored off Corbet's Point, the commissioners—Lieutenant General James Robertson, Chief Justice William Smith, and Lieutenant Governor Andrew Elliott—were informed that General Nathanael Greene was present to receive General Robertson and his aide, but that the others should not land.

Robertson, when he returned to the *Greyhound,* wrote Clinton of his exchanges with Greene. "He said that there was no treating about Spies. I said no Military Casuist in Europe would call André Spy, and I would suffer Death myself if Monsieur Rochambault or General Knyphausen would call him by that Name." Greene declared "the Army must be satisfied by seeing Spies executed—but there was one thing would satisfy them—they expected if André was set free, Arnold should be given up. This I answered with a Look only, which threw Greene into Confusion. I am persuaded André will not be hurt."

William Smith, remaining on the vessel, wrote that "A long Conference ensued, while Murray walked elsewhere with Hamilton[,] Washington['s] Aid de Camp & two other Rebel officers." Perhaps during this stroll the letter was given to Murray, General Robertson's aide, and so reached Clinton. That would explain how, in spite of its anonymous signature, the missive was identified by the British as Hamilton's.

If Hamilton penned the disputed letter, as Clinton and Simcoe supposed, he masked his hand, for the writing differs markedly from his familiar script. He later told Laurens that "a Gentleman [not himself, for he spurned to do it] took occasion to suggest this expedient" (exchange for Arnold) to André, "as a thing that might be proposed by him. He declined it. The moment he had been capable of so much frailty, I should have ceased to esteem him." However, the honorable refusal of André did not impugn the proposition if advanced by another, as indeed it was advanced by Greene on Washington's authority, and seemingly also in the message carried by Ogden to British headquarters. As will have been noticed, some of the language of the disputed letter is similar to the phraseology that Hamilton used when writing to Laurens. Also, in a known instance, in an exceedingly private communication with James Reynolds, Hamilton disguised his handwriting. But these clues are not conclusive, and the authorship of the letter remains a mystery.

Hamilton drafted Washington's letter (September 29, 1780) to the board of general officers with instructions for the trial of André and decision on his punishment. The prisoner, Hamilton said, "frankly confessed all the facts relating to himself; and upon his confession without the trouble of examining a witness, the Board made their report." This was that, in view of the secrecy and deception he practiced within American posts, "Major André, Adjutant General of the British army, ought to be considered as a spy from the enemy; and that, agreeable to the law and usage of nations . . . he ought to suffer death."

Hamilton "urged a compliance with André's request to be shot [instead of hanged] and I do not think it would have had an ill effect . . . When André's tale comes to be told, and present resentment is over, the refusing him the privilege of choosing the manner of death will be branded with too much obduracy." No answer was made to André's entreaty. This was "to spare him the sensations, which a certain knowledge of the intended mode would inflict."

The British position, maintaining André's innocence, was several times stated, most explicitly by Sir Henry Clinton in a letter to General Washington on October 4, 1780, after the American commander in chief had informed him of the decision of the court-martial. "I will . . . very freely declare my Sentiments . . . which positively are that under no Description Major André can be considered as a Spy; nor by any Usage of Nations at War, or the Custom of Armies, can be treated as such." Clinton asserted that André went north at the request of Arnold,

at that Time in the American Service and Commanding Officer at West Point. A Flag of Truce was sent to receive Major André, with which he went on shore and met Major General Arnold. To this Period he was acting under my immediate Orders, as a Military Man. What Happened after was from the entire Direction and positive Orders of Major General Arnold, your Officer Commanding at West Point. . . . Major André can merely be considered as a Messenger and not as a Spy.

This was no better than Arnold's application to Washington for André's release, in hope that "the respect due to Flags and the Law of Nations may be . . . understood and observed."

Hamilton condemned such sophistry:

Nothing could have been more frivolous than the plea which was used. The fact was that besides the time, manner, object of the interview, change of dress, and other circumstances, there was not a single formality customary with flaggs and the passport was not to Major André, but to Mr. Anderson. But had there been, on the contrary, all the formalities, it would be an abuse of language to say, that the sanction of a flag for corrupting an officer to betray his trust ought to be respected. So unjustifiable a purpose would not only destroy its validity but make it an aggravation.

And further, "André himself has answered the argument by ridiculing . . . the idea in his examination before the board of officers. It was a weakness to urge it."

Though the "maxims and practices of war are the satire of human nature" and "countenance almost every species of seduction as well as violence," Hamilton could not forgive André for his willingness "to prostitute a flag."

Apparently Hamilton would have liked to see André escape punishment. Lines in a letter to Elizabeth Schuyler (October 2, 1780) became a memorial to him: "Poor André suffers to-day. Every thing that is amiable in virtue, in fortitude, in delicate sentiment, and accomplished manners, pleads for him; but hardhearted policy calls for a sacrifice. He must die . . . ." And elsewhere Hamilton said, "There was in truth no way of saving him. Arnold or he must have been the victim; the former was out of our power."

André's execution, on a hilltop a few hundred yards from his place of confinement, was described by Hamilton, but he did not witness it, as Washington and his staff were not present. Hamilton testified that day at the trial of Joshua Hett Smith, who at length was acquitted for lack of evidence "of his being privy to . . . Arnold's . . . traitorous . . . designs." After release by the military he was arrested by the civil authorities, escaped confinement, and went to the British in New York. As a necessary formality, Varick and Franks, Arnold's aides, were investigated to discover whether they had guilty knowledge of Arnold's plot. They were cleared. Hamilton was among those making deposition of Varick's innocence; Varick was thereafter assigned to supervise the transcribing of Washington's military papers.

Peggy Shippen Arnold was escorted to her family in Philadelphia by Major Franks. At Robinson's house she received every consideration from Washington and his staff, who then had no suspicion of what later appeared. When Sir Henry Clinton's papers were available, it was learned that some of Arnold's guilty correspondence had passed through her hands. In light of her complicity, her delay of an hour after Arnold's flight before beginning her convulsive ravings was to allow her husband time to escape.

The full extent of Arnold's duplicity was not revealed until Sir Henry Clinton's papers were explored a century and a half later. These papers disclosed that a full eighteen months before the climax, Arnold had informed Clinton that he wanted to quit the American cause, join the British, and, for a price, render signal service to the British. His profession of motives of principle was canceled by his stipulation that he must profit by his treason. Arnold said he was irked because other major generals were advanced ahead of him, but one wonders whether any rewards would have made him honest. Under assumed names and by devious means he revealed American military operations to British headquarters.

In July 1779 Arnold was told the account he had given to Clinton of Sullivan's expedition against the Indians was acceptable; however, it "has but a very indirect influence here and does not enable us to distress or counteract." Later that month André notified Arnold that Clinton preferred "an accurate plan of West Point, with the new roads . . . what . . . gun Boats . . . are in the North River . . . Sketches or descriptions of Harbours to the Eastward which might be attacked and where Stores and Shipping might be destroyed." Not until a year after, when Arnold had the prospect of the command on the Hudson, could he propose, "If I point out a plan of cooperation by which S[ir] H[enry] shall possess himself of West Point, the Garrison, &c., &c., &c. twenty thousand pounds Sterling I think will be a cheap purchase for an object of so much importance."

The importance to the British was unquestioned. A prearranged, successful "attack" there would undo plans of Washington and Rochambeau for an assault on New York, would capture four thousand men, valuable stores, and perhaps finish off the war. But for this coup Clinton must be certain of Arnold's identity, and he therefore acceded to Arnold's demand that Major André be sent to him for concert of plans. (Arnold had corresponded with British headquarters for eighteen months, but through intermediaries.) Clinton would have preferred to send General William Phillips, but Phillips was a prisoner of the Americans on parole. Clinton's disappointment at failure of the plot was embittered by the fate of André. Clinton unjustly blamed Washington personally for putting André "to a most ignominious death," ignoring the fact that the British had visited the same on Nathan Hale.

11

Petulant Departure

 In the autumn of 1780 the lull, not to say depression, in America's military outlook made Alexander Hamilton again restless for a change of scene from deskwork at headquarters. Charleston had been in enemy hands for six months, as had Savannah, despite the attempt a year earlier by D'Estaing and Lincoln to retake it. Plans for the campaign of 1781 had not taken shape. As immurement in winter quarters approached, Hamilton reflected on the advancement of friends who held field commands.

Then the ever-enterprising Lafayette revived the idea of attacking New York, which would stimulate French support of the American cause. Fort Washington, so disastrously lost four years before, would be the first object of assault. Hamilton was obliged to answer, for Washington, that the attempt was beyond the army's means. Soon the project was resumed in different guise. Hamilton, Lafayette, and Tilghman spent nights in concerting plans. Boats with muffled oars would land a thousand men on Staten Island. Hamilton was in no way deterred because back in January 1780 he had crossed to Staten Island on the ice with Lord Stirling, who had been commanding more than twice as many troops, only to have the expedition repulsed to the mainland.

Now, however, Washington so far consented as to direct Lafayette to consult with Lieutenant Colonel Jean Baptiste Gouvion, the engineer, who proved to be "charmed with the beauty
and propriety of the thing." Hamilton, if Washington approved,
was to share in the attack, heading two hundred men. "Tomorrow"—that would be November 23, 1780—Lafayette wrote,
"we must carry your private affair. Show me your letter [to
Washington] before you give it." Together they worked out the
request. Hamilton reminded the general that he had twice before been refused opportunities for combat command. A year
previously, when his application to go to the south had been
denied, Washington had promised to gratify his ambition when
better opportunity presented. In the brief adventure to Staten Island he had had no command. The present undertaking was
not liable to old objections. His small body of men, a detachment from several corps, would not be beyond his rank. Headquarters work would not suffer, for he was to be absent anyhow, to be married. (Evidently his intended bride could wait
to be embraced, while he smote the British.) He hoped to as-
sail Bayard's Hill, the fortification on lower Manhattan
whence he had retreated after the battle of Long Island. If the
Staten Island feint brought him too late for Bayard's, he wished
to be put in the van of another attack. He put his plea in writing in order to avoid the possible embarrassment of being turned
down in a personal interview. The general did not have to refuse him, for the whole scheme was suddenly abandoned.

Hamilton's friends Lafayette, Greene, and John Laurens did
not forget his ambition to be excused from headquarters, and
sought his appointment to honorific official posts.

General Greene observed to the commander in chief that if
Colonel Alexander Scammell chose to return to his regiment, "a
new adjutant-general will be necessary; and I . . . suggest the
propriety of giving this appointment to Colonel Hamilton."
Greene knew Washington's dependence on his principal aide at
his elbow, and ventured "His services may not be less important

. . . in your family business, if he only employs a deputy extraordinary." Perhaps Washington would have fallen in with this proposal, but he had to reply that "without knowing Colo. Hamilton ever had an eye to the office of Adjt. General," he had already recommended Brigadier General Edward Hand for the post. Anyhow, the adjutant general took rank of the subinspectors, the assistants of Inspector-General Steuben, and full colonels among these would object if a lieutenant colonel were put over them. Lafayette, to Washington, praised both Hand and William Stephens Smith, his own adjutant, but urged that Hamilton "would suit better than any other." Hamilton's knowledge of the commander in chief's arrangements, his facility in French (important when the two armies operated together), and "his uncommon abilities" peculiarly fitted him. Since the adjutant general "ought allwais to be with the commander in chief," Hamilton would remain in the general's official family. However, Lafayette wrote Hamilton, "this curs'd way of a letter you have insisted upon has been the Cause of my miscarrying." Gouvion had tried to deliver Lafayette's letter to Washington at New Windsor, but found the general gone to Morristown, where "another misfortune threw Hand in his way; and remembering your advice . . . he hastened to make him the proposition, and in consequence . . . wrote his letter to Congress." Then Lafayette went directly to Washington and offered to send an express to recover the recommendation of Hand, but the general, especially as Hamilton had supported the nomination of Hand, let the matter be.

Another and more consequential assignment for Hamilton loomed, as special minister to France to secure desperately needed assistance. Hamilton had proposed Lafayette for this critical mission, which might be decisive for the American cause. But the marquis preferred field command, opposing Cornwallis in Virginia. Lafayette, returning the compliment, hurried to Philadelphia, where he busied himself in an effort to have Congress name Hamilton the envoy. "I have already spoken to many members," he reported. Lafayette said he was encouraged by the reception of his recommendation, and that he would spend two more days "in paying visits." If Hamilton were selected, Lafayette said he would send for him by express, and hasten him to France with "many private letters." John Laurens, too, diligently lobbied for Hamilton's appointment. He himself was favored, but fended off the election. More than a year earlier he had declined being named secretary of the legation in Paris; he did not wish to desert active service at home until Savannah, where he had fought fiercely, had been retrieved. Now he begged that Hamilton be chosen as "superiorily qualified in every respect" to solicit the French court. "But, unfortunately for America," Laurens wrote to Washington, "Colonel Hamilton was not sufficiently known to Congress to unite their suffrages in his favor." Laurens, "assured that there remained no . . . alternative than the total failure of the business," was induced to renounce participation in the southern campaign, and was unanimously elected special minister to France, December 11, 1780.

Either young soldier was eligible "for the special purpose of representing the present state of our affairs and soliciting the necessary succours." Both, as aides of Washington, intimately understood the military posture. Both were friends of the French officers in America, were personable, and spoke French fluently. John Laurens, as son of the recent president of Congress—who was at that time a British prisoner in the Tower of London [1]— enjoyed a family prestige that Hamilton did not possess.[2] Laurens had been educated in Europe, which gave him prior ac-

---

[1] John Laurens had seen his father off (mid-August 1780) as minister to Holland to borrow money and negotiate a commercial treaty; the small vessel was captured in September on the Newfoundland banks by the British armed ship *Vestal*. Henry Laurens' imprisonment lasted from October 1780 through the year 1781, when he was released on bail and some months later was exchanged for Lord Cornwallis.

[2] However, within days after this, Hamilton married the daughter of General Philip Schuyler.

quaintance there. He had been more in political circles in America than had Hamilton, and was one year older. Congress made no mistake in choosing John Laurens. Hamilton was glad to see his friend trusted and honored.

While John Laurens was waiting for a ship—he was not able to sail until February 13, 1781, in the *Alliance*, under the famous captain, later commodore, John Barry—it was suggested that General Washington himself furnish the envoy with a letter to be presented to the French ministers, explaining the reasons for his mission. Lafayette agreed that this would carry special weight. Hamilton prepared the letter, and Washington copied it without change, to give it the authenticity of his own hand. Hamilton's presentation has been called by a knowing judge, Douglas Southall Freeman, one of the finest letters of the Revolutionary period. It illustrates the conviction that candor, laying all the cards on the table, constitutes high diplomacy. The portrayal of this country's economic disabilities and the means of their removal, while perfectly endorsed by Washington, better originated with Hamilton. A decade later, in the treasury, he acted on the expedients now outlined for the French authorities.

In five years of war, Hamilton began, the country had exceeded its natural capacities. While mistakes had been made in the finances, the decay of public credit was due primarily to lack of wealth, or of funds with which to redeem the paper money. The paper currency having sunk into contempt, efforts to support the army by direct collection of food and forage had proved unworkable. Domestic loans yielded little, while the few men of means chose to invest more profitably elsewhere. The distresses of the army required speedy relief or disaster would follow. He referred to recent mutinies; the worst, in the Pennsylvania line at Morristown, had happened January 1, 1780, only a fortnight earlier. Burdens of the struggle made the people wonder whether they were not enduring oppression from their own government.

This situation, said Hamilton, demanded "an immediate, ample and efficacious succour of money; . . . enough to be a foundation for substantial arrangements of finance, to revive public credit and give vigor to future operations." The coming campaign must deliver a fatal blow to the enemy, or American resistance was finished. The plain implication was that France must salvage all that was furnished before, by furnishing more now. "Next to a loan of money a constant naval superiority on these coasts is the object most interesting." A cordon of French warships would cut off the enemy's supplies from Europe and permit the allies to assume the offensive.

France must not conclude that American determination for independence was extinguished; nor were material resources to achieve success exhausted. Patriot fatigue could be banished by generous, timely assistance from outside. The new nation was a good risk. Americans could repay, for "Our debts are hitherto small. The vast . . . tracts of unlocated lands, the variety and fertility of soils; the advantages . . . we possess for commerce, insure to this country a rapid advancement in population and prosperity and a certainty, its independence being established, of redeeming in a short term of years, the comparatively inconsiderable debts it may . . . contract." He ended on this reassuring note.

Though John Laurens was accustomed to the rules of polite society, he was not prepared for the delays and indirections of diplomacy in a European court. His impatience was born also of the urgency of his mission. However, in the end Laurens was furnished most that he sought. With half the amount put at his disposal, he freighted four vessels with war supplies, three of which reached America safely. In addition he secured French guarantee of a loan of 10 million livres to be negotiated in Holland. Of even greater consequence, Laurens obtained the ordering of de Grasse's splendid fleet to the American coast, which made possible the victory at Yorktown. Laurens, after an impeded voyage, reached Boston August 25, 1781, bringing

2,500,224 livres, 18 sous (every sou counted!) in silver, say $500,000.

Hamilton's service in Washington's military family had lasted for almost four years of daily association with the commander in chief when their companionship was temporarily interrupted in mid-February 1781. The occasion was a trifling incident which provoked Hamilton to act on accumulated dissatisfaction with his station at headquarters. Aside from a momentary outburst by Washington, which he at once repented, the fault was wholly Hamilton's.

Knowledge of what happened is almost entirely from Hamilton's self-justifying account in his letter to his father-in-law, Philip Schuyler. Commander in chief and aide passed each other on the upper floor of headquarters at New Windsor.

He told me he wanted to speak to me [Hamilton related] I answered that I would wait upon him immediately. I went below, and delivered Mr. Tilghman a letter . . . of a pressing . . . nature. Returning to the General, I was stopped on the way by the Marquis de La Fayette, and we conversed together about a minute on a matter of business. He can testify how impatient I was to get back, and that I left him in a manner which, but for our intimacy, would have been more than abrupt. Instead of finding the General, as is usual, in his room, I met him at the head of the stairs, where, accosting me in an angry tone, "Colonel Hamilton," said he, "you have kept me waiting . . . these ten minutes. I must tell you, sir, you treat me with disrespect." I replied, without petulancy, but with decision: "I am not conscious of it, sir; but because you have thought it necessary to tell me so, we part." "Very well, sir," said he, "if it be your choice," or something to that effect, and we separated. I sincerely believe my absence, which gave so much umbrage, did not last two minutes.

Characteristically, Washington within the hour sent Tilghman, "assuring me of his great confidence in my abilities, integrity, usefulness, etc., and of his desire, in a candid conversation, to heal a difference which could not have happened but in a moment of passion." Now was the instant for the aide to respond to this magnanimous invitation with his own apology,

223

which indeed should have been offered first. Instead, still smarting, he gave Tilghman the return message that his resolve was fixed, and he begged to be excused from a mutually disagreeable interview. He would not inconvenience Washington's business until absent aides returned, and promised in the meantime not to refer to the episode. The general let it rest at that, with thanks for proffered interim assistance.

Anxiety and fatigue had led to Washington's sudden reproof and Hamilton's unlucky retort. They had worked to a late hour the night before on dispatches to be forwarded "very early in the morning" to Rochambeau and other French officers at Newport. Would cooperation of allies bring rescue from alarming portents in the patriot effort? The treasury was empty, troops had mutinied, recruits came in slowly, the traitor Arnold was ravaging Virginia of supplies desperately required by Greene in the Carolinas.

Besides, for Hamilton's part, he had been disappointed in two applications for field command, and proposals for his appointment to other posts had gone awry. Hamilton explained to Schuyler that he had "always disliked the office of an aid-de-camp as having in it a kind of personal dependence," which made him, early in the war, refuse invitations of two major generals. It was only his esteem for Washington's character which "overcame my scruples." This much was understandable, but he went on unworthily: "It was not long before I discovered he was neither remarkable for delicacy nor good temper, which revived my former aversion to the station . . . and it has been increasing ever since." For three years past, "I have felt no friendship for him and have professed none," plainly preferring "to stand rather upon a footing of military confidence than of private attachment." This seems to have been contrary to his behavior, but Hamilton did worse in supposing that his "pride of . . . temper" hurt Washington's self-esteem. If this were true, Hamilton accused himself by putting it in words. Actually, Washington's appreciation of Hamilton, during the war and atterward in the national government, denies the imputation. Biographers of Washington have theorized that the general, with no son of his own, gave his paternal solicitude to Lafayette. By all signs, Hamilton had his share of it. Also, in his present angry mood, no sooner had Hamilton belittled his patron than he in effect, though grudgingly, repaired his error. "The General," he went on to Schuyler, "is a very honest man. His competitors have slender abilities, and less integrity. His popularity has often been essential to the safety of America, and is still of great importance to it . . . . I think it is necessary he should be supported." He hoped that his own alienation would not impair Schuyler's friendship for Washington.

Washington "complied religiously" with Hamilton's expressed wish that neither should tell others of the rift between them, and found it "extraordinary" that his aide "was communicating it himself." That Hamilton confided in his wife, in her father, General Schuyler, and in Lafayette is understandable. Later Hamilton wrote of it briefly to General Greene, and Major François Louis Fleury, and doubtless others knew of the impending separation. Schuyler earnestly begged Hamilton not to quit his post, especially since he assisted Washington as interpreter to the French officers and minister. Lafayette went further and interceded with Washington in efforts to heal the breach. Doubtless Tench Tilghman also acted as intermediary between commander and aide. Mrs. Hamilton, with perfect breeding, behaved outwardly as though nothing had happened; she "served . . . Tea with much grace" to Washington, Knox, and the headquarters aides when the special guest was Baron Jean von Closen, who had come with letters from the French allies at Newport.

Hamilton in no way relaxed his diligence in the ten weeks following the quarrel that he remained as Washington's aide. After his petulant break at New Windsor on February 16, 1781, and his refusal to be mollified, he reported to his father-in-law that he was "no longer a member of the General's family."

However, he said he had assured the commander in chief that "I did not wish to distress him or the public business, by quitting him before he could derive other assistance by the return of some of the Gentlemen who were absent." As only he and Tilghman were at headquarters—and the latter was just recovering from illness—he would continue to serve until Humphreys and Harrison got back. For two months, until the middle of April, he helped Washington prepare for the Virginia campaign, which ended in the surrender of Cornwallis. Then he moved across the Hudson to DePeyster's Point (adjacent to Beacon), where his wife joined him. A fortnight later he was summoned back to New Windsor to assist Washington in a letter of much delicacy, which required a conference beforehand. After his tiff with Washington he had said, "I was persuaded that when once that nice barrier, which marked the boundaries of what we owed to each other, should be thrown down, it might be propped again, but could never be restored." Though Hamilton (not Washington) was nursing a grudge in this interval, his forecast for the longer future was in error.

At Washington's order Hamilton drew up recommendations for revising punishments in the army and prescribing practices of furlough and discharge intended to reduce desertions. The main point was that the punishments were too harsh and therefore disciplinary measures were seldom successfully applied. The death penalty was often invoked where a hundred lashes, the maximum number then authorized, were judged insufficient for certain crimes. But capital sentences, thus imposed, were usually rescinded, and this mercy, it was believed, tempted more serious infractions. Five hundred lashes, though extended over a period, would be savagery. Hamilton suggested avoiding resort to such a penalty by putting the guilty on public works. Deserters could be transferred to the navy, where they would have less opportunity to run away from their duty. Other methods of preventing desertion were proposed. Hamilton was surely mindful that brutal corrections had been complained of by Washington's critics in the Conway cabal. Congress referred the report to a committee.

In June 1782, when Hamilton had left active service, he was still on the theme of mercy. He was one who intervened to cancel the threatened execution of young Charles Asgill, whose plight resulted from the capture and hanging by Loyalists of Captain Joshua Huddy in New Jersey. Washington, his council of officers, and Congress held that the charge against Huddy was false, and they called on Sir Henry Clinton (and afterward Sir Guy Carleton) to surrender Captain Lippincott, leader of the guilty party. Meantime Washington ordered that a British captain in American hands be chosen by lot and sent to headquarters as a hostage. Asgill, entirely innocent, provoked the more pity because he was a mere boy, of titled family and excellent prospects. When the British, instead of giving up Lippincott, acquitted him, Captain Asgill was appointed for death.

Washington seemed obdurate against all remonstrances. Through General Knox, Hamilton urged on Washington the impolicy of the retaliatory execution; in Europe it would be condemned as "wanton and unnecessary," and "unfavorable to the General's character." The war was practically won, no further provocation was likely to happen; why close the chapter with an act of inhumanity? Hamilton's warning of the ill effect on America's allies was justified when Lady Asgill appealed to the king and queen of France to save her son. Count Charles Gravier Vergennes, the French foreign minister, expressed the royal entreaty to Washington, Congress found a face-saving formula, and the doomed youth was liberated.

Of critical importance, Hamilton was at his chief's side in early March 1781 on the return visit to Rochambeau and Destouches in Rhode Island. On the result might hang the success of operations in the southern quarter. Admiral Le Bardeur de Tilly had sailed from Newport three weeks before with a ship and two frigates, but this proved too small a force to dislodge Benedict Arnold—now a brigadier general in the British army

—from Portsmouth, Virginia. At Washington's first stop, near the Connecticut line, he learned that Admiral Destouches planned to renew the attempt against Arnold with the whole French fleet and eleven hundred troops. Hamilton sent ahead the American commander's thanks by express. If the new French expedition hastened, it might reach the Chesapeake before the British Admiral Marriot Arbuthnot could arrive from Gardiner's Bay. In that event, Lafayette and Steuben, already watching Arnold, would hopefully be able, with naval support, to rout and capture the traitor. More might be accomplished than clearing the enemy from Virginia. Cornwallis, following the capture of Charleston in May 1780, was in the midst of his campaign to subjugate the whole region from Georgia to Pennsylvania. If with French cooperation they could dispose of Arnold, Lafayette and Steuben could move into North Carolina to "intercept . . . Cornwallis and relieve General Greene and the Southern States."

When Washington's party arrived on the heels of this message, Hamilton was surely his interpreter in conferences at the French headquarters. While Destouches was preparing his expedition, Washington reviewed the French troops and received a glowing address from the citizens of Newport, to which Hamilton penned Washington's appreciative response. More than a personal acknowledgment, it spoke official gratitude to the French forces and nation, and promised the "antient town" restoration of the damages it suffered during enemy occupation. On March 8 he rode with the commander in chief and his hosts to the point to see Destouches' fleet sail before a fair wind. Thereafter Hamilton must have sped to his wife and the Schuylers at Albany; Washington's return route to his "dreary quarters at New Windsor" was out of Hamilton's way, and his letters were written by himself or by Tilghman.

When the "old Secretary," Colonel Robert H. Harrison, who had resigned to be chief justice of Maryland, returned to New Windsor to make his farewells March 23, Hamilton was still in

Albany. A fortnight later, however, he returned to headquarters for his final service as aide to Washington. He wrote for the general about exchange of prisoners. He conveyed also the shortage of available commands; even Lafayette, if he chose to leave Virginia, would probably not receive a new field assignment. And Hamilton must have realized that this did not bode well for his own chances of receiving a field command. He inquired of Greene whether there were any post for him in the southern army, for he would "hate to be nominally a soldier." He also wrote two secret letters for Washington to Lafayette, dated April 21 and 22, in which the commander in chief revealed that probably "the weight of the war this campaign will be in the Southern states, and it will become my duty to go there in person . . . . The danger to the Southern states is immediate and pressing; it is our duty to give them support." Hitherto, Washington had taken great pains to conceal this fact. For nearly a year, Washington told Noah Webster afterward, he had "determined . . . to . . . cause it to be believed . . . that New York was the destined place of attack," while actually his design was against the British either in Virginia or at Charleston.

Had Hamilton accompanied Washington back from Newport to New Windsor, he could not have saved his superior from an embarrassing slur on the cooperation of the French. In a private letter on March 28, 1781, to Lund Washington, his kinsman and manager of his Mount Vernon estate, the commander in chief asserted that if Destouches had dispatched his fleet "when I first proposed it to them; the destruction of Arnold's Corps would then have been inevitable before the British fleet could have . . . put to Sea. Instead of this the small squadron . . . was sent, and could not, as I foretold, do anything without a Land force at Portsmouth." This letter, with its sour postmortem reproach, unluckily was intercepted by the enemy [3] and

---

[3] It could not have been Washington's best day. One letter in the packet intercepted, to Governor Benjamin Harrison of Virginia, revealed military plans concerted with Rochambeau.

promptly "hung up in Rivington's Gazette" in New York. Lafayette, a special link between the Americans and their allies, while on his way to Virginia learned of Washington's lapse. "A letter from you relating to the delays of the French makes a great noise at Philadelphia. Indeed it gives me pain on many political accounts."

Washington was almost never indiscreet; Hamilton frequently was. But now the younger man, who had so recently given his superior a sample of his own impulsiveness, was haled to help compose an apology. Other skillful aides at headquarters (Humphreys and Tilghman) wrote a half-dozen letters for Washington that day—actually including one, of a routine nature, to Rochambeau. But Hamilton had been present at the conference at Newport, could check the general's recollection of what had passed, and had long since proved his aptness with his pen. The French commander had entered a dignified protest, enclosing a copy of Washington's letter as printed. Rochambeau said that the letter, if not a forgery, was overthrown by the facts, which he then recited to show that he and Admiral Destouches had not been disobedient to Washington's wishes.

Washington's letter to Rochambeau began with a profession of "extreme pain" that any expression of his should have given offense. Perhaps, Washington suggested, the enemy had fabricated parts of the letter, which had happened frequently before, but of this he could not judge, as he had no copy of his letter to Mount Vernon. (It later appeared that the British had not altered this letter; Washington's own words were sufficiently damning for their purpose.) He candidly acknowledged to Rochambeau that "I believe the general import to be true," but pointed out that his comments were to a private friend, and declared that "No idea of the same kind has ever gone to any public body." [4] He did complain of delay in executing the enterprise, but agreed that his *formal* proposal" of a larger expedition

[4] Washington had written similarly to Philip Schuyler, Joseph Jones, William Fitzhugh, and John Armstrong.

did not reach Rochambeau until after the smaller squadron had been dispatched, though his oral suggestion was made earlier. He said that he had later learned that the cause of delay was a want of supplies for the fleet. He hoped that this explanation would persuade Rochambeau of his "sincere esteem and attachment." Washington made only two minor amendments in Hamilton's draft. Washington's regrets to Rochambeau for having offered comfort to the enemy doubtless pointed his protest, the same day, against somewhat similar conduct by his Mount Vernon manager. He had just learned from Lund Washington that the British sloop-of-war *Savage*, Captain Richard Graves, had anchored off Mount Vernon, taken seventeen slaves, and threatened pillage and arson. Lund, to prevent this, went on board with refreshments and begged release of the general's slaves. George Washington dressed down his cousin for choosing to mollify "a parcel of plundering Scoundrels." He would have preferred to hear that in consequence of Lund's refusal to parley, "they had burnt my House, and laid the Plantation in ruins."

12

A Command in the Light Corps

The antecedents of the siege of Yorktown
—where the war reached its catastrophe for the British, and
Hamilton finally had his chance for brilliant battle exploit—
were reflected in Hamilton's headquarters correspondence for
the commander in chief; not always in forward planning,
however, for unexpected events at a distance in space and time
wove themselves into the dramatic pattern. The disastrous defeat of Gates at Camden, August 16, 1780, Washington successfully struggled to overcome through the persevering campaign of
General Greene in the Carolinas against Cornwallis. Two decisive victories, at King's Mountain and Cowpens, were grateful
gifts, of which the commander in chief had the news weeks
afterward.

Cornwallis, after clearing South Carolina of major opposition, found himself in the late summer of 1780 in much the
same condition as Burgoyne in the woods of northern New
York three years previously. In a hostile interior, which afforded
him no supplies, his comrade commanders in nearby Virginia

were destroying flour but sent none to him, and he was hopelessly removed from the main British base in New York. Just as Burgoyne had sent a side expedition under Lieutenant Colonel Friedrich Baum into New England to win friends and collect horses and cattle, so Cornwallis detached Major Patrick Ferguson to rally Tories in the upcountry of the Carolinas. And as mountain militia led by Brigadier General John Stark destroyed the Hessians on the hilltop of Bennington, so the spontaneous attack of highland men of the South under their local colonels surprised and wiped out the force of Ferguson at King's Mountain.

In the extreme western part of North Carolina there are historical markers in the defiles through which mounted militia rode to the kill. Bands of a few hundred each were led by Colonel Isaac Shelby, Colonel John Sevier, Colonel William Campbell, Colonel Benjamin Cleveland, and Colonel Charles McDowell. They collected at Sycamore Flats on the Watauga River (near what is now Elizabethton, Tennessee) to catch Ferguson before he could carry his raids to their homes over the mountains. Ferguson thought he had eluded his pursuers when he encamped his 1,100 Tories on the flat top of King's Mountain (near present Gastonia, North Carolina). The steep, rocky declivities fell sixty feet to the plain. But the "backwatermen" surrounded his citadel (October 7, 1780), tied their horses in the woods, and scaled the heights. Taking advantage of every cover, with their long rifles they repelled the bayonet charges of the enemy above. From every side the frontiersmen swarmed to the summit. They were slaughtering their penned foes, but the brave Ferguson refused to give up. Then he was killed. The survivors among his men surrendered, but even then Campbell's cries to the furious attackers did not at once stop them. Of the thousand-odd Tories in the fight, 157 were killed, 163 of the worst wounded were left on the field, and all the rest, 698, were taken prisoners. The attackers lost 28 killed and 62 wounded.

The stunning victory of the patriots at King's Mountain alarmed Cornwallis, at Charlotte, for the safety of his posts in South Carolina. On October 14 he quit North Carolina in a painful retreat to Winnsboro. King's Mountain was the eruption of the westerners into the Revolution. Some of those who had destroyed Ferguson fought later under Greene, but most were content to return to their frontier homes, which they had protected.

General Greene had only the troops, fewer than two thousand, who reassembled after the disaster of Camden, and could not attack Cornwallis' main body. The constant annoyance given Cornwallis by the South Carolina partisans, especially Francis Marion and Thomas Sumter, persuaded Greene to divide his own little force into two partisan bands. The larger, some eleven hundred, he took to Cheraw in the northeast, where Marion was his nimble collaborator. The smaller contingent of nine hundred he entrusted to Daniel Morgan to threaten the British posts at Augusta and Ninety-six. By Greene's unorthodox strategy, Cornwallis was compelled to divide the British force. He had to maintain his hold on the upcountry, where Morgan was on the loose, and keep watch on the Americans at Cheraw, who might cut the British off from the coast.

Cornwallis dispatched Tarleton to catch and crush Morgan. At Cowpens, January 17, 1781, hard by the scene of Ferguson's ruin at King's Mountain three months before, the American champion, his light troops ably seconded by the cavalry of William Washington, dealt Tarleton a humiliating defeat. Another commander than Daniel Morgan would not have succeeded on the ground and with the plan of battle he chose. At Quebec he had led the assault on the lower town, at Saratoga he and Arnold had done the work for which Gates took credit. At Cowpens Morgan's independent fame was established.

Of Greene's own engagements and maneuvers in the Carolinas, it has been truly said that he encountered tactical defeats for the sake of strategic victories. He was content, with his defec-

WAR IN THE SOUTH

MOUNT VERNON

Charlottesville

James R.

Richmond

Yorktown

Portsmouth

Potomac R.

Chesapeake Bay

V I R G I N I A

Hillsboro

Guilford C.H.

N O R T H   C A R O L I N A

Salisbury

CAPE HATTERAS

Charlotte

COWPENS   KING'S MOUNTAIN

Cape Fear R.

Wilmington

Winnsboro

Camden

Ninety-six   **S O U T H**

C A R O L I N A

Eutaw Springs

Georgetown

Atlantic Ocean

Augusta

Savannah R.

Charleston

G E O R G I A

Savannah

0   50
Scale of Miles

tive resources, if he could weaken the enemy or otherwise place him in a disadvantageous situation. The classic example was Greene's retreat northward, drawing Cornwallis after him to Guilford Court House (near Greensboro, North Carolina), far from the British commander's source of support. The battle here (March 15, 1781) left the British in possession of the field, but with loss so heavy that withdrawal to Wilmington, the nearest point of contact with the fleet, was the only course. Similarly, Greene lost the fight at Hobkirk's Hill, just north of Camden, only to fall heir to the town when Lord Francis Rawdon, to maintain communication with the coast, retired to Monk's Corner near Charleston. Minor strongholds of the British fell to Marion and Henry Lee, Augusta being taken by the latter. Greene's siege of Ninety-six was frustrated by Rawdon, who made a two-hundred-mile march to its relief, but the British commander could not remain so far from the seaboard, so he later abandoned the place and retreated to the low country. Both armies rested during the hot Carolina summer. The closing scene, September 5, 1781, the battle of Eutaw Springs, fifty miles north of Charleston, was again a British victory, followed, however, by refuge in Charleston, the only place in South Carolina remaining in enemy hands.

In the Carolinas Cornwallis fought first Lincoln, then Gates, then Greene and Greene's lieutenants. In Virginia, until the closing scene at Yorktown, he marched much but fought little, because the weak American force kept beyond his clutch. In October 1780, when Greene went south to replace Gates, Washington ordered Steuben to assist in that quarter where "there is an army to be created." Greene placed Steuben in command in Virginia to collect and forward troops to him in the Carolinas, then join him to the south. But enemy movements in Virginia kept the baron in that state. First the traitor Arnold, who had been sent by Sir Henry Clinton to Portsmouth, ascended the James River, burned a foundry at Westham, above Richmond, and public buildings in the capital. Steuben received help in March 1781, when Lafayette, who took command, arrived at Annapolis with twelve hundred light troops to cooperate with a French fleet, which had brought an equal force. Prospect of a successful attack on Arnold at Portsmouth vanished, however, with defeat of the French fleet and arrival of reinforcements to the British under General William Phillips. A plan of Steuben's and Lafayette's to join their troops with Greene's army in pursuit of Cornwallis after the Guilford battle was frustrated, because the Virginia authorities refused to allow troops and arms to leave the state while the enemy was on her soil. Virginia had been woefully unprepared for defense until it was too late. Phillips ravaged at will.

Cornwallis, drawn rather than pushed from the Carolinas by Greene, decided to pursue his campaign in Virginia, though he sought in vain to persuade Sir Henry Clinton to make that state thenceforth the focus of British operations. With the troops already in Virginia, Cornwallis had an army of five thousand. Lafayette, reinforced when Wayne was ordered down from Pennsylvania (June 10, 1781), had about the same number, but mostly militia. Cornwallis boasted that "the boy cannot escape me." Lafayette not only escaped but continued to hang on the British army in its marches and countermarches in the valley of the James. Cornwallis sent Tarleton to Charlottesville to capture the legislature and Governor Jefferson, but he was a few minutes too late to prevent their flight. Cornwallis, as before in the Carolinas, after his incursion felt it prudent to move nearer the sea. He proceeded from Richmond to Williamsburg, and the first week of August he began entrenching his army, now numbering about seven thousand, at Yorktown.

When Hamilton applied to General Washington for a command in the line in the impending campaign, he realized that it might be the final one of the war. In a long letter to Robert Morris, urging rescue of the finances through a national bank, Hamilton declared, "All we have to fear is that the want of money may disband the army, or so . . . enfeeble our operations as to create in the people a general disgust and alarm, which may make them clamor for peace on any terms." But for the capture of Charleston and the victory of Camden, which permitted the British ministry to procure a loan of 25 million pounds, the enemy "would have been in the utmost embarrassment for the supplies of this year." With increasing aid from France, America had the prospect of "stopping the progress of their conquests, and reducing them to an unmeaning and disgraceful defensive"; this must destroy their "expectation of success, from which the ministry draws their resources." As for patriots, "The game we play is a sure game, if we play it with skill . . . . Many events may turn up in the course of the summer to make even the present campaign decisive."

This dispassionate review of the situation, economic and military, was sent to Morris on April 30, 1781, having been prepared in the fortnight since Hamilton's departure from headquarters. Back in February, when restiveness in his situation as aide had produced his difference with Washington, he was quick to tell Schuyler, "I cannot think of quitting the army during the war." He balanced "a project of re-entering into the artillery" against "a handsome command for the campaign in the light infantry," should one offer.

For the former he might take the place of Lieutenant Colonel Thomas Forrest, who wanted to retire on half pay. This would mean, however, that Hamilton would return to the artillery as the youngest of his rank instead of the eldest, which he would have been had he not left the corps to become an aide. Return to the artillery also promised to "be more solid and permanent; but as I hope the war will not last long enough to make it progressive, this consideration has the less force." A command for the campaign only would "leave me the winter to prosecute studies relative to my future career in life," evidently referring to the law.

Since artillery was his original field service, Hamilton would have needed no special intervention of the commander in chief to return to the corps. But appointment in the light infantry, which he now determined to seek, depended entirely on Washington's discretion and goodwill. Though repeatedly refused earlier, Hamilton now tried again, choosing, because of the strain in his relations with Washington, to put his plea in a letter (from DePeyster's Point, April 27, 1781). He began by reminding Washington that he was clearly eligible for field service under the resolution before Congress giving that capacity to aides [1]—a right for which, incidentally, he had always contended. How would the commander in chief be able to employ him in the forthcoming campaign? "Unconnected as I am with any regiment, I can have no other command than in a light corps, and I flatter myself my pretensions to this are good." (The light corps were *ad hoc*, picked, officers and men, from regular organizations for special assignment.) To secure such a coveted post, however, he must counter objections, well known to him, "that have opposed the appointment to commands of some other officers not belonging to what is called the line."

His own case was peculiar, Hamilton continued. He had begun in the line early in 1776, and if he had continued there, his rank might have been higher than it now was. He hoped his conduct had warranted the esteem of officers of the army in general (he knew, but did not say, that some had been jealous of him as too much the favorite at headquarters). He could not suppose, he said, that anyone would be so ungenerous as not to be glad to see him again in a situation to continue his service to the United States. True, the light infantry was already formed,

---

[1] May 25, 1781, Congress ruled that "officers not annexed to any line, serving . . . as aids de camps with . . . general officers, retain the rank they now hold, and shall be eligible to command upon detachments." More than a year earlier (January 15, 1780) Washington himself had taken this position. Otherwise "the Rank given these Officers would be a mere sound" and mockery of their services.

yet the army going south would doubtless require a detachment for the vanguard.[2]

Washington's answer the same day brought no comfort to his former aide, and doubtless gave the general pain to write. He said that Hamilton must remember "the ferment in the Pennsylvania line the last Campaign," when Major William Macpherson was given a command in the light infantry. Hamilton also was aware of the complaints "at this moment" of New England officers because Major William Galvan and Lieutenant Colonel Jean Joseph Gimat had been similarly named, under conditions of "absolute necessity."[3] In the unlikely event of formation of another advanced corps, it would be small, composed almost entirely of eastern troops, and to give a place in it to an outside officer of Hamilton's rank would bring disagreeable consequences. Washington did not retreat from his right to make such appointments, but said he must not push it too far at so critical a juncture as the present one. While agreeing that none could dispute Hamilton's merits, Washington pointed out that previous objections had been not to persons but rather to the preferment of officers who had not undergone the trouble of training the troops they were to command. Washington was

[2] Incidentally, this allusion shows that, like very few others, Hamilton knew at this early date that Virginia, not New York City, was to be the object of the campaign now preparing.

[3] Major Macpherson held a brevet commission. When he was appointed to light infantry, August 1, 1780, officers in the Pennsylvania line complained of prejudice to their rank and threatened to resign. Ten days later in a long letter to Generals Wayne and Irvine, over Washington's signature, Hamilton justified the assignment. Undoubtedly he had his own claims in mind when he wrote, "Military rank and an eligibility to military command . . . cannot be separated." Macpherson, in fact, performed commendable service in the Virginia campaign. Hamilton had said that his own application for a command in the light infantry differed from the cases of others, which had provoked objections. Washington relied on the trusted Baron Steuben to make tactful remonstrance to Major Galvan against the latter's "disobliging behavior," which had given "the greatest disgust in all the [light infantry] Corps," to which he was assigned. Unless Galvan complied, Washington said he would be obliged to relieve him. The protest against Galvan did seem to be on personal grounds.

concerned lest Hamilton impute his refusal "to other motives than these I have expressed," which he disavowed.

Hamilton delayed his reply for several days, and surely did not pursue the question in person when on April 30 he was called back to headquarters to help frame Washington's apology to Rochambeau.

General Washington's inability to grant the plea of his former aide for command in a light corps was a blow to Hamilton's hope. He wrote the commander in chief five days afterward (May 2, 1781), professing to renounce his plea for field command in order "to obviate the appearance of having desired a thing inconsistent with the good of the service." Yet he returned to the issue in some detail. Contending that the objections expressed to the assignments of Macpherson, Gimat, and Galvan could not apply to him, he said that he still hoped he might be appointed in a light corps should one be formed. While declaring that he could not agree with Washington's position, he ascribed it to the best motives only, and concluded by saying that "I am incapable of wishing to obtain any object by importunity." So rested for the time being his desire for service in the upcoming campaign.

His father-in-law, Philip Schuyler, was not at all dismayed by Hamilton's failure to gain a command. Schuyler had suffered his own disappointments after arduous military service. Hamilton had devoted five years in the same behalf; his wife Elizabeth was three months pregnant. Mrs. Schuyler had recently given birth, and Angelica Schuyler Church, Elizabeth's sister, was about to be fetched to Albany for the late months of pregnancy. Schuyler, the head of this increasing tribe, always sensible of his family responsibility, was ill with quinsy (severe tonsillitis) and could only now swallow a little broth. Under these circumstances he would be relieved to see Hamilton in toga rather than in martial tunic. Schuyler would meet the legislature the following week, and he assured his son-in-law that

"I believe you may prepare yourself to go to Philadelphia as there is little doubt but you will be appointed [to Congress]." The *pater familias* was on the same theme three months later (September 1781). Again he was sure that Hamilton's friends in the New York legislature would propose him for Congress. Even if Cornwallis were not forced to surrender, and the war continued, Schuyler said, he would wish Hamilton in Congress in preference to remaining in the army, "for reasons that are obvious."

Not so Lafayette. From Head of Elk (now Elkton, Maryland) he had written early in April that Hamilton would be more useful at headquarters, "But if you don't stay there you know what you have promised to me." He outlined a plan for "a new corps of light infantry," which would be taken south by water from Philadelphia. He named the officers he would wish, though Hamilton was not among them. Writing six weeks later from Richmond, Virginia, he again discussed his need for a light corps but, perhaps knowing by this time that Hamilton had been refused such employment, urged that he come down to command the artillery.

Following failure of his plea to be placed in a light corps, Hamilton seems to have remained nevertheless in the vicinity of Washington's headquarters at New Windsor, perhaps to be at hand if any chance for active service offered. He did not go to Albany, for Schuyler knew of his doings only by letter. Early in June Schuyler expected to meet him at Fishkill, and it was from there, five weeks later, that Hamilton dated the first number of his series of essays, "The Continentalist," that appeared in Samuel Louden's New York *Packet*, which was published at Fishkill during the British occupation of New York City. His interval away from military duties gave him leisure to reflect on the political shortcomings of the country and their effect on the fortunes of the war. The first four numbers came out within six weeks, the last two not until a year later. The earlier ones were probably written at DePeyster's Point or Fishkill, though perhaps after he rejoined the army at Dobbs Ferry. From the latter place he wrote his wife (July 13, 1781) that he had nothing to occupy his attention, spent a great part of his time in company; he missed Elizabeth.

Hamilton's preachment in the "Continentalist" essays was that America's military perils flowed from a want of power allowed to Congress and the want of independent revenue to permit the central government to discharge its responsibilities. He sketched the distresses

that threaten our immediate safety. Our whole system is in disorder; our currency depreciated, till in many places it will hardly obtain a circulation at all, public credit at its lowest ebb, our army deficient in numbers, and unprovided with every thing, the government, in its present condition, unable to command the means to pay, clothe, or feed their troops, the enemy making an alarming progress in the southern states, lately in complete possession of two of them, though now in part rescued by the genius and exercions of a General [Nathanael Greene] without an army, a force under Cornwallis still formidable in Virginia.

In reality, Hamilton argued, the country had ample means to secure victory. The enemy's whole force in the United States was little more than fourteen thousand effective men. Since commencement of the war, the population of America had grown, and the quantity of its specie had increased. America abounded with all the necessaries of life, and had an improved stock of warlike materials. Now five thousand auxiliary troops had been furnished by an able and willing ally. Why, then, was the struggle taking so long to win? Not because of disaffection in the people; they had steadfastly endured every hardship; and the enemy could not at this moment attract a thousand volunteers from the populace. The answer was "impolicy and mismanagement." If success in the war came soon, America could not rest on its laurels and continue to refuse to give competent authority to Congress, and he forecast the weakness of the Confederation following the peace. If, on the other hand, "a more general and more obstinate war" seemed likely, it was necessary without delay to

enlarge the powers of Congress. Every plan, of which this is not the foundation, will be illusory. The separate exertions of the states will never suffice. Nothing but . . . exertion of the resources of the whole, under the direction of a common council, with power sufficient to give efficacy to their resolutions, can preserve us from being a conquered people now, or can make us a happy people hereafter.

Congress should have the capacity to regulate trade, imposing import duties both for revenue and to encourage industry. Congress should have the proceeds of moderate land and poll taxes, the disposal of all unlocated land, and a proportion of the output of all mines. Congress should appoint all military and naval officers.

Every nation at war was obliged to borrow money at home and abroad. The rebel Colonies were no exception. Congress had to borrow five or six million dollars annually. To secure these loans, Congress required sure revenue to pay the interest currently and to set aside each year the funds to discharge the principal. With such resources, twenty years of peace would suffice to wipe out the public debt.

The writing of these essays, however, could not compensate in Hamilton's mind for more active service. Resolved to give his project of a command in the next campaign yet another try, he visited Washington's camp at Dobbs Ferry on July 8, 1781. His wish must have been relayed to the general by one of his many friends with immediate access to headquarters—perhaps General Benjamin Lincoln, or one of the comradely aides, Tilghman or Humphreys. When he had no prompt response, "I wrote the General a letter," he informed his wife, who was at Albany, "and enclosed him my commission." Washington was now persuaded in his favor.

This morning [July 10] Tilghman came to me in his name, pressed me to retain my commission, with assurance that he would endeavor by all means to give me a command nearly such as I could have desired in the present circumstances of the army. Though I know my Betsy would be happy to hear I had rejected this proposal, it is a pleasure my reputation would not permit me to afford her. I consented to retain my commission and accept my command.

Hamilton's letter of resignation to the commander in chief has been lost. From the grudging tone of his acceptance, when his desire was to be substantially gratified, it may be inferred that he had been emphatic in his determination to quit. He may have recited the refusals that had met all of his attempts to be given field service. Though Hamilton may well have been captious, Washington, in spite of a hundred cares, again treated him with consideration and, on this occasion, with indulgence. Throughout their years of close association, both during and after the war, each appreciated the other's qualities, including dedication to the public good. The difference was that Washington was unselfish, while Hamilton often thought of the advantage to himself that Washington's influence could confer, not so much in terms of benefits to himself personally, as to the policies he held dear.

While he waited for particular assignment, Hamilton was invited by General Lincoln to share his quarters at King's Bridge, some ten miles from the main camp. But he was no doubt at the camp daily, seeing his brother-in-law, Church, who had come from Newport as a contractor with the French army, and zestfully renewing interrupted associations, including those with French officers. Soon he took lodgings for himself, presumably nearer headquarters. From Schuyler's farm at Saratoga came two of his horses, one for riding, the other a "portmanteau horse." [4] In the fortnight that he waited at Dobbs Ferry

---

[4] Hamilton's "Old Gray Horse," Schuyler reported, after appearing to be in high order, had suddenly died, and "The black is thin and I believe too aged or too Infirm for future service." Someone, faulting Hamilton generally, said he was a timid horseman, preferring quiet mounts. However, in reconnaissances and longer journeys with the commander in chief, who was notably a splendid rider, the aide seems to have kept up. Hamilton was continuously in the saddle on liaison errands prior to the battle of Monmouth, and was disabled in that fight because he was thrown when his horse was wounded.

for his command, his servant's saddle became unfit; as no new one could be purchased there, would Pickering, the quartermaster, furnish a substitute or have the old one repaired? But Hamilton did not want this if the like was not done for other officers.

On July 28 Hamilton was a member of a court-martial that tried Captain David Livermore of the First New Hampshire regiment. The captain was charged with threatening and insulting Lieutenant Colonel John Barnard Murnan, his superior officer, "in a most outrageous manner," and, not content with verbal abuse, was said to be guilty of "Striking him with his own Espontoon and after having broken that with striking him with that of another officer." Washington approved the sentence of dismissal from the service. (However, Livermore, evidently a resourceful as well as a fighting man, was reinstated the same month and did not retire until March 1782.)

Hamilton's long-sought assignment was published in general orders July 31, 1781. Thanks to General Washington's solicitude, it was exactly to his wish:

The Light Companies of the first and second regiments of New York (upon their arrival in Camp) with the two companies of York Levies under command of Captains [William] Sackett and [Daniel] Williams will form a Battalion under command of Lieutenant Colonel Hamilton and Major [Nicholas] Fish. After the formation of the Battalion, Lieutenant Colonel Hamilton will join the Advanced Corps under the Orders of Colonel [Alexander] Scammell.

Later, in place of the New York levies, Hamilton's battalion received two Connecticut companies. Commanders of the three other light infantry battalions were Lieutenant Colonels Ebenezer Huntington, John Laurens, and Edward Antill, all under Brigadier General Moses Hazen. Hamilton was delighted to have his friend Nicholas Fish as his major, and to be under the immediate direction of the universally popular Colonel Scammell, formerly the adjutant general.

Hamilton lost no time seeing to the equipment of his battalion, recalling the care for his artillery company five years before. He needed from Quartermaster Pickering two wall tents for his field officers, also an orderly book and stationery; as to the last, he wanted to know what allowance was made, so he could "regulate the consumption accordingly." The camp kettles and pails had been ordered but were not delivered. Hamilton had applied to Tench Tilghman, Washington's aide, for an order for shoes for the two companies of levies. Tilghman thought that the order could not be issued, as the state was to clothe its own troops. Hamilton recalled, however, that in the last campaign a distinction was made in favor of the advanced corps, and cited Colonel Philip VanCortlandt's regiment as an example. Inquiry of others confirmed his memory, and he felt justified in going directly to General Washington, with the argument that the service of an advanced corps, more active than that of the line, and in rough country, made "the article of shoes . . . indispensable." He was concerned for the efficiency of his corps, which was also of personal importance to him. The men had spent their bounty of thirty pounds each, could not purchase shoes for themselves, and as the state sent them forward shoeless, they required a supply from Continental stores. Clothing might be refused, but shoes, please, his men must have. Washington promptly agreed, enjoining strict accountability.

Washington had consulted with the French generals, Rochambeau and Chastellux, at Wethersfield, Connecticut, late in May 1781. Unfortunately, Vice Admiral Louis Barras de Saint-Laurent was detained with his squadron at Newport. He had made it plain that his fleet was not strong enough to permit him to convoy the French troops from Rhode Island to the Chesapeake and there cooperate with the land forces to expel Cornwallis from Virginia. It was judged impracticable for Rochambeau to march his army the 450 miles to Virginia, since he was short of teams for the supply train and the weather would be hot. A new element, however, had entered the calculation: A large French fleet under the command of Admiral

François Joseph Paul de Grasse was sailing from Brest for the West Indies. Its admiral would detach a vessel to escort a small reinforcement of six hundred troops for Newport, but beyond this was the stirring possibility that Comte de Grasse, when his mission in the Caribbean allowed, would bring his many mighty ships to the Atlantic coast. This fleet, superior to the British, might give Washington command of the sea—an event for which he had yearned through six years of war. If this godsend should arrive, the allies could combine against the enemy at New York or to the south. Rochambeau, it was decided at Wethersfield, would leave a protecting force at Newport, and join Washington with the main body of the French army on the lower Hudson. The allies would then attack New York. This was a prime object in itself, and menacing New York would draw off strength from Cornwallis and relieve Greene and Lafayette in the southern theater.

Shortly after his return from Wethersfield, Washington wrote to Lafayette in Virginia:

Upon a full consideration of our affairs in every point of view, an attempt upon New York with its present Garrison (which by estimation is reduced to 4500 regular Troops and about 3000 irregulars) was deemed preferable to a Southern operation as we had not Command of the Water . . . but above all, it was thought that we had a tolerable prospect of expelling the enemy or obliging them to withdraw part of their force from the Southward, which last would give the most effectual relief to those States. The French troops are to March this way as soon as certain circumstances will admit.

He was begging the states to fill their battalions, and hoped that those of New England especially would respond to their favorite project, the capture of New York. This disclosure of the plan of campaign, sent by the regular post, was intercepted by the enemy June 3. Sir Henry Clinton rewarded the captor and boasted of his stroke of fortune. Before Washington knew his revelation to Lafayette had been seized, he had written similarly to Greene, adding, "I can only give you the outline of our plan. The dangers to which letters are exposed make it improper to commit particulars to paper." However, when he learned of Clinton's glee at possessing the allies' secret, Washington made light of it, telling Rochambeau that "The enemy can gain no material information from my letters." Thereat Sir Henry began to wonder whether the intercepted dispatch was a ruse. Hamilton is reported by his son to have given a double twist to puzzle the enemy. An American spy, found to be in British pay, was allowed at headquarters to see a map marked for a pretended land and naval attack on New York. To be sure, the spy inquired of Hamilton the destination of the army. Confident that crooked people expected crooked answers, and that the truth would be most misleading, the aide replied, "We are going to Virginia." This may have helped confirm Sir Henry Clinton in his precautions for New York.

The question arises, when did Washington discard New York as the object, and pitch on the southern campaign? The usual answer is that he was hesitant between the two as late as July 19, 1781, when he gave a formal opinion to Rochambeau that New York should be the target, but that by August 1, when he could count on de Grasse's early appearance, he was inclined to attack Virginia instead. On this date he recorded in his diary, "I turned my views more seriously (than I had before done) to an operation to the Southward." This design was hastened two weeks later, on August 14, when it was reliably reported by Barras that de Grasse was coming to the Chesapeake with twenty-nine warships and three thousand troops. But de Grasse could not remain on this coast beyond October 15, so not an hour was to be lost in preparations to cooperate with him against Cornwallis.

This is the contemporary testimony. On the other hand, seven years later, when asked by Noah Webster to say when he resolved on a concentration in the south, he replied: "it was determined by me (nearly twelve months before hand) at all hazards to give out and cause it to be believed by the highest military as well as civil officers that New York was the destined place of attack, in order to spur the Eastern & Middle states to greater exertions in furnishing specific supplies, and to render the enemy less prepared elsewhere."

His words meant that the commander in chief shared his true intention, early conceived and persistently held to, with nobody —not with Greene, nor Lafayette, nor Rochambeau, nor Robert Morris (recently appointed superintendent of finance), nor with the president of Congress. These and all others not only were kept in the dark as to his genuine purpose but were induced to expect that New York was the aim, until necessary arrangements for the actual movement commenced. If so, Washington was indeed being subtle and deep. Perhaps, in declaring himself some years after the event, his previous waverings of choice were blotted from memory by the glorious success of his final decision.

Hamilton must have known well in advance what was in store, though in the first half of July he was assuring his wife of his safety since there was "little prospect of activity." A few days before mid-August he wrote her that he had taken command of his corps and was glad to have with him Major Fish, whom he prized "both as a friend and an officer." A few days later, breaking the news to her gently, by letter and through her father, he said operations were preparing. Not until he was actually on the march, at Haverstraw, August 22, did he tell her that he was with that part of the army bound for Virginia. He cautioned her not to mention their destination. She should write him in care of Richard Peters, secretary of the Board of War at Philadelphia. He had supplied her with money and arranged for her to have additional funds from his small stock; he thought he need not draw on her father, as Schuyler had offered, or use an order on Robert Morris. He said he would be back in October, or in November at latest.

The French troops, about 6,000, had come down to the Hudson during the last fortnight in June. Washington and Rochambeau planned a combined assault on the outer defenses of New York for July 2. How serious it was intended to be, without naval support, is not known. At any rate, the advantage of surprise was frustrated; the enemy safely withdrew across the Harlem River, and all the allies achieved was a closer knowledge of Sir Henry Clinton's strength on Manhattan island. Washington moved his force from New Windsor across the Hudson to Dobbs Ferry, nearer to New York in case a further attack was to be tried; the French were encamped to the east. The allied force amounted to little more than Clinton's. Washington was embarrassed and anxious because, having promised Rochambeau that he would muster 10,500 troops, he actually had only 5,800 Continentals, rank and file, fit for duty, and in spite of entreaties to the states for militia, none had come to him. Wagons, draft animals, cavalry horses, and forage, required for the French as well as Americans in any major operation, were distressingly lacking, as were food and clothing in Washington's camp. The Continental paper money would buy nothing, as Hamilton was lamenting just at this time, and no specie was available to Quartermaster General Timothy Pickering. Impressment was the only means of obtaining men and supplies, though this method produced much resentment.

At the end of July Lafayette notified Washington that forty British transports were in Hampton Roads, presumably to bring reinforcement from Cornwallis to Clinton. Instead, twenty vessels from Europe that reached New York August 12 increased enemy strength there by 2,400 Germans, raising Clinton's total of rank and file to 15,000. The development was overshadowed, however, by the arrival of the frigate *Concorde* at Newport, with the shining news that de Grasse was to have sailed from Santo Domingo on August 3 with twenty-five or more ships of the line and additional land forces. Washington, writing on August 15, told Lafayette to expect de Grasse to appear in the Chesapeake momentarily. Lafayette should keep the troops he had, including hopefully General Anthony Wayne's

Pennsylvanians, to prevent Cornwallis from retreating into North Carolina. He also was to conceal the expected arrival of de Grasse's fleet as long as possible, lest the enemy decamp. As soon as de Grasse appeared, Lafayette was to plan a joint action with de Grasse "until you receive aid from this quarter . . . . You shall hear further from me as soon as I have concerted plans and formed dispositions for sending a reinforcement from hence." This dispatch to Lafayette, written in suppressed excitement, was forwarded with directions that "a trusty, active Express" should "ride Night and Day and . . . call on the Magistrates, or Military Officers for Horses and assistance, and . . . deliver the Letter to the Marquis at the earliest possible period."

The promised "reinforcement" to enable Lafayette to hold Cornwallis on the Virginia peninsula at Yorktown was no less than the whole of the American and French armies on the Hudson, with the exception of a detachment left with General William Heath to protect the river posts. Washington "concerted plans and formed dispositions" to trap his lordship with astonishing speed. De Grasse's fleet, blocking the mouth of the York River, was essential to success. The admiral would tarry only two months, until October 15, before returning to the Caribbean. Thus propelled, Washington was ready, five days after he knew de Grasse was coming, to commence his southward movement. Before leaving, much had to be done. Hamilton's friend General Alexander McDougall having declined command of the American force, General Benjamin Lincoln, with whom Hamilton had recently lodged, was given it. General Heath was carefully instructed for the safety of West Point; he should prevent the enemy in New York from detaching to the south, and keep up as long as possible the pretense that the allies would attack New York. Nearby states were to be reassured for their security.

Executives of Rhode Island and Connecticut were urged, if their credit was exhausted, to impress vessels to move fifteen hundred barrels of salt meat and thirty hogsheads of rum to

Newport; Admiral Barras would convoy these supplies to Virginia when he brought down the French siege guns. Patrols must give earliest word of any movement of the enemy in New York. The Superintendent of Finance was told that three hundred barrels of flour, as many of salt meat, and some hogsheads of rum would be necessary in Elk River; as many vessels as possible should be collected at Baltimore for carriage of the troops down Chesapeake Bay. Equally important, and even more difficult, a month's pay in specie would help to overcome the reluctance of the soldiers to go south. Admiral de Grasse was begged to send to the head of Chesapeake Bay all his frigates, transports, and light vessels to supplement those available locally to convey French and American troops to the expected scene of action. Routes for the two armies were worked out; proper places for night camps, about fifteen miles apart, were indicated for Rochambeau; Lafayette should inform Washington of the number of wagons and horses to be had in Virginia for use when the armies reached his vicinity Above all, Washington repeated his "most earnest Wish . . . that the British Army may not be able to escape you." Colonel Elias Dayton was to furnish a guard for bake ovens for the French to be built at Chatham, New Jersey; this extensive bakery was established to deceive the British into thinking Chatham would be a base of operations against New York.

These were major features of Washington's preparations for combined land and sea movements that were to end in the bagging of Cornwallis. This was by far the most ambitious project in concentration of forces from several quarters that General Washington undertook, and its success made it the last.

Just before quitting the camp at Dobbs Ferry, Hamilton's battalion was joined by "Two Companies each [consisting] of a Captain, two Subs [subalterns], four Sergeants and Fifty Rank and File," which were "to be immediately formed from the Connecticut Line . . . it is expected that the companies will be composed of good men engaged either for the War or three years." Apparently this was a net addition to Hamilton's command. The American columns, some 2,500 men, set out August 19 for King's Ferry. The next morning they began to cross the Hudson, and in twenty-four hours all, including baggage and artillery, were on the west shore. Washington, expecting the French on August 21, remained to assist their ferriage. They had been delayed by poor transport, and did not get over the river until August 25. As though he had not enough else to do, "During the passing of the French Army," Washington recorded, "I mounted 30 flat Boats (able to carry about 40 Men each) upon carriages as well with a design to deceive the enemy as to our real movement [the enemy would expect such boats to be used to cross to Staten Island prior to an attack on New York], as to be useful to me in Virginia when I got there."

The Americans marched through upper Jersey by two routes. The light infantry, including Hamilton's battalion and the First New York regiment, kept to the east by Kakiate, Haverstraw, Paramus, Second River, and so to Springfield. The other column, encumbered by baggage, artillery, and stores, went inland by Pompton and Chatham. The French passed to the west, by Suffrans (Suffern), Pompton, Whippany, Somerset Courthouse. The allied forces joined at Chatham, where Washington wrote to the deputy quartermaster general, explaining why he had delayed ordering boats to be gathered at Trenton until this moment; "because I wished to deceive the Enemy with regard to our real object as long as possible, our Movements have been calculated for that purpose and I am still anxious the deception should be kept up a few days longer, untill our intentions are announced by the Army's filing off towards the Delaware." Even in the American army, Dr. James Thacher recorded, curiosity was "wrought to the highest pitch," and bets were taken on the destination of the march. Washington took every means of discovering what Sir Henry Clinton was making of the game. Clinton's spies were active; the boats, trundled along overland and giving trouble on bad roads, persuaded many of them that the allies were making for Staten Island or Sandy Hook. Actually Sir Henry Clinton, writing to Cornwallis as late as September 1, was in the dark about Washington's purpose. The American commander feared the British would chase after him, once it was clear he was not coming against New York, but they made no such move.[5]

Washington directed that Hamilton's battalion, and others of the light corps, were "always . . . to be fit for action and free from every incumbrance." He had advised them, immediately after they crossed King's Ferry, to deposit at West Point "every article of Baggage which they can in any wise dispense with"; this included "such of the Women as are not able to undergo the fatigue of frequent marches." Hamilton's wife had procured for him "camp equippage"; Pickering had provided a "wall tent." From orders it appears that he shared a covered wagon with several other officers for carriage of his gear. The other light troops moved on the route nearest New York City, screening the main body from a possible attack by Clinton. Every direction given by Washington was inspired by his anxiety to reach Virginia and close with Cornwallis at the earliest possible date. Nagging at his mind was the fear that Cornwallis could not be contained before de Grasse had to return in mid-October to the West Indies. Washington was constantly making plans for transport by land and water, and arranging for the deposit of forage and provisions along the route to be followed. He hastened ahead to learn the condition of roads, and ordered repairs to permit artillery and heavy baggage to press on. "The success of our enterprise depends upon the celerity of our Movements," he ad-

[5] Doubts about Washington's intended destination aside, Sir Henry Clinton wrote in his memoirs, "I could not have prevented his passing the Hudson under cover of his forts at Verplank's and Stoney Points. Nor (supposing I had boats properly manned) could it have been advisable to have landed at Elizabethtown, in the face of works which he might easily have occupied, as they were only seven miles from his camp at Chatham, without subjecting my army to be beat *en detail*. Nor could I, when informed of his march toward the Delaware, have passed an army in time to have made any impression upon him before he crossed that river."

monished Lincoln; "delay therefore, may be ruinous to it." His anxiety showed in the details he took on himself. For example, to speed progress, "every horse and Oxen should be Swam over the Delaware. A few Boats above and below the place they are made to enter the River, to give them a proper direction, will remove all difficulty and greatly facilitate the passage across." By his orders reveille sounded at three o'clock, and the troops were to be in motion by four.

Hamilton, eager to enter the campaign, also worried about getting to Virginia in time. On August 22, at Haverstraw, he wrote that "It is ten to one that our views will be disappointed by Cornwallis retiring to South Carolina by land." However, this was in a letter to his wife, and may have been designed to reassure her that only distance, rather than danger, would separate them.

At Chatham, August 28, Washington ordered Lincoln to form the American army under his immediate command into three brigades under Scammell (a light infantry brigade, this included Hamilton's battalion) and Brigadier Generals James Clinton and Moses Hazen. For the morrow's march toward Trenton, these brigades formed the left column, with their baggage and six fieldpieces. The right column consisted of the main artillery, the boats and supplies, escorted by the corps of sappers and miners. Hamilton's column was to go through Westfield and Lamptown to Raritan landing above Brunswick; the next day, August 30, they were to march the sixteen miles to Princeton, and the following day to proceed to Trenton.

It is not known how Hamilton and his battalion went from Trenton to the Head of Elk (Elkton, Maryland). Since the boats available at Trenton were sufficient to carry only a few troops, in addition to the heavy cannon and supplies, Rochambeau offered to have his men march all the way. Hamilton may have been among the Americans who went by water to Philadelphia, or, for that matter, on down to Christiana, on the creek of that name below Wilmington, and thence the few miles by land to Head of Elk. If he were at Philadelphia, reached by the American van September 1, he would have been in the dusty procession that passed through the city September 2, followed by the French a few days later. The honors done to Washington, Rochambeau, Major General François Jean Chastellux, and the allied armies—the city illuminated, the president of Congress and the French minister standing uncovered to review the troops—were cheering. But Washington could not be inwardly composed. He had repeated his plea to Robert Morris "to procure one month's pay in specie for the detachment . . . under my command; part of those troops have not been paid any thing for a long time past, and have upon several occasions shewn marks of great discontent. The service they are going upon is disagreeable to the Northern Regiments. . . . If the whole sum cannot be obtained, a part of it will be better than none." Morris had not been able to comply.

In the most crucial operation of the war, of unexampled magnitude, on which the fate of the country hung, Washington had no money. The empty war chest was the lightest piece of baggage. The commander in chief was obliged to beg the financier for traveling expenses—petty cash, really—of officers sent on special details, and for more to compensate secret informants, whose dangerous duties could not be rewarded with promises. Reluctantly, he issued general warrants for impressment of wagons, teams, and forage.

Washington's anxiety was heightened by posthaste messages from Brigadier General David Forman, keeping unfailing watch on British shipping at Sandy Hook. On August 27 Forman reported "eighteen large ships of war . . . standing in . . . their colours was discovered British." He mistakenly believed it was Admiral George Rodney's fleet from the West Indies. With the eleven fighting ships of Admiral Thomas Graves already at New York, the enemy had twenty-nine, equal to the number de Grasse was bringing. Subsequent dispatches reduced the British naval strength by a few ships and placed them under Admiral

Sir Samuel Hood instead of the dreaded Rodney. Then came word that on August 31 all had sailed out of the bay. Were they going to intercept the squadron of Barras, on his way to Virginia with siege guns and provisions? Or were they making for the York River, to relieve Cornwallis before Barras or de Grasse, of whom there was no further news, could arrive? Washington pointedly inquired of Forman whether the British fleet included transports, in which case reinforcement of Cornwallis would seem the object.

At Chester, on September 5, both of Washington's worries were relieved. The lesser one first, though Washington did not know of it until he reached Head of Elk; Robert Morris had followed the French, hat in hand, and at Chester borrowed, with Rochambeau's approval, twenty thousand dollars, and five hundred guineas for Washington's "particular use." The real news came from General Mordecai Gist, who forwarded de Grasse's dispatch of three days before that he was within the Virginia capes. Of Washington at this moment the duke Armand Louis de Lauzun said, "I never saw a man so thoroughly and openly delighted." He immediately sent his congratulations to Comte César Henri de La Luzerne, the French minister, and to Congress; the next day he wrote his own plans to de Grasse, and in general orders gave the news of the French admiral's safe arrival in the Chesapeake.

Hamilton, at Head of Elk, knew of this good fortune before it was publicly announced. He wrote his wife on September 6, saying that he would embark for Yorktown the next day. "Circumstances that have just come to my knowledge, assure me that our operations will be expeditious, as well as our success certain," he said.

Now followed an unavoidable check in the hitherto "expeditious" progress southward. The assorted vessels at Head of Elk (what the French wrote in their itinerary as "Head-Ofelke") were not of number or size to transport more than a part of the army down the bay to Annapolis, where they were to be transferred to frigates from de Grasse's fleet for the sail to Virginia. The lack "of transports to carry our whole Force and Apparatus from this place at once, is a great Misfortune," Washington lamented. Most of the small craft of the Eastern Shore men had been destroyed or captured by the British. Consequently only siege guns and light troops, which would be the first needed in Virginia, were embarked at once. The French grenadiers, chasseurs, and infantry of Lauzun's legion, a thousand men, out of politeness were given preference, but room remained for eight hundred of the American light corps, Hamilton's battalion included. The thirty boats that had been wheeled from the Hudson would be a valuable supplement if they should reach Head of Elk in time for the first fleet, but otherwise there was no waiting for them. All else must go by land to Baltimore; some could use such meager shipping as was found there, though most must await the return of the vessels that took the advance troops from Head of Elk. If this second trip could not embark all, the rest were to be put on their march, for, as Washington urged Lincoln, "The Time is fast slipping away; the most expeditious Mode should be taken to collect our whole Force at the Point of Operation." Actually, the boats at Baltimore were judged unfit, without dangerous crowding, so the toilsome march was continued (September 13). Fortunately, they got only as far as Elkridge when word came that de Grasse had sent transports to take all aboard at Annapolis.

Hamilton's voyage from Head of Elk to Annapolis, in a crowded open boat, the winds light or contrary, required an exasperating week (September 7 or 8 to 15). Here the flotilla was held in port by disturbing news. Washington traveled by land; on his ride south from Mount Vernon, where he and his companions had stopped briefly, he got word that de Grasse had put to sea from the Chesapeake. Nobody knew why, except that the British fleet had been reported ten days earlier off the mouth of Delaware Bay. It was unthinkable that de Grasse had abandoned his strategic station bottling up Cornwallis and had sailed back to the West Indies. More likely there was a naval engagement, with less fear for the superiority of de Grasse than that Barras might be involved. Or had Barras, bringing down his precious cargo of cannon and salt provisions, already fallen victim to the enemy?

13

"Cornwallis and His Army Are Ours"

 Until the Chesapeake was again safe, the American and French armies on their way from Head of Elk must interrupt their course. The miserable worry of the allied commanders vanished when it was learned that a severe battle in the open ocean had favored the French. Rodney, ill and homeward bound, had given over to Admiral Graves, who with Admiral Hood was chasing Barras when sighted by de Grasse. Both Graves and de Grasse suffered casualties, before the English, with some ships disabled, returned to New York and de Grasse resumed his station in the Chesapeake. Providentially, Barras had slipped by, ignorant of his peril.

The French and American troops at Annapolis proceeded south by water on September 18. While he waited at Annapolis, Hamilton had dismal reflections. He wrote his wife: "How checkered is human life! How easily do we often part with it for a shadow!" The best cheer he could give was that "our operations will be so conducted, as to economize the lives of men. Exert your fortitude and rely upon heaven." He would have been more distressed had he then received Schuyler's letter, written from Albany about this date, saying that Elizabeth "was so sensibly affected by your removal to the southward that I apprehended consequences"—meaning a miscarriage. However, Schuyler was able to add, "she is now at ease."

Hamilton, with his battalion, must have quit, with no regret, the nondescript flotilla that had brought them to Annapolis, and boarded one of the ampler, faster vessels sent up by de Grasse. Otherwise they could not, in company with the rest of Scammell's light troops, have been the first to arrive at College Landing (then called Archer's Hope) on a tributary creek of the James only a mile from Williamsburg. This was on September 20, and was not accomplished without further trials, for their vessel ran aground on the way. They spent a night helpless, until next morning, when they transferred to a smaller craft to navigate the creek. Even then violent winds were against them, but by dint of much tacking, they were at length safely ashore.[1] The French soon landed at Burwell's wharf at the mouth of the creek Hamilton's boat had threaded, while the artillery and stores were unloaded at nearby Trebell's wharf, closer to their destination of Yorktown. By September 26 the entire American and French force from the north had joined Lafayette's army, and the three thousand troops under General Claude de Rouvroy Saint Simon were at Williamsburg, a dozen miles from Yorktown.

Here Hamilton surely enjoyed his reunion not only with Lafayette but with two more fast friends. Lieutenant Colonel John Laurens was serving on Washington's staff, having recently

---

[1] The diary of Lieutenant Reuben Sanderson, of the Fifth Connecticut Continentals, assigned to Scammell's light infantry corps, chronicled the march from the Hudson to Yorktown. Sanderson's vessel, on leaving Annapolis, "sailed about thirty miles. Came to anchor off Pople point." Next day, at sunrise, "waid anchor, sailed about 35 miles, came to Anchor off the Potomock." Two days later, favored by a strong wind, they made York River, 80 miles. In spite of light airs they got around to the mouth of the James September 19, and with difficulty were off Williamsburg at sunset of September 20. His troops camped near the shore, and did not march the short distance to Williamsburg until September 24.

returned from his successful mission to France. The other special intimate was Lieutenant Colonel Francis Barber, his teacher in the Elizabethtown academy.

Barber's service during the summer with Lafayette had turned him "something of the colour of an Indian," and he was as thin as he was brown. He found the same dearth of food at the great concentration of troops at Williamsburg. No sooner had Washington arrived, September 14, than he set about summoning delivery of flour (and clothing and entrenching tools also) from distant quarters. "The Army here have already experienced a Want of Provisions, especially of the Bread kind," he wrote, "and I fear they will be in Danger of greater Distress, when the whole force I expect is assembled, unless the most vigorous measures are taken to prevent it." Warfare had already swept the local area bare, except for standing corn; soldiers were forbidden to rifle cornfields, except those "appropriated [by the quartermaster] to the use of the Troops." Fortunately Barras had arrived a month earlier with his fifteen hundred barrels of salt meat, and he also convoyed some American vessels with provisions.

If Admiral de Grasse could remain "to the close of a regular Operation," a siege, the result might be slow, but would, as Hamilton had said, conserve the lives of men. If, "from the fear of losing the Aid of the Fleet, the operations by Land are precipitated faster than . . . prudence . . . will warrant," the outcome "must be bloody and precarious." A long siege would require more supplies of food and powder.

Arrival of the light troops, with the main armies on their heels, encouraged Washington to write, "in a few Days I hope to find myself before the Works of the Enemy." Lord Cornwallis, however, "is incessantly at Work on his Fortifications, and is probably preparing to defend himself to the last Extremity." Every day that was allowed to the enemy's "unremitting labour" to strengthen his position seemed to Washington an age, and "may cost us many Lives to encounter."

Why did Cornwallis, judged by many the ablest general of

King George in America, having left Yorktown three weeks earlier, choose to return there in the first days of August 1781? He had embarked part of his troops to go to the aid of Sir Henry Clinton at New York when the latter felt himself threatened by Washington and Rochambeau on the Hudson. Then Clinton countermanded this order, and instructed Cornwallis to fortify a coastal point in Virginia for the protection of British shipping. His lordship obeyed, thinking to recruit his strength and with Clinton's cooperation to renew his campaign in cooler months. Consequently he took command of the force at Portsmouth (giving him a total of some seven thousand troops), abandoned that place, and surveyed Old Point Comfort for a naval station. But this seemed unsuitable, due to the great width of Hampton Roads, and he chose Yorktown. Here, by fortifying also Gloucester Point, only half a mile across the York River, he could give better defense to a good anchorage. In the controversy between the two generals, after Cornwallis' surrender, Clinton repeated his direction that Yorktown was to be fortified only as additional protection to Old Point Comfort. Had Cornwallis possessed Old Point Comfort, he might have escaped via Portsmouth into North Carolina when de Grasse's fleet appeared. In any event, he was not compelled, militarily, to retreat to Yorktown; he did not intend to make it more than a temporary stop.

Cornwallis, reporting to Clinton the day after the surrender, said,

I never saw this post in a very favorable light; but when I found I was to be attacked in it, in so unprepared a state, by so powerful an army and artillery, nothing but the hopes of relief would have induced me to attempt its defence; for I would either have endeavored to escape to New York by rapid marches from the Gloucester side, immediately on the arrival of General Washington's troops at Williamsburg, or, I would, notwithstanding the disparity of numbers, have attacked them in the open field.

But, assured by Clinton that every means would be used, by army and navy, to relieve him, he rejected such desperate at-

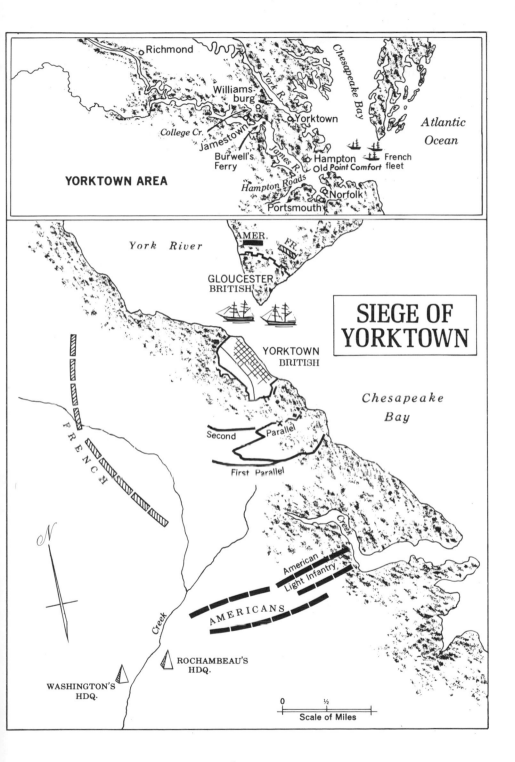

YORKTOWN AREA

Richmond

Williams-
burg

York R.

Chesapeake Bay

Yorktown

College Cr.

Jamestown

Burwell's
Ferry

James R.

Atlantic
Ocean

Hampton
Old Point Comfort

French
fleet

Hampton Roads

Norfolk

Portsmouth

York River

AMER.

FR.

GLOUCESTER
BRITISH

YORKTOWN
BRITISH

SIEGE OF
YORKTOWN

Chesapeake
Bay

Second

Parallel

First Parallel

F R E N C H

Creek

N

Creek

American
Light Infantry

A M E R I C A N S

Creek

ROCHAMBEAU'S
HDQ.

WASHINGTON'S
HDQ.

0   ½
Scale of Miles

265

tempts, withdrew to his inner works, and hoped to hold out until help came. Construction of his defenses, thought by Washington to be strong, had to be continued under enemy fire, with fewer than four hundred entrenching tools.

In preparation for moving the army to Yorktown, Washington on September 17 paid a visit to Admiral de Grasse on the *Ville de Paris* off Cape Henry. His delay of several precious days in getting back—one vessel ran aground, the substitute was balked by headwinds in the James—was not begrudged, since de Grasse was ready to give substantially the cooperation required for the siege. For six weeks, if need be, his great fleet would block the mouth of the York River against entrance of an enemy squadron to rescue Cornwallis. This was an extension of his former limitation, October 15, to the end of that month. He would furnish as many as two thousand soldiers if a bold stroke were in view, and he offered some cannon and ammunition. He was disinclined to heed Washington's plea that he force some ships up the river above Yorktown to close that exit and assist passage of allied land forces to Gloucester. But Washington could bear this disappointment.

Then a week later, on the eve of commencement of the siege, came from de Grasse an alarming reversal of his promises. Washington had notified him of British Rear Admiral Robert Digby appearing on the coast with transports and a few ships of the line. The general had no fears on this account, but de Grasse had already received the news and magnified Digby's strength to equal his own. The headquarters messenger, Baron Jean Closen, returned with a dispatch from de Grasse painful in every word of the translation. De Grasse was resolved to put to sea after Digby, and said the issue of the expected conflict might prevent him from resuming his station in the bay. This last minute defection would ruin Washington's design. Closen, seeing the French admiral thus restless for cruising, was as disgusted as Washington, whose dismay was shared by Rochambeau.

John Laurens, serving Washington in Hamilton's old capacity

at headquarters, drew the commander in chief's reasoned, earnest protest, and Lafayette, no less, delivered it to the admiral's flagship. The agonizing uncertainty, not the first in negotiations with the sea dog, ended in complete relief. The result of de Grasse's council with his officers was that "the plans I had . . . for getting underway, while the most brilliant and glorious, did not appear to fulfil the aims we had in view . . . to . . . act in concert for the good of our operation." Instead of sailing off on a dubious adventure, "the major part of the fleet should proceed to anchor in York River, sparing four or five vessels to patrol the James."

Washington did not pretend to be adept in naval warfare. His longest sea voyage had been to Barbados in his youth. He was a son of the soil. But in his instant correction to de Grasse's vagary he proved himself every whit the commander in chief, the master manager of a combined marine and land concentration. Happily, this was the last major crisis of the war that Washington must endure, for, as he told de Grasse, "the enterprise against York under the protection of your Ships, is as certain as any military operation can be rendered by a decisive superiority of strength and means; . . . is in fact reducible to calculation."

Just prior to surmounting this peril, the American army was brigaded. Hamilton's battalion remained in Colonel Alexander Scammell's corps of light infantry, which was incorporated into a brigade commanded by General Moses Hazen.

On Thursday, September 27, 1781, the order of battle was set. Next morning at five o'clock the army would march from Williamsburg to invest the enemy at Yorktown. The American troops, composing the right wing of the combined armies, were formed in three divisions. Hamilton's battalion, with the other light infantry (Peter Muhlenberg's and Hazen's brigades) were to be in advance on the right, the division being commanded by Lafayette. Wayne's brigade and Mordecai Gist's Marylander brigade constituted the division of the center under Steuben. The brigades of General James Clinton and Colonel

Elias Dayton formed on the left the division of Lincoln, who was in immediate command of the entire American wing. The American Continental force (5,500 total) was completed by the artillery under Knox, sappers and miners, and some detached contingents, bringing up the rear. The militia, about 3,000 and including a corps of mountain riflemen, all Virginians, were commanded by their governor, General Thomas Nelson.

The left wing of the combined armies was composed of French troops under Lieutenant General Rochambeau. Since he would make his own dispositions, these were not given in general orders. He had 7 regiments of infantry, 600 artillerists, and the same number of horse and foot in Lauzun's legion, for a total of 7,200. The French regiments figured under their descriptive titles—Bourbonnois, Royal Deuxponts, Saintonge, Soissonais, Touraine, Agenois, Gatenois. Rochambeau's major generals were Baron Antoine Charles de Vioménil, Count Charles Joseph de Vioménil, François Jean Chastellux, and Saint-Simon.[2]

The besiegers, the largest force ever commanded by Washington, numbered, with 800 marines from the fleet, about 16,500. Cornwallis' troops, with about the same complement of marines, were half as many, some 8,300, but all veterans.

The march from Williamsburg on September 28 to a position a mile from the Yorktown defenses was uneventful but slow, the road bordered by woods with now and then a clearing for tobacco or corn. Hamilton's light corps, as part of Hazen's brigade, was in second place of the van. The French, as the destination was approached, turned left to the location they kept throughout the siege. The Americans, taking the right, were held up that weary evening because a bridge across the Great

---

[2] Among the officers in the French army, two were particular friends of Hamilton's: Marquis François Louis de Fleury, previously serving in the American army, had pulled down the British flag at Stony Point, and Hamilton sought, though unsuccessfully, to have him allowed to keep it as a trophy; the Vicomte Louis Marie de Noailles was a brother-in-law of Lafayette. Hamilton's own brother-in-law, John B. Church, was with the French at Yorktown in his capacity as a commissary contractor.

(or Beaverdam) Run, which spread into a marsh south of York-town, had been destroyed. A party of British dragoons offered less interference, for they promptly retired in face of a few cannon shots. The battalion, bivouacked in the woods, got little rest that night, ordered as they were to lie on their weapons. Next morning Hamilton drew up his troops behind the marsh bordering Great Run, and crossed the now-repaired causeway to within a half-mile of the outworks. Hamilton's unit must have suffered one of the first casualties, for, so close to the enemy, a cannon shot carried away the leg of one of his men. Hamilton obeyed Washington's orders that the troops should throw up light embankments for immediate protection of the camp guards.

The besieged village of Yorktown is situated on a bluff forty or fifty feet above the York River, projecting a gently rounded shoulder into the south side of the stream. Gloucester Point, half a mile opposite, is low but sharper. Yorktown commands the river—hence Cornwallis' choice of it—but is vulnerable to attack from the land side, though the latter area has little superior height. Immediately before the town, to the southeast, is level ground, half a mile wide, enclosed by two streams running to the river between steep banks—Yorktown Creek to the left (as one faces the town), and Wormeley's Creek to the right. At the time of the siege these streams were more considerable than now, and collected their waters, particularly the former, from marshy grounds. The gorges furnished natural protection to besiegers while at a distance, but their nearer approach must be over the intervening little plain. This narrow avenue of advance for attackers was advantageous to the defenders, and correspondingly a limitation to the besiegers. Cannon in four British works could sweep this "gap" of level ground.[3]

[3] During the economic depression of the nineteen-thirties the boys of the Civilian Conservation Corps commenced restoration of the Revolutionary battlefield (not the allies' trenches, but certain of the British earthworks), and progress has been made since. Unfortunately for the visitor wishing to discover the features of the siege in 1781, the scene is marred by the presence of well-

The allied army encampment stretched in a semicircle from the riverbank above the town around to the river below it, at about a mile distant. The French were on the left of Great Run, the Americans on the right, except for Washington and Adjutant General Edward Hand, whose headquarters were in the French area, doubtless to be near Rochambeau.

Washington spent September 29 in reconnaissance of the enemy's defenses, especially the outer works, to determine how they might best be circumvented. Next morning he was agreeably surprised to find that these redoubts had been evacuated in the night. Many allied officers and not a few of the British, Clinton and Tarleton included, were sure that Cornwallis was guilty of serious error in abandoning these strongholds before they were ever attacked, as with them he could have protracted his defense by several weeks. The besiegers guessed that the withdrawal meant he would attempt to escape up the river; he had a hundred vessels of various sorts in the anchorage, many of which could have been used as transports under protection of the two warships, the *Charon* and the *Guadeloupe*. His real reasons, it transpired, were that he needed to concentrate his relatively small force, while he relied on Sir Henry Clinton's promise, just received, that a formidable fleet with five thousand soldiers would sail from New York October 5 to his relief. If this force arrived in time, he wrote, "York and Gloucester will be both in possession of his Majesty's troops."

The allies instantly occupied the vacated forts and adapted them to attack. This was not accomplished, however, without the capture and mortal wounding of Colonel Alexander Scam-

preserved Confederate fortifications, which in fact cover the line of inner British defenses. However, the British advanced redoubts, the storming of which precipitated Cornwallis' surrender, have been reconstructed. The approach to both is now greensward, but no more open than when the valiant assaults were made. However, while eighteenth-century Williamsburg is in good part a replacement, the village of Yorktown, or what remains of it, is principally original. The illustrated pamphlet by Charles E. Hatch, Jr., *Yorktown and the Siege of 1781* (Washington, D.C., National Park Service Historical Handbook Series No 14, revised to 1957) is accurately informing.

mell, Hamilton's immediate superior, who as officer of the day was inspecting the deserted works. The Americans believed that Scammell was shot after he was seized by three of Tarleton's dragoons. He was given first aid in Yorktown and paroled, but died a week later in the hospital at Williamsburg, greatly lamented. A change in command now had to be made in the "Regiment lately commanded by Colonel Scammell." Lafayette proposed to Washington that Hamilton's battalion be enlarged to equal Huntington's; he should "put the eldest of the two lieutenant colonels [Hamilton] upon the right [i.e., leading position] of the brigade." If this change were made, it would reinforce Hamilton's later claim to command the attack on a British redoubt. But whether the alteration in Hamilton's favor was made is uncertain. In the event, Lafayette, to whose division of light troops the assault was committed, did not at first prefer Hamilton for the attack. Also, the general orders of October 8 formed the troops that had been commanded by Scammell into two battalions, one under Lieutenant Colonel Ebenezer Huntington and Major Nathan Rice, the other under Lieutenant Colonel John Laurens and Major John Noble Cumming.

As an artillerist, though now in charge of a light infantry corps, Hamilton must have been absorbed in all the preparations of earthworks and batteries for the siege. His men, like all others, took their turn in fatigue duty, construction work. Fortunately for the diggers, the soil was sandy, but by the same token the embankments, to resist the enemy's cannon, had to be reinforced with gabions and saucissions (wicker baskets and cylinders, filled with earth), and fascines (bundles of poles). Troops otherwise off duty were kept busy in the woods fashioning these materials of uniform dimensions; every unit had its quota to be constantly available to replace the daily consumption. Hamilton's battalion must always have on hand 21 gabions, 70 fascines, 21 saucissions, and 210 pickets for staking down the cylinders. This was fewer than demanded of other units, except Huntington's and Laurens'.

Washington believed the enemy could not be starved out in the interval before the French fleet was due to depart. Therefore Cornwallis' works must be demolished by artillery or, in the last resort, stormed. A regular siege approach by trenches and construction of redoubts and batteries was to be the method. For this the commander in chief relied, among his own officers, on the skill of the engineers, Colonel Louis Duportail and Lieutenant Colonel Jean Baptiste Gouvion, and on the practical experience of Steuben, gained in Europe.

The first "parallel" was a trench 3½ feet deep and 7 feet wide, the earth from which formed the embankment strengthened by gabions, etc., previously prepared. It was opened on the dark, rainy night of October 6, and extended in a gentle outward curve across the level land in front of the British works, for a distance of more than a mile. It may be that the men of Hamilton's battalion, being on the right of the brigade, were among the 4,300 Americans and French put to work on the first night. The digging and shoveling was done by 1,500 men —say 12 feet of trench to a man—while the others sat (to be as much protected as possible) on guard. Strict silence of the workers was enjoined, and troops of Saint-Simon on the extreme left created a diversion that took British attention, so the first parallel, well advanced by morning, was a surprise to the enemy. The left portion was 600 yards from the British center, while the right extension reached the river 800 yards from two advanced British redoubts, known as numbers 9 and 10. These enemy positions made closer approach of the first parallel, on the right, dangerous.

An overelaborate list of "Regulations for the Service of the Siege" was issued in general orders the day before the first parallel was opened. The fifty-five articles, or directions, were evidently translated for the Americans from a French manual, and must have been something of a puzzle to officers altogether new to siege warfare. In spite of all of the prescriptions of safety, expedition, and exactitude, it was later necessary to prevent soldiers, not assigned to the trenches, from entering them as curious onlookers who got in the way of the fatigue parties. In addition, country people from the neighborhood insisted on being "sidewalk superintendents" at close quarters with the diggers. The siege was the most spectacular operation that had ever happened in that vicinity, and like other military engagements of the Revolution (and of the Civil War too, for that matter) drew numbers of civilian spectators.

Work was pushed forward on six redoubts and batteries in the first parallel. The most pretentious and earliest completed was the French "grand battery" on the left of the line. To conserve ammunition, Washington would not begin bombardment until enough guns were in place to give the cannonade substantial effect. A delay of three days was required to drag the heavy siege guns six miles across the peninsula from Trebell's landing on the James River. The soft roads were an obstacle, coupled with shortage of ox teams and horses; extra mounts of officers were pressed into service. However, General Henry Knox, who five years before had brought the guns of Ticonderoga on a longer, harder journey to Dorchester Heights overlooking Boston, had all ordnance mounted by the afternoon of October 9. The artillery included mortars and howitzers for high trajectory shells, and cannon with greater muzzle velocity. The allied arsenal included some large twenty-four-pounders, while the largest British cannon were eighteen-pounders.

The French began the bombardment at three o'clock in the afternoon. Firing continued through the night and into the next morning. The cannon were aimed at embrasures in the enemy's defensive works, with the result that reply of the British guns was reduced. Thomas Nelson, elderly uncle of the governor, who had long been secretary of the commonwealth, and lived in Yorktown, was sent out under a flag of truce. He brought word that works and village were damaged and that the besieged were killing horses they could not feed. However, Nelson said, Cornwallis would hold on tenaciously, since he expected a relief fleet within a week. The French battery on the allied left, commanding the river, set the British *Charon* warship afire with red hot shot. She burned to the waterline, and the conflagration spread to other vessels. De Grasse thought better of his refusal to send a few ships up past the town, to prevent retreat that way.

The allies had to get closer to the British defenses before they could attempt to storm them. Therefore, October 11, a zigzag communication trench was dug from the left of the first parallel to permit construction of the second parallel, which would halve the distance from the enemy works to some 350 yards. As this was extended toward the riverbank, however, fatigue parties would come under fire from the two redoubts advanced beyond the main, inner, British line. The engineers attempted to meet this problem by construction of an epaulement, or well-reinforced shoulder, for a battery that could bombard the menacing forts. If these were taken by the allies, not only could the second parallel be completed, but the guns of these forts could be turned against and enfilade the principal enemy works.

Meantime both sides redoubled their fire, with the two key enemy redoubts, pounded by all guns within range, suffering considerable destruction. The one to the allied left, Number 9, was the larger of the two, garrisoned, it transpired, by 120 British and Germans. Number 10 on the riverbank was defended by 45, also Germans and English. Both had earthen ramparts, surrounded by deep ditches. The embankments measured some 20 feet from top to bottom and had heavy, sharpened stakes set halfway up at an angle to impale assaulters. Each fort was further protected by a barricade, 25 yards wide, formed of felled trees, whose thrusting, tangled branches had been sharpened.

By afternoon of Sunday, October 14, the engineers believed these works had been damaged enough to risk an assault. The attack on Number 9 was committed to the French; Rochambeau assigned to it chasseurs and grenadiers under Baron de Vioménil. Number 10 would be assailed by American light infantry of Lafayette's division. The marquis chose for command of the American force his former aide, Lieutenant Colonel Gimat, who had been with him through the Virginia campaign. Though his battalion was to be included in the assault, Hamilton craved to lead the whole attacking force. Nothing less would satisfy his long ambition for distinction in battle. He saw his last best chance slipping from him, for success in this enterprise would hasten Cornwallis' surrender. He instantly went to Lafayette with his plea for preferment. True, his battalion, unlike Gimat's, which had dogged the movements of Cornwallis all summer, had "just come from the Northward," as Lafayette observed. But Hamilton was senior to Gimat, and was besides the duty officer of the day. Lafayette could sympathize with Hamilton in his demand. He himself, shortly before, had asked Washington for command of the American wing of the combined armies, displacing Lincoln; the latter, Lafayette had suggested, could direct operations across the river. Washington would do nothing so unjust, but had doubtless been glad to console Lafayette with charge of the storm of the riverside redoubt. Lafayette now took Hamilton's claim to the commander in chief, and Hamilton came along to argue his case in person.

The interview was brief. Hamilton burst from the tent, and, embracing Major Nicholas Fish, exclaimed "We have it, we have it!" Lafayette was content, for his own former aide, Gimat, would still play an important role in the attack as commander of the right column. Hamilton's men, pending the assault when darkness came, were directed to eat their dinner and rest behind the lines. It was probably then, in agreement with Hamilton, that Lafayette planned the attack. The vanguard of the right column should be led by Lieutenant John Mansfield, accompanied by a detachment of sappers and miners under Captain James Gilliland, who would remove obstructions. The left column, of eighty men, was to be commanded by Lieutenant Colonel John Laurens; they would circle the redoubt "to take the enemy in reverse, and intercept their retreat." Major Fish, commanding Hamilton's battalion, when the attack reached the barricade, was to veer off to the left to enter the redoubt from that side (the other side, immediately on the edge of the cliff, could not be approached). All would advance with unloaded arms, depend on bayonets only, and move as silently as possible to accomplish surprise.

General Washington visited both detachments, French and American, to give his personal encouragement. He found that Vioménil had given the command of four hundred light troops from the regiments of Royal Deuxponts and Gatenois to Count Guillaume de Deux Ponts, with Baron Claude de l'Estrade [4] as his second. Gatenois troops, under Count Rostaing, formed the reserve. Then he rode over to Hamilton's party. He had not been able to speak to the French in their language, and was short but earnest in exhorting the Americans. By this time the whole army was expecting "something grand to be done by our infantry."

The attacks that night were to be simultaneous, signaled by six quick bursts from a French battery. Saint-Simon would stage a demonstration on the left flank to distract enemy attention to that distant quarter, and General Claude Gabriel Choisy, commanding on the Gloucester side of the river, would feign an assault there.

Soon after darkness fell, at the signal, the detachments sprang from their trenches and advanced without a word spoken. The French were detected first. When a Hessian guard got no reply to his challenge, "Wer da?" the redoubt burst into musket fire. The Americans got closer to their objective before they were discovered. They did not wait for their axmen to cut through the barricade of trees, but struggled over it, pitched into the ditch, and swarmed up the rampart, pulling out the thrusting stakes. Hamilton himself was the first over the parapet into the redoubt, the men of Gimat's battalion on his heels. Laurens en-

---

[4] He must have been the oldest man in either party, for he had seen forty years' service; he was assigned with the idea that he would steady young Deux Ponts.

tered from the open rear of the redoubt, and personally captured the commander, Major Campbell. Fish, leading Hamilton's battalion, came in from the flank in time to participate in the assault.

Seizure of Redoubt Number 10 took only minutes. Hamilton's attackers relied entirely on the bayonet. The storm of Number 9 by the French required longer, about half an hour. This was because the alarm at their advance was earlier given, and the barricade was in better condition than had been expected, forcing the attackers to chop their way through. Also, the French party, of the same number as the American, encountered a much larger enemy garrison.

Washington, from a position near the front line, watched, or rather heard, the attacks, and when it was evident that the redoubts were captured, said, "The work is done, and well done. Billy [his body servant], hand me my horse." In his diary, orders, letters to Congress and to other generals, Washington praised the action in high terms: "The bravery . . . was emulous . . . . Few cases have exhibited stronger proofs of Intrepidity, coolness and firmness than were shown upon this occasion." Considering that this was "the first combined attack of the allied Arms," he added that "The General reflects with the highest degree of pleasure on the Confidence which the Troops of the two Nations must hereafter have in each other . . . . The possession of these two works which we have united to our second parallel gives us infinite advantages for the position of our batteries, and circumscribing the place."

Hamilton, in his report to Lafayette, said, "The rapidity and immediate success of the assault are the best comment on the behaviour of the troops . . . . I do but justice . . . when I . . . assure you, there was not an officer nor soldier whose behaviour, if it could be particularized, would not have a claim to the warmest approbation." He did single out the conduct of each of the leaders—Laurens, Fish, Mansfield, Gimat, Stephen Olney, Hunt, Gilliland, Kirkpatrick—by whose swift gallantry "The redoubt was in the same moment invelopped and carried in every part." Nor did he omit the aid of Colonel Charles Armand and several members of his partisan corps who joined the attack as volunteers, at the head of the right column. Lieutenant Mansfield, who led the vanguard, had Hamilton's special acknowledgment. Hamilton also had more than tactful commendation for Lieutenant Colonel Gimat, whom he had displaced in command of the storm: "I sensibly felt at a critical period the loss of the assistance of Lt. Col. Gimat, who received a musket ball in his foot, which obliged him to retire from the field." Captains Thomas Hunt and Stephen Betts of Laurens' corps suffered bayonet wounds, and Lieutenant Captain Kirkpatrick of the sappers and miners was wounded after entering the ditch.[5] A sergeant and eight privates were killed, and twenty-five privates were wounded. Of the garrison in the redoubt, who were "intitled to the acknowledgement of an honorable defence," eight were killed or wounded. "Incapable of imitating examples of barbarity, and forgetting recent provocations, the soldiery spared every man, who ceased to resist." [6] The major, a captain, an ensign, and seventeen others were made prisoners, and the remainder escaped.

Hamilton left it to others to extol his own leading part in the

[5] Not mentioned in Hamilton's report, Lieutenant Colonel Barber and Major William Barber were slightly wounded.

[6] Dr. William Gordon, whose loose tale-bearing Hamilton had earlier resented, related in his contemporary history of the United States that Lafayette, with Washington's approval, ordered the storming party "to remember New London [Benedict Arnold's raid], and to retaliate by putting the men in the redoubt to the sword after having carried it." He added that the humanity of Hamilton, Laurens, and their followers compelled them to disobey the command and spare the prisoners. Twenty years later, when the canard on Lafayette and Washington was revived in newspapers in America and Europe, Hamilton contradicted it publicly in explicit fashion, for which Lafayette thanked him. Dr. James Thacher, who was called to the wounded in the redoubt "even before the balls had ceased whistling about my ears," had a variant account. Washington, Lafayette, and the massacre of prisoners by Arnold's men at New London did not figure, but a captain, of New Hampshire, threatened to kill Major Campbell to avenge the death of his friend Colonel Scammell, but Hamilton interposed.

exploit. Two days beforehand he had written to his wife, "Thank heaven, our affairs seem to be approaching fast to a happy period. Last night our second parallel commenced. Five [7] days more the enemy must capitulate or abandon their present position." Even if they chose the latter course, Hamilton said their surrender could not be deferred beyond ten days longer. His next letter to his wife told of the attack. "Two nights ago, my Eliza," he wrote on October 16, "my duty and my honor obliged me to take a step in which your happiness was too much risked. I commanded an attack upon one of the enemy's redoubts; we carried it in an instant, and with little loss. You will see the particulars in the Philadelphia papers." Lest she be alarmed for the future, he assured her "There will be, certainly, nothing more of this kind, all the rest will be by approach, and if there should be another occasion, it will not fall to my turn to execute it."

The French, in their capture of Redoubt Number 9, had suffered fifteen killed and seventy-seven wounded; the enemy lost eighteen killed, and fifty were taken prisoner. For leading the assault, Deux Ponts received the title of chevalier in the Military Order of Saint Louis.

That very night the two redoubts were incorporated into the second parallel. Promptly their open sides, toward the enemy, were built up, and their guns played on Cornwallis' inner works at deadly range, 200 yards. The effect on Cornwallis foreshadowed his surrender. October 15, the morning after, he wrote to Sir Henry Clinton, perhaps from a cave under the cliff where he had taken refuge:

Last evening the enemy carried two advanced redoubts on the left by storm, and during the night have included them in their second parallel, which they are at present busy in perfecting. My situation now becomes very critical; we dare not show a gun to their batteries, and I expect that their new ones will open tomorrow morning. Experience has shown that our fresh earthen works do not resist their powerful

[7] He first wrote "four," but his estimate of five was an exact forecast.

artillery, so that we shall soon be exposed to an assault in ruining works, in a bad position, and with weakened numbers. The safety of the place is, therefore, so precarious that I cannot recommend that the fleet and army should run any great risk in endeavoring to save us.

According to Tarleton, the British cavalry leader, "A retreat by Gloucester was the only expedient . . . to avert the mortification of a surrender, or the destruction of a storm."

The British officers, but probably not rank and file, felt that honor compelled them to make at least one sortie against besiegers, no matter how forlorn the hope. The allies had been on guard against such an eruption from the British works. It did not come until predawn of October 16, when 350 of the enemy, in two parties, entered uncompleted French and American batteries of the second parallel. With bayonet points they spiked six cannon—Cornwallis claimed twice as many—but were driven off by grenadiers under Vicomte de Noailles, with casualties on both sides. As Cornwallis reported, "The action . . . proved of little public advantage; for the cannon, having been spiked in a hurry, were soon rendered fit for service again."

The allied bombardment reached its peak during the afternoon and night of the sixteenth, with a hundred guns firing and receiving little answer from crumbled enemy defenses. Cornwallis had but one chance left—to ferry his main force across the river to Gloucester, leaving a detachment to capitulate with the sick and wounded. This he attempted in sixteen boats, beginning at ten o'clock on the night of October 16, but even the elements were against him, for a violent storm of wind and rain, suddenly descending, dispersed the crowded craft. When they were collected the morning of the seventeenth, and the men were returned to Yorktown, the plight of the besieged was desperate. "We . . . could not fire a single gun," Cornwallis lamented; "only one eight-inch and little more than a hundred cohorn shells remained . . . . Our numbers had been

diminished by the enemy's fire, but particularly by sickness."
The British works were now vulnerable to an infantry assault.

At nine or ten o'clock (accounts of the exact time differ) a
red-coated drummer mounted the parapet of the forwardmost
British breastwork and "beat a parley," a call for a conference.
In the smoke and din he was not noticed, and must have been
a glad herald when at length an officer came to his side and
waved a white handkerchief. Thereupon the guns fell silent.
The officer bore a brief message for General Washington. It
read:

Sir, I propose a cessation of hostilities for twenty-four hours, and
that two officers may be appointed by each side, to meet at Mr.
Moore's house, to settle terms for the surrender of the posts at York
and Gloucester.

I have the honor to be, &c
Cornwallis [8]

Washington permitted a two-hour suspension of the pounding
he was giving Cornwallis, not the requested twenty-four,
since there was still the possibility relief might arrive for his
lordship. In the surrender negotiations, Washington refused to
agree to Cornwallis' proposal that his troops, prisoners of war,
be returned to England and Germany. Instead, they would be
marched to locations in America best able to feed them. On the
other hand, Cornwallis was permitted to send the armed sloop
Bonetta to New York with dispatches for Sir Henry Clinton.
The victors agreed to let the vessel leave without examination,
although they knew this would give Cornwallis an opportunity to save some soldiers from being captured. The favored soldiers were some 250 deserters from allied ranks, whom Washington had ordered shot, and who, in the formal capitulation,
were not to be treated as prisoners of war.

On October 18 Lieutenant Colonel John Laurens and Vi-

[8] Among the most momentous documents in American history, the original
(or an autograph copy, perhaps) is in the remarkable collection of Yorktown
materials in the Pierpont Morgan Library, New York City.

comte Louis Marie de Noailles from the allies and Lieutenant
Colonel Alexander Dundas and Major Alexander Ross from the
British, all field officers, worked for long hours on the precise
terms of the capitulation. The articles, signed by Cornwallis
and Captain Thomas Symonds, senior British naval officer, were
sent at eleven o'clock on the morning of October 19 to the
Number 10 redoubt, which Hamilton's corps had captured.
Here Washington, Rochambeau, and Barras (the last acting for
de Grasse, who was unfortunately ill and unable to attend) affixed their names.

The surrender ceremony on the Yorktown siege-ground
commenced at one o'clock, and was marred only by the absence
of Lord Cornwallis, who pled sickness and sent in his place his
second in command, Brigadier General Charles O'Hara. He ini-
tially mistook Rochambeau for Washington, but his error was
quickly corrected, and he presented himself, with Cornwallis'
excuses, to the commander in chief. Since his lordship had sent
a deputy, Washington referred him to General Lincoln, his own
second in command, to receive the surrender. In Trumbull's picture of the scene, Hamilton is mounted close to Washington.
This may have been friendship on the part of the artist, but, fact
or not, it was justice. He had been at Washington's side at headquarters during four years, expressing—and many times sharing
in—his superior's decisions. Then, only five days before, his capture of an enemy redoubt had been prelude to the surrender.

French hussars surrounded an adjacent field where the prisoners were directed by General Lincoln to lay down their
arms. Cornwallis' surrendered force, including seamen, numbered 7,241. Marquis de Choisy, allied commander on the
Gloucester shore, received the prisoners at that post.

The British and German regiments marched through the lines
of American and French troops with colors cased and their
bands playing an English air. "The World Turned Upside
Down" was one title of verses set to the tune. John Laurens,
in the negotiations, had insisted that the vanquished play one of

their own tunes, since the Americans, when they surrendered at Charleston, were not allowed to play the enemy's music. (The right to salute the victor—in this case by playing an American march—was coveted by the conquered as a sign that they had not sacrificed their pride.) The story told years later was that Hamilton saved the conquered another humiliation in the formalities. As officer of the day he was in charge of the surrender ceremony. When the color bearers objected to handing over their standards to sergeants, as had been planned, Hamilton tactfully directed that an ensign, a commissioned officer, accept them, then give them to the enlisted men. The tale, while true to his nature, is apocryphal. There is no evidence that Hamilton was officer of the day, or in charge of the proceedings of the surrender; the cased flags, as the knowledgeable Douglas Freeman concluded,[9] were doubtless grounded, as were the arms.

Hamilton was busy the last days of the siege and immediately after, winding up his responsibilities of command. His letters to his wife were perforce short. The day before the surrender he reported with joy, "Tomorrow Cornwallis and his army are ours. In two days after I shall in all probability set out for Albany, and I hope to embrace you in three weeks from this time." Schuyler, at Albany, told James Duane that Hamilton was sorry not to stop to see him on his way north, but "he thought of nothing but reaching [his wife] the soonest possible, and Indeed he tyred his horses to accomplish it, and was obliged to hire others to come on from Red Hook."

Hamilton had seen his last field service. There was no further fighting in the autumn and winter following Yorktown, nor serious prospect of it for the future. His friend Major Nicholas Fish, with the Second New York Regiment at Pompton, New Jersey, forwarded his camp belongings, which in his hurry to return to Albany, he had left behind. After his "Southern fatigues" Hamilton was "very sick" at Schuyler's home, and at

[9] *George Washington, a Biography*, 6 vols. (New York, Charles Scribner's Sons, 1948–54), V, 391.

the end of December was "still alternately in and out of bed." The Hamiltons' first child, Philip, was born January 22, 1782, which increased Alexander Hamilton's often-expressed inclination to renounce any public appointment and devote himself instead to domestic life.

Under a resolve of Congress (December 31, 1781) Hamilton was among the officers retained in service; General Lincoln, secretary of war, explained that he was included because of his "superior abilities & knowledge." Congress had provided that officers in Hamilton's situation—not belonging to the line of any state nor to any separate corps—were entitled upon retiring to the same emoluments as others. Under these circumstances, Hamilton informed General Washington, in the spring of 1782, that while he did not wish to resign his commission, he would like to be placed temporarily on inactive status. "I sincerely hope a prosperous train of affairs may continue to make it no inconvenience to decline the service of persons, whose zeal, in worse times, was found not altogether useless." If the need arose, he wanted to be able "to renew . . . [his] exertions in the common cause," said Hamilton. "I shall accordingly retain my rank while I am permitted to do it, and take this opportunity to declare, that I shall be at all times ready to obey the call of the public in any capacity civil, or military" which might contribute "to the final attainment of the object for which I embarked in the service." While the difficulties he had experienced in obtaining a field command in the last campaign deterred him from applying for such office again, Hamilton said that the bare possibility of his being further employed in the army did not justify him in accepting "any future emoluments from my commission. I therefore renounce from this time all claim to the compensation attached to my military station during the war or after it." (This renunciation of his pension rights caused difficulty for his widow years later, though she was finally fully compensated in lands and money.) In return for the privilege of keeping his commission without performing its duties, he gave up the claims to which active officers were entitled.

Actually Hamilton was promptly recalled to public service, but in the civil sphere, as collector of federal revenue in the state of New York. It was an important appointment, for the congressional purse was empty—as was plainly revealed when Washington's aide Tench Tilghman carried to Philadelphia the announcement of the surrender. Elias Boudinot recorded, "When the Messenger brought the News of this Capitulation . . . it was necessary to furnish him with hard money for his expenses. There was not a sufficiency in the Treasury to do it, and the Members of Congress, of which I was one, each paid a Dollar to accomplish it."

14

"Unfavourable Prognostics" at Newburgh

Alexander Hamilton would doubtless have succeeded in any profession or line of business enterprise he chose to enter after quitting military service. He had early thought of medicine, influenced probably by his patron in the West Indies, Hugh Knox, who was physician as well as clergyman. Though pious in his youth and a reader of religious works, the church as a calling was never in Hamilton's mind. He had been a clerk in Nicholas Cruger's store in Saint Croix, but did not wish to take advantage of mercantile connections in New York; in the backwash of war, business was disordered, and the city remained in enemy occupation. He had no landed inheritance; though he might have attached himself to the large estate of Philip Schuyler, he from the first showed independence of his father-in-law's bounty. On the other hand, such admired seniors as Elias Boudinot, William Livingston, and James Duane were lawyers, and his college mate Robert Troup was beginning legal practice in Albany. These examples, and Hamilton's own deep concern about the current problems of government,

naturally led him to prepare for the bar. Six months of intensive study after he repaired to Albany from Yorktown accomplished it.

Hamilton's preparations for the bar examination were interrupted to some extent by his service as receiver of Continental revenue for New York, a post to which Robert Morris, superintendent of finance, had appointed him. This practical experience, however, was an introduction to his later public career. It had immediate consequences, also. His main duty was to persuade the state legislature to meet the money requisitions of Congress, and this involved improving the New York tax system in all respects. In addition to local competence and ready response to the calls of Congress, he insisted that restoration of national credit required reform of the Confederation to give the central government adequate fiscal powers. Together with Schuyler, he induced the New York legislature to pass on to Congress a resolve in favor of a convention of all the states for this purpose.

The New York Assembly, impressed by Hamilton's endeavors, elected him a delegate to the Continental Congress in July 1782, and he took his seat in December. Hamilton was immediately plunged into the effort to get Rhode Island to consent to a national 5 percent duty on imports, which would enable Congress to discharge the war debt. Pressure on the smallest state might have succeeded had not the largest, Virginia, withdrawn her approval, so the project failed.

The sorry state of the finances was temporarily forgotten with the arrival of official news, two days before Christmas of 1782, that Great Britain was prepared to conclude peace with the "Thirteen United States of America." (Actually the preliminary treaty had been signed November 30, but this was not known in Congress until later.) To many, the acknowledgment of independence was the grand object for which this country had fought; it necessarily presaged peace, and particular matters in negotiation, compared to that, were minor. Hamilton suspended judgment. Three weeks later (January 12, 1783) he wrote to Governor Clinton:

we have received no further accounts from Europe, so that we remain in the same uncertainty with respect to the negotiations for peace. W[h]ether it will take place or not, is a problem of difficult solution. The duplicity and unsteadiness for which Lord Shelburne [the prime minister] is remarkable will not justify any confidence in his intentions; and the variety of interests to be conciliated in a treaty of peace, with the best intentions on all sides must render it a work of difficulty.

In the same letter he related another quandary. "We have now here a deputation from the army, and feel a mortification of a total disability to comply with their just expectations." The committee from the camp at Newburgh (Major General Alexander McDougall and Colonels Matthias Ogden and John Brooks) had been in Philadelphia since the last of December, and they circulated among members of Congress for a week before formally presenting their petition on January 6, 1783. Washington had warned, back in October, of the fear of the troops that they would be discharged empty-handed and without hope of future pay. Discontent was owing to "the total want of Money . . . and the prospect of poverty and misery before them." Then by mid-December Washington had exerted himself to moderate the tone of demands: "The dissatisfactions of the Army," he confided to his Virginia friend Joseph Jones, "had risen to . . . alarming height," but "by some address . . . their resolutions have been converted into the form in which they will now appear before Congress." The commander in chief had worked to good purpose, for the memorial, signed by General Henry Knox and a dozen officers of lesser rank, was restrained. However, the repression of language did not conceal the disgust that threatened to result in retaliation. Congress was respectfully applied to as "our head and sovereign," but "We complain that shadows have been offered to us while the substance has been gleaned by others . . . . Our distresses are now brought to a point. We have borne all that men can bear—our property is expended—our private resources are at an end . . . . The uneasiness of the soldiers, for want of pay, is . . . dangerous; any further experiments on their patience may have fatal effects."

The deputation from the camp grew more disgruntled by the day as they watched the struggle of Congress to raise a revenue for the treasury. The states, always reluctant to respond to requisitions, relaxed utterly as the prospect of further fighting faded. Hamilton, for his knowledge of the army and of public finance as well, was made chairman of a committee, with Thomas FitzSimons and James Madison, to contrive means of income. At best they were putting new wine in old bottles. "We are deliberating on some mode," he told Clinton, "to ascertain the quotas of the several states." This concerned the mere mechanics of collection, but Congress would remain impoverished while it could only request and not require taxes. "I dislike the principle altogether," Hamilton protested, "but we are tied down by the Confederation."

However, the ill wind of army importunity might blow good. Perhaps clamorous troops would convince sensible men that Congress could not find money without a genuine reform in the structure of government.

Congress had to come up with an answer to General Mc-Dougall's representations on behalf of the restive army. On January 22, 1783, Hamilton prepared the report of a grand committee, which perforce gave only additional promises. The superintendent of finance was to provide present pay "as soon as the state of the public finances will permit." The states should be called upon without delay to settle accounts of their respective regiments to August 1, 1780, and the superintendent of finance was to "take such measures as shall appear to him most proper" for effecting settlement since that date. These recommendations merely acknowledged the debts to the troops. Congress could furnish no security for actual payment by the states.

Its own obligations since August 1780 would be discharged when the states came forward with moneys sufficient to permit "funding the whole debt of the United States."

The officers had asked that their promised half pay for life be commuted into a lump sum. Hamilton, writing for the committee of Congress, recommended that officers have the option of claiming half pay for life or full pay for six years. It is not clear whether this was to be given them in a single sum one year after the conclusion of peace, or in six annual payments commencing then. It was probably the latter. Hamilton judged, on the basis of actuarial tables, that six years of full pay would equal half pay for life. In any event, payment was to be in money or in funded debt bearing annual interest of 6 percent. The committee said it would report later on what was due on account of deficiencies of rations and clothing, when more precise information on these subjects was obtained.

Congress rejected, then adopted, the first part of the report, but referred the questions of commutation of half pay of officers, and deficiencies, to a special committee, of which Hamilton was a member. All of this, obviously, was for the future, but no better could be offered at the moment.

Two days afterward Hamilton, evidently deprecating these shaky provisions for satisfying the just claims of the army, in a speech in Congress "went extensively into the subject" of raising funds for the United States. Permanent revenue must either (1) come from taxes laid within each state as the state chose, and be collected under authority of the state or of Congress, or (2) come from taxes extending "generally & uniformly throughout the U.S., & . . . be collected under the authority of Congs." Revenue of the second sort, levied and collected by the national government, was preferable. He showed why this was simpler, more certain, and more economical.

In the following weeks he continued to hammer away on this theme, the complaints of the unpaid army rumbling as an obbligato. When funds were under consideration, he wanted the doors open to the public. In mid-February he broached to General Washington the possibility that the discontent of the troops might be guided for their own and the public benefit. "The state of our finances," he began, "was perhaps never more critical . . . . It is probable we shall not take the proper measures, and . . . a few months may open an embarrassing scene. This will be the case whether we have peace or a continuance of the war." He did not mince matters. "If the war continues . . . the army must in June subsist itself *to defend* the country; if peace should take place it *will* subsist itself to *procure justice to itself.*" The army appeared to believe "that the disposition to recompense their services will cease with the necessity for them, and that if they once lay down their arms, they will part with the means of obtaining justice."

He entered on the "serious inquiry what will be the true line of policy." He relied, as he said, on Washington's willingness to receive his observations "as dictated by a regard to the public good." Further, Hamilton was more intimately acquainted with the shilly-shallying in Congress than the commander in chief could be. So the former headquarters aide suggested that the discontent in camp might actually be beneficial:

The claims of the army urged with moderation, but with firmness, may operate on those weak minds which are influenced by their apprehensions more than their judgments; so as to produce a concurrence in the measures which the exigencies of affairs demand. They may add weight to the applications of Congress to the several states. So far an useful turn may be given to them. But the difficulty will be to keep a *complaining* and *suffering army* within the bounds of moderation.

Hamilton sketched the role he believed Washington should play in this parlous posture. "Your Excellency's influence" should be exerted

not to discountenance their endeavours to procure redress, but rather by the intervention of confidential and prudent persons, *to take the direction of them.* This however must not appear: it is of moment to

291

the public tranquillity that Your Excellency should preserve the confidence of the army without losing that of the people. This will enable you in case of extremity to guide the torrent, and bring order, perhaps even good, out of confusion.

Hamilton, a month earlier, had been on the small committee directed to confer with General McDougall and his companions in the deputation from the camp. McDougall had befriended Hamilton from the younger man's first entry into the army, and indeed before that, when he was a student in King's College. Hamilton was also on cordial terms with Colonels Ogden and Brooks, especially Brooks, who had once made inquiries for him in a sensitive personal matter. So their discussion must have been perfectly frank, and doubtless influenced his next offering to Washington:

I will not conceal from Your Excellency a truth which it is necessary you should know. An idea is propagated in the army that delicacy carried to an extreme prevents your espousing its interests with sufficient warmth. The falsehood of this opinion no one can be better acquainted with than myself; but it is not the less mischievous for being false. Its tendency is to impair that influence, which you may exert with advantage, should any commotions . . . ensue, to moderate the pretensions of the army and make their conduct correspond with their duty.

This brought the writer to his constant insistence: "The great *desideratum* at present is the establishment of general funds, which alone can do justice to the Creditors of the United States (of whom the army forms the most meritorious class), restore public credit and supply the future wants of government." And he emphasized again that to this end the demands of the army, properly directed, could contribute. A postscript suggested a desirable intermediary: "General Knox has the confidence of the army & is a man of sense. I think he may safely be made use of. Situated as I am [i.e., in Congress] Your Excellency will feel the confidential nature of these observations."

To Governor Clinton he expressed the fear that "the Army

will not disband, till solid arrangements are made for doing it justice; and I fear these arrangements will not be made." A means of preventing civil commotions on the arrival of peace would be for the New York legislature to "set apart a tract of territory, and make a liberal allowance to every officer and soldier of the Army at large who would become a citizen of the State . . . . I believe a large part of the Army would incline to sit down among us, and then all we shall have to do will be to govern well." Hamilton was always anxious to increase the productive population. When New York City was evacuated by the British, he deplored the departure of many Tories who would have added to the wealth of the community. For the country at large he urged the immigration of Europeans, especially those skilled in "the mechanic arts."

Hamilton had inside information that the camp at Newburgh would soon flare into excited threats unless the troops were paid. This he may have received from his friend Colonel Walter Stewart of Philadelphia, who within a few weeks would provoke protests bordering on wholesale mutiny. In a conversation on February 20, 1783, with Madison, Daniel Carroll, Richard Peters, Nathaniel Gorham, and Thomas FitzSimons, at the home of the last named, Hamilton opined that "the army had secretly determined not to lay down their arms until due provision . . . should be afforded on the subject of their pay." Following a public declaration, "plans had been agitated if not formed for subsisting themselves." Hamilton also told the group that General Washington had become unpopular among almost all ranks "from his known dislike to every unlawful proceeding." Leading officers were said to be planning a movement to displace him in favor of a general whose name, in Madison's notes of the discussion, was crossed out. At this point, in a confidential company, Hamilton spoke of Washington's irritability, which comment, as always, was followed by appreciation of the commander in chief's noble qualities. Hamilton's words are worth quoting. He knew "Genl. Washington

intimately and perfectly . . . his extreme reserve, mixed sometimes with . . . asperity of temper both of which . . . have increased of late, had contributed to the decline of his popularity;
but . . . his virtue his patriotism & his firmness would . . .
never yield to any dishonorable or disloyal plans into which he
might be called; . . . he would sooner suffer himself to be cut
in pieces." This being his true character, Hamilton "wished
him to be the conductor of the army in their plans for redress, in
order that they might be moderated & directed to proper objects,
& exclude some other leader who might foment and misguide
their councils." He had taken the liberty to write in this vein to
General Washington.[1]

The outlook for money for the troops in this emergency had
been darkened when, a few months earlier, the resourceful
Robert Morris had notified Congress that he would resign as superintendent of finance June 1 unless the states provided adequate funds by that time. When the ban of secrecy on his intention was lifted, Hamilton told Governor Clinton, "This will
be a severe stroke to our affairs. No man fit for the office will be
willing to supply his place for the very reasons he resigns."

General Washington, distant from the political scene, was re-
markably unaware of the plight that exercised Hamilton; "so far
was I," he wrote, "from conceiving that our finances were in
so deplorable a state, *at this time*, that I had imbibed ideas . . .
that with the prospect of a loan from Holland we should be

---

[1] Apropos sufferings of the army, Hamilton was concerned for them not only
in his public capacity but as a private man. He wrote at this time to Samuel
Hodgdon, commissary of military stores: "The bearer Abby Mot is a soldiers
widow in great distress who wants to go to her friends in the Jerseys but has
not the means. If you could find her a place in some public waggon going
that way, you would do an act of charity." A few years later Hamilton paid the
funeral expenses for Abby Mott. Doubtless he attended to other similar applications. Those who regard him as hard and arrogant overlook his quick sympathy
with the unfortunate. Near what he knew might be the last hour of his life, he
interceded with a friend on behalf of a humble, poor man, and he made sure
that the woman who did washing for Mrs. Hamilton would be duly paid. He
himself as a young orphan had received generous charity, which was a tribute
to his own engaging qualities as well as to the kindness of his benefactors.

able to rub along." But he was acutely conscious of tendencies in the army, which might lead to "Civil commotions & end in blood . . . . God forbid we should be involved in it . . . . The sufferings of a complaining army on one hand, and the inability of Congress and tardiness of the States on the other [of which Hamilton had informed him], are the forebodings of evil," but he did not despair of prudence overcoming impetuosity. "In this however I may be mistaken, if those ideas which . . . are propagated in the Army, should be extensive." He had no proof, but suspected that "the old leven [the Gates-Conway cabal] . . . is again beginning to work, under the mask of the most perfect dissimulation & apparent cordiality."

Washington said he would pursue his "same steady line of conduct," relying on the discerning part of the army to credit his goodwill. Hamilton's suggestions for ruling the storm coincided with the general's own policy, which (doubtless with Knox as his agent) had thus far prevented desperate action. The immediate crisis might be surmounted, but Washington agreed with Hamilton that "unless Congress have powers competent to its *general* purposes . . . the distresses we have encountered, the expences we have incurred, and the blood we have spilt in the course of an Eight years war, will avail us nothing."

The camp near Newburgh seemed quiet enough when, on March 10, appeared an invitation to a meeting of general and field officers next day, and a stirring appeal to them to act on the representations McDougall's committee had taken to Congress. Both papers were anonymous. It was afterward known that they were circulated by Colonel Walter Stewart, who had been called from Philadelphia to camp to discharge his duties as inspector for the northern army. The addresses had been written by Major John Armstrong, Jr. Washington forestalled precipitate action by denouncing "such disorderly proceedings" and by appointing a meeting for March 15 to adopt measures "to attain the just and important object in view." The senior officer present should preside. This quashed the voluntary assemblage, but before that scheduled by Washington could be held, "a second address to the Officers" was "thrown into circulation." Composed with dangerous skill, it declared America had disdained the officers' cries. "If this, then, be your treatment, while the swords you wear are necessary to the defence of America, what have you to expect from peace, when your voice shall sink, and your strength dissipate by division?" If officers, thus spurned, could "consent to wade through the vile mire of dependency," then "Go, starve, and be forgotten." The present moment must be seized. "If your determination be in any proportion to your wrongs, carry your appeal from the justice to the fears of government." The army had its alternative. If peace ensued, "then nothing can separate [the people] from your arms but death: if war . . . you will retire to some unsettled country, smile in your turn, and 'mock when their fear cometh on.' " In other words, if peace came, the country had a bear by the tail; if the war continued, the army would desert its defense and perhaps set up a separate government in a remote region.

On March 12 Washington sent copies of all three papers to the president of Congress and wrote to Hamilton at length about the storm that "suddenly arose with unfavourable prognostics." He did not name Stewart, who had brought to the camp his insinuation of the wicked design of Congress to wait for peace, then dismiss the soldiers, unpaid, to fend for themselves. Washington knew his identity, as did Hamilton, but could only guess at the author of the inflammatory addresses. It was also suggested that "the public creditors looked up to [the army] for Redress of their own grievances, wd afford them every aid, and even join them in the Field if necessary." Further, "some members of Congress wishd the measure might take effect, in order to compel the public, particularly the delinquent States, to do justice." Washington was obliged, therefore, to call the official meeting "in order to arrest on the spot, the foot that stood wavering on a tremendous precipice."

"Let me beseech you . . . my good Sir," Washington concluded in his letter to Hamilton, "to urge this matter earnestly, and without further delay. The situation of these Gentlemen . . . is distressing beyond description. It is affirmed to me, that a large part of them have no further prospect before them than a Goal [Gaol], if they are turned loose without a liquidation of accts." The delegates of delinquent states should be told that "if any disastrous consequences should follow . . . they must be answerable to God and their Country for . . . ineffable horrors."

General Washington appeared before the meeting in "The Temple," a large wooden building erected by the soldiers for both religious services and social events. He was following Hamilton's advice to take direction of the ferment. He began by excusing his attendance on the officers' deliberations; he had not meant to be present, but felt obliged to come and read his own statement after the incitements of the anonymous addresses. The latter were "calculated to impress the mind with an idea of premeditated injustice in the sovereign power of the United States, and rouse all those resentments which must inevitably flow from such a belief." To pry pay from Congress with bayonets or to abandon America to its enemies was alike a despicable course. So far as was consistent with the great duty he owed his country "and those powers we are bound to respect," the army could freely command his services for rewarding all their toils and dangers. He trusted the officers would "place a full confidence in the purity of intentions of Congress." They would allow "posterity to say, when speaking of the glorious example you have exhibited to mankind, 'had this day been wanting, the world had never seen the last stage of perfection to which human nature is capable of attaining.' "

This was his climax; a practiced orator would not have gone on to read a letter from Joseph Jones, in Congress, explaining the vexations of that body. An interjected remark, however, proved more effective than his speech. The letter was closely penned, he stumbled through a few sentences, then reached for his new spectacles. "Gentlemen," he said, "you must pardon me. I have grown gray in your service and now find myself growing blind."

That did it; the casual remark evoked all the love that the army bore for its leader. With little opposition the officers passed the resolutions that Washington wished, repudiating the anonymous addresses, declaring faith in Congress, and asking the commander in chief to represent them. This assurance that the army would not disgrace itself was timely, for just then Captain Joshua Barney arrived with the text of the provisional treaty of peace, signed November 30, 1782.

Before he could know the result at Newburgh, Hamilton candidly told Washington that he had openly encouraged the army to make common cause with the other creditors in prodding the states, but that he eschewed use of force. He had opposed using a proposed import duty exclusively to raise payment for the army, since "it was impolitic to divide the interests of the civil & military Creditors," whose joint efforts were necessary to procure a general revenue. Hamilton soon secured action by Congress permitting officers entitled to half pay for life to commute this into a lump sum equal to full pay for five years, this to be discharged in money or in securities at 6 percent, the same as given to other creditors.

As to the preliminary articles of peace, Hamilton deprecated their conclusion with Great Britain without waiting for the consent of France. The French, he said, should be notified of the secret article favoring Britain's claim to West Florida. However, the secret article lost pertinence when, on March 24, 1783, Congress learned by a letter from Lafayette that Britain, France, and Spain had concurred in the preliminary treaty of peace.

In the following weeks Hamilton was constantly engaged on the problem of how to disband the army with fairness and safety in the face of an empty treasury. In the middle of April 1783 Washington wrote Hamilton, "I should do injustice . . . were I not to inform you, that [the army] consider you as a friend, Zealous to serve them, and one who has espoused their interests in Congress upon every proper occasion." The numbers of letters which passed in rapid succession between the commander in chief at Newburgh and Hamilton in Congress show that the young legislator was a principal instrument in liquidating the war. He helped persuade the superintendent of finance to hold on until the troops could be dismissed with three months' pay. He was concerned in evacuation of western posts by the British, with return of prisoners, and with provision of a small peacetime army. Looking to the near future, Hamilton urged on Washington that his exertions would be as essential in making independence truly a blessing as they had been in winning the country's freedom.

Turmoil continued in the army. Washington's appearance at The Temple meeting had quieted the officers, but rank-and-file grievances were brought to a head by a decision of Congress, to which Hamilton assented: that the men be furloughed to their homes, though the states had not furnished money to pay them even one month's wages. In the middle of June 1783 sergeants of new recruits in the barracks at Philadelphia remonstrated against accepting their separations until they were paid. Congress took no notice of this irregular proceeding. Major John Armstrong, Jr., author of the incendiary addresses circulated at Newburgh, was in Philadelphia, still stirring discontents, though there is no direct evidence that he made mischief among the sergeants. Mutiny ensued. John Dickinson, president of the Executive Council of Pennsylvania, sent to Congress letters that he had received from Colonel Richard Butler, commanding the Third Pennsylvania Regiment, and from William Henry of Lancaster. These told that eighty armed soldiers had broken away from their officers at Lancaster and were marching to Philadelphia "to co-operate with those now in the city . . . to procure their pay (or perhaps to possess themselves of money at any rate)." They hinted that they might "rob the bank, the treasury, &c. &c."—the latter impossible, since it was empty. Colonel

Butler's efforts to restrain them had been in vain. He had explained to them that to be paid they must remain at Lancaster. The defection, Butler believed, had originated in Philadelphia, where "the flame is supported by inimical . . . people." He sent officers after the decamping men to warn that "your presence at Philadelphia . . . will be justly construed into *menace*, rather than a proper mode of seeking justice."

Immediately Hamilton was named chairman of a committee, with Oliver Ellsworth and Richard Peters, to arrest the danger. In the trying days that followed, he threw himself into efforts to preserve the safety and dignity of Congress. Hamilton and his colleagues first went to the Executive Council of Pennsylvania, urging that a detachment of militia be sent to intercept the mutineers on their march before they could unite with the troops in the Philadelphia barracks. The council was reluctant to call out any part of the militia, since it was thought they would not respond unless and until "some outrage should have been committed by the troops." That attempt failing, Hamilton, for the committee, requested Major William Jackson, assistant secretary of war, to meet the marchers and persuade them to return to Lancaster and their duty. "You will represent to them, that their accounts cannot be settled without their officers whom they have left behind them at Lancaster." If they chose to stop where they were, they could have provisions. If they persisted in coming to town, Jackson must give Congress the earliest notice of their progress and temper.

The rebellious eighty, unheeding, pressed on and reached Philadelphia Friday morning, June 20, 1783. They united with the troops in the barracks, now numbering some five hundred. However, as none erupted from the barracks, Congress adjourned as usual Friday afternoon to Monday morning. Hamilton's committee arranged with the superintendent of finance for prompt payment of the Lancaster contingent when they had marched back to their post. General Arthur Saint Clair, commanding the Pennsylvania line, was summoned.

Saturday morning produced trouble. Elias Boudinot, president of Congress, was notified that the troops in the barracks had thrown off the authority of their officers and promised to raid the bank. Boudinot called the members of Congress to assemble in emergency session that afternoon. Sentinels were posted at the doors of the State House (Independence Hall), where both Congress and the Executive Council met. The building was surrounded by three hundred or more soldiers, armed and some of them drunk; fifteen or twenty were close to the windows of the council chamber. Congress lacked a quorum when Dickinson entered to announce that the mutineers had made demands of the council which the council unanimously rejected. The "noncommissioned officers and soldiers now in this city" required of the council "authority to appoint commissioned officers to command us and redress our grievances . . . . You will immediately issue such authority and deliver it to us, or . . . we shall instantly let in those injured soldiers upon you . . . . You have only twenty minutes to deliberate on this important matter." Seven sergeants commanded the rebels, who had bayonets fixed.

Meantime General St. Clair had reached Congress; he reported that veteran troops from Charleston, recently arrived, had been forced by the mutineers to join them in disobeying their officers and leaving the barracks. St. Clair planned to attempt to march the troops to their quarters. Congress sat surrounded for three hours, then rose, and the members passed without incident through the cordon. St. Clair calmed most of the mutineers by promising that they might appoint officers to represent them in dealing with the Executive Council. His success was incomplete, for the rebels seized the powder house and some other arsenals, acquiring several fieldpieces.

This increased the alarm of Congress, which met again that Saturday night. Hamilton appears to have drafted the resolution informing the Executive Council of Pennsylvania that the authority of the United States having been grossly insulted, and the peace of the capital being endangered, effectual steps must be immediately taken in correction. Hamilton's committee was to go back to the council, and if "prompt exertions of this State for supporting the dignity of the federal government" were not to be expected, Congress would meet next at Trenton or Princeton. The secretary of war was directed to ask General Washington to dispatch to Philadelphia a force to suppress any disturbances.

Hamilton and Ellsworth (Peters had been dropped from the congressional committee, perhaps because he was a Philadelphian) went to Dickinson that night, and were promised that the Executive Council would meet them at Dickinson's home next morning, Sunday. The council then declined to call on the militia unless it received assurance from militia officers that their troops would obey. The next day, Monday, the conference was resumed. The council refused to give an answer in writing to the committee, but said it would reply to a request from Congress itself. Orally, the council explained that the militia could not be relied upon. In case of actual violence to persons and property, doubtless a body of citizens would arm themselves, but the council did not know what measure of outrages would produce this protection. Commissioned officers, chosen by the mutineers to represent them, were negotiating for their submission. Hamilton and Ellsworth said Congress had felt compelled to use coercion. The rebels, far from subsiding, had written the officers acting for them, threatening them with death if they did not secure the soldiers' pay by whatever means necessary.

As the committee could put no reliance in the council to suppress the revolt, it had no option but to advise the president of Congress to shift the sessions to Trenton or Princeton.

Hamilton wrote a few days later (June 29, 1783) to Governor George Clinton: "The conduct of the executive of this state [Pennsylvania] was to the last degree weak & disgusting . . . they pretended it was out of their power to bring out the militia, without making the experiment. The feebleness on their part determined the removal of Congress from a place where they could receive no support; and I believe they will not easily be induced to return."

Major General Robert Howe led his fifteen hundred troops from West Point first to Princeton, to which place Congress had removed, then to Philadelphia. The mutiny melted away. The Pennsylvania council finally mustered five hundred militia to restore order. The troops were deserted by two officers who had instigated their rebellion: Captain Henry Carbery and Lieutenant John Sullivan, who fled to England. The remaining four officers of the rebels' committee were arrested. The Lancaster troops returned to their post.

Hamilton and Ellsworth had been reluctant to recommend that Congress flee Philadelphia; the spectacle of the federal government forced out of its capital would have a bad effect on the peace negotiations in Europe, and embarrass relations between national and state authorities. Dr. Benjamin Rush—this was sour grapes—charged a member of Congress, "If you remain one week longer at Princeton feeding one another with ideas of . . . wounded dignity . . . you may loose Philadelphia forever from your plans of continental revenue." And John Armstrong, Jr., rhetorical as ever, apprized General Gates: "The grand Sanhedrin of the Nation, with all their solemnity & emptiness . . . have removed to Princeton, & left a State, where their wisdom has been long questioned, their virtue suspected, & their dignity a jest."

The Pennsylvania Executive Council, by refusing to make Philadelphia safe for the national legislature, had done the city a disservice; Congress, in spite of appeals to return, moved to Annapolis in November 1783, to Trenton a year later, thence to New York City, and did not go back to Philadelphia until seven years after the mutiny that drove it out. Hamilton did not recommend departure in order to further the chances of New York to become the permanent seat of the central government.

However, he did alert Governor Clinton to "the advantages that will accrue to a state from being the residence of Congress." And President Boudinot, a Jerseyman, hoped his brother Elisha would bring his "Troop of Horse . . . to meet us at Princeton." This welcome "may fix Congress as to their permanent residence."

The mutiny in Philadelphia underscored the need of the national government for a preserve under its own control, which resulted in the District of Columbia. The experience influenced Hamilton's plans for a sufficient standing army and for a degree of federal power over the militia of the states. Furthermore, when Congress assembled at Princeton, Hamilton had ready a plea for a convention "with full powers to revise the Confederation." But when Congress achieved a quorum, it was apparent to Hamilton that the delegates were absorbed in business flowing from the mutiny and that the time was not auspicious for presenting his proposals regarding a constitution.

A sequel of the war was formation of the Society of the Cincinnati, named for the Roman hero who abandoned his plow at the call of military service. Limited to officers, it was a select company of men knit by experiences shared in camp and campaign. The membership was congenial to Hamilton personally, and coincided with his belief that the community should accept the leadership of an élite of proven patriotism and competence. Hamilton had more concern for the body of citizens than he had confidence in their wisdom, except on great issues that had been thoroughly explored and discussed. In interim decisions, he felt, the public welfare was best served by a small group of special fitness and responsibility.

Hamilton was not among the founders of the Society of the Cincinnati at the Newburgh encampment in the spring of 1783, for he had returned to civil life eighteen months before. He promptly became a member, and defended the organization against its critics, whether shrill or insinuating. In one of the few instances of his opposition to Washington's views he stoutly held to the provision of hereditary membership. He succeeded Washington as president-general of the Society and so remained until his own death.

General Henry Knox was the projector of the society. At West Point, April 15, 1783, he drafted a constitution, which, with some amendments, gave form to the society as organized May 10 at Newburgh, Baron Steuben presiding. The officers, about to disband, had little to take with them except their friendships, their pride in honorable service, and their devotion to the independence and unity of their country. Any officer, military or naval, American or foreign, who had been engaged for three years or was on duty at the time, was eligible, as were their eldest sons after them. Each contributed one month's pay, the interest from this fund to be used to relieve needy members or the families of those deceased. Washington was invited to be the first to put his name to the society's constitution and was at once elected president-general. Major Pierre Charles L'Enfant, whose artistry was often requisitioned in the new nation, designed the emblem of the order, a bald eagle covered and surrounded, front and back, by mottoes and symbolic figures, chiefly pertaining to Cincinnatus, the Roman farmer-soldier.

Immediately came an outcry, in print, from Aedanus Burke, Hugh H. Brackenridge, and Comte Gabriel de Mirabeau, and less publicly from John Adams, John Jay, and Thomas Jefferson. In varying degrees, they condemned the society as an attempt to establish a hereditary nobility in the American Republic. At the first general meeting of representatives of the constituent state societies, at Philadelphia in 1784, Washington went to the length of recommending that unless the grounds of popular complaint were eliminated, the society be terminated. When proposed changes were referred to branches in the states, Hamilton, as chairman of the New York committee to consider them, reported in favor of certain modifications, but insisted that the hereditary feature was essential to continuance of the organization. So many other states took the same stand that the society remained unaltered in this respect.

Protests against the character and objects of the Society of the Cincinnati soon died away, and the organization honorably and actively survives, the oldest originating in the American Revolution.

Just as Hamilton, in the army, was rapidly drawn to the center of action, at Washington's headquarters, so after the peace he soon became a figure in national political life. While still preparing himself for the bar, he served under Robert Morris as collector of congressional revenue in New York. Elected to his state legislature, he was sent thence as a delegate to the Continental Congress. Experience thus gained deepened his conviction of the necessity of reorganization to vest more power in the national government. The war had compelled a measure of cooperation between the states, but when hostilities ceased, disunity threatened. The states quarreled over territorial boundaries, injured each other for trade advantage, sent mostly second-rate men to Congress, and did not meet the interest on the national debt. Foreign governments, seeing the incapacity of Congress to honor commitments, declined to conclude commercial treaties. Had independence been won only to be followed by partitioning of the country between Britain, France, and Spain?

Alexander Hamilton was early and prominent among public men who insisted that the permissive Articles of Confederation be displaced by a constitution that would subordinate the states, in national affairs, to a central authority. The Annapolis Commercial Convention of 1786 was about to adjourn, confessing utter failure to lessen internal trade rivalries. Hamilton seized the moment of despair to draft a report calling on the states to meet the following year in Philadelphia for the larger purpose of revising the constitutional structure. As a delegate from New York, Hamilton's arguments helped to strengthen the federal government. The *Federalist Papers*, written by Hamilton, James Madison, and John Jay, were influential, and Hamilton's intensive efforts in the New York ratifying convention were decisive in securing approval of the new constitution by that state.

Chosen by President Washington as secretary of the treasury, Hamilton devised the solvency of the national government without which its sovereignty could not be supported. So excellent was his fiscal management that he was able to borrow in Holland at the lowest rates of interest paid by any government. To protect against smuggling at the ports, he established (1790) the service of revenue cutters, which was the origin of the United States Coast Guard. Hamilton's policies were opposed within the cabinet by Thomas Jefferson, secretary of state, and the two aired their differences before the country in a fashion that drew remonstrance from President Washington. Jefferson was jealous for the authority of the individual states, Hamilton for the power of Congress. Jefferson's political and economic views were libertarian; Hamilton was impressed by the need for social controls and deliberate planning. Jefferson's forte was democracy, Hamilton's was effective organization. These two became the leaders of opposing parties, Jefferson of the Republicans (later Democrats), Hamilton of the Federalists. Jefferson resigned from the cabinet in 1793, temporarily leaving official advantage to Hamilton.

15

Punitive Expedition

 The suppression of the Whiskey Insurrection in western Pennsylvania in 1794 was a military operation. Its purpose was to permit collection of the excise tax on domestic distilled spirits. In that formative period of American public life, vehement differences of view over the extent of national authority and the means chosen to uphold it inevitably gave the episode political significance. This earliest overt instance of vindicating central constitutional power set a precedent.

Hamilton directed the expedition, under President Washington's aegis. He acted primarily in his civil capacity as secretary of the treasury, because public revenue was being withheld, and in accompanying the troops he of course did not wear a uniform. It so happened that at this time he was also discharging the duties of the secretary of war, in General Knox's extended absence in New England on private business, so he was occupied beforehand with arrangements for recruiting, equipment, and supply of the punitive force. In the heart of the rebellious country he superintended the cavalry detachment that seized suspected leaders for trial. When Washington was obliged to return to the capital and handed over command to Governor Henry Lee of Virginia, Hamilton prepared Lee's instructions.

The excise tax on liquors distilled in this country (chiefly whiskey, but also rum and gin) was enacted in 1791 on Hamilton's recommendation. It was necessary to supply funds to permit the national government to assume payment of the war debts of the states. Besides other causes of antagonism, this purpose of the excise raised objection among states' rights advocates. At first glance one would suppose the individual states would be glad to have the federal treasury shoulder their burdens. But not so, since this was expected to aggrandize the central government, to which creditors of the states would now look and which would claim their chief loyalty. Also, those states that had made progress in repaying their debts contended they would be taxed to help meet the obligations of sister states that were laggard. This last, though vigorously urged, was a misunderstanding, for an equitable accounting scheme was adopted.

Actually the distillers along the Atlantic seaboard, primarily of rum from West Indian molasses, paid the tax with little opposition. It was the western, overmountain districts that in great part refused to comply with the law and defied measures of enforcement. Dissatisfaction in the back country of the Carolinas died down, but violence broke out in four counties of Pennsylvania—Washington, Westmoreland, Allegheny, and Fayette—and in Ohio County, Virginia. The mountain range formed a physical barrier, which became also a political division between the eastern region and the far frontier. Braddock's and Forbes' roads to Pittsburgh, each hastily cut for a single military need, had become mere tracks through the forests and mountain fastnesses, over which wagons could not pass for any distance. Packhorses could not carry such heavy, low-priced western products as grain, hides, and salt on the three-week, three-hundred-mile journey to the coastal markets. Such raw goods had to be floated on flatboats down the Ohio River and into the Mississippi. This was a slow and toilsome conveyance, and when New Orleans was at last reached, the Spaniards, likely as not, refused permission to land the cargoes for reloading on ocean vessels. This obstruction the westerners held to be a concession to Spain in return for trade advantages for eastern ports. The man who had engineered this prejudicial bargain was no other than John Jay, whose treaty with hated England was incurring heated opposition when the Whiskey Insurrection reached its height.

Though the Mississippi was effectively blocked, and the mountain trails were impracticable for bulky wares, the westerners could turn their grain into whiskey, swing two kegs of it over a horse's back, and sell in Lancaster or Reading for one dollar a gallon what had cost fifty cents in the Ohio valley. This was the principal means of getting cash for purchase of such few goods as the isolated region required from outside. If a tax must be paid on their whiskey, the profit, the westerners insisted, would be correspondingly lessened; in any event, they lacked money for taxes, since the economy of the interior operated largely on barter.

The overmountain district was mainly self-sufficient. What did the national government do for these remote settlers? The Indians raided cabins in the clearings, burning and murdering, for the two expeditions sent against them from the East, the first under General Josiah Harmar, the second under General Arthur St. Clair, were disgraceful failures. The British, undisturbed in their possession of the western posts, egged the savages on. The self-reliant men who had braved the wilderness were poor, democratic in their life as in their politics, and accustomed to defending themselves and their principles with their rifles. The combination of whiskey and gunpowder among simple folk out to protect what they held to be their dearest rights portended violence whenever they were aggrieved.

The westerners were encouraged in their antagonism to the national government by citizen Edmond Charles Genêt, the first minister of Republican France to the United States. Among other high-handed acts disrespectful to the American government and intended to favor his own, he had founded in Philadelphia a Democratic Society, which became the parent of forty others. In the eyes of the Federalists, these societies, especially influential in the West, were more inclined toward liberty, in the style of the French Revolution, than toward obedience to law. The societies of Mingo Creek and Pittsburgh were principal centers of resistance to the excise tax. Gatherings were difficult in a thinly populated district, so militia musters were apt to be occasions of political discussions.

Opposition commenced as soon as the law was passed. At first this took the form of meetings that adopted resolutions condemning the tax and declaring that the revenue officers would be held in public contempt. Delegates from the protesting counties, convened at Pittsburgh in August 1792, were particularly vehement against the excise and promised to use all lawful means to obstruct its enforcement. Hamilton, reviewing the protest of the westerners, pointed out that it was perfectly legal to take steps to repeal a law, but that to obstruct its operation was criminal. Albert Gallatin, who was developing his large estate on the Monongahela, was secretary of this meeting, and was believed to have drawn the menacing resolves. Since Gallatin was one of the few men of responsible leadership in that region, Hamilton never forgave him. Gallatin himself later called his part in this meeting, which helped rouse the insurgents, "my only political sin."

From talk, enmity to the law progressed to forcible interference, at first by vigilante bands. "Tom the Tinker," later identified as one John Holcroft, would shoot up the equipment of a complying distiller, and post a notice threatening that the same treatment should be expected by any other who paid the tax. Hamilton, in the treasury, took note of such doings. He recognized that an excise was historically held to be odious, that a similar law of Pennsylvania had proved a dead letter, and that the act he had drawn could be modified in ways that would help to meet the objections of the western people, though easterners had already paid a million dollars in obedience to the law as it stood. The secretary made administrative changes to serve local convenience, and secured from Congress amendments in the same behalf. These concessions, interpreted as retreat by the government, provoked more recalcitrance.

In justifying the proclamation he drew for the President (September 1792), warning against further infractions, Hamilton recited the acts of violent resistance to that time. Robert Johnson, collector for Allegheny and Washington Counties, was waylaid by men armed and disguised, who cut off his hair, tarred and feathered him, and took away his horse. The deputy marshal was afraid to serve processes, and turned them over to another, who was unhorsed, tarred, and tied for hours in the woods. The collector for Fayette and Westmoreland Counties was mistreated. One Wilson, mistaken for an inspector of stills, got the full treatment. He was dragged to a blacksmith shop, stripped naked, burned with irons, tarred and feathered, and "dismissed . . . in a very suffering condition." Washington's proclamation urging compliance and further easing the requirements merely incited more serious outrages. The home of General John Neville, inspector of the survey, was attacked by five hundred men under a major of militia, who made the few defenders surrender, then burned all the buildings. The inspector escaped with his records, and together with the marshal fled to Philadelphia by a circuitous route. The eastbound mail from Pittsburgh, thought to contain reports of such abuses, was seized by a mob. Inhabitants were afraid to rent their premises for offices of inspection.

Too late for Hamilton's chronicle was the muster of five thousand or more militia August 1, 1794, on Braddock's field. It was called by David Bradford, county attorney of Washington, who, dashing about on horseback, styled himself "general" of this frontier army. His troops spent a couple of days drinking and shooting at trees, then proposed to burn the nearby log town of Pittsburgh because intercepted letters showed that some of its citizens would beg the government at Philadelphia to suppress the disorders. Hugh H. Brackenridge, classmate of James Madison at Princeton, preacher, lawyer, and editor of the Pittsburgh *Gazette*, sped to the scene. He pretended to be on the side of the "whiskey boys," but with the purpose, he afterward declared, of dissuading them from attacking Pittsburgh.[1] Whatever his motive, he did not prevail. Fortunately the assailants, who would not listen to reason, succumbed to liquor; they were too drunk to do more than burn a barn, then submitted to being rowed across the Monongahela and started homeward.

George Hammond, the British minister, reported to his government, "The avowed pretext for these discontents is a dislike of the excise law, but the real origin of them is unquestionably a rooted aversion to the federal constitution, and to all the measures emanating from it." He could not guess what course the national authorities would adopt in "this emergency which is certainly the most . . . alarming that has yet arisen."

The secretary of the treasury was in no doubt. The time had come for military coercion. Invading recalcitrant counties, only five years after the Constitution was established, would be jeered at abroad. At home the Republicans would call it a violation of free speech and assembly, an excuse to flex Federalist muscles. What Hamilton contemplated was disciplinary action, but if foes proclaimed it civil war, that, however lamentable, was better than the destruction of government. This was a test case; if the national mandate, so near the beginning of the American experiment, was to be flouted by a tiny rebellious minority, more serious defiance could be expected in future.

President Washington was cautious when Hamilton urged

[1] Following the demonstration at Braddock's field, Brackenridge wrote to a treasury official, "Should an attempt be made to suppress these people, I am afraid the question will not be, whether you will march to Pittsburgh, but whether they will march to Philadelphia." More than the excise tax angered the insurgents; their detestation of the funding system was "ready to burst out . . . everywhere . . . the Chariot of Government has been driven Jehu-like, as to the finances; like that of Phaeton, it has descended from the middle path, and is like to Burn up the American Earth."

sending troops to the disobedient district. At an executive conference early in August of 1794 he recommended that Governor
Thomas Mifflin of Pennsylvania should "adopt some preliminary
measures under the State Laws." The President could not direct a military force to the scene unless Associate Justice James
Wilson of the Supreme Court certified that the civil authorities
were incompetent to compel compliance with the law of the
United States. Hamilton must have remembered that a decade
earlier, when deputed to secure protection of Congress from the
then head of this same state of Pennsylvania, he had been met
with refusal, and the national legislature, menaced by mutineers, had been obliged to quit Philadelphia for Princeton. His
fears of a repetition seemed warranted. Governor Mifflin was
reluctant to acknowledge guilt in his citizens. Alexander J. Dallas, secretary of the commonwealth, and a leader in the Philadelphia Democratic Society, raised technical difficulties about
calling out the militia, and said the judicial process had not been
exhausted. Joseph Harmar, the Pennsylvania adjutant general,
objected that units of the militia were unwilling to respond.

When President Washington then determined to take personal command of some fifteen thousand militiamen from Pennsylvania and the neighboring states of Maryland, New Jersey,
and Virginia, the local officials fell into line. Mifflin exhorted his
legislature, and toured the eastern and middle counties to fill the
ranks for the expedition. Dallas, just as suddenly converted,
went along on the march; he declared that dissenting politicians
like Albert Gallatin, William Findley, and John Smilie, so recently his allies, were "inconceivably obnoxious as the original
perpetrators of the doctrines which have . . . produced these
violences."

The army, said by critics to be excessively large, was judged
by Washington, Hamilton, and others to be no more than was
prudent to ensure success. Failure to overawe the rebels would
be a fatal outcome. The secretary of the impoverished treasury

was not apt to agree to the expense of the punitive force ($800,000), unless its size was compelling.

Hamilton was at Washington's side when on October 4, 1794, they arrived at Carlisle, with the governors of Pennsylvania and New Jersey, for the rendezvous of the troops of those states. He was active in all the planning. Though serving in his capacity of the civil officer chiefly charged with collection of the national revenue, he in effect resumed for the nonce his old duties as aide to the commander in chief.

He took part in two long interviews of western delegates with Washington. William Findley and David Reddick had hastened across the mountains from a chastened meeting at Parkinson's Ferry (Monongahela, seventeen miles south of Pittsburgh) in the vain hope of halting the troops at Carlisle. They asserted that the region was now quiet, determined to support the laws, and required no troops to compel obedience. They admitted that not all had signed their submissions, as invited to do, but this did not argue opposition. Hamilton particularly questioned the ambassadors from the insurgents to know whether distillers along the Monongahela would conform to the law and whether offices of inspection could be opened. Their answers were less persuasive since one of their witnesses was Judge Alexander Addison, whom Hamilton had held two months before to be "among those who had most promoted the opposition in an insidious manner." Washington refused to call off the march.

Hamilton went with the President to Williamsport and Cumberland, Maryland, to visit the southern wing of the army, thence back to the northern wing at Bedford, Pennsylvania, which was the easternmost point of disturbance. Here the President turned back to Philadelphia to meet Congress, but Hamilton continued in the four-week march over the mountains to Washington, Pennsylvania (since sometimes called "Little Washington"), and Pittsburgh. Hamilton opened public let-

315

ters to the President, referring military matters to Governor Lee, now in command. The secretary kept the President informed on all developments. He trusted that Congress would authorize five hundred infantry and one hundred horse "to be stationed in the disaffected country. Without this, the expense incurred [in the expedition] will be essentially fruitless."

This recommendation of a sufficient occupying force was carried out, Daniel Morgan—the very best officer for the purpose—being left in charge at Pittsburgh. The secretary knew from the first that to quiet the disturbances was not enough. Military policing for months to come would be necessary for efficient collection of the excise. Furthermore, since leaders of the rebellion would probably escape arrest, "they ought to be compelled by outlawry to abandon their property, homes, and the United States." Richard Peters, the district judge, and William Rawle, the district attorney, went along to deal with offenders when apprehended. As Hamilton anticipated, only the small fry could be netted. David Bradford, who had been chief insurgent at Braddock's Field, fled to Louisiana, but later returned with impunity to enjoy his considerable property. Gallatin was judged by the attorney general of the United States to have committed no indictable offense. Brackenridge gave evidence against others and so secured immunity.

As soon as General Morgan with the light troops crossed into Washington County, Hamilton directed them in the roundup of suspicious characters. Some 150 in all were seized and summarily turned over to the judiciary. Though the President, returning east, hoped that Hamilton would be "enabled by *Hook* or by *Crook*" to send the guiltiest "to Philadelphia for their winter Quarters," the method used—with no waiting for formal legal process of indictment—was a trespass on civil liberties. The justification offered was that any man might arrest a traitor. The line between military and civil action was blurred. Hamilton's task was more disagreeable because those taken were chiefly poor, ignorant fellows; the rebellion had ostensibly melted away, and his zeal in the aftermath was decried as vindictive. However, in view of the previously obstructed administration of the excise, he decided that back taxes would be collected for the last year only. He was not sure but what, in spite of all disciplinary efforts, violence would flare again. He recommended to General Henry Lee that only a few pieces of artillery should be left at Pittsburgh, "in so disaffected a Country." Also on his homeward journey, since his agency in the expedition was most resented, he was accompanied by a guard of six horsemen for the hundred miles from Pittsburgh to Bedford.

Convicted insurgents—a few were sentenced to death for treason—were all pardoned by President Washington, since the rebellion had been put down without bloodshed. However, the Chief Executive, in his speech to Congress, condemned the "self-created societies" which "fomented" the riots and "disseminated . . . suspicions, jealousies, and accusations, of the whole Government." The Senate, two-thirds Federalist, agreed with his strictures, but the House, evenly divided politically, debated for a week before a compromise response was accepted. The Republicans raised the alarm at Federalist policy to block political dissent by force. Washington's assault, though only verbal, was a curtain-raiser to the Alien and Sedition Acts of his successor.

The Whiskey Insurrection had other effects as well. Some months afterward the British, at war with France, intercepted a letter of Jean Antoine Fauchet, French minister to the United States, and passed it on to Secretary Oliver Wolcott in the treasury. Fauchet imparted that Edmund Randolph, secretary of state, had suggested loans to certain individuals who could expose British machinations to provoke the western rebellion. Peremptorily accused by Washington, Randolph as hastily resigned. He afterward cleared himself, but for the moment American resentment against France assisted acceptance of the Jay Treaty with England. This and other Federalist successes may have extended their tenure in the election of 1796, and they soon launched the quasi-war with France.

In the war between England and France that commenced in 1793, each of the contestants did its utmost to cut off the trade of the other without regard to the rights of neutrals. The United States, the chief neutral commercial power, was a gainer from the European conflict, but that did not lessen protests against depredations on American shipping. In the year following July 1796, more than three hundred American vessels were captured by warships and privateers of the battling nations. International law was honored in the breach, not the observance. Nor was there much to choose between the actions of England and France toward the United States.

The European conflict was reflected in the United States in fiercer rivalry between Federalist and Republican (Democratic) parties. The Federalists, whose strength was in the seaboard towns and leaned to the side of Britain, had the advantage. They were in office, they had negotiated the Jay Treaty of 1795, which substantially settled differences with Britain, and diplomatic relations with France were severed the next year when the American minister, James Monroe, was recalled and the French refused to accept a successor. The Republicans represented the agricultural interest and sympathized with France, whose ideological professions appealed to the average man. The Republicans declared that the Jay Treaty violated American obligations to France in the treaty of alliance of 1778. They opposed naval and military preparation because they saw that France was the object of resistance; they objected to the cost and to the enlarged powers the central government would exercise in the event of war. The Republicans constantly reminded that Britain had been America's enemy, while France was America's friend in the Revolution.

Beginning in the autumn of 1796 and running into 1799, Hamilton as Federalist leader published papers demonstrating the evil conduct of post-Revolutionary France toward the United States. These arguments increased in intensity and were aimed hardly less at pro-French sympathizers in America than at the stridence of the Directory and the ambitious career of Napoleon. Hamilton's first care was to disillusion the large number of his fellow citizens who were partial to France in her struggle with England because of the aid she had rendered in winning American independence. This attachment of Republicans, led by Jefferson, was the stronger because they held France to be—in spite of contrary behavior—the emblem of popular liberty for which their party stood. "The primary motive of France for the assistance she gave us," Hamilton declared,

was obviously to enfeeble a hated and powerful rival. A secondary motive was to extend her relations of commerce in the New World, and to acquire additional security for her possessions there, by forming a connection with this country when detached from Great Britain. To ascribe to her any other motives—to suppose that she was actuated by friendship towards us, or by a regard for our particular advantage, is to be ignorant of the springs of action which invariably regulate the cabinets of princes. He must be a fool, who can be credulous enough to believe, that a despotic court aided a popular revolution, from regard to liberty or . . . the principles of such a revolution.

In return for a nominal guaranty of American sovereignty, France had obtained an American pledge to protect her West India possessions, which might easily involve the United States in future wars "in which we may have no direct interest." He recited the record to show that France, after the peace, sought to keep us weak and distracted under the Confederation and to prevent us from "acquiring . . . a well-constituted and efficient government." He repelled French incitements against Great Britain; "it is not the interest of the United States to be engaged in any war whatsoever—much less do they desire to imbrue their hands in the blood of one nation to gratify the hatred . . . of another." He illustrated by examples France's "spirit of universal domination," her resolve "that her interest is to be the sole measure of the rights of the rest of the world."

Hamilton contradicted the favorite charge that in Jay's treaty with Britain the United States had broken its 1778 treaty with France. His argument was factual, but through it shone his ardent preference for English constitutional government as against the violent caprices of Gallic liberty. Here he was dealing not so much with the doings of foreign powers as with the contest in America between pro-British and pro-French parties. Hamilton had early anticipated the excesses to which the French Revolution conducted, perverting freedom into oppression and subjugation. He was temperamentally and by reason drawn to the English traditions of public life in which he was born, and which he adopted in his unquestioned American allegiance. He did not shut eyes to the trespasses of Britain on America's neutral commerce, but as between the political systems of Britain and France, his confidence was in the former. His resolve to overthrow French influence in America was aided by the progressive display of French dictatorial ambitions. He contended that under the guise of giving morals to the world, France hypocritically violated the very principles she professed.

America's "independence and liberty," Hamilton declared, were "threatened by the most flagitious, despotic, and vindictive government that ever disgraced the annals of mankind; by a government marching with hasty and colossal strides to universal empire, and in the execution of this hideous project, wielding with absolute authority the whole physical force of the most enthralled . . . nation on earth." The similarity of "cold war" thrusts at Lenin and Stalin in recent years to Hamilton's anathemas against Robespierre and Bonaparte is not to be missed.

He went so far as to assert that many of the French faction would "join the standard of France if once erected in this country." Since Americans might be obliged "at our very doors, to defend our independence and liberty," they must completely organize and bring into activity all the resources of America. To depend upon militia alone "against the enterprises of veteran troops . . . led by a skilful and daring chief" would be to invite disaster. The nation must "raise with the utmost diligence a considerable army," replenish the treasury, establish foundries, fortify its ports, create a naval force, and permit its merchant vessels to arm themselves. "Mental debasement is the greatest misfortune that can befall a people." America must prefer any peril or sacrifice rather than submit to oppression. "The honor of a nation is its life."

In 1797 President John Adams commissioned Charles Cotesworth Pinckney, John Marshall, and Elbridge Gerry to negotiate a treaty with the French government. The attempt to extort a bribe from the United States envoys (fifty thousand pounds and a large "loan") as a precondition of negotiation was grist to Hamilton's mill. He pooh-poohed the excusing suggestion that this insulting demand came from "swindling imposters," a designing mistress, or other unauthorized agents. He cited evidence that Charles Maurice Talleyrand, the French minister for foreign relations, and Pierre Augustin Beaumarchais acted for the Directory. When this attempt to compel America to buy immunity from French seizure of merchant ships and cargoes (the XYZ affair) was known in this country, President Adams was at the height of his resentment. He declared to Congress that he would never send another minister to France "without assurances that he will be received, respected and honored, as the representative of a great, free, powerful and independent nation."

Preliminaries put the country in a posture of defense. Early in March 1798, when Talleyrand's demand for a bribe was announced in dispatches of the American commissioners, the Republicans in Congress trapped themselves by joining in the resolve that the texts of the documents, as decoded, be laid before that body by President Adams. The full revelation, so far from offering even mitigated hope of settlement, in every feature excited patriotism when the dispatches were published. The fervid President Adams asked his cabinet whether he should plump for a declaration of war. His ministers were divided. Pickering was for it, but on consulting Hamilton (a frequent resort with Adams' secretaries), he received advice more temperate than the aroused mood of the President. Adams should address Congress in a "grave . . . and firm" review of our grievances against France, but leave "the door to accommodation open" and not proceed "to final rupture." He should urge "comprehensive measures of defence . . . calling forth and organizing all the resources of the country."

Doubtless Hamilton's circumspect recommendations, along with his own second thoughts, moved President Adams to a milder message than he had intended. The measures of defense he proposed were much those Hamilton had listed, and Federalists in Congress were quick in response. A separate Navy Department was established (Benjamin Stoddert, secretary), 12 ships of 22 guns each should be acquired, arms and ammunition be provided, and the regular army, at that time only 3,500, was to be increased. All commerce with France and her possessions was embargoed. Federalists could not attract Republican votes necessary to denounce the treaty of 1778 with France and the consular convention of 1788.

John Marshall returned from France (June 16, 1798) to a hero's welcome, saying publicly that honorable agreement with France was impossible. The toast was the defiance attributed to Pinckney, "millions for defense, but not one cent for tribute." Pinckney had gone to the south of France for his daughter's health, but Elbridge Gerry, encouraged by Talleyrand, lingered in Paris in the belief that France did not want war and that he in time could negotiate a satisfactory treaty. He was soon ordered home but remained for two months at his solo post waiting for his passports. Many Republican members absented themselves from Congress, while persons sympathetic with France and suspected of scheming to subvert the American government were pummeled with the Alien and Sedition Acts.

Hamilton did not share in the hysteria that inspired these laws. Just as immediately following the Revolution he opposed harsh measures that compelled Loyalists to abandon this country, so now he counseled against sending away foreigners indiscriminately. "Let us not be cruel or violent," he urged on Pickering, and to Wolcott, treason should not be defined to "establish a tyranny. Energy is a very different thing from violence," which would "give to faction body and solidity" and invite the very civil war intended to be prevented. Hamilton did consent in these repressive statutes, while he hoped for their amelioration as they were administered.

The credentials of all French consuls were canceled, the navy could capture French armed ships anywhere, and the President could commission privateers.

16

Preparations for Defense

In the spring of 1798, besides alerting the public to the French peril, Hamilton urged on his friends in President John Adams' cabinet means of defense the administration should sponsor in Congress. His policy in these advices was more circumspect than had appeared in his excited newspaper pieces. Vigorous military preparations, he said, should go hand in hand with further efforts at negotiation. To Timothy Pickering, secretary of state, he recommended a special session of Congress to appoint a three-man commission to France, to be composed of two stout Federalists, together with either Jefferson or Madison. At the same time Congress should recruit additional revenue, provide emergency military and naval forces, and authorize the arming of merchant vessels. He was not so exercised at French invasions of the neutral rights of the United States as to overlook similar British offenses. Informed of British orders in council of January 1798, he warned Pickering, "it is the true policy . . . of our Government to act with spirit and energy as well towards G Britain as France. I would meet [mete] the

same measure to both of them, though it should . . . furnish the extraordinary spectacle of a nation at war with two nations at war with each other. One of them will quickly court us . . . . It will evince that we are neither *Greeks* nor *Trojans*."

At this stage Hamilton did not favor alliance with Great Britain, which Lord William Wyndham Grenville, the British foreign secretary, was seeking to promote through Robert Liston, his minister in this country. Arming of American vessels would produce clashes with France "which must ultimately lead to . . . Open War." American conquest of Louisiana and Florida would have British blessing, while Britain, for her part, would take Santo Domingo. Pending agreement for cooperation, the British would avoid aggressions on American shipping. Liston laid these proposals before a responsive President Adams at his home in Braintree, Massachusetts. Liston's report was that Adams "conceived it to be the interest of this country as well as that of Great Britain to . . . concert plans of operation, for the joint conduct of the war against France." If it depended on him "he would enter into the engagements . . . without scruple and without loss of time." Liston suggested that America should provide seamen in return for British naval protection. Rufus King, the American minister to England, had contemplated something similar. Liston was encouraged because Adams, in reply to patriotic addresses, used the opportunity "to enflame . . . animosity against the French Republick." However, Adams told Liston he was obliged to wait for the decision of the people.

Hamilton was not less anxious to rouse the country to the crisis, for he feared the design of the anti-government faction to bring about an open alliance with France. This sentiment was strongest in the southern states. Hamilton wanted to bring Washington out of his treasured retirement into the arena. The master of Mount Vernon should make "a circuit through Virginia and North Carolina under some pretence of health &c. This would call forth addresses . . . which would give you an opportunity of expressing sentiments . . . which would throw the weight of your character into the scale of Government and revive an enthusiasm for your person that may be turned into the right channel." This channel might be more than exhortation, for, he told Washington, "In the event of an open rupture with France, the public voice will again call you to command the armies of your Country."

Washington, deeply concerned over portents, nevertheless turned down the proposed tour. Its object could not be veiled, as his health was never better. If partisans of France felt themselves sufficiently supported, they would attribute to him wrong motives; if they were weakening, his journey would not be necessary. In any event, he reminded with his usual modesty, his influence might prove less than Hamilton supposed. Actually, the people of Virginia, the Carolinas, and Georgia were voicing their attachment to the general government, and this "effervescence which is appearing in all quarters, and the desertion of their followers" must silence the pro-French leaders. The French Directory would be disabused of fatuous expectations from this source.

Washington could not bring himself to believe France would invade this country. If that should happen, the call for him to command the army must be unequivocal to induce him to respond, since "a man more in his prime" might be preferred. If the demand for his services was "so imperious as to leave me no choice, I should . . . go with as much reluctance from my present peaceful abode, as I should do to the tombs of my Ancestors." Further, he would like to know, before accepting, who would be his military helpers, and "whether [Hamilton] would be disposed to take an active part, if Arms are to be resorted to."

Hamilton in reply assured Washington that his leadership would be universally demanded. For himself, he would be willing to go into the army if in a station where his service would be in proportion to his sacrifice. "If you command, the place in which I should hope to be most useful is that of Inspector General with a command in the line."

Hamilton recommended through Wolcott, his former assistant who was now secretary of the treasury, a loan of ten million dollars and additional taxes to permit raising at once an army of ten thousand, already authorized, and officers for a reserve force of fifty thousand. Six ships of the line, twice as many frigates, plus a score of smaller armed vessels should be provided. A military and naval academy should be established. Pickering wished that Hamilton was at the seat of government where he could not only see all the cards, "but . . . play them."

Actually Hamilton's proposals were substantially accepted. On May 28, 1798, an act was approved authorizing the President to raise a provisional army. A month later, June 26, McHenry, the secretary of war, inquired of Washington, "You see how the storm thickens . . . may we flatter ourselves, that in a crises [*sic*] so awful . . . you will accept the command of all our armies? . . . you alone, can unite all hearts and hands, if it is possible that they can be united." At about the same time President Adams, lamenting to Washington that he had "no qualifications" for his martial duties, begged advice whether he should "call out all the old Generals, or . . . appoint a young Sett. If the French come here, We must learn to march with a quick Step, and to Attack." Adams was less direct than Mc-Henry in soliciting Washington's consent to command, contenting himself with "We must have your Name, if you, in any case will permit us to use it."

When Washington replied to both the secretary of war and the President, on July 4, he did not know he had that day been commissioned lieutenant general and commander in chief of the army they intended to raise. He answered in response to "a variety of hints" that if the country were invaded, so also must be his retirement. Both letters made the same points. He could not conceive that the French, however intoxicated, would attack the Americans on this continent. However, "In case of *actual* Invasion by a formidable force, I certainly should not Intrench myself under the cover of Age and retirement." The mode of

327

carrying on a war against the French must differ widely from that employed against the British. Therefore officers of the former army must be chosen for intelligence, experience, and proven capacity, without respect to grade. Washington spelled out the prime importance of having staff officers of ability and integrity, as they were, in effect, "so many limbs, or parts of the Commander in Chief"; it was "essential . . . that they should be agreeable to him." He knew fit men, who probably would consent to serve only under him.

Hamilton, surprised that Washington had not been consulted before appointment to chief command, begged him to accept. "It is evident that the public satisfaction at it is lively and universal," and it "will give an additional spring to the public mind." He suggested a course that Washington had already adopted, namely, that he would enter on active duty only if future events demanded, and meantime he should insist on an arrangement of officers that he could approve. President Adams' disposition, Hamilton plainly implied, was to choose in accordance with mere seniority.

Washington had not received this letter when the highest preference for Hamilton was urged on him by Timothy Pickering, who was ever Hamilton's enthusiastic admirer. "There is one man who will gladly be *Your Second*: but who will not, I presume, because I think he ought not to be, the Second to any other military commander in the U. States. You too well know Colo. Hamilton's distinguished ability, energy and fidelity to apply my remark to any other man." But to secure Hamilton's appointment, Washington must insist upon it, for, from conversations it appeared that President Adams was opposed to giving Hamilton his "proper station . . . *Second* to You; and *Chief* in your absence." Pickering believed Washington shared his (Pickering's) opinion, and should express it to the President. "Even Colo. Hamilton's political enemies . . . would repose more confidence in him than in any other military character that can be placed in competition with him." Particularly if Washington was unable to serve, the naming of Hamilton was "of such vast importance to the welfare of the country" that Pickering said he would risk any consequences in his endeavors to secure it.

Hamilton had wished that Washington would go to Philadelphia to settle on the officers and their order of command under him. Instead, Secretary of War McHenry went to Mount Vernon for several days of conference, July 11–14, 1798. In this period Washington answered the letters of both Pickering and Hamilton, sending his replies by McHenry. To the first he declared that Hamilton's services "ought to be secured at *almost any price.*" He did not know why the President opposed this. If General Charles Cotesworth Pinckney returned promptly from France, strong reasons urged giving him first place. If the French were mad enough to invade the United States, their operations would commence in the southern states, because this quarter was weakest, friendliest to France, had Negro slaves to be armed against their owners, and was nearest to the French islands and to Louisiana, which France coveted. If this was to be the enemy's plan, Hamilton could not be put ahead of Pinckney (of South Carolina), whose fitness in military skill and experience and influential family connections were estimable. In addition, Pinckney's late conduct in spurning the French demand for tribute gave him signal credit with the public. With these pretensions, and being senior to Hamilton, Pinckney would not accept junior appointment. His "disgust" would spread disaffection in the South where it was most to be avoided.

If Pinckney's return from abroad was delayed, Hamilton might be given the highest post, but he trusted that Hamilton would be satisfied with a commission as inspector general with a command in the line. Plainly, it was peril to the South that tipped Washington's preference to Pinckney over Hamilton. Washington wrote a few hours before McHenry was expected, so he did not know what instructions the secretary of war was bringing from President Adams.

Washington wrote to Hamilton at the end of McHenry's visit,

marking the letter "Private and confidential." His conditions in accepting command were what Hamilton knew, that the principal officers must have his confidence, and that he be not called to the field unless necessity arose. The pending bill, which might or might not have become law, provided for two major generals and an inspector general with that rank, plus three brigadiers. Evidently McHenry's persuasions, or his own further reflection, had induced him, in the list of officers he proposed, to name Hamilton first, then Pinckney, then Henry Knox, or, if either of the last named refused, Henry Lee.[1] That much said, Washington candidly expressed to Hamilton "a difficulty which has arisen in my mind relative to seniority between you and Genl. Pinckney; for with respect to my friend General Knox, whom I love and esteem I have ranked him below you both." So Hamilton should understand his perplexity, Washington recited the peculiar fitness of Pinckney in the event of invasion in the South. "Will he serve then, under one whom he will consider a junr Officer? and what would be the consequence if he should refuse, and his numerous, and powerful connections . . . in those parts get disgusted?" He added that Pinckney, more than any other officer of the old army, was reputed to have made tactics and the art of war his study.

"Under this view of the subject, my wish to put you first, and my fear of losing him, are not a little embarrassing. But why? for after all it rests with the President to use his pleasure." Thus resigning the final decision, he hoped that all, as they put the country's welfare foremost, would let smaller matters yield

[1] Those of less rank were surely such as Hamilton approved: brigadiers—Lee, if not major general, in which case John Brooks (Massachusetts), William S. Smith, or John Eager Howard (Maryland); for adjutant general, Edward Hand (Pennsylvania), Jonathan Dayton, Jr. (New Jersey), or Smith; for quartermaster general, Edward Carrington (Virginia); for director of hospitals, Dr James Ciaik. Washington gave to McHenry a tentative list of regimental officers, which contained many of Hamilton's trusted friends, including Caleb Gibbs, Jeremiah Olney, Nicholas Fish, William North, Benjamin Walker, Aaron Ogden, William Macpherson, and Thomas Pinckney.

to that purpose. No one could make a greater sacrifice of inclination than himself.

Hamilton visited Philadelphia, where he consulted with Pickering and surely with other Federalists about the part he was called on to play in the impending crisis; the encouragement he now received gave him the conviction, later frequently expressed, that Federalists and the public generally insisted he should have military responsibility second only to Washington. Now, however, when shown Pickering's correspondence with Washington, Hamilton was content to fall below Knox, "if thought indispensable," though not below Pinckney. Six weeks later (July 29), replying to Washington's notice that he had been placed at the head of the list, Hamilton was stiffening his resolve to stay there. He would accept the opinion of "a great majority of leading Federal men" that if Washington declined or was disabled, the command should devolve upon him. The others appointed should acquiesce. If either had a complaint, it was Knox, much senior in the old army to both himself and Pinckney, and better versed "in the tactics of a general." Hamilton was something less than cordial toward Pinckney's relative merits. Still, he said he was willing to waive his pretensions if the service was likely to suffer by the preference given to him.

Of more importance was McHenry's inadequacy as secretary of war. Hamilton was obliged to violate his longtime friendship [2] to have Washington understand in advance that McHenry's incapacity was sure to reflect discredit on the officers acting under him. Hamilton had gone to Philadelphia to try, tactfully, to assist McHenry in preparing for the larger scope in which he must now operate, but with little result. McHenry was cheerfully ignorant of his unfitness for his duties. Hamilton's forecast was abundantly borne out in the months that followed.

[2] They had been fellow aides in Washington's military family, McHenry was a guest at Hamilton's wedding, and was his constant political supporter.

In a considerate letter Washington informed Knox why he had been placed third in the rank of major generals; he hoped that relative positions in the old army would be forgot in the zeal of all to serve in the confronting crisis. Knox in his reply took deep offense at the "public insult and injury" and "degradation of character" now inflicted on him in spite of what he had supposed was Washington's trusting friendship. The arrangement intended disregarded the law preserving Revolutionary rank (in this Knox was unaware that the rule had been revised). He doubted that Pinckney would consent to fall below Hamilton. Knox refusing, New England, which must furnish most of the army if raised, would be left without a major general altogether, or have one of only junior rank, which might dampen the ardor of that section. Knox was in a depressed mood. Struggling to develop his large estate in Maine, he was seriously in debt; he had just buried another of his many children who had succumbed in infancy. Happily, he later overcame his resentment, and expressed to Washington his unimpaired confidence and affection.

In the emergency, Washington's choice of Hamilton to be next himself and in active charge of defense preparations seemed justified. Washington doubtless had not forgotten that four years earlier, when the punitive force against the Whiskey Insurrection was raised, Knox as secretary of war had been absent from his post on a protracted visit to New England, and Hamilton had supplied his place. Washington could not foresee that the threat from France was never as imminent as feared, and that in the actual course of events Knox as organizer of a provisional army would have served admirably.

Pinckney, when he returned from France, was as gracious as Knox had been truculent. He wrote to the secretary of war that he was sorry Knox had declined his appointment. For himself, though he outranked Hamilton in the former war, "it was with the greatest pleasure, I saw his name at the head of the list of Major Generals, and applauded the discernment which had placed him there." He so assured Hamilton. Further, to save Knox's feelings, Pinckney would change places with him if the arrangement should be reconsidered.

Shown Knox's letters to McHenry and others, Hamilton was pained to be the occasion of his old friend's umbrage. Perhaps Knox would accept appointment, pending review of the ranking as stemming from the Revolution. He included this suggestion in a letter to Knox drafted for McHenry's signature.[3] Nevertheless, he did not feel free to waive a preference proceeding from public demand. He clearly intimated to McHenry that the country's concern was for command of the army not only in the present, but in the future—which was to say, if and when Washington was no longer available.

Knox might have been put first, after all, but for Pickering. Washington's nominations were delayed one day in going before the Senate. In this interval Pickering received a letter from Hamilton saying that, if necessary to save embarrassment, he would be second to Knox. Yet, Pickering confided, "I concealed [your willingness], in order that the arrangement of nominations . . . by Genl Washington . . . which I saw would govern, might leave you . . . in the first place."

President Adams had not understood that Washington made not only the choice of principal officers, but their relative rank, a condition of accepting chief command. Not versed in military forms, he was evidently unaware that the order of listing carried this significance. He declared to McHenry that the sequence in nominations meant nothing, for what governed was "rank

[3] The following spring, months after Knox had refused his commission, Hamilton in a letter tried to heal Knox's hurt pride. He explained that he had balanced between regard for Knox and obedience to the judgment of others that he (Hamilton) should be subordinate only to Washington. Knox was not mollified, for a few weeks later he was still complaining of "the insult offered me. . . . The faction[,] the miserable animals who were the cause of it are known to me, and ere long they will be compelled to hide their heads in their original obscurity." Fortunately he escaped another humiliation which he feared; debts they jointly owed "must be paid or General Lincoln and myself must both be committed to goal [sic]."

according to antecedent services." Accordingly, he held that Hamilton should not rank ahead of any major general, and he should have no command in the line. Adams would "settle all decisively" by dating the commissions to give the order Knox first, Pinckney second, Hamilton third. This power was in the President, and he would exercise it. If the question went back to Washington, it would be further vexed. "I foresee it will come to me at last, after much . . . exasperation of passions & I shall then determine it exactly as I should now—Knox, Pinckney & Hamilton."

The secretary of war, in confidence, passed on to Washington the President's resolve. Washington replied to McHenry that by this news he was reduced, or soon would be, to submitting to Adams' "forgetfulness" (read disregard) of the conditions on which he (Washington) accepted appointment to command, or "to return him my Commission." He reviewed, for the record, the explicit character of what he had considered a compact. McHenry gave the President extracts from Washington's letter, and let Adams know that Washington had been informed of his determination on relative ranks. This afforded Washington "sufficient ground to proceed upon," and he wrote the President in his own hand a detailed remonstrance (some three thousand words, no less). Within the forms of politeness, it was a solemn rebuke and declared, in effect, that the President must conform to his requirements, or he would decline to serve. Since Adams had complained that intrigue had been at work, and he would not be the dupe of it, Washington laid it down that he, Washington, "had nothing more in view in making this stipulation than to insure the most eligible for these highly responsible Offices; conceiving that my opportunities . . . had enabled me to form as correct an opinion of them as any other could do." He came promptly to the point: "In the arrangement made by me . . . the three Major Generals stood, Hamilton, Pinckney, Knox; and in this order I expected their Commissions would have been dated. . . . But you have been pleased [in submitting the names to the Senate] to order the last to be first, and the first to be last." Adams also had made other appointments, in staff and line, without consulting Washington.

Washington maintained in his letter to Adams that rank in the army of the Revolution, which had been out of existence fourteen years, could have no relevance for the forces to be raised *de novo*, "farther than may be derived from superior experience, brilliant exploits, and general celebrity of character." Washington would defend his arrangement of the major generals. From varied and dependable sources he was convinced that the members of Congress, "and particularly . . . those from New England," favored Colonel Hamilton being second in command. "I have no hesitation in declaring, that if the Public is to be deprived of the Services of Colo. Hamilton in the Military line, that the Post he was destined to fill will not be easily supplied; and that this is the sentiment of the Public, I think I can venture to pronounce." Washington detailed Hamilton's qualifications.

Although [he] has never acted in the character of a General Officer, yet his opportunities, as the principal and most confidential aid of the Commander in chief, afforded him the means of viewing every thing on a larger scale than those whose attentions were confined to Divisions or Brigades, who knew nothing of the correspondences of the Commander in Chief, or of the various orders to, or transactions with, the General Staff of the Army. These advantages, and his having served with usefulness in the Old Congress; in the General Convention; and having filled one of the most important departments of Government with acknowledged abilities and integrity, have placed him on high ground; and make him a conspicuous character in the United States, and even in Europe. . . . By some he is considered as an ambitious man, and therefore a dangerous one. That he is ambitious I shall readily grant, but it is of that laudable kind which prompts a man to excel in whatever he takes in hand. He is enterprising, quick in his perceptions, and his judgment intuitively great: qualities essential to a Military character, and therefore I repeat, that his loss will be irrepairable."

335

Since President Adams had changed the order, which Washington "supposed *to be final*," and had placed Knox first, Washington explained why Knox should come after Pinckney. He expressed the warmest attachment to Knox; "there is no man in the United States . . . whom I have loved more sincerely . . . . But, esteem, love, and friendship, can have no influence on my mind when I conceive that the subjugation of our Government and Independence, are the objects aimed at by the enemies of our Peace; and, when, possibly, our all is at stake." If the French invaded, "their operations would commence to the Southward." Hence it was "all important . . . to engage General Pinckney." Between the lines it was easy to read Washington's fear that otherwise the people of the southern states, where partiality for France was strongest, might fail to offer stout resistance, or even defect to the foe. He had been disappointed in his efforts to have General Knox understand this reasoning.

Washington concluded with alarm at the delay that had been allowed to occur. "We are now, near the end of September [1798], and not a man recruited, nor a Battalion Officer appointed." The enthusiasm of a month or two earlier would have promptly enlisted the best men, while with further postponement few, and those of the worst sort, would respond. Could the United States meet "veteran Troops inured to conquest" with militia or raw recruits?

Washington sent the rough draft of his reproof of the President to McHenry, who had been the go-between, with the express cautions not to divulge its contents, unless Adams refused to comply, which would make it necessary for Washington "to proceed to the final step"—that is, return his commission. "You will readily perceive," he enjoined, employing understatement, "that even the *rumour* of a misunderstanding between the President and me, while the breach can be repaired, would be attended with unpleasant consequences." If Adams continued his recalcitrance, "the Public must decide which of us is right, and which wrong." Washington let it go at that. The outcome of such a contest, while the protection of America hung on the issue, was obvious.

President Adams must now eat humble pie, for neither he nor the country could afford to have Washington resign leadership of the defense army. The surrender was especially galling to Adams, because in abandoning his boast that he would have his own way, he must elevate Hamilton, whom he detested.[4] "That man," said Abigail Adams, the loyal wife, "would in my mind become a second Buonaparty if he was possessed of equal power." Years later, still resentful that he had been compelled to place Hamilton in active command, Adams, paraphrasing a line of Jonathan Swift, stigmatized Hamilton as "a bastard Bratt of a Scotch Pedlar." This aspersion, when Hamilton had been long in his grave, was in contrast to Adams' boast of his own ancient ancestry, which he traced to the Saxon conquest. "A more . . . virtuous and more irreproachable race of people," he declared, "is not to be found in the world."

Adams' retraction to Washington (October 9, 1798) was not only complete, but as much as claimed, untruthfully, that he had not been in opposition beforehand. He said he had signed the commissions of the major generals on the same day, hoping these men would amicably agree on relative rank, but "if . . . any one should be so obstinate as to appeal to me from the judgment of the Commander in Chief, I was determined to confirm that judgment." Further, any rule of preferment in the old army had no application to the new one.

On the surface the contenders in this controversy may appear to be paper soldiers struggling for command of a paper army. Actually, the dispute involved more than the personal ambitions or vanities of individuals, and it served as prologue to a drama in

---

[4] The word is that of Alexander DeConde, in *The Quasi-War . . . with France* (New York, Charles Scribner's Sons, 1966), which see for its revealing account of the climax of the personal and political struggle between Hamilton and Adams.

American history. The action was political rather than military, but the backdrop was that of war—genuine and fierce in Europe, only prospective in this country. The episode, as it was played to the finish, signaled the end of Federalist rule and the arrival to power of the Republican (now the Democratic) party. One stage in the nation's progress was completed, another commenced. Hamilton was to make his exit, Jefferson his entry.

With the wisdom of hindsight, and seizing on plausible explanation, it has been contended that Hamilton's summoning of an army, or the beginnings of one, to fight against France had the motive of preserving Federalist control. The repressive Alien and Sedition Acts, expelling suspected foreigners and hushing critics of "the establishment," fitted into this design. An army, growing perhaps to fifty thousand, or to more if eighty thousand militia were embodied, could be the instrument of insuring and perpetuating Federalist authority. Overtones in the controversy were preference, on the one hand, for English principles, and on the other, for French ideology.

In this interpretation of Hamilton's actions, he is presented as having always thirsted for military glory—and not only as a defender of the United States. It is suspected by some historians that Hamilton wished to use the new army to enlarge this nation's territory by seizing French and Spanish possessions on this continent, and perhaps with the cooperation of the British navy, to liberate colonies in South America from European sovereignty.

This is the picture posed after the event. It surely contains elements of truth, but is it faithful to the purposes on which men acted at the time? Were leading figures, however disingenuous, that deliberate in their contriving? Did they see their own situations, their opportunities and objects, in such clear light? There is some evidence to the contrary.

Preparation against feared invasion was blessed by Washington, to whom no one could attribute ulterior motives. He believed the French menace was real. He frequently expanded on this, and only deep conviction that American safety was threatened could have persuaded him, after a lifetime given to the public, to come out of his Mount Vernon retirement. As already seen, it was Washington, acting on his knowledge of Hamilton's fitness, and in response to what he found to be the general demand, who insisted that Hamilton have chief responsibility for defense plans. His anxiety proved to be overdrawn, but with his calm mind profoundly disturbed, the worry of others may be readily understood.

Hamilton was similarly apprehensive, or he would not have made the sacrifice of leaving his rewarding law practice, which was the support of his large family. Also, he several times offered, if need be, to serve under General Knox.

Moreover, it is not possible to speak of a selfish design of Federalists to use the war scare to keep their party in power as though they were all of a piece. Latent division within the party became prominent as moderate Federalists, the majority, cooled to the urgings of so-called "High Federalists" such as Hamilton, Pickering, Wolcott, Fisher Ames, and George Cabot, mostly concentrated in New England. These leaders, as the emergency lessened, were unable to keep their lieutenants in line, to say nothing of the run of Federalist voters. If Hamilton and his coterie passed from honest concern for the country to unworthy artful exploitation of the crisis for party purpose, their expectation was soon disappointed. Some have said that their objection to Adams' choice of William Vans Murray to manage the final negotiation that brought peace with France was prompted not by distrust of his ability but by fear that he would succeed. It comes down to the question whether Hamilton and his friends wanted war or peace. Perhaps they feared, at this juncture, a peace dishonorable to America. French overtures for settlement had been made for some eight months before Murray was appointed in February 1799. But were these approaches designed to prevent alliance between the United States and Great Britain? Would the French satisfy the grievances of this country?

In any case, hardly had defense preparation been authorized when the prospect of adjustment of differences began to loom. President Adams, who had been so heated over the XYZ insult to his government, never gave hearty support for the provisional army. In other words the interval in which display of armed force could be turned to party purpose was at best short and equivocal.

The split in the Federalist party, opened by Hamilton's injudicious published attack on President John Adams, was both personal and political. Moderate Federalists supported Adams, the incumbent, as the logical candidate in the bid for a second term. They applauded him because by patient diplomacy he had settled the quarrel with France. He was especially the hero of all but a few in his New England bailiwick. Federalists of the stricter sort followed Hamilton, who had long opposed Adams as vain and vacillating. In the heat of the national campaign of 1800, Hamilton's parade of evidence of Adams' unfitness for the presidency was, of course, seized upon and gleefully circulated by rival candidates, especially by Aaron Burr. Adams' failure to win re-election, however, should not be attributed solely to Hamilton's indiscretion in assailing his party's standard-bearer. The Federalists had been in office for twelve stressful years. They had succeeded in bringing order and prosperity out of the post-Revolutionary confusion, but they had carried through their policies by what an increasing number of the electorate considered a high hand. The very progress and security the Federalists had brought about now emboldened those of the popular, more democratic party to displace them.

One meets the confident assertion that Hamilton—the "Little Mars" as some Jeffersonians dubbed him—attacked Adams because he was furious that the President, by reaching agreement with France, had canceled his chance for military exploit. Hamilton was capable of ill-considered enterprise prompted by emotion rather than sense, though generally his intelligence and feeling of responsibility saved him from pettiness. The evidence, however, is that chagrin at vanished warlike ambition did not inspire his thrust at Adams. His judgment told him that a negotiated peace with France was the right course for this country. Also, in this same election, he fiercely opposed Aaron Burr, with no room for suspicion that he was actuated by vindictiveness.

So much, pro and con, for motives personal, political, and patriotic.

17

General Hamilton

 Hamilton was commissioned inspector general and major general July 19, 1798. At the same time he and the other general officers were notified that they would receive no pay or allowances until called into active service by the President. This suited Hamilton personally, for he could continue his law practice full-scale, but he did not believe it had come about through the intention of Congress or for the good of the service. McHenry needed help, really a directing hand. Hamilton had discreetly suggested to McHenry means of increasing his efficiency, but, though Hamilton feared he had been blunt, the secretary of war did not take in what was meant. Hamilton had also tried, through Washington, to prod the secretary by asking for a report on the available military supplies and on what he was doing to secure the additions necessary. "It is impossible for McHenry to get through all that is now upon [him] in a manner honorable to himself, satisfactory to the public, or proportioned to the energy of the conjuncture." At that time (early August 1798), Hamilton said, his "participation in the preliminary arrangements [was] only occasional and very limited," but he plainly implied to Wolcott and Pickering that constant and original collaboration with McHenry was required or the gov-

ernment and all concerned would be discredited. This meant that Hamilton must receive the salary attached to his office. Washington from the first was at liberty to draw all or any part of his salary.

Washington told Hamilton he had been on the point of writing "very seriously" to McHenry on several matters, among them shortcomings in his office. (Washington when President had appointed McHenry secretary of war, but early found him "unequal to great exertions, or deep resources," though these qualities were not expected, for McHenry had been "a Hobson's choice.") Washington hoped that Hamilton now, even before it was required of him, could devote time to "recruiting *good* men, and the choice of *good* officers." [1] Washington would try to impress on McHenry the need for accepting Hamilton's assistance, and of course beginning his full pay. "Delicacy," Washington added, "if matters become serious, must yield to expediency. The stake we play for, is too great to be trifled with."

Wolcott's response to Hamilton's regretful complaints of McHenry was that he should come on at once, "with the expectation of being *Secy of War in fact.*" McHenry did pass on to the President Hamilton's proposal that he and General Knox (who had not yet definitely declined his commission) be called forthwith into active service, and attendance at the War Department. Hamilton answered that he could be frequently at the seat of government, but asked that he not be compelled to quit his residence in New York unless the danger of war in-

---

[1] Washington had been and continued to be surprised at some of McHenry's choices of general and staff officers contrary to his wishes. "By what circuitous rout did you come at, Severe in the wilderness [John Sevier, then governor of Tennessee]?" Washington supposed him "better qualified to *cut off Indians* than to discipline an Army, or lead a Brigade in the mouths of cannon." Later he was still expostulating to McHenry that Sevier "never was celebrated for anything (that ever came to my knowledge) except the murder of Indians," and his strictures on another who had also been commissioned a brigadier were more vehement. He admitted that he "might have mistaken [Sevier's] character," which was the case. Sevier did chastise Indians, but was a valiant leader, as shown in the victory of frontiersmen over Major Patrick Ferguson's force of Tories at King's Mountain (October 7, 1780).

creased. (Actually he continued throughout to have his headquarters in New York.)

Hamilton had to taper off commitments in his law practice as his military duties increased. By this time he was leader of the New York bar, had important obligations to clients, which could not suddenly be terminated, and besides he needed the income. At the same time, it became clearer as time went on that preparations for war would move with energy and dispatch only if Hamilton was at the seat of government. James Gunn, of the committee of Congress to report measures of defense, said that Hamilton must command the army, direct the War Department, "and . . . the legislative aid necessary to . . . support . . . that department must be arranged by yourself." Hamilton recognized that to press forward the business "in all its extent" more than part-time attention, though with "Frequent visits and constant communication" with the capital, was necessary. Under the circumstances, the work was not impeded by President Adams' absence in Quincy, to which he retreated when Congress was not in session, for relations between them were strained; Hamilton operated through cabinet ministers, though this involved surreptitious maneuver. Hamilton needed two aides for secretarial assistance, but they had not yet been appointed. He promised to take his nephew, Philip Church, as one, but for the other required an experienced officer. Meantime routine correspondence and copying fell on him, along with essential planning.

The great obstacle to Hamilton's preparations was the contingent nature of the threat. Hamilton himself did not want to go too fast in the beginning (December 1798), since "a prospect of peace is again presented by the temporizing conduct of France." Such intervals of hesitation increasingly recurred. Besides, there was steady opposition from the Republicans, who did not fail to put the most favorable interpretation on hopes of conciliation. "Why all the war measures," cried the leading Republican newspaper, the *Aurora*, "pregnant with such oppres-

sion . . . when there exists a conviction that peace is at our
will?" And a month later (March 1799) a Virginian queried
the secretary of war whether "orders will be suspended untill
it is known whether the present Mission to France will succeed." Furthermore, the suspicion was proclaimed in unfriendly
quarters that the augmented army was not to confront a foreign
foe, but to clamp down on political dissent at home.

Color was given to this charge by pains taken to appoint
officers and recruit for the ranks only those believed to be loyal,
and in this effort patriotism might be confused with Federalist
sympathies. "A Virginian" in the hostile *Aurora* reported restric-
tions laid by McHenry on a militia officer of that state. The
officer was instructed not to enroll volunteer companies "composed of disaffected persons who might from improper motives
. . . intrude themselves into the army, under the pretence of Patriotic Association." The correspondent declared that the Federalist "Pretorian Bands" were to be the instruments of "Party
Persecution"; every member prepared to "imbrue his hands in
the blood of a fellow citizen, a neighbour or a brother, should
the president or his Little Mars think proper."

General Washington steadily insisted that officers chosen exclude any with French leanings. In submitting a list of supposed eligibles he cautioned, "There may be among the foregoing some of bad political principles, and others whose true characters I have mistaken." The whole of them required to be investigated. When one Friget was recommended to him, Washington replied that if hostilities should be against France "I do
not suppose that [he] would incline to take an active part against
his own Country. Nor that it would be the policy of this to
employ him."

Hamilton of course required that all in the army be faithful to
the government, but he did not demand that all in the officer
corps be Federalists. McHenry was told that several of Hamilton's nominations were rejected by the Senate because they
were "anti federal," "opposed to the Government and of

French principles," or "nobody." Refusal to accept Caleb Gibbs gave Hamilton particular regret. He had been a captain of Washington's bodyguard in the Revolution, was rated in Washington's list of availables as "good," and Hamilton considered him admirable to command a Massachusetts regiment. Gibbs was out of place in civil life and repeatedly applied to Hamilton for military employment.

Hamilton did not balk at alien, even French, birth where the candidate possessed special merit. He recommended his old friend Major Louis de Tousard for the critical post of inspector of artillery. Tousard had lost an arm in the battle of Rhode Island in his one-man charge on a British cannon, and had remained in this country. President Adams demurred at Tousard's nomination, though conceding that Hamilton's judgment should have great weight. To McHenry, Adams dissented emphatically; he did not know why Hamilton proposed Tousard, but "an angel with the name & tongue of a Frenchman would not in a French war have the confidence of this nation." John Rutledge, Jr., of a community with many French families, believed he had argued away the President's fears, and urged Tousard to pursue his application with Hamilton, whose "mind is much too great to be susceptible of any of these prejudices which unfortunately exist in the fountain of Power." However, Tousard was an exception, for Hamilton was determined "that none but natives shall be enlisted for the cavalry," and he wished that the same rule should apply to the artillery.

The shoe was on the other foot when it came to Aaron Burr, who offered himself as a brigadier. Adams wanted him appointed, but Washington refused, because Burr, though brave, was an intriguer, and Hamilton was of the same opinion. Adams protested that Washington "had compelled me to promote, over the heads of Lincoln, Gates, Clinton, Knox, and . . . Pinckney, one of his own triumvirate, the most restless, impatient, artful, indefatigable and unprincipled intriguer in the United States, if not in the world, to be second in command under himself, and [who] now dreaded an intriguer in a poor brigadier." Adams, partial to one son-in-law, William S. Smith, was cautious of another; he refused to sign the commission of Major John Brooks until sure he did not damn "me and all my children and grandchildren."

Recruiting for the twelve additional regiments, Hamilton's first care, began late and then lagged. Districting of the states and commissioning of line officers were delayed, and men for the ranks would not respond while the clothing contractors failed to deliver uniforms. Gleefully, the hostile *Aurora* knew not where thousands of enlistees were to come from. Most of those in the existing small army, the newspaper declared, were alien Irish, "and the sons of American yeomen, are not fond of . . . the barbarous Prussian code which we have adopted." The reference was to Steuben's regulations, a merit of which, as a matter of fact, was that they had been purposely simplified to adapt to American preference.

Washington, though not to be pulled from retirement unless danger became imminent, had offered to keep an eye on preparations. Hamilton must have flinched under his remonstrances, official and private, in March 1799:

If the augmented force was not intended as an interrorem [*sic*] measure, the delay in recruiting it, is unaccountable, and baffles all conjecture. . . . The . . . enthusiasm . . . excited by the Publication of the Dispatches of our Commissioners at Paris (which gave birth to the Law authorizing . . . the twelve Regiments, &c.) are evaporated. It is now no more, and if this dull season, when men are idle . . . and from that cause might be induced to enlist, is suffered to pass away also, we shall . . . set out as a forlorn hope, to execute this business.

He continued at length in the same vein. Though Washington did not know it, President Adams just then nominated the new commission to France, which further diluted military zeal. Virginia was not districted for another three weeks, when Washington complained "Not an Officer in this State . . .

has yet received his commission, to the dissatisfaction of *all*, & relinquishment of many." Washington spoke not of the army, but "more properly of the embryo one, for I do not perceive . . . that we are likely to move beyond this."

While preparations for an increased army dragged, the navy expanded rapidly from an original 3 vessels to 55 of all sorts, which had been built, bought, or begged. For much of the time France, knowing our naval weakness, relied on privateers in American waters, supported by a few frigates. The principal American operations were in the Caribbean, where, in spite of semi-piratical sea rovers, some 85 French vessels were captured. Captain Thomas Truxton, in his flagship, the *Constellation* (38 guns and a crew of 320), became the hero of the naval war. He chased, fought, and captured two French frigates, *Insurgente*, (February 5, 1799) and *La Vengeance* (February 1, 1800), each of heavier armament than his own, and was awarded a gold medal by Congress. As a result of this and other spirited operations, French depredations were so reduced that marine insurance rates on our vessels were cut in half, and American commerce, especially in the Caribbean, revived and flourished. The conflict with France, to the degree that it was such, was naval. The act of Congress of May 28, 1798, authorizing the President to use naval force against French attackers of American ships, was the nearest thing to a declaration of war, strengthened in the following July by suspension of existing treaties. While John Adams wavered on land defense, his support of naval activity was constant.

Within a couple of months after Washington's remonstrance at slow recruiting, Hamilton reported his hope "that in the summer and fall the army will be at its complement." Nine hundred workers were making uniforms, and hired civilian drummers and fifers in streets of towns and villages were calling to the colors. It was enough to recruit for the additional regular regiments without President Adams' orders that officers be selected and volunteer companies be accepted for the provisional force. However, the choice of these officers lay with senators from the states, and was not Hamilton's immediate responsibility.

When Hamilton had been secretary of the treasury, he had refrained from recommending direct taxes, relying for federal revenue on import duties and taxes on domestic distilled spirits. These, with borrowing, would serve the needs of the government then, and public opinion was not matured to approve direct levies now. To pay for the defense program, however, he urged taxes on all houses to raise $1 million; stamp taxes on insurance policies and collateral inheritances, to yield $500,000; a graduated duty on hats ($250,000); a flat rate on saddle horses, to produce $250,000; and a salt tax to yield the same amount. He eschewed a land tax unless war actually broke out, and opposed a tax on slaves as such, except for slaves included in the category of "all menial servants for luxury, as coachmen, footmen, cooks, etc." The taxes he outlined would amount to $2 million. Besides, he would have the government open a loan for $5 million, at a rate as high as 8 percent, to be repaid within 5 years. Later, on the eve of passage of the revenue act in July 1798, he modified these proposals to increase the income.

Hamilton was willing "to lay hold of [direct taxation] now" since "The leaders (Findley, Gallatin, Madison, Nicholas) of the opposite party favor it now perhaps with no good design. But it will be well to take them while in the humor, and make them share the responsibility. This will be the more easy, as they are inclined to take the lead." The taxes Congress imposed and the loans contracted were substantially what Hamilton had proposed.

Violent protest against the new taxes appeared in March 1799 in Northampton, Bucks, and Montgomery counties in eastern Pennsylvania, where the people, largely of German descent, expressed their thrift by abusing collectors. When two resisters were lodged in jail at Bethlehem, John Fries, well known in the region as an auctioneer, led some 140 mounted men, armed with rifles and swords, to "spring" the culprits. Overawed, the federal marshal surrendered them. Adams, in what Hamilton had called "the ardor of the President's mind," hastily issued his proclamation denouncing the rebels for committing acts of treason. He requested and then, following delays, ordered Governor Mifflin to call out militia to put down the insurrectionists who made war on the United States. McHenry, transmitting the President's direction that Hamilton should send regular troops to the scene, explained that this would reduce the demand for Pennsylvania volunteers (under Brigadier General William Macpherson), and that the regulars would be more effective than militia in quieting the disorder. McHenry had ordered units from Frederick Town, Maryland, Carlisle, Pennsylvania, and Fort Mifflin, and Hamilton was to dispatch others from West Point, New Brunswick, Morris Town, and perhaps elsewhere. Hamilton should take charge of the whole correctional force.

Repeating his policy in suppressing the Whiskey Insurrection, Hamilton was for decisive, prompt action with an unquestionably sufficient body of troops. He advised the secretary of war, "Beware of magnifying a riot into an insurrection by employing in the first instance an inadequate force. 'Tis better far to err on the other side. Whenever the Government appears in arms it ought to appear like a *Hercules*, and inspire respect by the display of strength . . . expense is of no moment compared with the advantages of energy," though judgment must be exercised. He believed additional troops should be put under provisional marching orders. Auxiliary cavalry might be had from New Jersey, New York, Delaware, and Maryland "without interfering with farming pursuits."

Wolcott, within a few days, lamented to Hamilton that the delay in suppressing the disturbance had allowed it to expand and deepen. Everything at the seat of government was "languor & indecision," since "we have no Pres[iden]t here [Adams had departed for Quincy]" and "The Governor [Thomas Mifflin] is habitually intoxicated every day & most commonly every fore-

350

noon." But Hamilton had not dallied. Immediately on getting his orders, he commanded Captain John Henry, nearest at hand, to set out from Fort Jay (in New York City harbor) with 100 horse. Soon Macpherson was going forward with 240 cavalry and 2 companies of artillery; United States District Judge Richard Peters went along to commit the accused to prison.

A month after Fries had released the two prisoners from the jail at Bethlehem, Macpherson notified Hamilton that order was restored and he had dismissed his militia. Regulars under Hamilton's command, however, should remain for a time at Reading, Allentown, and Easton.

John Fries was arrested and taken to Philadelphia for trial. The prosecution contended that by taking a prisoner from the United States marshal by force, Fries, and two with him, had levied war on the government and were guilty of treason. The defending counsel denied that Fries had intended to war on the United States, maintaining that the crime was only a misdemeanor. Judges James Iredell and Peters sentenced the accused to be hanged, as, on appeal, so did Justice Samuel Chase of the Supreme Court. Adams' cabinet was for carrying out the sentence, at least of Fries, but the President, on further inquiry, determined that obstructing the laws by force was not treason unless against the military. He pardoned the condemned.

"No wonder," Hamilton complained, "that the public was thunderstruck at such a result." Shortly before the pardon, Hamilton was informed, Adams had declared "with no small ostentation," that Washington's clemency after the Whiskey Rebellion was "the cause of the second insurrection, and that he would take care there should not be a third, by giving the laws their full course against the convicted offenders." The reversal of judgment was "the most inexplicable part of Mr. Adams' conduct."

The explosive President Adams, in this case as in others, on reflection corrected himself. Hamilton, though peculiarly sensitive to defiance of the laws "in the vital article of revenue," responded too eagerly to the command to send troops to the disturbed counties. He must obey the President's orders, but he was too quick to suspect that a riot, unless summarily punished, would become a rebellion guided by "the intrigues of factious men, who may desire to . . . overthrow the government." The district involved, unlike that of western Pennsylvania, where the Whiskey Insurrection had occurred, was in fact generally of Hamilton's Federalist party. In distempered times Hamilton was overwrought, though he could not have shared the implausible conjecture of some Federalists that French machination was at work among "Pennsylvania Dutch" farmers.

Hamilton, meanwhile, continued to be involved in planning for the existing army as well as the additional regiments to be raised. As inspector general, he was continually receiving appeals for decisions on all sorts of details. Many of these questions could have been handled by subordinates if only he had had them. As it was, his one aide was really only a clerk with no military experience, and he could not impose on the friendship of William North, the adjutant general, who had his own duties. Though he must have chafed at annoying trivia, his correspondence did not betray it. A post commandant begged discharge of his son, enlisted as a drummer, because the boy had a swelling on his neck. Lieutenant Zebulon M. Pike had fetched a lad, son of a soldier, from the Mississippi to Pennsylvania. Could he, following downriver custom, draw rations for his protégé?

A remonstrance against the change of buttons on the artillery uniform from yellow to white metal more properly claimed Hamilton's notice, for he was always anxious to satisfy the troops with their dress. It was complained that the white metal was more apt to be tarnished by powder. Hamilton himself protested to McHenry and commanding officers that "the Hats . . . received by our Recruits are not three cornered but round Hats; sans buttons, loops, cockades, or bands, and of . . . base stuff," and of poor workmanship at that. "Nothing is more necessary than to stimulate the vanity of soldiers," he admonished. "To this end a good dress is essential," or "the soldier is exposed to ridicule and humiliation." The men could not be expected to procure accessories for themselves; the hat "ought to be delivered with its furniture complete."

He had insisted that ordnance should be concentrated so far as possible for protection of principal harbors. Already serving on a citizens' committee with Aaron Burr and Colonel Ebenezer Stevens, he was officially charged to supervise the laying out of a legislative appropriation of $150,000 for the defense of New York. Nowadays that sum, notwithstanding its higher value then, would not begin to pay for a preliminary survey. It was inadequate at the time, or unwisely expended, for when Hamilton gave over as inspector general, Fort Jay on Governor's Island was reported to be unable to withstand the attack of a single gunboat.

A good pupil of Steuben, Hamilton required that commandants give him regular and exact reports on troops, arms, supplies, discipline, and works. He also wanted to expand Steuben's manual of regulations to include discipline and tactics for artillery and cavalry. After special study, he supplemented in much detail what applied to the infantry, and sought the criticism of General Pinckney and two colonels on the portion covering regimental maneuvers. He pursued this aim even after it was clear that mobilization would be discontinued. To determine the most desirable length of the infantryman's marching step at different rates of speed, he consulted British and French manuals, and directed practical experiments that took into account such factors as the nature of the ground, height of the soldiers, weight of the pack, and distance traversed in different periods of time. He concluded that the stride increased with speed, and preferred a pace intermediate between the extremes of foreign practice. On his orders Major Tousard, Major Simon Hoops, and Captain George Izard worked for six months on the section for artillery, while Brigadier General William Washington and Lieutenant John DeBarth Walbach handled the section on cavalry.

He drew specifications for new uniforms, and was probably the author of a "Bill for the better organizing of the Troops of the United States," passed to second reading in Congress January 1, 1800. As always, he planned ahead; most likely, printed "Rules and Regulations respecting the Recruiting Service" were by him, as were certainly—for they are in his hand—"Alterations and Additions to the Recruiting Instructions" and "A complete revision of the articles of war." A memorandum, in another hand, of "Measures in the War Department which it may be expedient to adopt," may be his; it begins with reorganization of the militia into five classes.

During his inspector-generalship Hamilton gave impetus to the beginnings of the United States Military Academy at West Point, which he had been among the earliest to promote. The purpose was to fit especially engineering and artillery officers, who required training in mathematics, "natural philosophy" (physics), and chemistry, as well as practice in gunnery and construction of fortifications. Hamilton had received his own technical preparation for his commission as captain of a New York artillery company through special coaching by the mathematics professor in King's College, Robert Harpur. In his eyes artillery and engineer officers enjoyed a distinction in possessing scientific knowledge, which demanded more study than the requirements for other military branches. As the few American colleges were devoted primarily to the classics and moral philosophy, this country in the Revolution was dependent on foreigners for engineers, and for many, though by no means all, of its artillerists. Hamilton in the war was intimate with numbers of these specialist volunteers, among them Louis Duportail, Pierre Charles L'Enfant, and Louis de Tousard. Hamilton's ardent concern to advance manufacturing in America also attracted him to the "mechanic arts." As a member of the New York legislature

he had helped establish the Board of Regents to foster all education in the state; in drafting Washington's Farewell Address, he
defined the need for a national university; he was a trustee of
Columbia College.

Hamilton's involvement with plans for a military academy
dated from his service in the Continental Congress immediately
after the war. He was the member oftenest turned to for recommendations on military matters, particularly since most of his
experience had been directly under the commander in chief at
headquarters. In the summer of 1783, for a committee, he prepared a detailed report on a military peace establishment. He
provided for instructors within the corps of artillerists and engineers, but at this time, contrary to his later view, he believed
military academies "rarely compensate for the expence—that
military knowledge is best acquired in service." Instead, he favored enlisting professors—of mathematics, chemistry, natural
philosophy, civil architecture, and drawing—into the army
with the pay of majors. The professors would serve "those
branches . . . which are of a more scientific nature," and "produce substantially all the utility to be expected from academies,"
he said. However, academies of a broader sort might be considered in the future. He included proposals that later became part
of his plan for an academy. Congress should "establish founder-
ies of cannon, manufactories of arms, powder &c.," making the
country self-sufficient in these essential munitions, and artillery
soldiers could help produce them. In the artillery corps he provided for artificers—founders in brass, iron, blacksmiths, wheel-
wrights, cutlers, powder makers, masons, and others.[2]

---

[2] Hamilton, for the committee, had queried General Washington for his
ideas on the proper peace establishment, who in turn required the views of
officers at the New Windsor encampment. Brigadier General Ebenezer Huntington and Colonel Timothy Pickering recommended a military school at West
Point. The latter proposed that "it might be made a rule, that vacancies in the
standing regiment" be filled by those who had studied in the academy. Students
so scheduled to become officers should be subsisted at the public expense, and
be taught "military discipline, tactics, and the theory and practice of fortification and gunnery." But General Knox was the main proponent of "a complete

Hamilton, as secretary of the treasury, in 1790 recommended the purchase of West Point from the private owner of the land, who had petitioned Congress to this effect. Hamilton cited a report by General Knox of four years earlier, explaining the uniquely advantageous features of West Point for defense of the Hudson River.

President Washington had always favored a military academy. In 1793, when he had proclaimed the neutrality of the United States in the war between England and France, it was nonetheless clear that this country must be prepared to defend its position with arms. In November Washington discussed with the cabinet the message he would deliver to Congress the following month. Jefferson, in his memorandum of the meeting, objected to

The clause recommending . . . a Military Academy. I opposed it, as unauthorized by the Constitution. Hamilton and Knox approved it without discussion. Randolph was for it [he had drafted the speech], saying that the words of the Constitution authorizing Congress to lay taxes, &c., for the common defence, might comprehend it. The President said he would not choose to recommend any thing against the Constitution, but if it were doubtful he was so impressed with the necessity of the measure that he would report it to Congress, and let them decide for themselves whether the Constitution authorized it or not. It was therefore left in.

As a result, Congress in May 1794 approved a bill enlarging the corps of artillerists and engineers (actually Hamilton's old artillery company, stationed at West Point) to four battalions, to each of which eight cadets would be attached. Under this plan the senior officers at the post would serve as instructors. But nothing came of this, nor of another act, in 1798, empowering President Adams to appoint four instructors. Some cadets were

system of military education which would embrace the whole theory of the art of war." Each of two academies, for army and navy, should have forty students and its own superintendent. Five years earlier, in 1778, at his artillery park at Pluckemin, New Jersey, Knox, from a platform in a special building, had regularly instructed his subordinates in what he termed "the academy."

collected, but Adams was unable to hire any Americans—and he wanted no others—who were competent to teach military engineering.

Hamilton's full exposition of his plan for a military academy was given to the secretary of war at the end of November 1799. Hamilton had consulted with Tousard and, doubtless, others beforehand, and sent his proposals to Washington for the commander in chief's revisions. Washington, in the last letter he ever wrote, two days before his death, was unable to comment in detail, but cordially endorsed the purpose and the design. "The Establishment of an Institution of this kind," he said, "upon a respectable and extensive basis, has ever been considered by me as an object of primary importance to this Country." He trusted Congress would "place it upon a permanent . . . footing."

In the plan that he gave to McHenry, Hamilton declared that the formation of a military academy in the United States was especially important, since the country was not expected to maintain a large standing army. Therefore, it was necessary "to substitute the elements of an army for the thing itself." "Proper nurseries" must prepare a competent number of officers, who, in emergencies sure to arise, could expand the organization, and be, as he said elsewhere, "the bones of an Army in case of need."

Hamilton proposed that the academy have five "schools"— one for fundamentals, in which the students would spend two years before going on to specialized schools for engineers and artillerists (two years), for the navy (two years), or for infantry or cavalry (one year each). Under a director general for the whole should be directors for each of the five divisions, all of them officers. He would provide six professors of mathematics, three of physics, one of chemistry, two architects, two drawing masters, plus a riding master and a fencing master.

It is evident from Hamilton's detailed suggestions for the staff and curriculum that he gave a great amount of thought to the plan. For example, courses in the introductory two years would include, in addition to principles of tactics, "Arithmetic, algebra, geometry, the laws of motion, mechanics, geography, topography, and surveying, designing of structures." Following this, those choosing to prepare for engineering and artillery would have advanced courses in mathematics, including "Fluxions, conic sections, hydraulics, hydrostatics, and pneumatics." Here Hamilton surely took the advice of Tousard. Other subjects for these more technically trained students were chemistry (especially mineralogy), fortifications, sapping and mining, theory and practice of gunnery, fabrication of cannon, and "composition of artificial fires." Significantly, he forecast service of the engineers to the community at large in peacetime, recommending that they be taught to construct aqueducts and canals as well as to build bridges for use in war. (He had previously engaged the engineer L'Enfant on the waterpower for the Society for Useful Manufactures at Paterson, New Jersey.) Training for infantry and cavalry would be less specialized, but those expecting to enter the navy would be taught "Spherics, astronomy, navigation, and the doctrines of the tides," in addition to naval architecture. Manifestly, his chief care was for the branches requiring what was lacking in this young country, the application of scientific knowledge. All appropriate instruments were to be provided (as they had not been furnished to that time), including apparatus "for philosophical and chemical experiments."

Remembering his own educational experience, he stipulated that students entering with previous training should, on examination, be allowed to spend less or no time in the introductory work and pass to their chosen specialties. Also, short refresher courses would be offered to commissioned and noncommissioned officers, who would attend the academy in rotation. Hamilton was always attentive to the functions of sergeants and corporals. The former would be trained in numbers sufficient to supply an army of fifty thousand men.

He did not designate West Point as the preferred location of the academy, but his specification that the site be on a navigable waterway for naval purposes, and his requirement of a gunnery range, fit the features of that place. Also, close to iron mines, forges, and foundries, West Point would be suitable for manufacture of cannon and small arms, affording object lessons for the cadets. He pointed out that in the earlier, unsuccessful attempts to found a military school, proper residences for directors and professors, barracks for cadets, and laboratories had not been constructed; this must now be done. He also noted that while studies for artillerists and engineers had much in common, the two were sufficiently distinct to warrant the formation of two corps, united under one head, with separate officers. This was enjoined from European experience and from his own observations and reflections. Military mechanics, instead of being distributed to companies, would form one corps within the corps of engineers and artillerists, and their officers would rank and rise as others did.

Hamilton did not want this plan to end as a paper scheme merely because it might appear too ambitious for immediate realization. He suggested, therefore, that the academy be provided for, in law, "in its full latitude," but that the President be allowed to begin it, at his discretion, on a limited scale.

McHenry made this paper his own, as Hamilton intended, and President Adams transmitted it with his approval to Congress. McHenry in March 1800 asked Hamilton's aid in preparing what became, with Tousard's help, "A Bill for Establishing a Military Academy, and for better organizing the corps of Artillerists and Engineers." However, McHenry was dubious of the bill's prospects for passage, telling Hamilton that every bill involving "the army is in some way . . . counteracted," while the navy (the favorite of the President), seemed likely to "ingulph everything." So it was; the bill was twice read in the House, but Congress adjourned without acting on it.

However, Hamilton had a hand in the advancement of Louis de Tousard to a position to benefit military education. He prevailed on McHenry to recommend Tousard, as the oldest major in that service, to be lieutenant colonel of the Second Regiment of Artillerists and Engineers and inspector of artillery. At once Colonel W. S. Smith, President Adams' son-in-law, an infantry officer who persuaded himself that he could readily convert to the artillery, applied for command of the regiment. Asked by Adams for his candid opinion, Hamilton expressed personal and military regard for Colonel Smith, but said he was sure the preferment of Smith would provoke criticism from artillery majors of superior pretensions. Adams gracefully acquiesced and promoted Tousard.

Jefferson, when he became President, was less the "strict constructionist" than when secretary of state. He changed his view that a military academy was unconstitutional. At the President's urging, the secretary of war, Henry Dearborn, ordered Tousard to take command at West Point (September 1801), where he was to assist, also, in the instruction of the dozen cadets. Within three months Jefferson recognized the importance of the school by naming Jonathan Williams, a scientific coworker of Benjamin Franklin's, as chief engineer and superintendent of the academy. The law of March 1802 provided that the Corps of Engineers, by then distinct from the artillerists (as Hamilton had proposed), should be stationed at West Point and "constitute a military academy." The following year Jefferson appointed professors of French and drawing. But the school did not prosper. Instruction was desultory, partly because the superintendent was often absent inspecting fortifications. It is generally agreed that the academy did not take its enduring shape until the superintendency of Sylvanus Thayer, 1817 to 1833. A portrait of Hamilton is on view at the academy as one of its founders.

Hamilton was concerned with more than domestic defense, for an interlude in plans for the provisional army was Hamilton's qualified response to proposals to attack French and Spanish possessions on this continent and, in cooperation with Great

Britain, to free South American colonies from Spanish rule. The mover in the latter project was Francisco de Miranda (1750–1816), a professional revolutionist, especially in behalf of his native Venezuela. Miranda, in the United States in 1784, and excited by the success of independence here, confided to Hamilton and Henry Knox his ambition to promote a filibustering expedition. As Spain had assisted North American Colonies to wrench away from Britain, it would be but justice if Britain joined this country in destroying Spanish power in the southern continent. Hamilton and Knox, passively it seems, furnished Miranda with a list of eligible officers and an estimate of probable cost of the Venezuelan's cherished enterprise.

Fourteen years later (1798) Miranda, then in England, revived his excited overtures to Hamilton, who in his position of military authority could be a powerful coadjutor. Miranda found new inducement when Talleyrand urged Spain to allow France to send troops to take over the Floridas and Louisiana before the Americans could make themselves masters there. Miranda wrote Hamilton that "the entire Spanish-American Continent seems prepared to throw off the yoke . . . and to enter into an alliance with the United States and England . . . . I believe that we will ultimately gain a victory for our cause and thus promote the happiness of the New World as well as the tranquillity of the Old." This act of salvation was "entrusted to us by providence." He had agreed with the British on a suitable form of joint government for the emancipated regions, doubtless what his admired Federalists would approve. French principles must not be allowed to poison freedom in the Western Hemisphere. Hamilton, said Miranda, must alert Henry Lee and Knox for invasion of Mexico and Peru. Primarily, "we should like to have you *with us* for this important object." Hamilton must not refuse.

Hamilton wrote an answer to Miranda's appeals, and sent it to Rufus King, American minister in London, "to deliver or not, according to your estimate of what is passing in the scene where you are." Hamilton had to be as cautious with King as with Miranda, for King was ardent for the scheme. "I should personally," he warned, "have no participation in it unless patronized by the government of this country." The public temper in the United States was unfavorable, he said, but if it ripened, Britain should supply the fleet, the United States the army. The command of land forces, he told King, "would very naturally fall upon me, and I hope I shall disappoint no . . . anticipation. The independence of the separate territory under a moderate government, with the joint guaranty of the co-operating powers, stipulating equal privileges in commerce"—that is, of the United States and Great Britain—"would be the sum of the results to be accomplished."

Rufus King did deliver Hamilton's letter to Miranda, who replied that "we [evidently his party of revolutionists] await only the fiat of your illustrious Pres. to leave like lightning." The fiat of President Adams was not forthcoming. He delayed for six weeks any consideration of Miranda's dispatches to him, then told Pickering, secretary of state, that it "will not be in character for me to answer," and he questioned whether any notice should be taken of the proposition. "We are friends with Spain," he said, "and even if we were enemies, the project would not profit us." Years later he recorded that events in revolutionary France had warned him against "engaging . . . my country in most hazardous and expensive and bloody experiments to excite similar horrors in South America."

Hamilton himself had limited the project to seizing adjacent Spanish territory, forestalling the evident intention of France to attach the Floridas and Louisiana. He advised Harrison Gray Otis, a lieutenant in Congress, that of course this would end the state of semihostility and precipitate war, but securing "the key to the Western country" would be worth it. He had long considered acquisition of these territories "essential to the permanency of the Union."

For this purpose Brigadier General James Wilkinson would be

an instrument. From experience during the Revolution, Hamilton had every reason to distrust him. In command of United States troops in the Southwest, and guardian of the frontier against Spain, he was in Spanish pay. Despite this, Hamilton decided that if Wilkinson's zeal were rewarded by promotion to major general, he would be of increased use to the government as senior officer in the field. Hamilton summoned Wilkinson on the long journey from the lower Mississippi, and the two went to Trenton to conclude arrangements with the secretary of war.

McHenry, for once not under Hamilton's thumb, had warned him that Wilkinson would not deserve confidence unless he severed his commercial, and perhaps political, connections with the Spanish. Hamilton should "avoid saying any thing to him which would induce him to imagine the United States government had in view any hostile project, however remote or dependent on events, against any of the possessions of Spain. I require this caution on good grounds." Hamilton disregarded this admonition. His agenda with Wilkinson began with directions to preserve peace on the frontiers, but went on to provide, in case of rupture, for forces necessary for "attacking the two Floridas." A watchful eye by Wilkinson on Spanish military capabilities, and care to build up his own, were to be expected, but discussion of means of transporting three thousand troops down the Mississippi hinted at more aggressive action. Wilkinson reported that "The imbecility of the Spanish Government on the Mississippi" made it possible to capture New Orleans in one hour, which was probably true, but beside the point. President Adams would have nothing to do with such schemes, and Washington opposed any threat to the Spanish—as in stationing troops at Natchez—unless war were declared.

Like all else that concerned the provisional army, ambition to attach foreign territory hung on political contingencies. Hardly had Hamilton assumed his duties, when President Adams received evidence from sources official and unofficial that France desired peace with the United States. General Thaddeus Kosciusko, who in the Revolution had won America's gratitude, and Dr. George Logan, a Philadelphia Quaker whose Republican zeal did not lack patriotism, undertook private peace missions to Paris. The French revoked decrees against American commerce and released American seamen seized as Englishmen. Talleyrand instructed Louis Pichon, a junior diplomat who had served in the United States, to make overtures to the American minister in Holland, William Vans Murray. President Adams credited these signs, considered he had assurances that a new envoy to France would be respectfully received, and (February 18, 1799) announced his intention of appointing Murray for that purpose.

The President's decision to renew efforts for peace, taken with minimum consultation with his cabinet, astonished Hamilton, "if any thing from that quarter," he wrote to Pickering, "could astonish . . . *Murray* is certainly not strong enough for so immensely important a mission." However, as the move was to be made, it "must go into effect with the additional idea of a commission of three." Pickering preferred to stiffen Murray by joining with him Hamilton and George Cabot. Instead, President Adams chose Chief Justice Oliver Ellsworth (of Connecticut) and Governor William R. Davie of North Carolina. As Murray was a Marylander, the three sections of the country were represented.

The strict Federalists, the leaders, were taken aback. There is question whether they genuinely distrusted any French professions, or designed to prolong the semiwar as means to party unity and continued power, though it might conduct to open war, preferably declared by France. Hamilton was caught midway of mobilization, such as it was, but Washington favored resuming negotiations, and so did less ardent Federalists. France had a new Directory, which might or might not honor tentative commitments of the former one for conciliation. Hamilton desired for this country cessation of hostilities, if honorably concluded. His tactic at the moment was to delay departure of the mission; he tried in vain to persuade Ellsworth to refuse to go.

He wrote to Lafayette (January 1799), "I join with you in regretting the misunderstanding between our two countries. You will have seen by the President's speech that a door is again opened for terminating them amicably. And you may be assured that we are sincere, and that it is in the power of France, by reparation to our merchants for past injury, and the stipulation of justice in the future, to put an end to the controversy." Shortly afterward to Harrison Gray Otis, a hawkish member of Congress, he expressed the wish that the President be empowered, if negotiation was not on foot or had failed by the following August, to declare war with France. "This course of proceeding, by postponing the event, and giving time for the intervention of negotiation, would be a further proof of moderation in the government, and . . . tend to reconcile our citizens to the last extremity, if it shall ensue." And further, "If France be really desirous of accommodation, this plan will accelerate her measures to bring it about. If she have not that desire, it is best to anticipate her final vengeance, and to throw whatever weight we have into the scale opposed to her."

When the Ellsworth mission was about to depart (October 1799), President Adams reluctantly left Quincy for Trenton (at that time the seat of government because of yellow fever in Philadelphia) to settle with his cabinet on instructions for the envoys. He had become distrustful of what the cabinet might do in his absence, but had not yet come to dismissing Pickering and McHenry. To Adams' disgust, this was when Hamilton appeared in Trenton with Wilkinson on their business with the secretary of war, but also surely hoping to influence the nation's diplomatic posture. Pickering, McHenry, and Wolcott opposed the mission, while Benjamin Stoddert, secretary of the navy, and Charles Lee, the attorney general, favored it. Hamilton paid a call on the President to urge delay. According to Adams, Hamilton argued that a rapprochement with France would induce

Great Britain to declare war on America, and that turmoil in the Directory was hastening to restoration of the monarchy, which would repudiate gestures of accommodation. Adams rejected Hamilton's pleas. Ellsworth and Davie sailed early in November 1799 and reached Lisbon within the month. It was expected that during the leisurely journey from Portugal to Paris —by ship and shore it consumed two months—they could gather information on what lay before them. While they were at sea in November, Napoleon overthrew the Directory and established himself as first consul, and thenceforth was master of France and of much of Europe.

The decision of President Adams to make a fresh attempt at settling differences with France spelled the end of General Hamilton's project to take the offensive against that country and her ally, Spain. Nevertheless, Hamilton continued to cherish the hope that the United States would, somehow, gain sovereignty over contiguous Spanish, and soon French, territory. He was gratified, as many strict Federalists were not, when shortly thereafter Louisiana was purchased by President Jefferson.

Though President Adams blamed Hamilton for so much as the thought of aggression against Spain, Adams himself sought to separate the colony of Santo Domingo from Spain's ally, France. Moreover, this was done in collaboration with Great Britain, with which France was locked in war. Adams dispatched Hamilton's close friend, Dr. Edward Stevens, to Santo Domingo as consul general with diplomatic powers to negotiate with Toussaint L'Ouverture, at just the time that Adams, in the Ellsworth embassy, was responding to Talleyrand's beckonings for peace. How so, asked Hamilton of Pickering? Where was either consistency or good faith? Toussaint, extending his revolution of Negroes in the western part of the island (Saint Domingue, later Haiti), dominated the whole. He considered his government independent, but—a confused historical holdover—acknowledged obligations to the sovereignty of France. The British had lost a large army in the attempt to take the island, but lingered in the hope of obtaining from Toussaint important trade privileges. For this purpose Sir Thomas Maitland visited Philadelphia and concerted plans for cooperating with Stevens in securing safety for British and American vessels in Santo Domingan waters. As Toussaint, when it suited him, professed himself still under French authority, he could not openly receive Maitland as emissary of France's enemy, but Maitland worked through Stevens and, undercover, directly with Toussaint. A hitch was that Toussaint was continuing to fight a civil war with Benoit Joseph Rigaud, who headed mulatto (credited by Pickering as French) resistance to Toussaint. The United States ensured the defeat of Rigaud by warring on French ships entering his ports, and soon by shelling the forts guarding Rigaud's harbors. Toussaint had thus expelled, with American help, the last disputant of his control of the island. President Adams issued two proclamations (April and September 1800) opening first part and then all of Santo Domingo to American trade.

This was a lifesaver to Toussaint, whose regime was starving for all sorts of goods, including munitions, because of the British blockade and the, until then, American embargo. Matters had not gone this far when, at the beginning in 1799, Pickering, as so often, appealed to Hamilton for guidance. A new law (February 9, 1799) permitted the President to open intercourse with any part of the French dominions, if the safety and interest of the United States would admit of it. Toussaint had taken measures to suppress the French privateers, and, if assured of restoration of American commerce, he would declare independence. The British (in spite of Lord Grenville's quailing at the prospect of a free Negro government) would approve this blow to France. Pickering observed that the United States could not favor Santo Domingan independence unless Toussaint should establish a reliable administration, provide for a succession, and contrive sufficient revenue.

Aside from Pickering's habit of turning to him, Hamilton's help was begged as pertinent for several reasons. He had grown up in the West Indies, as military commander had favored striking at France's Caribbean colonies, and was eminently equipped to give counsel on plans of government and public finance. Hamilton replied at once with advice on policy. The laws provided ample grounds for resumption of trade, but "The United States must not be committed to the independence of St. Domingo. No guaranty . . . nothing that can rise up in judgment" upon America if France, as now seemed likely, were prepared to settle differences with this country. Toussaint must first declare independence, but then he could be assured, verbally, that the United States would trade with him as long as he prevented molestation of American vessels. Hamilton promised to answer more fully, but delayed until reminded by Pickering that Dr. Stevens awaited only his instructions before departing on his mission to Toussaint. Even then Hamilton protested that haste prevented him from offering "any thing worth having."

He applied the maxim of Montesquieu "that a government must be fitted to a nation, as much as a coat to the individual," and outlined for Santo Domingo a military autocracy. His suggested scheme would have been pie to his Republican political opponents had they got wind of it, for they would have been tempted to overlook the slave history and inexperience of the people for whom it was intended. "No regular system of Liberty," Hamilton posited, "will at present suit St Domingo. The government if independent must be military—partaking of the feodal . . . . A hereditary Chief would be best," but since this seemed impracticable, he proposed "A single Executive to hold his place for life." His successor should be the officer next in rank, or one chosen by the commanders of regiments. All males within certain ages should be "compellable to Military service" on pain of forfeiting tenure of land. The supreme judicial authority should be in twelve justices chosen for life by the chief military officers, with trial by jury in criminal cases. Laws specifying corporal punishment or imposing taxes should originate with the executive but be subject to approval by the assembly of commandants. "All other laws to be enacted by the sole authority of the Executive," who alone would also have powers of war and treaty. The head of government would advise with three ministers—of finance, war, and foreign affairs—who would be approved by the generals. From his own experience in observing and reviewing the sentences of courts-martial, Hamilton cautioned that these tribunals must be composed with care. Revenue would come chiefly from duties on imports, and exports, and from taxes on land and buildings.

Pickering's own West Indian connections taught him that the island could not be a republic, but he flinched from Hamilton's prescription of a dictatorship.[3] The question, however, was not Pickering's to decide, and President Adams, Pickering told Hamilton, would do nothing to encourage Toussaint to declare independence, but would open commerce when Stevens certified that privateering was at an end.

Hamilton might as well concern himself with projecting a military government for a Caribbean island, for his work of military organization at home was at an end.

Augmentation of the militia, whether by 30,000 or 50,000, was only a paper project. The twelve additional regiments, authorized in mid-July 1798, the "provisional army," were finally officered by the last of April 1799, and were assigned their stations in November. This had been a slow process, for many, chosen from all of the states, had declined their commissions. Recruitment for the ranks, the full complement of each regi-

---

[3] The subsequent history of Haiti bore out Hamilton's prescience that a strong hand at the helm was indicated. More than a hundred years later (1905) the United States felt obliged to exercise a customs receivership, continued until 1941. In 1915 the Haitian congress was forced to yield to more comprehensive control; two years afterward the United States naval commander dissolved the congress and dictated a new constitution. As late as 1921 a U.S. Senate investigating committee found that the purpose of preparing the people of Haiti for self-government had not been achieved. For a century and a half the military, as Hamilton foresaw, played a dominant role, ending, rightly or wrongly, not with native generals, but with United States Marines.

ment to be 1,000 men, was far from complete at the last consolidated returns (November 4, 1799), when total enlisted strength was only 3,399. No regiment was as much as half filled, and many numbered fewer than 300. Some did not commence recruiting until August 1799. Then by act of Congress, February 20, 1800, further enlistment was suspended. Probably the provisional army, at maximum, did not consist of more than 5,000. The undertaking had lost all momentum by the time (May 14, 1800) the additional regiments were ordered disbanded. This order went into effect June 15. All officers and men were honorably discharged with 3 months' extra pay. The convention of peace with France was concluded September 30, 1800, and, ratifications having been exchanged, was promulgated by the President December 20, 1801.

Hamilton had devoted a year and a half actively to mobilization for a land war, which only briefly appeared to be developing and which in the view of none was ever imminent. To the degree that American military preparations helped to persuade France to abandon her hostility, a result that Hamilton all along wished, his work was not in vain. Still, as a military operation, due to the clearing of political skies, the enterprise was marked by delay in commencement and shortcomings in execution. The program never had the cordial support of the country. The Republican party, waxing in strength, was openly antagonistic, and moderate Federalists were in no better than passive agreement. Hamilton had previously been creative in national accomplishment. Under Washington's sponsorship, and striving to meet the evident needs of the new government, he overcame opposition. One might suppose that the threat of war would have united the people and surrounded his defense assignment with enthusiasm. But not so. Political dissent diluted fear. To France, plunging deeper into her European struggle, American anger at her actions was of peripheral concern. President Adams, who urged preparedness, was soon engaged in efforts to obviate the need for it. Except momentarily, the whole undertaking of expanding the army to meet possible, though unlikely, invasion was halfhearted.

Desiring peace with France, dissolution of the provisional army was not a personal defeat for Hamilton. He could write off that episode of misapplication of his energies. His defeat was political, and he invited it himself by his vehement opposition to President John Adams for reelection in 1800.

Because peace, engineered by Adams, canceled mobilization that was Hamilton's responsibility, many then and afterward laid Hamilton's enmity to attempted retaliation. Said John Quincy Adams, "conflict between a French war and a pacific mission was the immediate cause of that schism in the Federal party which accomplished their political ruin and the fall of my father's administration." The "abortion of the army of fifty thousand men, was the cause of the inextinguishable hatred of Hamilton and Pickering to my father." In his filial loyalty John Quincy was too specific in his blame. Faults on both sides were various and had been long in maturing.

Unless Hamilton was prepared to repudiate the Federalist party, he should have restrained himself from precipitating mischief within it. But the election of Jefferson that resulted, and Republican (Democratic) sway for the next quarter-century, was timely. Happily, Alexander Hamilton, recently willful and erring, retrieved himself by a magnificent act. When the election in the House of Representatives, after repeated ballots, hung evenly balanced between Jefferson and Aaron Burr, Hamilton begged fellow Federalists to vote for Jefferson, his political foe, and reject Burr, whom he deeply distrusted.

This closes the story of Alexander Hamilton's military career. His efforts in arms, commencing in his college days, were inseparable from his resolve to see this country independent and united. The success of the Revolution was necessary before he could apply himself to strengthening the young nation economically and politically—in the Continental Congress, the Constitutional Convention, as first secretary of the treasury, and as Federalist party leader. In these services of statesmanship he was, as in war years, aide to Washington. Similarly, Washington's continuing trust was essential to Hamilton's program. What each contributed in their collaboration of two decades is expressed in Washington's *Farewell Address*, which (Hamilton playing the subordinate role of draftsman) was their joint counsel for America's enduring greatness.

Though at the time of the *Address* (September 1796) Washington was within three years of his death, and Hamilton was to survive him for five years, the farewell of the father of his country was hardly less *l'envoi* of a favorite son. The two were again associated, in preparation for the national defense, but this was postscript to their earlier achievements.

Hamilton's mortal wound in his duel with Aaron Burr, July 11, 1804, was the sequel to his constant striving for the public integrity and welfare. Believing that Burr would use the position for unworthy purposes, Hamilton had blocked his election to the presidency in 1801. Burr sought to console himself with the governorship of New York, but again found Hamilton astride his path. Burr's challenge to the duel—in which Hamilton did not fire at his opponent—was the tragic revenge.

Selected Bibliography

Among printed materials, the following will be found useful for an understanding of Alexander Hamilton's military career:

Adams, John. *Works of . . . with a Life of the Author . . .* by Charles Francis Adams (Boston: Little, Brown, 1850–56. 10 vols.).

Clinton, George. *Public Papers*, Hugh Hastings, compiler (New York and Albany: published by State of New York, 1899–1914. 10 vols.).

Hamilton, Alexander. *The Papers of Alexander Hamilton*, Harold C. Syrett, editor; Jacob E. Cooke, associate editor (New York and London: Columbia University Press, 1961–   ). When all volumes have appeared, this will be the most complete collection of Hamilton's writings. Letters and papers written by Hamilton but signed by another (chiefly letters as aide to Washington) are briefly calendared; certain more important letters to Hamilton are included. Scholarly footnotes, besides identification of persons and places, offer, where needed, environing circumstances.

———. *Works*, J. C. Hamilton, editor, 7 vols. New York: J. F. Trow, 1850–51. As compared with the above this set contains more letters to Hamilton.

———. *Works*, H. C. Lodge, editor (New York and London: Putnam, Federal Edition, 1904, 12 vols.).

King, Rufus. *Life and Correspondence*, Charles R. King, editor (New York: Putnam, 1894–1900, 6 vols.).

Lafayette, Marquis de. *Letters . . . to Washington, 1777–1779*, Louis Gottschalk, editor (New York, privately printed by Helen F. Hubbard, 1944).

———. *Memoirs, Correspondence, and Manuscripts* (London: Saunders & Otley, 1837, 3 vols.).

Lee, Charles. *The Lee Papers, 1754–1811* (New York: New-York Historical Society Collections, vols. 4, 5, 6, 7; 1871–74).

Sullivan, John. *Letters and Papers*, O. G. Hammond, editor (Concord: New Hampshire Historical Society Collections, vols. 13, 14, 15; 1930–39).

Washington, George. *Writings*, John C. Fitzpatrick, editor (Washington: U.S. Government Printing Office, Bicentennial Edition, 1931–44, 39 vols.). This, with the Syrett and Cooke edition of Hamilton's own papers, forms the most valuable source; Fitzpatrick identifies those of Washington's writings drafted by Hamilton.

———. *Correspondence Concerning the Society of the Cincinnati*, E. E. Hume, editor (Baltimore: Johns Hopkins Press, 1941).

Webb, Samuel B. *Correspondence and Journals*, W. C. Ford, editor (New York: Wickersham Press, 1893–94, 3 vols.).

Records and Proceedings

American Archives . . . (Washington: M. St. Clair Clarke & Peter Force, 1836–46, 4 vols.); often referred to as Force.

Dickinson, John. *Report to Assembly*, in 4th series, 3 Pennsylvania Archives, pp. 905 ff.

New York, *Journal of the Provincial Congress . . . Committee of Safety, etc.*, 1775–77 (Albany: Thurlow Weed, 1842).

———. Office of State Comptroller, *New York in the Revolution as Colony and State*, J. A. Roberts, compiler (Albany: Brandow Print Co., 1898).

Pennsylvania. *Minutes of Executive Council* (Harrisburg: Theodore Penn & Co., 1853).

———. Archives, Series 2, Vol. 4. (Harrisburg: Clarence M. Busch, 1896).

Society of the Cincinnati, Institutions of (New York: J. M. Elliott, 1851).

United States Continental Congress, *Journals*, 1774–89 (Washington: U.S. Government Printing Office, 1904–37, 34 vols.).

United States Courts: *Proceedings of a General Court-Martial . . . for the Trial of Major-General* [Charles] *Lee, July 4th, 1778* (New York: privately reprinted, 1864).

United States Inspector General [Steuben, F. W. von], *Regulations for . . . Order and Discipline of the Troops of the United States, Part I* (Philadelphia: Stymer and Cist, 1779).

Pamphlets

"Cassius" [Aedanus Burke]. *Considerations on the Society . . . of Cincinnati* (Philadelphia: Robert Bell, 1783).

Mirabeau, H. G. R., Comte de. *Considérations sur l'ordre de Cincinnatus* (London: J. Johnson, 1784; English translation, same, 1785).

Selected Bibliography

Autobiography, Recollections

Duer, William A. *Reminiscences of an Old Yorker* (New York: W. L. Andrews, 1867).

Graydon, Alexander. *Memoirs of His Own Times* (Philadelphia: Lindsay and Blackiston, 1846).

Kent, James. *Memoirs and Letters*, William Kent, editor (Boston: Little, Brown, 1898).

Ogden, Aaron. *Autobiography*, annotated by Wm. Nelson (Paterson, N.J.: Press Printing Co., 1893).

Wilkinson, James. *Memoirs of My Own Times* (Philadelphia: A. Small, 1816, 3 vols.).

War Diaries, Letters

Anderson, Enoch. "Personal Recollections of an Officer in the Delaware Regiments in the Revolutionary War" in 16 *Historical and Biographical Papers of Delaware* (Wilmington: Historical Society of Delaware, 1896).

André, John. *André's Journal. An Authentic Record of the Movements . . . of the British Army in America, June 1777 to Nov. 1778* (Boston: H. O. Houghton & Co., 1903).

Boudinot, Elias. *Journal or Historical Recollections of . . . Events During the Revolutionary War* (Philadelphia: F. Bourquin, 1894).

Bourg, Cromot du. "Diary," in 4 *Magazine of American History*, p. 205 ff.; Vol. 7, p. 283 ff.

Brissot de Warville, J. P. *New Travels in the United States* (New York: T. and J. Swords, 1792).

Chastellux, François Jean, Marquis de, *Travels in North America, 1780–82* (London: G. G. and J. J. Robinson, 1787, 2 vols.).

Clinton, Sir Henry. *The American Rebellion*, W. Wilcox, editor (New Haven: Yale University Press, 1954).

Deux-Ponts, W. de. *My Campaigns in America*, trans., edited S. A. Green (Boston: Wiggin and Lunt, 1868).

Feltman, William. *Journal . . . 1781–82, including the siege of Yorktown* (Philadelphia: H. C. Baird, 1853).

Gallatin, Gaspard de. *Journal of Siege of York-Town* (Washington: U.S. Government Printing Office, 1931).

Haven, C. C. *Thirty Days in New Jersey Ninety Years Ago* (Trenton: State Gazette Office, 1867).

Heath, William. *Memoirs of the American War*, R. R. Wilson, editor (New York: A. Wesscls Co., 1904).

Krafft, J. C. von. "Hessian Military Journal, May 1776–January 1784," in 15 *New-York Historical Society Collections*, pp. 1–200.

Laurens, John. *Army Correspondence . . . 1777–78*, edited with memoir by William Gilmore Simms (New York: Bedford Club, 1867).

Lee, Henry. *Memoirs of the War in the Southern Department* . . . (New York: University Publishing Co., 1869).

Riedesel, Baroness von. *Letters and Journals Relating to the War of American Independence* (New York: G. & C. Carvill, 1827).

Riedesel, Major General von. *Memoirs during Residence in America*, translated by W. L. Stone (Albany: J. Munsell, 1868, 2 vols.).

Rochambeau, Comte de. *Mémoires Militaires* . . . (Paris: Fain, 1809, 2 vols.).

Simcoe, J. G. *A Journal of Operations of . . . the Queen's Rangers* (Exeter: privately printed, 1787).

Tarleton, Banastre. *A History of the Campaign of 1780 and 1781 in the Southern Provinces of North America* (London: T. Cadell, 1787).

Thacher, James. *A Military Journal during the American Revolutionary War* (Boston: Richardson & Lord, 1825).

Trumbull, Jonathan, Jr. "Minutes of Occurrences Respecting the Siege . . . of York in Virginia" in ser. 1, Vol. 14 *Massachusetts Historical Society Proceedings*, pp. 331–38.

Secondary Materials

Alden, John R. *General Charles Lee, Traitor or Patriot?* (Baton Rouge: Louisiana State University Press, 1951).

Aptheker, Herbert, *The Negro in the American Revolution* (New York: International Publishers, 1940).

Baldwin, Leland D. *Whiskey Rebels* (Pittsburgh: University of Pittsburgh Press, 1939).

Boyd, G. A. *Elias Boudinot* (Princeton: Princeton University Press, 1952).

Boynton, E. C. *History of West Point* (New York: D. Van Nostrand, 1863).

Callahan, North. *Henry Knox: General Washington's General* (New York: American Book Co., 1968).

———. *Daniel Morgan, Ranger of the Revolution* (New York: Holt, Rinehart, and Winston, 1961).

Chinard, Gilbert, *Honest John Adams* (Boston: Little, Brown, 1933).

Custis, G. W. P. *Recollections and Private Memoirs of Washington* (Philadelphia: J. W. Bradley, 1861).

De Conde, Alexander. *The Quasi-War . . . with France, 1797–1801* (New York: Scribner's, 1966).

Duer, W. A. *Life of William Alexander, Earl of Stirling* (New York: Wiley & Putnam, 1847).

Fleming, T. J. *Beat the Last Drum, the Siege of Yorktown, 1781* (New York: St. Martin's Press, 1963).

Flexner, James Thomas. *George Washington* (Boston: Little, Brown, 2 vols., 1965–68); see especially Vol. 2.

Forman, Sidney. *West Point: A History of the United States Military Academy* (New York: Columbia University Press, 1956).

Freeman, Douglas Southall. *George Washington, a Biography* (New York: Scribner, 6 vols., 1948–54).

Ganoe, W. A. *The History of the United States Army* (New York: Appleton, rev. ed., 1942).

Greene, G. W. *The Life of Nathanael Greene* (New York: Putnam, 3 vols., 1867–71).

Hamilton, Allan McLane. *Intimate Life of Alexander Hamilton* (New York, Scribner's, 1910).

Hamilton, J. C. *History of the Republic . . . as Traced in the Writings of Alexander Hamilton* (New York: Appleton, 7 vols., 1857–64).

———. *Life of Alexander Hamilton* (Vol. 1, New York: Halsted & Vorhies, 1834; Vol. 2, Philadelphia: Appleton, 1840); no more vols. published.

Humphreys, David. *Life of . . . Israel Putnam*. (Philadelphia: W. McCarthy, 1811).

———. *Conduct of Washington Respecting Asgill* (New York: Holland Club, 1859).

Kapp, Friedrich, *Life of William von Steuben* (New York: Mason Brothers, 1859).

Lossing, B. J. *Life and Times of Philip Schuyler* (New York: Sheldon & Co., 2 vols., 1873).

Manucy, Albert. *Artillery through the Ages* (National Park Service Interpretive Series, History No. 3, Washington: U.S. Government Printing Office, 1949, pp. 42, illus.).

Marshall, John. *Life of George Washington* (Philadelphia: C. P. Wayne, 1804–07, 5 vols.).

McCarthy, E. J. "Lieut. Col. Francis Barber of Elizabethtown," in 50 *New Jersey Historical Society Proceedings*, pp. 373–84.

Miller, J. C. *Alexander Hamilton, Portrait in Paradox* (New York: Harper and Row, 1959).

Mitchell, Broadus. *Alexander Hamilton* (New York: Macmillan, 2 vols., 1957–62).

Palmer, J. M. *General von Steuben* (Port Washington, N.Y.: Kennikat Press, 1966).

Panagopoulos, E. P. *Alexander Hamilton's Pay Book* (of his New York Artillery Company) (Detroit: Wayne State University Press, 1961).

Patterson, S. W. *Horatio Gates* (New York: Columbia University Press, 1941).

Pickering, Octavius. *The Life of Timothy Pickering* (Boston: Little, Brown, 4 vols., 1867–73).

Robertson, W. S. *The Life of Miranda* (Chapel Hill: University of North Carolina Press, 2 vols., 1929).

Schachner, Nathan. *Alexander Hamilton* (New York: Appleton-Century, 1946).

———. "Alexander Hamilton Viewed by his Friends; the Narratives of

Robert Troup and Hercules Mulligan," in *William and Mary Quarterly*, 3rd ser., vol. 4, no. 2, pp. 203–25.

Smith, Page. *John Adams* (Garden City, N.Y.: Doubleday, 1962, 2 vols.).

Thayer, Theodore. *Nathanael Greene, Strategist of the American Revolution* (New York: Twayne Publishers, 1960).

Tilghman, Oswald. *Memoir of Lieutenant Colonel Tench Tilghman* (Albany: J. Munsell, 1876).

Tousard, Lewis. *American Artillerist's Companion* (Philadelphia: C. and A. Conrad, 2 vols., 1809–13).

Tuckerman, Bayard. *Life of . . . Philip Schuyler, 1733–1804* (New York: Dodd, Mead, 1903).

Wallace, D. P. *Life of Henry Laurens, with a Sketch of the Life of . . . John Laurens* (New York: Putnam, 1915).

War Histories

Bill, A. H. *The Campaign of Princeton, 1776–1777* (Princeton: Princeton University Press, 1948).

Bliven, Bruce. *Battle for Manhattan* (New York: Henry Holt and Co., 1956).

Cronau, Rudolf. *The Army of the American Revolution and Its Organization* (New York: G. Cronau, 1923).

Godfrey, Carlos E. "Organization of the Provisional Army . . . in the Anticipated War with France, 1798–1800," in *Pennsylvania Magazine of History and Biography*, vol. XXXVIII (1914) No. 2, pp. 129–82.

Gottschalk, Louis, *Lafayette and the Close of the American Revolution* (Chicago: University of Chicago Press, 1942).

Johnston, H. P. *The Campaign of 1776 around New York and Brooklyn* (Long Island Historical Society Memoirs, vol. 3, Brooklyn: 1878).

———. *The Yorktown Campaign and Surrender of Cornwallis* (New York: Harper, 1881).

Lossing, B. J. *Pictorial Field Book of the American Revolution* (New York: Harper, 2 vols., 1850–51).

Lowell, E. J. *The Hessians and other German Auxiliaries . . . in the Revolutionary War* (New York: Harper, 1884).

Smith, Samuel Stelle. *The Battle of Monmouth* (Monmouth Beach, N.J.: Philip Freneau Press, 1964).

———. *The Battle of Princeton* (Monmouth Beach, N.J.: Philip Freneau Press, 1967).

———. *The Battle of Trenton* (Monmouth Beach, N.J.: Philip Freneau Press, 1965).

Stillé, C. J. *Wayne and the Pennsylvania Line* (Philadelphia: Lippincott, 1893).

Stryker, W. S. *The Battle of Monmouth*, W. S. Myers, editor (Princeton: Princeton University Press, 1927).

————. *The Battles of Trenton and Princeton* (Boston and New York: Houghton Mifflin, 1898).

Trevelyan, George Otto. *The American Revolution* (4 vols. extends only to 1778. New York and London: Longmans, Green & Co., 1926–29); continued in Trevelyan, George Otto, *George the Third and Charles Fox* (2 vols. New York and London: Longmans, Green & Co., 1921–27).

Ward, Christopher. *The War of the Revolution*, edited by John Richard Alden (New York: Macmillan, 1952, 2 vols.).

Whiteley, Emily S. *Washington and His Aides-de-Camp* (New York: Macmillan, 1936).

Wilkinson, Norman B. "The Forgotten 'Founder' of West Point" (Louis de Tousard) in *Military Affairs*, Vol. 24, No. 4, winter 1960–61, pp. 177–88.

André-Arnold

André, John, Defendant. *Minutes of Court of Inquiry upon Case of . . . André, with . . . Documents* (Albany: J. Munsell, 1865).

Dawson, H. R., editor. *Record of Trial of Joshua Hett Smith . . . for alleged Complicity in . . . Treason of . . . Arnold* (Morrisania, N.Y.: 1866).

Flexner, James T. *The Traitor and the Spy* (New York: Harcourt, Brace, 1953).

Hart, A. B., editor. *The Varick Court of Inquiry* (Boston: Bibliophile Society, 1907).

Inglis, Charles. *The Case of Major John André, . . . who was put to Death by the Rebels* (New York: James Rivington, 1780).

Smith, Joshua Hett. *An Authentic Narrative of . . . Death of Major André* (London: Mathews & Leigh, 1808: New York, E. A. Duyckinck, 1809).

Van Doren, C. C. *Secret History of the American Revolution* (New York: Viking, 1941).

Local History

Benedict, W. H. *New Brunswick in History* (New Brunswick: privately printed, 1925).

Bolton, Robert. *History of County of Westchester* (New York: Alexander S. Gould, 1948, 2 vols.).

Hufeland, Otto. *Westchester County During the . . . Revolution* (New York: Knickerbocker Press, 1926).

Pine, J. B. *King's College and the Early Days of Columbia College* (New York: Columbia University Printing Office, 1917).

Reynolds, Helen W. *Dutch Houses in the Hudson Valley . . . Before 1776* (New York: Payson and Clarke, 1929).

Schuyler, Georgina. *The Schuyler Mansion at Albany* (New York: DeVinne Press, 1911).

Stokes, I. N. Phelps. *Iconography of Manhattan Island* (New York: R. H. Dodd, 6 vols., 1915–28).

Whiskey Insurrection

Brackenridge, Henry M., *History of the Western Insurrection, 1794* (Pittsburgh: W. S. Haven, 1859).

Brackenridge, Hugh H. *Incidents of the Insurrection in the Western Parts of Pennsylvania in . . . 1794* (Philadelphia: John McCulloch, 1795).

Craig, Neville B. *Exposure of . . . Misstatements in . . . Brackenridge's History of the Whiskey Insurrection* (Pittsburgh: J. S. Davison, 1859).

Ewing, R. M. "Life and Times of William Findley," in *Western Pennsylvania Historical Magazine*, Vol. 2, No. 4, pp. 240–51.

Findley, William. *History of the Insurrection, in the Four Western Counties of Pennsylvania* in . . . M.DCC.XCIV (Philadelphia: S. H. Smith, 1796).

Pennsylvania Archives, 2nd series, Vol. IV, J. B. Linn and Wm. H. Egle, editors (Harrisburg: B. F. Meyers, 1878); pp. 5–550 devoted to Whiskey Insurrection.

Proceedings of Executive of U.S. respecting the Insurgents (Philadelphia: John Fenno, 1795).

Index

Index

Scott, General Charles, 151, 153, 155
Seabury, Samuel, 5
Sevier, John, 233, 243 n.
Shelby, Isaac, 233
Simcoe, Colonel J. G., 211
Six Nations, expedition against, 186 ff., 215
slaves, as soldiers, 125 ff.
Smith, Joshua Hett, 199, 200, 204-205, 206, 207, 214
Smith, William, 199, 211, 212
Society of Cincinnati, 304-306
South Carolina, 127, 129 and n., 130, 256
Stanwix, Fort, 92
Stark, John, 91-92
Staten Island, N.Y., 8, 217
Steuben, Baron F. W. von, 39, 131 ff., 146, 171, 179-180, 228, 347, 353
ambition of, 138-140, 141
pension of, 143
in Virginia, 236-237, 240 n., 267, 272, 305
Stevens, Ebenezer, 24
Stevens, Dr. Edward, 366, 367
Stewart, Walter, 104, 158, 293, 295
Stirling, Lord (William Alexander), 6, 8, 26, 35, 40, 118, 150, 152, 159, 217
Sullivan, General John, 16, 186 ff., 191, 197
Sumter, Thomas, 234

Talleyrand, Charles Maurice, 321, 322
Tappan, N.Y., 202, 209, 210
Tarleton, Colonel Banastre, 234, 270, 280
Tarrytown, N.Y., 113, 201
Teller's (Croton) Point, N.Y., 200
Thacher, Dr. James, 254
Thompson, Lieutenant Thomas, 12, 67
Ticonderoga, 89-90, 99, 104, 105, 114, 122
Tilghman, Tench, 22, 55, 56, 59, 68, 156, 165, 171, 217, 223, 225, 230, 244-245, 285
"Tom the Tinker," 311
Tories, 293
Tousard, Major Louis de, 346, 353, 354, 357, 358, 359-360
Trenton, N.J., 302, 303
battle of, 20, 41 ff.
Troup, Robert, 17, 118, 286
Truxton, Captain Thomas, 348

Valley Forge, Pa., 38, 81, 117, 122, 131, 133, 136, 170
Varick, Richard, 200-201, 203, 214
Varnum, General James M., 137, 158
Vergennes, Count Charles Gravier, 227
Verplanck's Point, N.Y., 115, 202, 204, 207, 255 n.
Vioménil, Baron Antoine Charles, 268, 274
Vulture, 200, 202, 205, 207

Wadsworth, Jeremiah, 136
Walker, Benjamin, 137, 142, 180
Ward, General Artemas, 64-65
Warner, Seth, 101
Washington, Fort, 24, 43, 217
Washington, General George, 32
aides of, 54-55, 58 ff.
Arnold's treason and, 199 ff.
authority given to, 48-49, 81
character of, 224-225, 293-294
commanding in N.Y., 8, 15, 19
and complaints of troops, 291 ff.
encounter with Lee, 165-166, 167
Fabian tactics of, 76
Farewell Address of, 62, 75, 372
fortification of Dorchester Hgts., 7
H. favored by, 20, 54, 56-57, 245-246, 335
at Harlem Heights, 21-22
money need of, 257
and Monmouth battle, 146 ff., 156 ff.
and quasi war with France, 326 ff.
reconnoiter in Delaware, 77-78
relief from Saratoga, 98 ff.
retreat across N.J., 25 ff.
and Society of Cincinnati, 305
and Steuben, 143
and storming of redoubts, 277
and Sullivan's expedition, 188-189
and surrender of Cornwallis, 281 ff.
tiff with H., 223 ff.
Trenton battle and, 41 ff.
Whiskey Insurrection and, 308 ff.
Wayne, Major General Anthony, 80-81, 86, 104, 135, 146, 150, 153, 157, 166, 183, 190, 251-252, 267
Webster, Noah, 249
Weedon, George, 66
West Point, N.Y., 199 ff., 215, 252, 358-359
Whiskey Insurrection, 308 ff., 352
Whiteley, Emily, 54-55, 62

385